BETWEEN OURSELVES

An Introduction to Interpersonal Communication

GRAEME BURTON AND RICHARD DIMBLEBY

THIRD EDITION

Hodder Arnold

A MEMBER OF THE HODDER HEADLINE GROUP

First published in Great Britain in 2006 by
Hodder Education, a member of the Hodder Headline Group,
338 Euston Road, London NW1 3BH

www.hoddereducation.com

Distributed in the United States of America by
Oxford University Press Inc.
198 Madison Avenue, New York, NY10016

British Library Cataloguing in Publication Data
A catalogue record for this book is available from the British Library

Library of Congress Cataloging-in-Publication Data
A catalog record for this book is available from the Library of Congress

ISBN 978 0 340 809532

3 4 5 6 7 8 9 10

Typeset in 10/13pt Adobe Garamond by Servis Filmsetting Ltd, Manchester
Printed and bound in India

What do you think about this book? Or any other
Hodder Education title? Please send your comments to
the feedback section on www.hoddereducation.com.

Contents

3 Social interaction and social skills

4 Culture and communication

5 Self-presentation

6 Transactional analysis

7 Communication in groups

8 Critical perspectives

Preface to the third edition

It is now ten years since the second edition of this book came out, and we are pleased that it is still of value to student readers out there. While we have retained the basic structure and direction of this work, we have tried to respond to the changing critical climate, not least in respect of the growth of interest in cultural dimensions to communication.

So we have written a new chapter which examines facets of communication and culture, including cross-cultural communication. This recognizes the increasingly global dimensions to all our experiences of communication in society. We have taken on areas to do with identity and technology. All the chapters have been revised to some extent, though we also retain a belief in the usefulness of critical approaches such as that afforded by TA theory. Naturally, reading lists and the glossary have been revised to bring the material up to date.

At the same time, we still see human communication as being dominantly a dynamic process in which meanings about ourselves and our world are negotiated and constructed. We are still concerned with giving this book a pragmatic edge – communication in action. The process of communication affects our social and working lives. It happens in everyday contexts. It is possible to improve mutual understanding through knowing what is going on, and by developing our skills in the use of verbal and nonverbal language.

We have largely rewritten the final chapter in order to relate communication theory to those major critical perspectives out there which also inform disciplines such as media studies and sociology. This chapter, in effect, gives an abbreviated account of the main thrust of those perspectives. In this way we are trying to provide some sort of integration for courses and disciplines, believing that they have less singularity than they have interests in common.

How far we have succeeded in all these ambitions is up to you, the reader, to judge. We hope that you will have an interesting read and a useful read, and that you find what we have to say helpful if you are undertaking a formal course of study. Once more we invite you to give us feedback via the publishers, however critical this may be. This would reinforce our view that both communication and learning are a continuous part of life's experience.

Graeme Burton & Richard Dimbleby   April 2005

Introduction

This book is about communication between people, whether they are in pairs or in groups.

We hope that what we have written will help explain how and why this communication is carried on, as well as help encourage more effective communication practice.

We believe that understanding what happens when we interact with others is of value in itself, but can also be useful in giving us more control over our own communication.

So this book is also about understanding what influences and governs interaction between people, and about how such understanding may lead to more constructive and sympathetic control of that interaction.

We believe that there are identifiable communication skills, which in the area that this book covers would be described as social and perceptual. These skills can be recognized, understood and absorbed with benefit to our working and social relationships.

This book is very much about people, not least because communication is such a fundamental human activity.

Although we do make reference to the evidence of research, you will not find that this book catalogues research in great detail. What we have tried to do, where appropriate, is to bring together the evidence and significance of relevant research and of communication practice. This is related to the topics identified in each chapter. We hope that readers will find this a book in which ideas are explained thoroughly and are seen to make sense in their own experience.

We have written for a range of students on various academic and vocational courses where interpersonal and group communication is an object of study and practice. We also believe that other people, not least teachers, will find this a useful point of reference for their work and for their interests. So we hope that all you readers will, indeed, find that this book contains something of value to you, both in your work and perhaps for yourselves.

To you, the reader

You may well be involved with a communication course at college, at school or at university; whoever you are, we hope that you will find this work accessible and relevant. We would like you to use it in understanding what happens when we communicate at work and in leisure. You should find explanation and examples that reveal this, and which positively help students in their studies.

Understanding people and their communications is not straightforward in many ways. Yet as we learn to read and to write, so we learn to produce verbal and nonverbal communication for others, and to understand what they produce for us. It is a fascinating process, full of ambiguities and problems of meaning. We hope that you enjoy trying to unravel it, and that we have given you some help in doing so.

Please be clear that this is a book for courses, not specifically a course book. There is nothing to stop you working through it from beginning to end if you want to. But we have organized our work so that you can take what you want from it. So far as teachers are concerned, we see this book as supporting their role in promoting active learning. What you as a student have, we hope, is a straightforward and structured piece of writing that gives you a base from which to work: here is a point of reference, here is a means of checking what you may have missed or understood imperfectly. You will find ideas about human communication brought together from a variety of sources apart from ourselves, together with references and cross-references. Most of all, we hope you will find that we have made these ideas clear through examples that relate to authentic experience.

Communication study, communication behaviour and communication theory

The study of communication has often been described in three main ways. These may be described as the **process** approach, the **semiotic** approach and the **cultural** approach. They are not mutually exclusive and each of them will be used at times in this book. They can be described briefly as follows.

- The process approach involves the holistic view of looking at everything that is considered to be part of a given communication situation or transaction. It tries to describe all these variables and their contributions to the communication.

- The semiotic approach is more specifically concerned with the production and meaning of signs and 'texts' and with the structuring of the interaction.

- The cultural approach is concerned with the creation of distinctive culture through communication, and with how that culture is maintained and transmitted through communication.

The final chapter of this book, Critical perspectives, deals in more detail with these three theoretical approaches to the study of communication. This chapter also discusses other recent perspectives on communication and culture, such as feminist, Marxist and postmodernist viewpoints.

In talking about study and theory, it is worth remembering that there is a reciprocal relationship between this and behaviour. That is to say, one might agree that interaction, communication and behaviour have a great deal in common, even if they are not strictly synonymous.

It is also worth remembering that our theory must come out of observation of behaviour, and is only verifiable through such observation or through making enquiries – which themselves require communication to take place. Whether one is trying to describe characteristics of groups or the mental processes behind any communication, we need to look at communication itself in order to see if we are correct in what we suppose. This means, happily, that theory and practice need to be seen as equally important and as complementary to one another.

This study of communication and concern with actual behaviour is also underpinned by the fact that one is looking for what is significant, and that what is significant is usually that which is repeated. So it is that a great deal of communication study returns to a key concept of **convention**. Conventions show themselves through repeated behaviour (or content and treatment of material). It is worth bearing in mind, then, that much of what is in this book is, in effect, about patterns – patterns of behaviour that seem significant because they *are* patterned, and perhaps because they are frequent. Think about this when you are reading our work and when you are using it to make sense of what you see people doing as they communicate. Look for the patterns. Question what we say. And always be prepared to ask the most important question of all, with reference to what you read or what you observe – 'So what?'

We have also written this book on the premise that all communication is about **meaning**. That is to say, about how meanings are constructed in the mind, about the exchange of meanings through verbal and non-verbal communication in particular. You will see that we begin by looking at communication within the person, where meanings are made, where we make sense of a world that for all of us is, most importantly, about people.

Assumptions underlying this book

In what we have said so far in this Introduction we have already told you some of the assumptions on which the book is written. Here are a few more.

The book is based on the assumption that readers are interested in understanding how and why communication takes place, and in developing communication skills. A further premise is that the study of communication should be directed towards helping these interests.

We also think that such study can be approached through a three-part notion of **description, interpretation** and **practice**. That is to say, we can describe what happens when communication takes place, and we can then try to make sense of what we have described. This understanding can then, with practice, lead to more effective and more appropriate communication with others.

Perhaps the most important assumption we make is that readers do have a basic level of knowledge and understanding as represented in our previous book, *More Than Words: An Introduction to Communication Studies* (Dimbleby and Burton 1992). Reading of the three relevant chapters in that book would be helpful, though not essential. There is some overlap of topics in this book. However, we do not, for example, reproduce very basic communication models. And we do assume understanding of terms such as 'perception'.

How this book is organized

Throughout the book we try to provide at least brief explanation of terms in passing as they are introduced. However, in order to maintain a flow in the development of ideas, some concepts are not dealt with in detail until later in the book. If you do decide you want to know more about various concepts mentioned only briefly in Chapter 1, you will probably find it helpful to read Chapter 8 just after you have read Chapter 1, as you will find explanations in Chapter 8 of various key concepts such as critical perspectives. However, you may prefer to read the whole book first and then consolidate your understanding by reading Chapter 8 at the end.

The book starts with an examination of the Self, of the individual as communicator. Then we move to ideas about how we interact with others, and develop these points into an examination of communication in groups. Thus we move from a point within the Self, to ideas about the Self relating to others.

Before we look at groups in particular, we deal with the theories of self-presentation and of transactional analysis (after Goffman and Berne respectively), because these offer some stimulating ideas about motivation and regulation of interaction.

In this third edition we have added a separate chapter on culture and communication (Chapter 4), which discusses a number of issues, including cross-cultural communication and also the impact of technology on interpersonal communication.

As mentioned above, the final chapter (Chapter 8) is about critical perspectives. It partly draws together what has gone before and partly summarizes alternative ways of interpreting the communication process.

At the back of the book, you will find a glossary of main terms, and a section referring to further reading and to some relevant learning/activity materials.

Finally, you will find an index. Don't forget to use this (and the table of contents), to find your way quickly around this work. Books for study are there to be used, not necessarily to be read from cover to cover. It is your book, so make it work for you.

To this end, we have tried to make each chapter clear in structure as well as in style. Notice that there is a review/summary at the end of each chapter. It will be a simplification, of course, but it should also answer the question, 'What were the main points that I was meant to get out of that chapter?'

Within the chapters, look out for the key statements and main concepts that appear in bold. We want to help you learn by sorting out some of the material for you. This is why we have provided at least some case situations/stories that incorporate concepts in a live context in order to make their application and meaning more clear.

This is what we hope that we have done. If you want to comment on this piece of communication then feel free to give us some feedback via the publisher of this book.

Acknowledgements

We should like to thank those many friends and colleagues who have helped us practically, creatively and intellectually, in the making of this edition of *Between Ourselves*. Thanks in particular are due to Nick Dimbleby for finding time for an additional photoshoot in his busy schedule; and to Terry Williams for his inimitable cartoon style. We also want to say thank you to Deborah Edwards and Jaimee Biggins for keeping us on course and for being patient as deadlines became slippery. Editorial support matters – dare we say it – as much as that home support from philosophical partners. So thanks again to Gill and Judy, who might have missed some of the interpersonal communication that we were so busy writing about.

The publishers and we would like to thank those listed below for their permission to reproduce copyright material.

Fig 1.4, from Larry Barker, *Communication* (Published by Allyn and Bacon, Boston, MA. Copyright © 1986 by Pearson Education); Nick Dimbleby for Fig. 2.1, 3.1 and 7.1; Alexandra Fitzsimmons for Fig.1.1; Jacky Fleming for Fig. 3.5 and 8.1; Images.com/CORBIS for Fig. 5.1; Photodisc for Fig 4.1; Terry Williams for Fig. 6.1; The McGraw-Hill Company for Fig 1.6, the Luft model for the Johari window; John Wiley & Sons for Fig 2.2, the March & Simon model of perception.

Every effort has been made to trace all copyright holders: our apologies to those in cases where this has not proved possible.

Fig. 1.1 The ideal Self – we are not always seen as we would like to be seen

Chapter 1

Intrapersonal communication

Everybody has private thoughts and feelings that differ from those they express publicly, and everybody behaves differently in different situations . . . Everybody also has more access to and interest in their own lives and feelings than they do to other people's. In this sense, you are bound to know more about yourself than other people do.

(Reid and Hammersley 2000)

1.1 What is intrapersonal communication?

Introduction

This chapter is much concerned **with the Self, which is at the beginning and end of all communication**. Although we will deal separately with the Self, we acknowledge the artificiality of such an exercise. The process of communication is really one whole thing: all our acts of communication and our experiences have a bearing on one another. And we ourselves must be part of all this. However, what we are going to do is to examine parts of the communication process separately, in order to describe them and to explain how they work together. Similarly, this book is a whole thing, but you have to work your way through it, and connect one part with another in order to make sense of it as a whole. We hope that we will help you to do this by describing separate concepts and by explaining their significance for the whole communication process.

What we have to say about the Self and intrapersonal communication does have a bearing on everything that follows. All the communication activities and processes that are described in subsequent chapters must be related back to those described in this chapter. It therefore seems to make sense to start with who we are, how we come to be the kind of people we are, and why this matters in terms of making sense of communication.

Elements and activities

Let's start by saying simply that we define intrapersonal communication (IRPC) as **communication within the Self, and of the Self to the Self**. So, for example, thinking about this paragraph and making notes on it would both count as examples of IRPC (as we will abbreviate it from now on).

The main elements in IRPC can be described as follows:

- There is the **core of self**, which can be divided into a number of different elements, the most important of which are: how we see ourselves, how we value ourselves, and our personality.
- There are the **needs (motivations)** that drive that Self to generate communication, to interpret communication and to change the way it presents itself in different sorts of interactions with different people. The Self and its personality are not static and unchanging, but rather active and dynamic.
- There are internal activities by which we make sense of the world, which is called **cognition**. We develop internal cognitive maps that we can then apply to various situations when we are trying to interpret and make sense of what is happening. We call on these past experiences and the ideas, values and concepts we have made a part of ourselves to interpret other people's communication activities and to generate our own acts of communication.
- There are **emotional feelings and responses** to our inner thoughts and to what happens around us. The Self is continually aware of these and we learn to manage and control these impulses and to share or hide them from others. Sometimes we find it difficult to control our emotions and then we may feel overwhelmed by them or let them out in ways that may help or hinder our communication with others.
- There is the internal activity **of monitoring the reactions of others to our communication**. The Self is continuously interacting with the outside environment, including other people. We are constantly obtaining and checking feedback from others, that is, information that tells us about the effects of our actions on other people.

In Fig 1.2 we have tried to illustrate this model of the Self and to indicate how processes of intrapersonal communication also influence communications with others. Our cognition processes, our attitudes and our motivations reflect and influence our self-image, which, in turn, is affected by feedback from others. We have not yet discussed all the concepts referred to in this diagram. These will be discussed later and are also explained in the glossary (see page 297).

Encoding and decoding

The Self is in a constant state of activity in giving and receiving messages, that is, in trying to express our own meanings to others and interpreting what others are consciously or unconsciously doing around us. These active elements of encoding and decoding are crucial to IRPC. This is discussed in more detail in Section 1.6 of this chapter on Intrapersonal processing.

- **Encoding** is about the composition of the communicative signs within the brain, and then their external expression (through speech, for example).
- **Decoding** would be about the physical acceptance of external signals (through hearing, for example) and then understanding (or the construction of meaning from those signals).

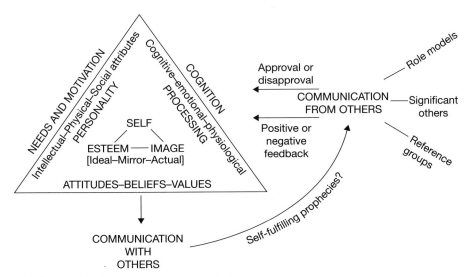

Fig. 1.2 A model for intrapersonal communication

In this way all communication involves intrapersonal processes. Whatever the Self is, with its various characteristics and needs, it must work through the intrapersonal processes of encoding and decoding if there is to be any contact with others.

IRPC activities

IRPC activities can be divided into two kinds: those that are entirely internalized and those that have external manifestations. The following examples are by no means exhaustive, but they should make sense of what we are talking about.

- **Internal activities** are those thought processes that are not spoken out loud – for which we have labels such as reflection, evaluation, problem solving. Communication is within the Self and addressed to the Self. Any time you sit and think about what you want to do tomorrow, or come to a decision about buying a pair of shoes, or think about an argument that you have had with someone, you are engaged in intrapersonal communication.

- **Externalized examples** may involve talk, but could just as easily require some other form of communication. We all talk aloud to ourselves in private, especially when emotionally aroused or dealing with a tricky physical task. Cars often get repaired to the accompaniment of someone saying to themselves 'Now, maybe if I tried to . . .' If we do not have someone else to bounce ideas and problems off then we are just as likely to talk to ourselves about them. Again, we may write – keeping a diary is an intensely intrapersonal activity. Or we may draw a plan of a room to see if we can change its layout. In this case, too, the communication is from ourself and to ourself.

If you try to extend this list of examples for yourself, you will realize that we do indulge in a great deal of IRPC activity.

KEY QUESTIONS

What is intrapersonal communication?

1. Use the model in Fig. 1.2 to analyse your own intrapersonal communication processes during a conversation with (a) your mother or partner about why you cannot have dinner with her/him next Saturday, and (b) with your work colleague, asking her/him to come on holiday with you.

2. Analyse your intrapersonal communication processes while you are deciding whether to stay in and do some work tonight or go out with friends.

We suggest that you make some written notes of the processes that you identify, with headings such as: motivations, emotional issues, attitudes and values, and your desired self-image.

1.2 Self-drives

Communication, whether it is to our self (intrapersonal) or between our self and other people (interpersonal), must be motivated by something. There are reasons why we choose to initiate thought processes or interaction with others. One kind of motivation is discussed in section 1.4 of this chapter, where we offer some ideas about how we use communication to maintain and evaluate our ideas about our Self. Here we are motivated to keep on checking as to whether or not our own view of what we are like actually seems to hold true in the light of the ways that others communicate with us. We check their reactions, or **feedback**.

Needs and motivation

The notion of **needs** as the driving force behind human activities is well established, with Maslow's (1984) hierarchy of needs often quoted. He proposes that such needs have to be aroused and unsatisfied in order for them to motivate behaviour (including communication). These needs are described as:

- physiological needs

- safety needs

- social needs

- esteem needs (that is, the need to achieve a sense of worth, perhaps from others' communication with us), and

- self-actualization needs (that is, needs to achieve fulfilment and potential).

Such needs, as they become less important to physical survival, also become more sophisticated and more important to the psychological well-being of the individual.

Schultz (1966), on the other hand, suggests a rather more simple set of three needs. Two of these fit other comparable categories, that is, the need to control and the need for affection. But he also proposes a 'need for inclusion', which is defined as a need to be recognized as an individual by others.

From all this it can be seen that there is general agreement that certain needs are geared to satisfying a sense of the Self, to defining that Self with relation to others, and to producing a sense of esteem and worth for that Self. From this motivation, communication follows.

In particular, and with relation to our need for self-esteem (see below for definitions and further discussion of this), it may be argued that **we are motivated to** construct a Self that is attractive to others. Yet again, we would argue that such a Self only becomes apparent when it communicates. This motivation would take account of both personal and social needs. That is to say, if we want to get on with others, if we want to form relationships, if we want to think well of ourselves, then we want to present ourselves in such a way that we will be liked. In Chapter 5 we look at Goffman's views on self-presentation and discuss them in relation to communication. But even here it must be apparent that communication is a crucial bridge between ourselves and others. **We can only be known through our communication.** Within the bounds and the values of our culture, we learn what is attractive to others and what will allow us to join groups. We learn that to be a certain kind of person who behaves in certain kinds of ways will bring success and satisfaction in social relationships.

So these various motivations, mainly described as needs, initiate the formation of a certain kind of Self. They also stimulate that Self to initiate external action – communication.

KEY QUESTIONS

Self-drives

Think back to the most recent face-to-face or telephone conversation you initiated. Describe the needs/motivation that led you to start this.

Describe yourself in terms of your clothes, hair, facial appearance/make-up and posture and analyse how far you use these to define your concept of self for yourself and others.

1.3 Elements of the Self

Influential theories about the Self

Psychology is a relatively new science, dating back just over 100 years. Prior to that it was philosophers, novelists and dramatists who wrote about people and their behaviour, and analysed why people behave in certain ways. But close analysis of individual personalities, and the formation of theories about them, are usually seen as early twentieth-century developments. Two thinkers from this era continue to have influence on how we think about the Self. Much that has been written about the Self and its workings in the past 100 years is either continuing or challenging the ideas of Sigmund Freud and Carl Gustav Jung. As an introduction to elements of the Self, we shall therefore very briefly say something about the ideas about the Self that were developed by these two men.

Sigmund Freud, a doctor working in Vienna from the end of the nineteenth century, became famous for developing a method of working with his patients called 'psychoanalysis'. In this type of therapy the patient is encouraged to make 'free associations' and thereby to help the analyst delve into the patient's early life experiences that may have been repressed from the conscious mind. (Free association was a technique developed by Freud in which the patient was asked to talk about his/her thoughts with the doctor/analyst as honestly and freely as possible, without censoring the immediate ideas or words that first came into their minds. Freud and later psychoanalysts found it hard to get patients to do this at times, as they would suppress what they considered embarrassing or frightening thoughts.) Freud believed that many psychological problems were caused by early life experiences and, in particular, the repression of some experiences into the unconscious mind. One of Freud's most important contributions to our ideas about the Self is this notion of there being **conscious and unconscious parts of our personalities**. The Johari window (see page 51) is a more recent idea that uses this idea to explore things hidden from us.

Freud believed that dreams were a way of accessing the unconscious part of the personality, and one of his earliest books was called *The Interpretation of Dreams*. Many of his analyses of dreams involve repressed sexual thoughts, and we now refer to 'Freudian symbols' such as sticks, knives and other pointed objects representing the penis; boxes, chests and other containers representing the womb; movement up and down ladders representing having sex, and so on. In the past people have analysed advertisements and works of art as sources of Freudian symbolism.

Freud was interested in the ways the adult personality was formed from childhood experiences. His work led him to formulate a theory that the Self is made up of three parts: the id, the ego and the super-ego. Each represents different ways that we think and feel. They are Freud's way of explaining the apparent conflict he saw between the different levels of consciousness.

- The id he described as the primitive, unconscious part of the mind that we are born with. It is a dark, inaccessible area with instinctive urges and selfish, pleasure-seeking needs. As the child grows up it realizes that it cannot always instantly have what it wants. And so it begins to suppress the urges of the id to fit in with society and other people's expectations. Freud believed that the suppressed desires of the id are commonly expressed in dreams.

- Freud said the ego (the Latin word for 'I') was the part of the mind that reacts to external reality and which we think as the Self. The ego makes sense of the world around us, it is practical and rational, and makes decisions. Freud believed that the ego constructs unconscious defence mechanisms to protect it from the urges of the id.

- The super-ego is a sort of internalized parent, which gives us our sense of right and wrong. It gets us to act in ways that are acceptable to society and thus gives us guilt feelings if we think we are going against our internalized norms. It is a controlling part of our mind and seems to demand perfection.

As we can see, according to Freud's theory of the Self we seem to be subject to inner conflict and anxiety. Conflicts between these different parts of our personality result in anxiety and stress. Freud identified three types of anxiety:

- realistic anxiety, which arises from real events in the external world perceived by the ego;
- neurotic anxiety, which arises from the id and often seems unfocused but reflects a source of inner conflict;
- moral anxicty, which arises from the super-ego as a sort of voice of the conscience, telling us when something is improper in terms of the values we have learnt.

At the root of these conflicts is Freud's idea that we are torn between a 'pleasure principle' that seeks immediate gratification of our urges and desires and a 'reality principle' that involves conscious, logical thinking and leads us to delay gratification.

Freud's theories about the Self came from his experiences in treating disturbed and neurotic patients and seeking to explain the causes of their problems. His ideas have been influential in the way we have subsequently thought of ourselves and our behaviour and have had an influence on art and culture.

Carl Jung, a Swiss doctor and disciple of Freud who later split off and developed his own theories, is most famous for his theory of the **'collective unconscious'**, which he believed was a part of each individual psyche. (Jung uses the term 'psyche' to refer to the whole of someone's mind or spirit, both conscious and unconscious.) Like Freud, Jung was interested in the unconscious and developed his own theories of the Self, following on from the ideas developed by Freud. Jung developed his own process of 'analytical psychology' (different from Freud's psychoanalysis).

As a result of work with his patients, Jung came to believe that the human mind seems to produce universally recognizable symbols and imagery, and he coined the term 'archetypes' to describe these. He described the collective unconscious as having two main aspects:

- archetypes that help us to understand our unconscious ideas, and
- instincts that are innate biological drives determining our behaviour, for example, hunger, aggression and the sex drive.

These instinctive energies he referred to as 'libido' (a term that for him meant more than simply sexual energy).

In Jung's terms the ego refers to the centre of consciousness and gives us our sense of who we think we are. The ego has a balancing influence on the conscious and unconscious. He also uses the term 'shadow' to refer to an unconscious part of the personality that we cannot admit to having, mostly the dark, uncivilized part of our nature. The ego and the shadow work as a balancing pair. Jung also identified the public face of our psyche as the 'persona' – which is like a mask that the ego creates to hide our true nature from society and other people.

Jung divided people into two basic types of personality: **introvert and extravert**:

- Introverts are more interested in their own thoughts and feelings and behaviour. They need privacy and personal space.

- Extraverts are more interested in external things and relationships. They are more outgoing and need action and other people around them.

Both Freud and Jung had ideas of instinctive unconscious forces that we need to control as part of growing up as socialized adults. Through their observations of people they collected reliable data about people's inner lives that showed that many of our thought processes are unconscious. Such ideas have been influential throughout the twentieth century but are now often challenged as a result of research that sheds different light on the workings of the brain. Their ideas have, however, been considered useful in trying to understand some of the processes of intrapersonal communication that may operate at both conscious and unconscious levels within ourselves.

Self-image or self-concept?

One problem in dealing with the Self is that different writers attach different terms to the word to describe the same thing. For example, Turner (1982) refers to self-image as a part of a self-concept. The concept he suggests is relatively firm. The image shifts from situation to situation and draws from the concept. The one may differ considerably from the other. This bears a close relationship to the debate about personality – do we have a fixed core personality (a 'true' Self), or is our personality a flexible notion, with certain features predominating at certain times? There is an increasing body of evidence for the latter view. We will use the term 'self-image' from here on, and regard self-concept as a synonymous term.

The nature of Self also reflects the society and culture in which a person has grown up. If we accept the model of Maslow's hierarchy of needs, then in a society, or a section of a society, where physiological and safety needs are still major preoccupations, the concept of Self may be less developed and group social needs may be more significant. Maslow's highest need in the hierarchy is the product of a Western, industrial, individualistic culture where 'self actualization' (being able to fulfil your own needs and wants, both physical and emotional, and to achieve a sense of freedom) is the ultimate motivator.

In a culture where social cohesion and mutual cooperation, or equality of treatment for all, are the highest values, the ultimate need of the Self may be inner peace and harmony through the service of others and the subduing of your own personal needs and wants.

Public and private Self

This idea of **shift in the emphasis of self-image** is illustrated by the fact that it is common for people to display a different Self in public and private situations. Some people also believe that they have a private Self within them that is at variance with the one that is commonly displayed to others, even to friends.

Gahagan (1984), in referring to self-awareness, touches on the public and private Self. She identifies various forms of self-awareness, including awareness of private physical and psychological events, and awareness of ourselves as public objects and characters. In the first case we are aware of internal pain or a state of guilt. Pain messages are transmitted along the nervous system. Guilt notions are rationalized through the nervous systems of the brain. In the second case we may find ourselves watching our own performances. Many people become self-aware when they have to stand, literally, on a public stage. They monitor their performance – that is, what is being revealed of themselves to others in this public situation. 'There is usually a difference between the public self and communicative performance which happens when we collect some prize with due gravity and gratitude, and that private intrapersonal communication when we are on our own and give vent to our feelings of joy and satisfaction.' (Gahagan 1984)

So, the Self has its public and private dimensions. We may communicate with ourselves about our Self even in a public situation. But in a private situation this communication with the Self may be externalized – talking to our self about what we have done. And we will feel that the Self that operates in private is rather different from the one that is represented in public. The cultural conventions about intrapersonal communication in public are powerful. Put simply, people who talk to themselves in public are considered to be eccentric. They are performing a private activity and revealing a private Self in a public place.

Self-image

In general, self-image is about how we see ourselves. It is about ways in which we categorize ourselves. The way we categorize ourselves also depends on how we believe that we are categorized by others. To this extent the self-image, however private a construct, must be in a dynamic relationship with the outside world. The link with the outside world is communication.

Many people see the Self in terms of **role** and **personality traits**, for the most part. Dominant roles are, not surprisingly, those of occupation or family relationship. In terms of personality, there is some evidence that things such as confidence, intelligence and social worth predominate in many people's views of themselves. You could try for yourself offering a group of people cards with statements on them covering possible areas of personality, and see which ones are most frequently chosen. The only problem is that someone may choose a statement about, for example, their capacity for leadership because they feel that they *ought* to choose it because of the value that our culture appears to place on this quality. They may not feel privately that leadership is an important trait in themselves at all. We will have more to say about personality under 'Personality traits' below.

Three kinds of attribute

One pretty well agreed set of categories to describe self-image comprises those identified as **physical, intellectual and social attributes**.

One example of the **physical image** that we can have of ourselves is demonstrated by sufferers of anorexia nervosa. Among other beliefs, these people think that they are fat even when they are not. They have an obsession and have acquired a distorted self-image. They cannot recognize themselves objectively.

The pressure on young women, and increasingly on young men, to develop a particular body shape, as portrayed by media celebrities, can have a strong effect on people's self-image. Many teenage girls can develop low self-esteem if they believe they do not have a supermodel-like body shape and face. Many teenage boys can develop low self-esteem if their lifestyle seems to prevent them from having toned muscles, a 'six-pack' stomach and chiselled facial features.

Physical self-image also relates to other definitions of self-image, as described in the rest of this section. For example, it is well known that many of us will reveal, when describing ourselves, a tendency to exaggerate our height (evidence of the ideal image). Obviously any optimistic views of our physical selves will also reflect on our communication behaviour, for better or for worse. If we see ourselves as being devastatingly attractive to the opposite sex then we will probably behave as if we really are!

Intellectual attributes of self-image are to do with problem solving, reasoning, analysis, logical thinking. These may be related directly to a description of intellectual skills, such as the ability to correlate pieces of information and to draw conclusions. Such attributes become valued and recognized through education to a fair extent. Your reading of this text is part of this educative process. How you approach the text is partly predicted by your existing view of your intellectual Self. Putting it colloquially, if you do not see yourself as being very clever then you may well approach reading books like this with a negative attitude that is not justified. If you were only to reappraise yourself you would realize that, like everyone else, you do have the capacity for reading and understanding if you were prepared to give it a try.

Emotional attributes of Self can refer to fleeting emotions that are a short-lived response to a particular situation. However, without even defining particular emotions, some people see themselves (and are seen by others) as being 'emotional'. That is to say, they have a propensity for responding emotionally to situations, especially those involving tension and conflict. Such responses may range from rage to fear to misery. Again, one has to emphasize that the frequency and quality of such responses is often misjudged. Others who fear rage may, for example, judge other persons to have an 'angry Self' even if they have only seen that person lose their temper a couple of times. People who have panicked once or twice in a crisis may feel that they always panic. In many ways, the emotional Self is the one that it is most easy to misjudge.

What we have just said also indicates how **it is easy to confuse temporary Self conditions with more permanent ones**. It is possible that certain individuals will tend to certain kinds of emotional behaviour. But there are other behaviours that are particular to particular circumstances. In essence, we are saying that when judging ourselves, or when others judge us, it is important not to assume permanent characteristics of Self from a temporary condition.

With all these three sets of attributes that may be said to compose the Self, it is important to remember that they work together. Barker (1984) talks about the 'need to maintain a unified conceptual system': we are more than the sum of our parts. We communicate at any given time out of the whole of our Self. Views of the Self that emphasize a few attributes and ignore the rest are, in truth, stereotypes. We may stereotype ourselves as much as others may stereotype us. This is why there is a strong argument for developing self-awareness through studying communication or other subjects, so that we become more objective and obtain a more complete picture of ourselves.

Ideal and realistic image

Another common way of describing self-image is through the pairing of ideal and realistic self-image. These two coexist within the consciousness. It is argued that many of our actions, including communication, are motivated by a desire to bring the one closer to the other. Both may be described in terms of the attributes already referred to. Ideally, we would like to be one kind of person. In fact, we know realistically that we are another. How objective we are about our realistic image is open to question. Probably no one is entirely truthful with themselves.

It is possible for people to see themselves as being dull and incompetent because they are ineffective at managing social relationships. But, in fact, they may be extremely competent at a range of tasks, from model building to dressmaking. These people have fallen into the traps of generalization and of undervaluing themselves. A realistic appraisal of the Self would distinguish attributes, might well raise self-esteem, and could lead to a more positive attitude towards dealing with those areas in which such a person could improve performance.

Looking-glass Self

One common definition of Self is described through a phrase of Cooley (1902) – 'the looking-glass Self' – that is, we see ourselves reflected in how others see us. Communication is crucial here, because we only 'know' how others see us through their verbal and nonverbal communication. This may be direct feedback, as in a conversation. It may be indirect comment, as when we overhear others talking about us. Obviously, this version of Self underlines the importance of feedback and perception. To construct a looking-glass Self, we must have evidence to work on, and we must process that evidence. Such processing is an act of intrapersonal communication.

Self as seen by others

A variation of this description of Self was proposed by Mead (1934) when he pointed out that people have a view of themselves constructed from the view that they believe others have of them. This view is achieved by putting ourselves in the position of that other person – **the Self as seen by others**. Interestingly, this kind of mental act identifies with the social skill of empathy, where we are also said to view the world as viewed by another person, as well as to experience their feelings and attitudes. This ability to stand outside the Self and at least attempt to see it as others see it is clearly an attempt to be objective. Of course, in describing the Self as seen we are making assumptions about the person who is perceiving us. Those assumptions are only as good as our perception of them. Nevertheless, we will continue to communicate on the basis of those assumptions.

Self and role

Finally, there is a description of the Self in terms of roles. We develop these sets of attitudes, values and behaviours, which orientate us towards others, as we grow up. Some roles are **ascribed**, that is, given us by others – for example, we will all be either a daughter or a son. Others are **achieved**, that is, earned and learnt – for example, work roles such as counter assistant. It is also true that some aspects of achieved roles are also ascribed by others. So, if one was appointed assistant manager at work, then one would have achieved this role knowing what was expected of someone in that role. One would also behave within the role according to qualities that others also ascribe to it (their expectations).

The roles that, from one view, add up to our self-image can be categorized in terms of family relationships, religion, political affiliations, age, sex and occupation. We will communicate out of the role that dominates in a given situation. We see ourselves as having that role, as having qualities attached to that role, as behaving in ways appropriate to those qualities and to that role in general. This **role performance** is likely to have characteristic verbal and non-verbal communication. Someone who sees the role of sister as being characterized by loyalty may defend a sibling fiercely in some argument. On the other hand, that same person as supervisor may not defend one of the work team who has got into an argument with a colleague.

A number of books, for example Coates (1991), Glass (1992) and Tannen (1991), have analysed Self and role in interpersonal communication by focusing on gender differences. The use of language and nonverbal behaviour patterns is contrasted between men and women.

Lillian Glass was used as an adviser to the actor Dustin Hoffman as he prepared for his role in the film *Tootsie*, in which he played the part of a male actor, Michael Dorsey, who adopts a female persona as Dorothy Michaels and becomes a famous 'actress'. Glass, in her book *He Says, She Says*, contrasts the acting required to convey masculine and feminine Selves:

> In the scene where Dustin (as Michael) is in his agent's office, he is abrupt in his physical movements and vocal tones. His movements are angular, broad and away from his body, while his legs are spread apart when he sits down. In essence it takes up more room. His speech is faster, more clipped and staccato, and even more nasal, since he barely opens his mouth or his lips when he speaks. He uses hardly any facial animation, even though his most openly expressed emotions appear to be anger and hostility as a result of his frustration at being unable to get work as a 'male' actor.
>
> In contrast, recall the scene in the Russian tearoom when Hoffman, as Dorothy, first enters to meet 'her' agent. Her gestures are more delicate, smaller and directed towards her body. When she speaks she puts her hand on her upper

chest, smiles more and uses more facial animation, which makes her appear more receptive and acquiescent. She uses a soft, breathier voice with upward inflection at the end as she declares: 'I will have a Dubonnet on the rocks with a twist'. This upward inflection makes her statement sound as though she is asking a question. It is an all too common female communication pattern which may give the illusion that the woman is tentative, weak, unsure of herself or even a helpless victim.

Clearly, Dustin Hoffman as actor in a role was 'programmed' by Lillian Glass to express these culturally expected male and female 'personalities', perhaps in a rather exaggerated way. You might like to watch a factual TV programme, such as news or documentary, with the sound turned off to observe the nonverbal expressions used by men and women.

KEY QUESTIONS

Many people become self-aware when they have to stand, literally, on a public stage. Describe the feeling of self-awareness you have when you have to stand up in front of others to give a talk.

We have suggested that our self-image comprises physical, intellectual and social attributes. Describe yourself using those three categories, first as you believe your boss or teacher sees you, and second as you believe a friend sees you.

Self-esteem

This important aspect of self-image qualifies one's view of the various kinds of Self already described. It defines how we value ourselves, how we rate ourselves, what we think of ourselves. If we have high self-esteem then we think well of ourselves. Such esteem necessarily depends on a value system that is also part of the Self. That value system is learnt through communication with others as well as through observing others. We learn what other people think is desirable or not, attractive or not, worthwhile or not, important or not, and so on.

Although it is possible for an individual to come to value behaviours or personality traits that most other people do not, **on the whole what we esteem represents a fair measure of agreement with what other people esteem** within our own culture. We take up attitudes towards our Self that approve or disapprove of various aspects of our self-image. Self-perception and attitudes towards Self operate, it is supposed, in much the same way that we perceive others, and form attitudes towards them. There is more about this in later sections of this chapter, as well as in Chapter 2. One fundamental criterion, however, is a scale of liking or disliking that we have of ourselves. Those with low self-esteem do not like themselves very much.

This prompts the question of what it is that is liked or disliked. To a fair degree this is defined in terms of **perceived competence**. We see ourselves as being more or less competent in terms of motor skills, social skills, intellectual skills. For example, a student may have low self-esteem in respect of his or her sporting abilities, esteem themselves highly in terms of getting on with other people, but see themselves as only averagely capable in their academic work.

What self-esteem depends on

Self-esteem also depends on self-image to the extent that one may approve or disapprove of one's attributes (as one believes they are). People who have been brought up to believe in the virtue of self-control may despise themselves for a perceived attribute of becoming emotional in times of stress and crisis. Other people may see themselves as being both clever and good-looking, and will esteem themselves highly for these attributes. In short, the positive or negative qualities of the self-image will bear a relationship to the degree of self-esteem that we have. The degree of esteem will relate to our use of communication. Without wishing too much to turn on a single example, one could show a possible contrast of self-esteem in two kinds of request approach, one of which runs: 'Have you got a left-handed thimble in stock?' and another that runs, 'I don't suppose by any chance you've, um, got something like, um, a left-handed thimble?'

    Self-esteem also depends on the approval of others. This approval will be communicated, in particular, nonverbally. If you were to greet a couple of friends in a restaurant and then receive strong nonverbal signs that your presence was not welcome, two things might follow. One could be that you deduce a message about not interrupting a precious moment. The other might be that you then feel incompetent for not perceiving their relationship and for offering inappropriate behaviour. Low self-esteem follows. It may not last for long if you have a strong and positive self-image. It is likely that you will have felt this way as a result of the disapproval offered by others early in your life. This early response from others will contribute to the construction of various kinds of self-image.

    Even an ideal image will have been constructed, at least partly, out of the responses of parents and others to the young person's behaviour. Coopersmith (1967) found that there was a positive correlation between high self-esteem in teenage boys and the degree of affection and approval shown towards them by the parents when they were younger. Boys whose parents were authoritarian, offered less approval and showed less recognition of the worth of their sons, were distinctively lower in self-esteem.

    Because **most people would prefer to think well of themselves rather than not** (see also personal needs), they will also seek the approval of others. In effect they will adjust the kind of Self that is presented so that it fits social values or the norms of a particular group. This may mean adjustment of physical, emotional, intellectual or personality attributes. This selective adjustment of self-image happens internally in the first place, because self-image is an internal construct. But, again, it must be manifested externally for it to be known. Such self-presentation means communication. The most common example of this adjustment in order to gain approval is when people dress up and adopt certain behaviours that they think will make them attractive to others. If they receive feedback that confirms the success of this behaviour then not only will their esteem have been strengthened, but also their awareness of their attributes will have been confirmed. In the first place it could be that being kind to others is something of an experiment by a child. But when it receives approval for kind acts this will firm up kindness as an attribute. Kindness will rate high in self-esteem.

Such approval and feelings of self-esteem are a strong motivating force. High self-esteem brings satisfaction that can be described in other terms, but which still depends on that esteem to a large extent. 'In large measure the "pursuit of happiness" is the pursuit of self-esteem' (Patton and Griffin 1981). It is beyond the scope of this book to discuss what might be called 'disturbed self concepts' or to get into the realms of psychotherapy. However, Carl Rogers' book *On Becoming A Person: A Therapist's View of Psychotherapy* (1990) provides some very stimulating explorations of self-concept and self-esteem. Carl Rogers is credited with being the originator of 'client-centred' (or 'person-centred') therapy, which approaches clients' problems by seeking to develop in a positive self-concept in the client.

In order to be self-confident communicators, do we need to like ourselves? Carl Rogers suggests one way of looking at self-esteem that makes it clear it is not a form of arrogance or superiority:

> We have established the fact that in successful psychotherapy negative attitudes toward the self decrease and positive attitudes increase. We have measured the gradual increase in self acceptance and have studied the correlated increase in the acceptance of others. But as I examine these statements and compare them with our more recent cases, I feel they fall far short of the truth. The client not only accepts himself – a phrase which may carry the connotation of a grudging and reluctant acceptance of the inevitable – he actually comes to *like* himself. This is not a bragging self-assertive liking; it is rather a quiet pleasure in being one's self.
>
> (Rogers 1990)

When self-esteem varies

Self-esteem is a variable factor – that is to say, it varies in general and in particular cases, and it varies on some assumed scale. So, one may talk of **a general level** of self-esteem for an individual, but also of **particular levels** in particular circumstances. We have all come across that person who seems in general to have weak self-esteem, to be reticent and withdrawn. Put that same person in a canoe and it turns out that they have a gold badge and can tell everyone else a thing or two about handling the canoe. Their confidence blossoms.

Equally it is the case that self-esteem is not something that simply appears or disappears. We have a notion of **degrees of self-esteem**. The problem for an observer is how to define the scale used. It is an internal construct, like self-esteem itself, but we can only use communication to recognize and evaluate it. Psychologists must produce a form of words and then ask people if that phrase corresponds to something in their consciousness. So while it may be agreed that there are various levels of self-esteem, it is difficult to measure these. There is no clear agreement about using descriptive terms as scales of measurement, though notions of high and low are fairly well defined. Thus the work of people like Rosenberg (1965) does show a correlation between his subjects' estimate of themselves and the estimates of others of those subjects. And there was agreement about terms of reference in that, for example, subjects with low self-esteem were seen as being easily discouraged and either avoided social situations or remained detached from them.

Self-esteem and communication

To develop this point about behaviour and to conclude this section, it is useful to come back to self-esteem's representation through communication. **High and low self-esteem is represented through communication style** as much as through particular phrases. It takes a collection of characteristics to add up to this style.

People with high self-esteem tend to talk firmly, with a relative lack of hesitation, and through a wide and flexible vocabulary. Their talk contains phrases that acknowledge others and their views, such as 'I take your point'. They may use phrasing that admits responsibility and misjudgement: 'I'm sorry, I shouldn't have said that'. Their nonverbal communication is open and assured. They are concerned for others and show other social skills such as empathy. So, they are not self-regarding and their view of Self is firm enough that they can accept failure and criticism.

Those with low self-esteem communicate in a contrasting way to the above. They are defensive about their Self, and this is shown in extremes in slack body posture, protective gestures and lack of animation in expression. In short, they do not appear confident, and are reluctant to take risks in social encounters. They are defensive in their approach to social interaction, may talk about themselves with persistent deprecation, and about others in terms of envy. Their very speech patterns may be hesitant and/or heavily larded with the phrasal habits of their peer group, from which they desire approval. Tics such as often using words like 'like' and 'you know' are probably the most recognizable examples of these. Not surprisingly, such people tend to have a pessimistic view of their social skills and of the outcomes of activities in which they are involved.

Our self-esteem is not a fixed state that is imposed on us. As with our self-concept and self-image, we can change our self-esteem through the ways we think about our self and our relationships with others. Raj Persaud (2005) sets out ten steps to greater self-esteem:

> Low self-esteem comes in many guises: learn to recognize it for what it is.
> Don't think praise is given so as not to hurt your feelings.
> Don't let the past determine your future.
> Don't let others' opinions matter more than your own.
> Don't project your own dislike of your self on to other people.
> High self-esteem means you can risk failing.
> Stop comparing yourself with others as the only way of sensing your worth.
> Recognize your own achievements.
> Low self-esteem means you don't trust yourself.
> Aim to make a small improvement each day in yourself.
>
> (Persaud 2005)

KEY QUESTIONS

Self-esteem

Make a list of positive or complimentary adjectives you would like other people to use to describe you.

Using this list of adjectives, adapt them to reflect how the same ideas of your self-esteem might be viewed by someone who you believe does not like you. For example, what you consider as 'confident' someone else may consider to be 'arrogant'.

Self and the media

In this section we want to take a brief look **at the relationship between the media and people's notions of Self**. It is often suggested, or assumed, that the media offer models for the construction of self-image as well as for interactive behaviour. Surprisingly, hard evidence for such aspects of socialization is not so easy to come by. (The term 'socialization' refers to the ways in which we assimilate the values, attitudes, conventions and norms of behaviour of the society in which we live. Our self-image and how we relate to other people are influenced by our responses to these processes of socialization. The media are one of the key agents of socialization, but their actual effect is a matter of debate.)

This problem is bound up with media effects, debates and research, in which much has been hypothesized about the influence of the media on us, but relatively little has been demonstrated to be true, even under specific circumstances. Indeed, in many ways research into the connection between media and people has been very much concerned with the idea of effects above everything else, and, even now, with the idea that effects are about what the media *do* to people. In fact, there is plenty of evidence that people do things with the media – take things from reading and viewing to satisfy internal needs. Equally, there is evidence that people can distinguish fiction from reality and are well aware that the media construct a world that is not life. This suggests that audiences do not so easily internalize qualities of Self or imitate forms of interaction. On the other hand, this need not stop us from making propositions even if they need effective testing. For example, it may be proposed that people construct notions of an ideal Self from admired performers or characters in the media. One can also propose that the media offer models for social behaviour – how to perform in romantic encounters, for example.

Some evidence does, at least indirectly, support the notion of connections between media and interpersonal activity. For instance, we know that people in Britain spend an average of four hours a day watching television. It is also the case that Livingstone (1987) found that 60 per cent of viewers surveyed said that they became identified with the lives of soap characters. If one takes this on face value, it is possible to accept that this degree of identification could also lead to degrees of imitation or assimilation of examples of social behaviour. Duck (1993) also refers to Livingstone when he says that her work 'seems to suggest that viewers acquire a certain belief system associated with sex-roles'. The notion of role is bound up with role behaviour – so there may be a connection between the example of television material and the way that men and women behave, including communicative behaviour.

In terms of one's sense of role or of internalization of self-image, it is also relevant to point to what the media do not say. In a cultural context, if there is an absence of material that one can recognize, as an immigrant Bangladeshi or a Glasgow teenager, then a number of things may follow. Media could be dismissed as being irrelevant to one's sense of Self and of culture. One could turn more strongly to other cultural experiences, such as religious practice or activities based on a style of music. Or one could feel subconsciously resentful or damaged or cheated because one's sense of culture is being denied.

To sum up, it is assumed that because the media influence our beliefs and attitudes, that they therefore shape our sense of Self. It is assumed that we borrow from the media in terms of how we communicate. It is assumed that the media shape our sense of cultural identity. It is much less easy to be certain how this happens, to what degree and in what way.

Attitudes, beliefs and values

Although they have necessarily been referred to already, these still need to be dealt with separately, however briefly, as another distinct element of the Self. They are an important part of intrapersonal communication, serving as kinds of reference points when making judgements about the Self, and about information perceived as relevant to the Self.

We have attitudes towards our Self and attitudes towards others that are also part of that Self. (We also have attitudes towards other things such as types of behaviour or public issues.) With regard to people, **these attitudes are positions that we take up towards the person being dealt with,** and that we have before we start to deal with them. They have much to do with self-esteem because, fundamentally, attitudes are either favourable or unfavourable. They are based on a collection of beliefs – perhaps about ourselves. Once acquired, these beliefs will affect communication because they create a negative or positive position towards the subject. Clearly it matters as to whether or not we feel negative or positive about ourselves.

Beliefs are not only about the Self. But some are, and this is important. **Beliefs may be defined in terms of what we think is true,** and how far we agree with a statement or an opinion. So we must have beliefs about our Self, what we believe its main features are. Indeed, it could be said that to have a view of the Self is to have beliefs about the Self. As with attitudes, our other beliefs are also part of the whole Self and will affect perception when interacting with others. Beliefs are more or less strongly held, and are more or less important to ourselves. Beliefs about the Self are strong and important for the obvious reason that a well-formed and firm view of the Self brings a sense of security and certainty. People will confidently make statements about their qualities and abilities based on such beliefs, and are prepared to argue with others about this: 'but you don't know me, I'm not like that really'. We even have beliefs about our ability to communicate. Such beliefs have external effects. Nothing succeeds like success. Positive beliefs produce positive behaviour, which, in turn, reinforces this belief. The more we believe that we are good at communicating, the more likely we are indeed to be that good. Of course, some people's beliefs are not geared to their abilities. If they believe their ideal image is much like their realistic one then they may 'fool' themselves into believing that they are great communicators. The correlation between belief and behaviour is referred to by Gahagan when she writes of the idea that 'we try actively to get others to behave in ways which accord with our main beliefs about ourselves' (Gahagan 1984).

Values have to do with morality and ethics. They are ideas we have about what is good and bad – indeed, about what is relatively good and bad. Once more the idea that we have such values as part of our Self must be connected closely with self-esteem. As Myers and Myers (1992) put it, values are 'conceptions . . . of the relative worth you attribute to the things, people, and events of your lives'. And we have already defined self-esteem in terms of the degree of worth that we feel about ourselves. Clearly the terms are synonymous if not actually identical. **Values, like other concepts that we have described, are learnt**. We are not born with them. Once learnt they are quite persistent. We don't give them up easily. As part of a trinity with beliefs and attitudes, they are important in the intrapersonal processes because they offer standards by which we may weigh up experience, including communication from others. Equally, as good, sceptical communication students we have to recognize that values are relative. What is valued in a person in one culture may not be so valued in another. What is valued at one time is not so valued at another time. Differences in values occur because of different needs and different environments, social and physical. For example, in Northern European and American cultures it is accepted as 'right' that old people should go to retirement homes or nursing homes. In many Southern European cultures this is seen as 'wrong'. In these cultures one could say that part of people's self-image includes a Self who will, and should, look after elderly relations until they die. There are historical and cultural reasons for such a difference. We make no moral judgement on such values. But clearly they are crucial to external and internal communication processes.

The concept of personality provides a way of us describing our own or other people's characteristics or personal traits. The psychotherapist Carl Rogers came to the view that personality is a kind of mask that we adopt to deal with other people and to display the self-concept we have developed. From his experience as a therapist he believed that it was important that this expression of personality should reflect the concept we have of ourself. If we feel we are displaying a false view of ourselves it is likely to decrease our self-esteem because we feel rather a sham. Our concept of ourself and of our personality may be a limiting factor in our communication with others. For example, if you have a concept of yourself by which you perceive yourself as introverted and shy, this will affect how you deal with other people.

Peter Hartley, in his book *Interpersonal Communication* (1999), usefully sums up his own view of personality and its influence on communication as follows:

My own view of personality follows these developments (i.e. of recent psychological research) . . .

- we do possess a range of personal character traits
- these traits do influence how we behave and communicate
- these traits are *only one* influence upon our behaviour

Following this line of argument, I suggest that your personality influences your communication in two main ways:

- Predispositions: our personality characteristics predispose us to behave in certain ways.
- Limitations: our personality characteristics establish very broad limits for our communication.

One also has to be aware of how **contradictory messages about values could cause conflict in the developing self-image of the young person**. For example, a father may imbue his children with the idea that it is good to tell the truth. Then the children hear him lying to cover up the fact that he has forgotten an appointment (euphemistically called 'making excuses'). Hence, a child may have got a key value of honesty and never telling lies as part of their self-image, but then learn that some untruths are considered to be acceptable.

The concept of **ideology** also relates to attitudes, beliefs and values. You will come across this concept later in relation to the media and communication in particular, so we do not propose to spend much time on the topic here. But it is important to realize, at least, that the implications of ideology exist within the self-consciousness. These are, for example, that there are 'natural' social and power relationships in our society. It is communication that carries messages about what is 'natural'. We assimilate beliefs about the naturalness of the social position of women or about class from what the media and people say to us from an early age. We process these beliefs intrapersonally, and they become part of the Self out of which we communicate to others.

Personality traits

First, it has to be said that the idea of personality is largely synonymous with that of self-image, and that to some extent we are dealing with it only because it is such a familiar term. Its precise meaning is arguable. Its most distinctive meaning seems to assume **a set of traits that are largely permanent and that are distinctive to the individual**. The traits or features of a given personality are assumed to be linked. The term 'attributes' may reasonably be used to substitute for traits. With reference to the notion of a coherent personality, Argyle and Trower (1979) dismiss it thus:

> Many studies have shown that people are not as consistent in their behaviour as a personality theory would have us believe, but we go on believing in personality because it makes the world a more secure and predictable place.

One straightforward and useful notion that research into personality did throw up was that there are two key pairs of factors: dominance and submission, friendliness and hostility. These are accepted as traits that most people have in some degree, and traits that we like to assess in others before and during interaction with them.

Having said this, **there is still no effective distinction between use of the words 'traits' and 'attributes'**. Terms used to describe traits can be categorized within the **three kinds of attribute – physical, social and intellectual**. What we can say, as with attributes, is that what are described as personality traits will hinder or aid communication. For example, a person who is open-minded will be a good listener and will tolerate views and arguments that do not fit with his or her view of the world. The opposite would be true of someone who is dogmatic. The communication style of this latter person would be opinionated and assertive. Their speech might include phrases such as 'any fool can see that'. Yet again, the Self affects interpersonal communication. And the intrapersonal processes are likely to involve degrees of self-justification given this type of personality. This kind of person will rationalize errors of judgement internally as being, for example, based on false information from others, rather than actually being misjudgements.

The emotional self

Our map of ourselves includes an area for emotion. **We attribute emotions to ourselves**. Those who use the term 'personality' would identify certain emotions as traits in the personality. We are fond of referring to ourselves and others as, for example, good-natured or passionate. But once more, the idea that there are fixed and dominant traits within individuals vanishes the more closely one looks at it: people simply do not behave this way. We think they do. They may think they do. But if one examines their behaviour over a range of situations it usually becomes evident that they do not, for example, represent passion or strong feelings the whole time. Whether one is talking about perception of the Self or of others, it seems that there is a distorting factor by which the perceiver fastens on some behaviour, ascribes meaning to it and sees the behaviour as frequent and dominant when in fact it is not.

Obviously there is an emotional element to the Self; it is represented strongly through nonverbal communication. We cry in sorrow, laugh in pleasure and shout in rage. In many ways our words for emotion seem to define the behaviour as much as the state of Self. Research into emotion finds it difficult to pin down. The most acceptable description of the intrapersonal state simply identifies a state of arousal. Which way that arousal will express itself is less certain – as we often say, laughter is next door to tears. Research by Schachter (1964) tends to confirm his theory that there is, first, a state of generalized physiological arousal in the person, which then has to be labelled and directed. Cognitive labelling follows. The effect of Schachter's research was to prove that, once aroused, his subjects' emotion could be labelled as euphoria or anger, depending on how he manipulated the social interaction of the situation. Essentially this is a cognitive approach to explaining emotions, in which emotions are attributed rather than being a distinctive physiological experience.

People do not have consistent descriptions of their internal states when feeling emotional. They describe emotion largely in terms of external signs – which brings us back to communication. In this case the medium and the message are thoroughly mingled.

Research by Ekman (1982), who showed photographs of expressions to subjects in a wide range of cultures, did confirm a considerable degree of agreement in reading the emotions of anger, fear, contempt, surprise, disgust, sadness and happiness. In his recent book *Emotions Revealed: Understanding Faces and Feelings* (2003), Paul Ekman has described 'all that I have learned about emotion during the past forty years that I believe can be helpful in improving one's emotional life'.

Paul Ekman's extensive research into emotions and their expression has led him to identify four essential skills to help us manage our own and other people's emotions:

1. Becoming more consciously aware of when you are becoming emotional, even before you act or speak. Developing this skill allows you to have some choice about when you are emotional.

2. Choosing how you behave when you are emotional, so you can achieve your goals without damaging other people. The purpose of emotional episodes is to help us to achieve our objectives quickly, whether to draw people to comfort us, scare off a predator, or some other of thousands of goals.

3. Becoming more sensitive to how others are feeling. Since emotions are at the core of every important relationship we must be sensitive to how others are feeling.

4. Using the information you acquire about how others are feeling carefully. Sometimes that means asking the person about the emotion you have spotted, acknowledging how she or he is feeling, or recalibrating your own reactions in light of what you have recognized.

(Ekman 2003)

Ekman says that he set out with the belief that emotions and their expression were socially and culturally learnt. However, his researches have convinced him that seven key emotions and their expression through facial expressions are universally understood.

Ekman has studied facial expressions and developed a Facial Action Coding System (FACS) to analyse the expressions of emotions. He suggests that a face can make more than 10,000 expressions and has identified the changes in the mouth, eyes, eyebrows, nose and forehead that we use as signals of our own emotional state and read as signals of the emotional states of other people. We can detect when someone is smiling only with their mouth because their eyes indicate this is a contrived rather than a genuine smile. These facial expressions are also accompanied by physical actions and changes in the voice.

Research conducted by Ekman and Davidson (1994) found that making a smile produced many of the changes in the brain that occur with enjoyment. This was not true of just any kind of smile, but only the smile that truly signified the feeling of enjoyment. (There is one difference that separates enjoyment smiles from non-enjoyment smiles: a genuine smile also activates a particular set of eye muscles.)

These discoveries have led Liz Hodgkinson to develop a view that smiling can form a sort of personal therapy to make you feel more emotionally positive. Her popular book *Smile Therapy: How Smiling and Laughter Can Change Your Life* (1987) suggests that smiling (genuinely) makes you feel better and encourages others to smile back at you, contributing to your feeling of well-being.

Taking this evidence that external signs feed back to internal states, you might test this simply by making a rule that you will smile as much as seems socially sensible for a given morning. See if you actually feel happier by the end of the morning than at the beginning. Your feelings might have to do with the expression (though, of course, some good things might happen to you as well that make you smile).

Obviously we do not feel like smiling all the time and it would not be appropriate to smile when situations that you and others are facing are a cause for sadness, fear, anger or other negative feelings. We develop a sensitivity to our own and other people's emotional states from observing their facial and physical behaviour.

It is clear that emotion is an important element of the Self, but that its origin and nature is not clearly understood. What is most clear is that emotions are recognized through communication and that once recognized by either the producer of the emotion or by the receiver, judgements about the state of that Self are confirmed or adjusted.

Emotional intelligence and other intelligences

In the past few years the phrase **'emotional intelligence'** has come into common use as a way of describing **a range of intrapersonal and interpersonal characteristics and skills**. This is perhaps in growing recognition of the ways in which our emotions either enable us or hinder us from living contentedly with our self and with others. As Ekman (2003) succinctly expresses it:

> Emotions determine the quality of our lives. They occur in every relationship we care about – in the workplace, in our friendships, in dealings with family members, and in our most intimate relationships. They can save our lives, but they can also cause real damage.

Emotional intelligence (EQ) has been developed as a concept partly to show that a person's intelligence, as measured by intelligent quotient (IQ) tests, is often not a good predictor of success in life nor of emotional health. Raj Persaud (2001) defines emotional intelligence as a measure of your ability to perceive correctly your own and other people's emotions, and to use this information shrewdly. An element of the process of intrapersonal communication is to be aware of, and to deal with, your emotions as they are triggered by your feelings and external situations.

The emotional quotient inventory was developed in the 1980s by Dr Reuven Bar-On who based it on five realms and fifteen scales. The five realms are:

- Intrapersonal: emotional self-awareness, assertiveness, independence, self-regard and self-actualization
- Interpersonal: empathy, social responsibility, interpersonal relationships
- Adaptability: problem solving, reality testing and flexibility
- Stress management: stress tolerance and impulse control
- General mood: happiness and optimism.

Steven Stein and Howard Book (2001), in their work *The EQ Edge: Emotional Intelligence and Your Success*, provide a full account of EQ and how it can be used for greater success in personal and work life.

Daniel Goleman is credited with popularizing the ideas of emotional intelligence for a wide audience. In his books, *Emotional Intelligence: Why It Can Matter More Than IQ* (1996) and *Working with Emotional Intelligence* (1998), Goleman has set out both the concepts and practical applications of EQ. He lists some of the characteristics and abilities of emotional intelligence as 'being able to motivate oneself and persist in the face of frustrations'; 'to control impulse and delay gratification'; 'to regulate one's moods and keep distress from swamping the ability to think'; 'to empathize and to hope' (Goleman 1996).

At the root of EQ are the processes by which we recognize our own internal thought processes (what some psychologists call 'metacognition') and our own emotions (sometimes called 'metamood'). It is a tool for self-awareness, for paying attention to one's internal states.

Goleman (1998) moves from the notion of EQ to the notion of **'emotional competence'**, which he defines as 'a learned capability based on emotional intelligence that results in outstanding performance at work'. He might have added that such competencies can also help in daily personal life too.

The Emotional Competence Framework that Goleman sets out in his *Working with Emotional Intelligence* provides a practical guide to effective management of ourselves and our relationships with others. Under 'Personal competence' he lists:

- 'Self-awareness including emotional awareness, accurate self-assessment, and self-confidence

- Self-regulation including self-control, trustworthiness, conscientiousness, adaptability, and innovation; and

- Motivation, including achievement drive, commitment, initiative, and optimism.'

Under 'Social competence' he lists:

- 'Empathy, including understanding others, developing others, service orientation, leveraging diversity, and political awareness; and

- Social skills, including influence, communication (listening openly and sending convincing messages), conflict management, leadership, change catalyst, building bonds, collaboration and cooperation, and team capabilities.' (Goleman 1998)

Emotional intelligence is now a part of the landscape of interpersonal communication. It takes some of the concepts of communication and social psychology and seeks to use them as ways of improving one's life experience and career. EQ could be described as a manifestation of the long tradition of self-help books that have been particularly popular in the USA and now, judging from the numbers of these books on sale in British bookshops, has become almost equally popular in the UK. Tom Butler-Bowden's book *50 Self-help Classics* (2003) summarizes some of the key ideas from fifty 'inspirational books to transform your life'. Many of these are based on issues of intrapersonal and interpersonal communication and, in particular, on ways of trying to enable you to feel better about your personal feelings and emotional state.

As a footnote to this reference to the tradition of self-help books, it is remarkable how large this industry has become – does this reflect feelings of personal inadequacy or a desire to seek quick fixes to make our life experiences more meaningful? Francis Wheen (2004) states that John Gray (author of *Men Are from Mars, Women Are from Venus*) had an income stream of $10 million in 1999, partly from 350 Mars and Venus facilitators who paid him for the privilege of distributing his books at monthly workshops. By the end of the twentieth century self-help publications were worth $560 million a year and the total self-improvement industry in the USA – from seminars, personal coaching, CDs and videos – was $2.48 billion. Wheen dismisses it all as 'lucrative twaddle', but to the student of culture and communication it is an interesting cultural phenomenon. In this context, self-help books also often deal with issues of intrapersonal communication and its role in developing identity (see Section 1.4 below). David Gauntlett, in his book *Media, Gender and Identity: An Introduction* (2002), discusses self-help books as tools that some people seek to enable them to develop identities and roles that they believe will help them to become 'successful and happy'.

Possibly as a spin-off from this concept of emotional intelligence (EQ), there is now also discussion of **'spiritual intelligence'** (SQ). This goes beyond understanding and managing our emotions to encompass a belief in the meaning and purpose of life. An individual who has developed a satisfying personal belief system about the meaning and purpose of her/his life is likely to be able to cope with personal crises and feelings of depression or alienation that many people experience at some moments in their life. From this personal base of inner calm, you may also be able to communicate a sense of meaning and purpose to others who are feeling in some sort of personal turmoil.

Danah Zohar and Ian Marshall, in their book *SQ – Spiritual Intelligence: The Ultimate Intelligence* (2000), define SQ as: 'the intelligence with which:

- we address and solve the problems of meaning and value
- we can place our actions and lives in a wider, richer, meaning-giving context
- we can assess that one course of action or life path is more meaningful than another'.

It is possible to analyse personal statements and opinions in terms of their personal origins, that is, to decide if they derive from an individual's intelligence, emotional or spiritual quotient, or a mixture of these.

Our emotional self is also a product of our achievements and other people's views of them. In Britain, and perhaps elsewhere, the ex-footballer George Best is recognized as having been a very talented player whose personal and working life has been damaged by alcohol and an indulgent lifestyle. He is alleged to have said: 'I spent 95% of my money on booze, birds and fast cars . . . the rest I just squandered'. This is clearly intended to be a humorous statement, but you might like to consider how far it challenges or reinforces some cultural and social norms. One might form a view from it that George Best, along with some other successful sportspeople, found it difficult to cope with his success and perhaps his self-concept was based very largely on his physical and footballing ability.

In addition to IQ, EQ and SQ, it is useful to add PQ – **physical intelligence**. Some people's key strength is in physical hand, foot and eye coordination. Such kinaesthetic coordination may also lead to talents of performance in drama, dance and music as well as sport.

Howard Gardner (1993) suggested that the accepted view of intelligence and ability was too narrow and that we should rather think of people as having **'multiple intelligences'**. He proposed seven types of separate human intelligences:

- 'Linguistic (spoken and written language, ability to learn languages)
- Logical-mathematical (capacity to analyse problems logically and investigate issues scientifically)
- Musical (skill in performance, composition and appreciation of musical patterns)
- Bodily-kinaesthetic (the potential of using one's whole body or parts of the body to solve problems or fashion products as with dancers or athletes, craftspersons or surgeons)
- Spatial (the potential to recognize and manipulate the patterns of spaces as with navigators, sculptors or architects)
- Interpersonal (denotes a person's capacity to understand the intentions, motivations, and desires of other people'as with teachers, religious leaders, politicians, psychologists)
- Intrapersonal (involves the capacity to understand oneself, to have an effective working model of oneself – including one's own desires, fears, and capacities – and to use such information effectively in regulating one's own life)'. (Gardner 1993)

In 1999, Gardner wrote a book called *Intelligence Reframed: Multiple Intelligences for the 21st Century*, in which he reconfirmed his views of these seven intelligences and considered three possible new candidate intelligences to add:

- Naturalist (expertise in recognition and classification of flora and fauna)
- Spiritual (this encompasses a concern with cosmic and existential issues, as well as achievement of a state of being and a concern for others)
- Existential (a concern with ultimate issues).

Gardner eventually rejected the final two here as separate intelligences, but added 'naturalist'. His theory of multiple intelligences has been challenged by various writers, but it does provide a useful way of reflecting on one's own talents and interests and one's concept of personal strengths.

KEY QUESTIONS

1. Taking Gardner's theory of multiple intelligences, consider each one with regard to your own interests and talents and ease of learning and rate them on a scale of 1–5, where 1 means least and 5 means most.

2. Complete the Multiple Intelligences Questionnaire in Figure 1.3, which will enable you to reflect on your personal interests and strengths and then to analyse these in terms of Gardner's list of intelligences. Does this result agree with your own self-reflection about your intrapersonal processes?

Complete the following questionnaire by assigning a numerical value to each of the statements that you consider represents you. If you agree that the statement very strongly represents you assign a 5. If the statement does not represent you at all assign a 0. Use the numbers 0–5 to grade each statement.

1. I enjoy being out of doors in the country.
2. I am skilful in working with objects.
3. I have a good sense of direction.
4. I can remember the words to music easily.
5. I have a natural ability to sort out arguments between friends.
6. I am able to explain topics and make them clear.
7. I always do things one step at a time.
8. I know myself well and understand why I behave as I do.
9. I can identify lots of different birds and flowers.
10. I enjoy community activities and social events.
11. I learn well from talks, lectures and listening to others.
12. When listening to music I experience changes in mood.
13. I enjoy puzzles, crosswords and logical problems.
14. Charts, diagrams and visual displays are important for my learning.
15. I am sensitive to the moods and feelings of those around me.
16. I learn best when I have to get up and do it for myself.
17. I need to see something in it for me before I want to learn something.
18. I like to identify different species of insects and bugs.
19. I like privacy and quiet for working and thinking.
20. I can pick out different individual instruments in complex musical pieces.
21. I can visualise remembered and constructed scenes easily.
22. I have a well-developed vocabulary and am expressive with it.
23. I enjoy and value taking written notes.
24. I have a good sense of balance and enjoy physical movement.
25. I can discern pattern and relationships between experience and things.
26. In teams I cooperate and build on the ideas of others.
27. I am observant and will often see things others miss.
28. I get restless easily.
29. I enjoy working or learning independently of others.
30. I enjoy making music.
31. I have a facility with numbers and mathematical problems.
32. I have a strong commitment to protecting the bio-diversity of the earth.

Multiple Intelligences: key to statements

Transfer the numbers that you assigned to each statement to these boxes (on page 28). Then add up the scores that represent your personal view of your use of the different intelligences.

Fig. 1.3 Multiple Intelligences Questionnaire

Intelligence type	Statements/scores	Total scores
Linguistic	6 11 22 23	
	Scoring	....
Mathematical and logical	7 13 25 31	
	Scoring	....
Visual and spatial	3 14 21 27	
	Scoring	....
Musical	4 12 20 30	
	Scoring	....
Interpersonal	5 10 15 26	
	Scoring	....
Intrapersonal	8 17 19 29	
	Scoring	....
Kinaesthetic	2 16 24 28	
	Scoring	....
Naturalist	1 9 18 32	
	Scoring	....

Fig. 1.3 cont.

3. Then try to review your own view with someone who knows you well, for example, a close and trusted friend, a family member or a teacher. Compare your own view with his or her view of your strengths of intelligences.

4. Taking the notions of IQ, EQ, SQ and PQ, consider your own self-concept in terms of these quotients.

5. While not suggesting these four should be equally balanced as an 'ideal', it is possible to consider that an athlete would have a greater proportion of PQ, a scientist a greater proportion of IQ. Consider a number of professions and roles, and suggest which quotient is likely to be the most developed, which second, which third and which least.

The self as free agent

One dominant view of the self, held by many in our culture at least, is that we are free agents. We have the power to make decisions, to change our lives. Strictly speaking, this is not so much an element of Self as a specific belief. But in so far as we are trying to describe that range of components of Self generated through intrapersonal communication and affecting interpersonal communication, then it is important enough to merit separate mention.

We are aware of something that we call our Self. **We see ourselves as decision makers. We see the Self as cause and our actions as effect**. 'We accept a partial responsibility for the consequences of our actions' (Bannister and Agnew 1977). We also recognize that, in part, others and external events may also influence our actions. But we may also influence them.

This belief in the individual Self and in responsibility is a version of the belief that we determine our own destiny. It strengthens a view of the Self that believes we have the power to influence what happens to us perhaps through influencing others. We attribute to ourselves qualities and competence that will tend to support this view. For example, people like to see themselves as being able to work things out and as being decisive. Conversely, people show distress and anxiety when actually denied control over their lives (and when presumably their view of themselves and their esteem suffers). For example, in a study by Schultz (1976) of old people in a residential care home, it was shown that those who were denied the right to arrange their own visiting times and decide their visitors had a lower level of morale and health than those who were allowed to do this. So, it appears that we believe in a certain kind of Self, we attribute certain qualities of Self, and we become distressed if that belief or that attribution is contradicted.

Self as moral person

The notion of responsibility extends to a moral sphere. **We also have a view of ourselves as a normal person making moral decisions**. This sense of morality (related to the values described above) has particular reference to social behaviour. Much social behaviour is, of course, communicative. In this case Gergen and Gergen (1986) refer to the notion of **social accountability** and describe the ideas of Shotter (1984). Shotter suggests that we are engaged in **social accounting** when we use nonverbal and verbal communication to convince others that we are 'normal'. We would contend that this normality has a moral dimension. We will adopt behaviours and make utterances that are seen as 'right and proper' by those to whom we are rendering accounts. If we make such an account and receive approving feedback then our sense of self as moral person with moral responsibility is strengthened. We have exercised that responsibility and have had it confirmed. For example, someone who clips their neighbour's car when backing out of their driveway, even without causing damage, will see themselves as morally responsible. They will go through an apology – for no material reason – because they see themselves as being socially accountable.

KEY QUESTIONS

Write down about ten beliefs and values that are important to you. Comment on how you think they affect how you deal with other people.

Do you see yourself as a 'free agent', and if so how does this affect your life?

1.4 The Self and identity

'Identity' is a term that adds to the overlapping set of words used to describe the Self. You may come across the term 'self-identity'. We will use it to draw attention to culturally inflected aspects of Self. It is a term that has a considerable literature of its own within the discipline of cultural studies.

Whereas some of what you have read in this chapter so far talks about the Self from a psychological point of view, other explanations talk more about the social self. We take identity as being to do with social and cultural aspects of the Self, its formation, maintenance and development. Chapter 3, in which we explain social interaction on the basis of Goffman's ideas, also connects with the social Self, and with ways in which we achieve a sense of identity through our dealings with others.

Cultural context

Because it is connected with culture and communication, identity also relates to ideas about the flexible and adaptive self. This contrasts with what are called **essentialist views** about people having a core personality. We are not arguing that there is no such thing as a stable self. It is generally the case that as a person develops their sense of what they value, what they are good at, how they see themselves, then they are also developing a sense of identity. But we have also said that people learn to put forward different aspects of themselves in different circumstances. Those circumstances, for example to do with family occasions or leisure activities, are deeply cultural. Identity operates within specific cultures. From this perspective, our sense of who we are is defined by such things as what we 'should' wear at a wedding, or how we expect to be treated because we are male or female. Everything around us bears in on identity formation. As Jorge Gonzales puts it (in Lull 2001), 'churches, schools, hospitals, museums, restaurants, dance halls, broadcasting organisations, and many other institutions play a strong role in shaping our very selves from birth'.

Identity, then, is talked about in terms of the **cultural context** in which a person grows up, in terms of how that person interacts with others within that culture. From this view, who we think we are cannot exist in isolation from others. **Our self is continuous with our culture**. We are not as individual as we might like to think we are.

In respect of **defining identity**, we may say that our sense of self is bound up with:

- our family history (and stories about past family members)
- our geography (where we live or perhaps where our family comes from)
- our ethnicity (a sense of group affiliations and the bigger history of 'our group')
- cultural practices (how we celebrate occasions or how we worship)
- our bodies (how we look, perhaps our age and, consequently, how others treat us)
- our gender (how 'male' and 'female' are understood and treated within our culture).

Such cultural factors may be linked to well-established theories of personality development, such as the stages of development in the young person described by Erikson in his influential book *Childhood and Society* (1972). He argued that a sense of identity is important for the well-being of the individual. In cultural terms, this is not just about who we are, but also about how we are located in terms of history, place and social practices.

Identity is also very much to do with **difference** – one might say, with *who we are not* when compared with others. Difference may be celebrated, or it may become a lever of oppression. It is one thing, for example, to enjoy family stories about one's grandparents' generation living in Barbados. This gives a sense of 'roots', of belonging, even if one is living a very different kind of life in a city. But it is another thing to be made by others to feel different (as inferior) because some of the family used to live in Barbados. In principle, difference may neutrally be about 'distinction from'. There are all sorts of reasons why one individual may be seen as being distinctive. More likely, one will be seen as being distinctive because of group affiliation, because of the beliefs, behaviours and material appearances that one shares with one group, but not with any other. But often that which is seen as being distinctive also attracts a 'ranking' within a society.

Cultural analysis is, in part, concerned with the reasons for such difference/distinction, with the practices that mark out difference. In this negative sense, difference therefore is to do with status and prejudice – and by extension, to do with one's sense of place in society. It is to do with a sense of self-esteem. Difference could be neutral, but so often it is not. Difference, as with stereotyping, may be culturally constructed around features such as class, gender and age, as well as ethnicity. A negative feeling of being different will be a consequence of ideologies at work, of dominant and subordinate value systems. It will be acquired through social interactions, and through a process of socialisation from an early age. Feeling subordinately different is something that comes from the ways others communicate with us, as well as through media of communication. Such difference becomes assimilated within one's sense of identity. To be a young British and Turkish male living in London is at least to feel different from a young Scottish female living in Oban. But it is to feel very different from a young Greek Cypriot male also living in London, with all the history of antagonism between Turkish and Greek communities. It is to feel different from the, generally speaking, white, middle-class politicians who run one's life. And threaded through all these feelings of difference are some feelings of superiority or inferiority that may be sharpened by dominant social attitudes.

It may be argued that **a sense of identity is sharpened by a sense of difference**. Groups pull together in the face of threats. Whenever Britain goes to war – the Falklands, Kosovo, Iraq – the popular press is full of patriotic discourse and identity terminology: 'our boys are doing it for their country'. In the same way, sports teams 'are flying the flag for Britain'. In certain respects one can be ambivalent about the value of identity. On the one hand, it is seen as securing the personality. It is accepted that everyone craves an identity. On the other hand, asserting and defending identity can be associated with conflict.

Pennington et al. (1999) refer to negative features of social identity when they model the effects of a given group differentiating itself from others, and favouring itself. They say that 'the presence of intergroup conflict is one of the strongest factors making social identity possible'.

The construction of difference is also understood in terms of the concept of **'the other'**. If one feels oneself to be the other, then one feels different. But this implies the idea of norms. One must be different from something, other than something. To be the other is then in some ways to be not within norms, and in some ways to be inferior or subordinated. The examples given above would still apply here. In particular, it can be argued, this means that the ethnic identity of the white person in this country is in fact 'invisible' – because it is of the norms: it is taken for granted. It does not have to be discussed because it is those who are not of 'white culture' who are the other. What is interesting in our increasingly multicultural society is that in some cities it is *not* the norm to be white. Also, what being British means is a matter of increasing contention. You do not have to be white to be British. And even if you are white, like many ethnic groups, it may be that your family has not lived in a given area for many generations. So, if the notion of otherness is a negative one in terms of identity, it is also being challenged by social change – immigration, geographical mobility, marriage across ethnic boundaries.

Discourses

Discourses are ways in which people use language to talk to, or about, their subjects. The term 'language' covers both nonverbal and even visual communication. We have certain vocabularies and styles of speech for talking about, or talking to, elderly people, for instance. The language of the discourse reveals what we think about that person, how we see them, how we rate them in the social structure. Do we talk about them as if they are incompetent, physically and mentally, for instance? If so, we are revealing our own notion of their identity. And if we talk to them in a condescending manner, then we may affect their sense of their identity.

In this view, to which we subscribe in this book, communication is a prime mover. **It is interactions that invoke social identities** – and, indeed, help define what they are. This view would also say that identities are something that is 'performed'. As with personality, one may suppose that a person possesses something labelled identity. But we do not know about that until they communicate. Identity is only an idea until it is given expression.

Although discourses about subjects such as gender may seem rather fixed and unchanging in their meanings, in fact most discourses are not fixed. So the effect of discourses expressing ideological positions is not as continuous as it might seem. And there are many discourses operating through our language systems. So, although identities may indeed be formed through the action of discourses, they also may change, adapt and be negotiated. The understanding of who we are within our society, culture and our immediate groups that we have when we are aged twenty, may well change, if not be overturned, by the time we are forty. Nonetheless, many older people now incorporate ideas of being active and adventurous within their identities. Changing discourses 'allow' for this. Changing social attitudes are part of this. Changing activities or practices also express this. For example, it has become a matter of some concern for those involved with road safety that a number of middle-aged males are killing themselves driving powerful motorcycles that they could not afford when they were younger. This new phenomenon has something to do with changes in identity linked with changes in the discourse of age and what this means.

These ideas also reconnect us with a dynamic model of communication, in which a range of factors interrelates to affect relationships and to produce meaning. This kind of **dynamic model of identity production and development** once more contrasts with essentialist ideas, for example of a 'core self-identity' (Layder 2004). Layder talks about 'core and satellite selves', while also recognizing the modifying effects of others and of context. He refers to the Self as being 'conditioned by life events, relationships and social circumstances'. He recognizes that social responses affect the evolution of identity. His view comes out of a sociological perspective rather than a cultural studies one, and privileges identity and Self as being located in the person as individual, rather than the person as a social and cultural being. In his view there are two kinds of interdependent reality that give rise to an identity which is within all of us. 'Personal identity is forged at the intersection between two distinct but overlapping universes or realities, that of individuals (psychological reality) and that of society, or social reality.'

A culturalist view would be that one cannot have an identity outside the sphere of culture. Cultural (and, indeed, social) experiences are everything. They give us meaning. The self cannot exist apart from the culture that helps form it, and within which it is expressed through social interaction and cultural practices.

Such ideas cause one to return to the concept of individual and collective identities as being continuous. This is where notions of the self and of group membership come together. In Woodward's view (2002), 'Identity has to be socially located because it is through the concept of identity that the personal and the social are connected'.

Identity positions may be understood in terms of what elsewhere is called 'group membership' – seeing oneself as 'a Jewish settler', for example, or as 'an environmentalist'. It is not, one could argue, possible to separate group affiliations and values from those that attach to other roles. The settler may simultaneously be a father and a farmer. This also brings us back to an argument that collective (or social) identities are really all that we have. The individual cannot be apart from life as it is lived, from their past, from their place. If we are to believe in the idea of the individual identity, then one also has to argue that the Self has the autonomy (freedom of action) to construct itself, apart from its cultural and physical environment. This argument is hard to sustain.

Our sense of who we are, where we are from, how we relate to others, is inevitably bound up with the belief systems behind our society and operating within social groups. In a loose sense, ideology is about a way of looking at the world and understanding it. This is true for all of us. **So, it is hardly possible to separate ideology from identity**. In Britain, at the time of writing (2005), it is, for example, impossible to be a farmer who had always hunted with the hounds, and not to feel that one's Self is bound up with beliefs in hunting and in a rural way of life. The farmer feels that this is a 'normal' and 'natural' way of looking at the world and of behaving. We are not saying that it is wrong. But we are saying that it is not natural just because the farmer thinks it is. 'Ideology functions to convince its audiences that the ideas it offers are timeless and ahistorical: that is to say, they have always been, and always will be' (Schirato and Yell 2000).

These naturalized beliefs become part of our identities. Cultural features are bound up with these beliefs and with identity. Even if we do not go to church, we may take it for granted that Sunday is 'different' from other days of the week. But this is not seen as being naturally true by some sections of the population. Their identity is bound up with making other days of the week special, and with conducting other rituals than a visit to the church or to the nearest shopping mall.

Schirato and Yell also point out that, following neo-Marxist arguments of critics such as Althusser and Foucault, **one can see people as being subject to the values contained within ideologies**. These views – always in the interests of those groups that have social and economic power – are, as it were, invisibly imposed upon us. 'To be a subject is to be subjected' (Woodward 2002). As we have said, the views and values are incorporated within our identities. In this way of looking at identity, it may be said that identities are also subjectivities. These are, as Schirato and Yell say, 'produced and made meaningful within a culture'.

This is not to argue that what we feel to be our identity is irrevocably imposed on us from birth. There are competing views and values out there. The 'problem' is to realize that they are there. The difficulty is to resist or criticize the pressure of what is called 'hegemony', the domination of one set of ideas above others. If you are British Asian and grow up in Lancashire, there are a lot of pressures conspiring to make you think about yourself in certain ways, not least by comparison with other social groups. What you think you are also affects how you are, how you treat others and how you deal with other social groups.

This leads us to make a brief comment on what is called **identity politics**. This refers to political statements and actions made by groups who feel diminished or threatened in their identities by dominant groups within society. This may involve kinds of protest, such as those in areas like Oldham or Hoxteth in London, which have made the national press, and which include what has been called a 'protest vote' in local elections supporting British National Party candidates. The protestors could be described as white, working-class people who feel that their way of life is threatened and their histories are being lost, as these areas become multicultural. They have lost social dominance. Like all threatened groups, they feel their identity all the more keenly.

The most obvious area of identity politics is that to do with sexuality. This is not simply to do with women and gender, which we will deal with more fully in Chapter 3, but includes identities that have to do with transsexuality, or homosexuality and lesbianism. Groups that identify themselves in these ways have been politically active in lobbying for reforms of laws that they feel have operated against their interests. They have been socially visible in marches and celebrations, particularly in London. These activities have been about gaining recognition, demanding equal treatment under the law, and asserting the validity of their identities in the face of a social history that has marginalized and oppressed them. Identity becomes obviously political when it is at the heart of social division and conflict.

A sense of oppression and the need for identity are probably most strong in those groups that have moved from one place to another – immigrants and migrants. This phenomenon is especially strong in this age of globalisation and the ease of travel across the planet. The sense of identity, the longing for a secure identity, is seen clearly in those communities that belong to what have been described as **diasporas.** This word describes a diffuse but strongly felt affinity between members of a group, such as the Roma or Jewish people, that is spread across a large geographical area and often uprooted, but which still shares common beliefs and cultural practices. For example, the need for identity is felt by Indians who go to the Middle

East as labourers, and by Filipina women who go to Britain or the USA to work as nurses or house servants. Diasporic identities are often built through common experiences of suffering or of threats to the original identity. The search for identity and security is well exemplified by the movements of Jewish people after World War II, coming from very different countries and going to Israel in order to seek 'the certainty of a shared past and of belonging to a kinship group' (Woodward 2002).

The human body is also a focus for understanding of identity because it can be a marker of characteristics and differences. It is certainly used in a negative sense to underpin racism, sexism, ageism. It is the body that operates forms of communication and conducts the interactions of everyday life. The body is what we look at when we interact and, indeed, when we regard our mirror selves. Bodily features are seized upon to provide immediate descriptions of others and ways of categorising them: facial wrinkles mean that you are old; breasts mean that you are female; brown skin means that you are Indian – or perhaps Egyptian? or perhaps . . .? It is at this point that it becomes clear that what you see may not be what you get, and what you look like may not be what you are. 'The human body is important . . . because it shapes our identities and structures our interventions in and classifications of, the world' (Shilling 1997).

People with lined faces have often said that they do not feel old. Men with slack bodies have as much breast tissue as many women. And skin colour is a very poor indicator of geographical and ethnic origin. All these things are no indicator at all of personality. Yet, through stereotyping and false perceptions, we so often assume that the body tells us about the person.

The meanings of the body are culturally generated. They are, once more, about ideology and power, about having or not having kinds of status within a culture. They certainly do reflect on identity formation, not least because others treat us in part according to the body that they see, and about which they make assumptions. We are asking you to recognize those assumptions for what they are.

The fit body is valued in our culture, especially in the sphere of sport. Media close-ups of footballers tearing off their shirts reinforce this. The popularity of gyms and weight training is evidence of this. Both men and women enter bodybuilding competitions. Yet looking fit does not make you a pleasant person or a good communicator.

The sexualized body is also valued, especially in women. Again, media representations emphasize their sexual features, and help socialize them into believing (unless they choose the path of resistance) that the sexual body is 'a good thing'. It becomes conflated with equally false ideas about what constitutes 'beauty'. It becomes incorporated within their personal and social identities. For everyone, the clothes that we choose to wear to enter into given social situations say something about the identity that we wish to project – and, indeed, reinforce the proposition that we do have flexible and multiple identities. But for women the choice of clothing is often one that is also about the presentation or suppression of sexuality. Low-slung jeans and uplift bras may be chosen for situations in which they wish to present themselves as being 'attractive' (another culturally relative term). Equally, trouser suits, neutral colours and less make-up may be chosen to suppress sexuality in, for instance, formal and work situations. What perhaps is most significant in terms of the female body and identity, however, is that, first, it is unlikely that a western woman will deny all signs of sexual identity in any situation; second, if this is the case, it is more likely in an older woman. The significance of this is not hard to decode.

It is also the case that sexuality should not to be confused with gender. Sexuality is biological, gender is social. And both terms are fraught with ambivalence. Thai 'lady-boys' pass for women, but may have both male and female sexual features. But then, in social terms, it is argued that gender is not about sex but about attitude, how one relates to others, how you feel about yourself. More importantly, gender is about social practices, about behaving as male and female. Statistically, for example, there are tall, physically strong women in the population who are as strong as men. But they may act as if they are weak and incapable because culture has defined their gendered identity in this way. 'Gendered practices and images of the body exert an influence which does not, then, remain at the level of consciousness or discourse. They become embodied and can affect people for life' (Shilling 1997).

KEY QUESTIONS

What factors have been important in shaping your sense of who *you* are?

In what ways are these factors separate from or connected to what you would describe as your personality?

1.5 Maintenance and evaluation of Self

Influential factors

These are described by Argyle (1973) **as the reactions of others, comparisons made with others**, roles played, identifications made with others. (See also reference to 'significant others' below.) So one can see that **it is other people who are most influential in respect of the building, changing or maintaining of the self-image**.

Reactions or feedback from others have most effect if the other person is seen to have status and expertise. So people will listen to therapists or counsellors because they are regarded as knowing what they are talking about. Anything that they say about a person's behaviour or inferred attitudes, for example, will be respected and may well cause adjustment of the self-image.

Comparisons are likely to be made with groups or sets of others as much as with individuals. But those who are the object of comparison are realistically chosen. Children compare themselves with members of their own class at school, not with those who are two grades higher up the school. Evidence suggests that people tend to grade themselves up rather than down. So if members of the second team play with the first team and do well, they revise their self-esteem upwards. If they play with the third team and perform poorly, they are more likely to put it down to an off day than to revise their personal rating downwards.

It appears that **taking on new occupational or social roles affects self-image**, though obviously there will be a simultaneous effect from the reactions of others to these roles played. People who are promoted to a new post at work adopt a self-image appropriate to that role, seeing themselves as newly competent or as having qualities that they did not have before. If they behave in a way appropriate to this self-image then, of course, their new view of, say, their leadership qualities will be endorsed. Clifford and Clifford (1967) refer to an increase in positive self-rating among boys on an Outward Bound course – because, in effect, they had 'proved' themselves. This is what leaflets for such activity courses mean when they say that the experience of such a course will be 'character building'.

Identification with models is concerned with the **ideal image** as much as the realistic self-image. Obvious examples are parents, teachers and stars. Young people for the most part infer attributes of that model person from their behaviour, whether in life or in fiction. They then build those qualities into an ideal image that becomes an object of aspiration; one on which they would model their own behaviour and one whose attributes they would like to develop in their realistic self-image. Again, we have a situation in which **the process of identification (and of attribution) depends on communication**. Indeed, given the fact that self-image can be made known only through communication, one could argue that people aspire to certain kinds of communication behaviour and habits of the model. They want to be seen to be acting like the model because the actions suggest the internalized image. The assumption is that a form of behaviour signifies a specific content of character.

Maintaining and changing (developing) self-image

There is a tension in ourselves between stability and change. It is more secure to seek to endorse and stabilize an established image of the Self. On the other hand, one needs to change and develop self-image to be able to cope with new situations. And there is even an element in the ideology of our culture that values growth and progress (however one defines these terms). Staying the same and changing are both desirable things to do, but they contradict one another, hence the tension.

With regard to stability we may operate **self-maintenance strategies** (see Gergen and Gergen 1986). Basically, these strategies operate a kind of bias inclining towards the ideal Self – or at least screening information that does not fit the realistic Self. **Biased attention** involves us preferring to notice feedback from others that confirms our view of ourselves. **Biased interpretation** involves us making sense of information that is obtained in ways that suit ourselves. **Selective affiliation and presentation** involves us in seeking friends and contacts who are likely to confirm our self-image, and in presenting ourselves in such a way that we are likely to get feedback that also confirms our self-image.

A clear implication of these three self-maintenance strategies is that intrapersonal communication must operate selectively in order to deal with external information selectively. There is evidence that this is indeed the case. One experiment indicated that people process information more quickly if it fits with the terms of reference for their self-image. Other research (Sentis and Markus 1979) also indicates that people better remember information that is consistent with their self-image.

A variation on this theme of bias is seen in another tendency, which is to form a lower opinion of those who indicate that they do not share our view of ourselves. This is **discrediting the source**. So if one's supervisor at work writes a poor progress report, then one's inclination is to say that he/she is a poor judge of character and performance anyway!

The ultimate device for maintaining Self is simply to ignore any evidence that does not fit what we want to believe. This is an extreme example of selective attention. At worst, this represents a pathological condition in which the person denies having heard what the other has said, or asserts that they did not say (or nonverbalize) what in fact they did say. Such a person may live in a world of their own, a world of delusion.

In summary, it may be that those who live a well-defined lifestyle, meeting with a selective and well-defined set of people, are in some measure engaged in protecting their self-image and may have low self-esteem anyway. A wide range of social engagement and new experiences mean that we must take some risks with our self-image. But those with firm self-esteem and a fairly stable view of the Self will feel able to cope with this, and be prepared to make adjustments as they learn more about themselves from others.

Change and self-image

If one is to change or develop one's self-image and to take the risks that this involves, then one must have good reason for doing so. You might want at this point to refer back to the section on motivation. However, we can give you **two good reasons** here. One is **to win the approval of others**; the other is **to cope with changes forced upon us**.

It is, in fact, difficult to draw a line between the ideas of building and of development if one believes that people develop throughout their lives. We have made a tacit assumption that change and development occur after building, after a period when the self-image has stabilized – in which case, examples from our two reasons would be:

- First, an occasion when we make a new group of friends, or perhaps meet someone who becomes special to us. We might then wish to change our behaviour to please them. Unless we are capable of keeping up a deceit, this change in the way we act and talk will be accompanied by a change in the way we see ourselves, presuming that the other(s) give us positive feedback for doing this.

- In the second instance, one could think of changing jobs or getting married. Either of these important changes in our life position means that we have to learn to get on with new people. Again, we would have to adjust our behaviour and our self-image.

The fact that such a change does mean something is summed up in phrases people might use, such as 'I just can't see myself working in that place' or 'I'm not ready to marry him, I can't imagine myself as a wife'. In both cases the speakers have recognized that they would have to change their orientation towards others and change their self-image.

Sometimes we volunteer for such changes, sometimes they are forced upon us (for example, being made redundant from our job). But one can be positive about it and argue that **the more change is risked, attempted and successfully negotiated, the more**

adaptable and open to change we become. Patton and Griffin (1981) refer to this when they say: 'There can be no guarantee of continued self-esteem as we attempt changes. We must risk our self-esteem with each attempt to improve it. Our doubts about our self-worth can be dissipated only by putting them to the test of self-exposure and feedback'.

The process of making changes to the Self absolutely depends on use of communication. If one accepts Radley's hypothesis of a **three-part change** (1974), then this may be seen to be true. In the first part the person has to be able to visualize what the changed Self will be like – a piece of storytelling. Then we may start to act out the new role experimentally – particularly to communicate the way we feel as this changed Self. Finally, at stage three, we may have practised this role with so much success that we really have either changed our Self, or at least added new dimensions to it which can be called up for that role.

Communication from others

It has already been made clear that **what we are and what we think we are depends as much on communication from others as on our own communication skills and style**. Now we will add a few more points explaining how received communication operates on our ability to construct, maintain and evaluate Self.

The research of Videbeck (1960), among others, provides support for the view that not only is the self-image learned through communication, but that also 'the evaluative reactions of others play a significant part in the learning process'. There are oft-quoted examples of experiments where a female has been the recipient of communication that treats her as if she has attractive qualities. The effect of this has been to influence the female so that she behaves as if she is indeed attractive, and may be assumed to have enhanced self-esteem. (You might like to try the same experiment with males!)

Myers and Myers (1992) define communication from others in terms of **confirming and disconfirming responses**. Further, they suggest that confirming responses can be described in five ways:

'1. acknowledging what is heard

2. agreeing with what is said

3. being supportive

4. offering and seeking clarification of what has been said, and

5. expressing positive feelings'.

Disconfirming responses are these seven:

1. ignoring what has been said

2. interrupting

3. saying something irrelevant

4. going off at a tangent

5. being impersonal or generalizing

6. not replying coherently or comprehensibly, and

7. offering non-verbal communication (NVC) that contradicts what is said.

This useful set of examples mentions specific types of verbal and nonverbal behaviour that may be interpreted positively or negatively as feedback, in terms of self-image and self-esteem.

At the same time as accepting the importance of communication from others, one has to remember the point previously made – that **communication from others only affects our self-image as far as we may 'allow' it to**. Eiser (1986) refers to the idea that people seek consensual validation for their attitudes and beliefs. In other words, **we may seek out communication from others that tends to fit our self-image**. This does not mean that people seek only praise. Someone with low self-esteem may actually seek critical comment from others because this confirms their low opinion of themselves.

Our ability to accept or reject statements relating to our Self, in particular, depends on our previously built image. If we cannot accept critical statements, then we will tend to privilege maintenance at all costs. If we are more resilient, then we can accept such remarks, deal with them and contemplate change in our behaviour and image.

Communication from others concerning our Self is often not intentional, and not put in explicit verbal terms. What people think of us is usually expressed in nonverbal terms (including paralinguistic features). It may be expressed through absence of communicative behaviour. Recognition by others of the Self that we present is very important to us as confirmation. Lack of recognition can be interpreted as rejection – 'What have I done wrong? You didn't talk to me today. I've passed you twice and you haven't even blinked!' The point to be made here is that the most apparently trivial smiles and greetings can act as confirmation and recognition. Indeed, this kind of communication, with its tenuously implied messages, is identified specially as **'phatic communication'** (see Glossary).

So, other people are important in a communicative sense to holding on to and even developing our understanding of who we are.

These other people

People whose utterances matter specially to us may be categorized in three ways. What we are saying here is that it is not only what is said that affects our self-image, but also who is saying it. Hayes (1984) talks of **'significant others'**. These are people (such as best friends, parents, respected team leaders) whose judgements we respect, who have status and who have some particular relationship with us.

Then there are **reference groups**. In this case it is the group norms and values (see Chapter 6) and group communication that matters, rather than individuals. The family lets you know what it thinks of your behaviour; the gang lets you know whether you 'fit'; the club offers approval or disapproval – by admitting you or not in the first place.

Finally, there are the **role models**, who may also be significant others. These are people whom we do not just respect or listen to, but on whom we may wish to model ourselves. These models may fall within the categories of role described above. So, for a girl, one particular person may be seen as a role model for being female, while of another person that girl may say, 'I hope I'll be as nice as him when I grow old'. Of course, role models do not just remain an external influence. At some point they become internalized, and that model for image and behaviour can be called up through intrapersonal communication.

Self-perception and self-attribution

The process by which the Self is maintained or changed also depends on how we view and evaluate what we believe to be our Self. One view of this process proposes that it is much the same as interpersonal perception (see Chapter 2). This approach suggests that our own behaviour is as important as the behaviour of others. In other words, **we watch ourselves and make inferences from this observation** (Bern 1967). In effect, we say, 'if I do that then I must be this or that kind of person'. There is no effective difference between this idea and that of self-attribution, where the principle of trying to explain observed behaviour by attributing characteristics to ourselves is comparable.

Cognitive dissonance

Last in this section we refer to a well-established theory (Festinger 1957) that can explain how we deal with the Self throughout our lives – and which, indeed, could just as well be seen as a basic drive for the Self. The simple principle of the theory proposes that **if we find that any of our attitudes, beliefs and values is inconsistent with our experience, or if they seem to contradict one another, then we feel so uncomfortable that we have to do something about it**.

Since we have already suggested that these same three elements are at least a part of the Self, it follows that to change any of them is to change the Self. The theory is attractive not least because our society and its moral positions are so often manifestly contradictory that individuals must adjust in some way to accommodate these contradictions. For example, the virtues of being employed and the rewards this brings are incorporated within the self-image of many people, especially males. So what do individuals feel if they do not, on the other hand, actually believe that the job they do is important or attractive? They feel that somehow it ought to be, but it is not. At the least they will feel unhappy. But then they may assuage this unhappiness by adjusting their self-image to that of a person whose efforts are justified because he is doing it for his family.

It can be argued that experience of this dissonance creates alternative models of behaviour with regard to what happens to our self-image. But people's experiences are so diverse that one cannot easily predict whether a person will respond to dissonance by 'holding on to what they have got' or by making a change in themselves.

The internal communication processes through which this change may occur are the subject of the next section.

KEY QUESTIONS

We have suggested that taking on a new occupational or social role affects self-image. Describe examples of these changes that have happened to you, or in someone you have observed, or if necessary imagine what they might include.

'Significant others', 'reference groups' and 'role models' may have a particular effect on our self-image. Give two examples from each of these categories that you believe have affected your self-image, and say how they have affected it.

1.6 Intrapersonal processing

In this section we deal with the key elements that make up active processing of communication within the Self. We will be coming back to these and adding points in the next chapter. However, although you should find it useful to refer to Chapter 2, remember that we also gave a general description of intrapersonal communication at the beginning of this chapter.

As a kind of opening proviso it also needs to be said that no one is very sure of what goes on inside our heads, though there are many ideas around. For instance, no one is perfectly sure of exactly how we remember things or of how we make guesses. On a basic level, it may be agreed that through these intrapersonal processes we must take in information, shift it to various parts of the brain that have various functions, do something with that information to make sense of it, perhaps store the information, and perhaps act on it – in which case, we may also formulate messages for action. What sounds so simple is, however, immensely complex.

What we will deal with now is a kind of map of intrapersonal activity that identifies the main landmarks. It could be argued that there are five main elements in the process, all of which overlap to some extent. These are: decoding or cognition, integration, memory, schemata or perceptual sets, and encoding.

Decoding

Decoding is that part of the process through which information (communication) is taken in to the brain and made sense of. The signs of communication have to be recognized and interpreted. 'Cognition' is another term that you will come across, which means very much the same thing as decoding. Literally, it refers to 'knowing'. But to know something one has to recognize it, and to recognize it one has to make sense of it. Hence the difficulty in truly separating the parts of the process.

Three kinds of processing

Barker (1984) refers to three kinds of processing in his model for intrapersonal communication (see Fig. 1.4). **Physiological processing** is concerned with messages from our body. In this case one is aware of continual feedback about things like outside

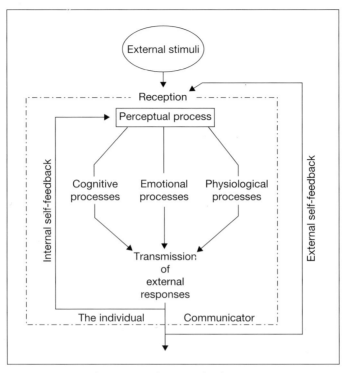

Intrapersonal communication

Fig. 1.4 Barker's model for intrapersonal communication

temperature, or pain from the table edge on which one has just bruised oneself – a kind of body monitoring. **Emotional processing**, which is also relatively subconscious and instinctive, is concerned with internal feedback about our emotional state (see earlier what we have already said about the attribution of emotions). **Cognitive processing** covers everything else, including the handling of information that comes in the form of messages from other people. But do not forget that messages handled in this way can also be generated intrapersonally. If you are making notes from this book, for example, then you are the initiator, the marker and the receiver of the communication that is your notes. You are communicating with yourself. Barker describes this processing as the 'storage, retrieval, sorting and assimilation of information'. And this leads on to the next point.

Integration

Integration refers to that part of the process through which the information identified is put together to make sense of it. One piece of information has to be related to another, comparisons have to be made, categorizing takes place, analogies are made, distinctions are drawn. In the end, a decision is made about what piece of information fits with what.

For example, if one were trying to make a sweater or a wooden storage box and things were going badly, one would have to decide what this failure meant in terms of one's view of the Self. It could be integrated with notions of one's physical coordination, or with one's ability to visualize, or with one's ability to plan and organize activities. Further integration of all three would probably take place so that conclusions could be drawn not only about the Self but also about what to do next.

Memory

Memory is the storehouse of intrapersonal communication. In it are kept all the referential parts of the process. It is not just a store of facts and events. It is a brain function that keeps attitudes, previous judgements and beliefs. Though the operation of memory is not truly understood, it seems that it is not really like a set of boxes in which we put things, but more like a set of messages moving around one tiny part of the brain, waiting to be tapped into the main message system. When we try to think about who we are, then some of these messages are collected together and organized into a pattern called self-image.

Because memory is also about competence and performance – that is, how to do things and what to do – it really is fundamental to our existence, let alone communication. The experience of those who suffer from types of loss of memory (aphasia) is tragically instructive in this respect. We have all read about those people who are found wandering, having forgotten everything about identity, usually after some trauma. But even sadder is the case of people who have lost parts of their long-term memory. In particular, they 'forget' about the death of a loved one. So, every time they are made aware of the death of this loved person they suffer anew the grief that goes with this knowledge.

Memory involves both the ability to store information and also to recall it. Both these subsidiary processes are selective. We have already indicated that there are things that we learn about ourselves and may choose to store, and others that we may not. This is allied to the idea of selective attention. Equally, there is plenty of evidence that we do store a lot of material without being aware of it. To an extent, the memory is more like a camera and a tape-recorder than we realize. It takes many things in. Whether or not we choose to take these things out is another matter. One experiment (Anderson and Williams 1985) asked a group of people to make a conscious effort to remember and recall positive thoughts and feelings. Another group had to remember positive actions and achievements, and consciously keep on calling them back again. A third group was the control group and was given a basically meaningless task. When all three groups were later given a standard test to rate self-esteem, the two active groups came out with markedly higher esteem ratings than the control group. The one that was asked to keep recalling private thoughts and feelings came out best. In this sense there can be a clear relationship between the active use of memory and our view of ourselves. Intrapersonal communication is a private, inward activity, but it seems it can be a very positive one. The two key groups in this case were, in effect, asked to involve themselves in a certain kind of IRPC, and doing so improved their view of themselves.

Three types of memory

As far as memory is understood it seems that there are three types of memory: **sensory storage, short-term memory and long-term memory**. In the first case, information is held only for a moment – a fleeting impression. This is why you see movies as moving – you hold the picture information for a fraction of a second, by which time the next image is coming in, and you assume that the sequences of still images must be moving. In the second case, information is held for a few seconds so that it can be identified, labelled and associated with other information. Only the third example is really a proper 'holding store' in which information is kept.

Of course, long-term memory is only as valuable as the use we are able to make of it, and this depends on our ability to retrieve information. When we recognize a person or an experience, this is a kind of retrieval-recognition. But to really use memory we have to recall fully the information and its relationship to other information. It is of little use to recognize someone in the street if we cannot remember their name, where we last met them, and so on.

We remember what has been communicated to us, what we have communicated and how to communicate. Remembering how to communicate is not just about the function of producing speech, for example. It is also about how we make sense of communication. We remember meanings and how we construct meanings. We remember actions as well as objects.

Schemata and perceptual sets

These two terms are effectively interchangeable. What they describe are **structures of thinking, ways of organizing information**. Through these sets certain pieces of information are interrelated – playing word-association games is some evidence of this. In terms of the idea of roles, we might say that each role has its own sets. We perceive ourselves in terms of these sets. Our image of ourself at work and in the work role relies on one set, and our evaluation of that image will be measured against that set and the expectations that it creates. **These perceptual sets can also be described as cognitive structures**. In principle, they would seem to be the same thing as those structures identified as **self-schemata** (Markus 1977). Eiser (1986), in referring to Markus's ideas, describes these schemata as 'cognitive structures embodying networks of meaning associated with particular attributes, that together coalesce to form the self-concept'. People might, for example, have one schemata for organizing masculine or feminine traits.

So, in effect, what happens in the intrapersonal process is that information being dealt with is assigned and organized according to these cognitive structures. They are pre-programmed plans for making sense of experiences that are built up, it is assumed, through learning.

Encoding

This is the final organizing part of the process, in which meaning has been assembled, and perhaps symbols have been arranged prior to some communicative act such as speech. Where interpersonal communication is concerned, the term is also taken to include the composition of the speech utterance itself – putting the words together audibly.

In this case we are concentrating on the prior mental activity in which that 'putting together' must already have taken place. It is perfectly possible to 'hear' words in the head or to 'see' pictures in the mind. For us to believe that we are so hearing and seeing we must have encoded the communication. We have done this intrapersonally, that is, within ourselves.

KEY QUESTIONS

Describe from memory a supermarket, or other type of shop, which you know well. Analyse why some areas of the shop are more clearly recalled than others.

1.7 The Self to others

In this section we want to say a few things about how the Self matters when we are communicating with others. So this is not a section about interpersonal communication, but it is about the Self in interpersonal communication.

Self-fulfilling prophecies

Or, **'what you want is what you get'**! We can say this because what we want affects how we communicate, and how we communicate affects others. If we affect them the 'right' way then we get what we want. A crude little formula, but consider seriously the fact that our self-image really does influence our communication behaviour. We have already referred to the way in which our general self-esteem may cause us to use a set of body-language cues from which others infer that our state of mind is depressed or miserable. And, if one behaves as if one is miserable then people will deal with one accordingly. Some people have a version of negative self-image that actually desires rejection and alienation – this confirms their negative self-image. One could almost say that they feel good about feeling bad. More likely you will come across the version of the negative Self in which someone simply feels sorry for themself and wants others to feel sorry for them. It is relatively easy to put on a performance that other people respond to with comfort and words of cheer. This is what we have been waiting for – a boost to our self-image. Someone else does the work of raising our self-esteem.

This is a self-fulfilling prophecy: **what we are affects how we communicate, and how we communicate affects what we are**. This is the principle on which all cheapskate psychological 'success courses' operate. This is why you hear phrases like 'think positive, be positive'. All you learn through such courses is that the principle of feedback works. If one is pleasant to people then they usually respond pleasantly, which feels okay – and so one has the courage to be even more pleasant another time – and so it is not really so hard to get on with people. Only do not try too hard, because although sincere effort is rewarded, plain deceit will be found out.

Langer and Dweck (1973) refer to a **circle of success or failure**, which is another version of the self-fulfilling prophecy (see Fig. 1.5). Basically their argument is that someone is likely

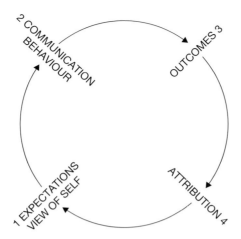

1. Believes in ability to manage the interaction successfully
2. Communicates in accordance with this belief
3. Sees the outcome of the interaction as successful
4. Attributes success to self and ability to manage interaction

Fig. 1.5 A model of the self-fulfilling prophecy

to be a success in dealing with others if they believe that they are the kind of person who is likely to be a success. The converse is true. In more detail, there are said to be four stages in the circle.

- First, the person has **expectations** of their success in, for example, persuading someone to go out with them.

- Then that person uses **behaviour** that should fulfil those expectations – that is, they will communicate in ways that they believe will make them attractive and will persuade the other person.

- Then, having either succeeded or failed to get the person to go out with them they take a **view of the outcome**. This means deciding whether or not they succeeded in what they set out to do.

- Finally there is **attribution**. Here, a lot depends on one's self-image. Someone with a positive self-image will certainly have this reinforced if they succeed in getting what they want. But even if they do not, it is entirely possible that this person will attribute failure to some fluke of circumstance rather than to themselves. They will still be able to approach another encounter optimistically. And nothing succeeds like success, or even partial success.

Saliency

This term refers to the idea that in a given situation some element or feature becomes more important than others – becomes more apparent. It refers to Self in two ways.

- In the first, general case it is observed that the Self and our awareness of this become more important in some situations than others. These kinds of situation are those where there is an audience and those where there is an element of assessment involved. These situations lead to greater awareness of Self – a state in which we are active intrapersonally as well as interpersonally, and are monitoring both our external behaviour and our internal states. For example, this is likely to happen if we have to stand up and make a speech at a wedding celebration, or if we are being sensitive to the kind of Self that we are presenting to others.

- In the second case one is dealing with particular features of the Self. Here, it may be noticed that the salient features of Self depend on situation. This kind of saliency may well be tied in with role. So, if someone is looking after children in a summer camp, then that person may adopt some kind of parental role – in which case it is possible to suggest that there will be salient features of Self displayed, perhaps a controlled demeanour coupled with directive behaviour.

Self-presentation

The reference to audience above should be related to presentation of Self. That is to say, the notion of audience applies to many situations other than those where a collection of people exist as an audience for communication from one other person. In the wider sense there are many situations in which a single person is an audience for a performance from one other person. When doctors deal with a patient they are, in effect, playing to an audience. They bring out certain features of Self through a selected kind of communication behaviour. Intrapersonal communication had played a part in bringing out that Self, and continues to be involved in the process of monitoring Self and receiving feedback from the patient.

At this point we would like to refer you forward to Chapter 5 on presentation of Self, which, you will see, picks up the remarks made in this last paragraph. Another example, perhaps, of why you need to read the whole book to get the whole picture!

1.8 The person and personal development

This section is concerned with the idea that understanding of the Self and intrapersonal communication may be of benefit to the individual. This benefit is not easily measured, but can be described in terms of having a sense of one's personal worth in most, if not all, situations. It is about being honest with oneself, yet without having to wear the heart on the sleeve. It is about having an adaptable Self that can adjust to one's own needs and to the needs of others. It is about being able to grow or develop that Self so that, without being smug, one is able to say, 'I knew myself pretty well and I know where there is room for improvement'. It is about understanding how one's Self relates to others and can be adapted to making those relationships happy and satisfying. This is easiest if, indeed, one does feel good about oneself.

Self-knowledge and self-control

In the first place there is a premise that – as for communication studies generally – **self-knowledge brings the possibility of self-control**. This is not control of Self in a repressive or defensive sense. Nor is it control in the sense of learning how to control oneself in order to control others. It is a control that leads to the benefits described in the first paragraph. It is a control that stops one, for example, thinking badly of oneself when there are achievements and qualities that, if recognized, should create satisfaction. It is a control that stops one unleashing blame on others, when the concept of blame may even be irrelevant. It is **a control that allows rather than denies because it makes possible an increase of self-esteem and an expansion of self-image**.

This view of knowledge and control is akin to consciousness raising. The more one is conscious of what is happening in one's life and how it happens, the more there is at least the possibility of deciding what happens. One does not have the option of using communication in any positive ways unless one is conscious of how it works.

Self-deception and self-concealment

One of the things we need to know is that **we are not always honest with ourselves about ourselves**. More often, we are not honest about ourselves *with others*. However, deceiving or concealing the Self is unproductive. It is also likely to create tension. People who are labelled 'poseurs' are trying to conceal something from others by giving off false cues. But the fact that they are recognized as poseurs suggests that such concealment is difficult. It creates tension all round. Trying to pretend creates tension in oneself, and makes others tense because they know that they are not dealing with the real You.

In proposing that one should recognize and avoid self-deception and self-concealment, we are not arguing for a kind of pretentious baring of the soul. Sometimes we tell lies to protect others' feelings. Sometimes we should not be perfectly honest about ourselves if it is going to embarrass someone dreadfully. Sometimes, temporarily, we need to conceal ourselves from others – perhaps in times of grief. This might be self-protection. The point is that most of us could probably be rather more honest than we are for some of the time. In being honest a lot depends on the way one goes about it. Putting it rather simply, if you have a friend who is a real exhibitionist and even makes a fool of themselves, it is one thing to say, 'Cut it out. You're a real pain in the neck!' It is another thing to say, 'I wish you'd stop doing that. It makes me feel uncomfortable'. **Honesty has to take account of circumstances and people, and of the way in which someone communicates**.

When we deceive ourselves we are denying knowledge of ourselves, and this is silly because one cannot run one's life on false information. We need to know what we are capable of in order to be able to plan ahead, to anticipate how we will cope with situations. It is also true that people are capable of a great deal more than they give themselves credit for. This is precisely because we do have the capacity for growth and change. The Self is not fixed. We may practise avoidance techniques because we feel that we cannot cope with certain social situations. But if we stop deceiving ourselves it may be possible to pin down *why* we avoid such situations. We may be able to reach a state where we can say, 'I've nothing much to lose really, if I'm honest with myself'. In this case it becomes only a small risk to engage in this situation and see how one gets on. If nothing too terrible happens then that is another small victory, and an expansion of the self-image.

To take one example, it is often difficult to say no to people. If some authority figure at work or college asks you to do something like running a personal errand for them which has nothing to do with your work or responsibilities, it can be hard to refuse. But then you might reflect on yourself and your avoidance of conflict. You might wish to change that part of your image that does not want to face up to the other person. You might decide to try asserting your belief in yourself for once and say, 'No, I don't mind helping you out once, but I'm not paid to run errands, and I don't think that it is reasonable to ask me to do that'. In this case you might well find that your superior adjusts his or her view of you more positively. Or they might resort to blackmail and threats – but if these are not backed by real power they can be ignored. If this person does have the power to, for instance, dismiss you without justification, then at least your choice is clear – and you can still feel good about yourself for having taken a stand.

The worst kind of defensiveness, and a common variety, is that where people take a rigid view of what they are and are actually not willing to change their view of themselves. Kelley (1969) talks of hostility expressed by such people: attack is a form of defence. Examples of this behaviour are to be seen in teachers who try to 'put down' pupils to prove to themselves that they are clever. Such people are also often too inclined to play clever teacher to other people in their lives, apart from the pupils. Their self-image is fixed. Their social interaction is inflexible. It causes conflict. It attacks the self-esteem of others. This is maintenance of Self gone to extremes.

So, **to achieve self-knowledge we may have to overcome certain kinds of self-deception and defensiveness techniques** that we have built up to protect a rigid view of Self.

The hidden Self and self-disclosure

Willingness to disclose information about one's **private Self** depends on a variety of factors apart from self-esteem. In the first place it depends on the values of one's cultural or subcultural group. If our culture discourages intimacy and conversation about one's personal feelings and private beliefs as a general rule, then this can be a real block to self-disclosure. Who the other person is matters a great deal. People of status do not like to reveal themselves to those without status. Men are less inclined to make disclosures than women (especially mothers).

Disclosure depends on trust, so we are more likely to talk frankly to those we trust. At the same time, making disclosures invites trust and can bond relationships. If one's work or social situation is one of competitiveness then it is much harder to make disclosures than if it is not. Equally, and especially on the basis of work done by Rogers and others since the 1960s, it is recognized that **some degree of self-disclosure benefits relationships, leads to more self-esteem and develops the stability of the self-image**. Self-disclosure may not be a skill, but in moderation it appears to be a practice that benefits the individual. It is, in effect, about the practice of communication.

In particular, it has been noticed (Altmann 1972) that self-disclosure encourages the building of a relationship. First, it is more likely to take place at the opening of a relationship than later on. Second, it seems to encourage reciprocal disclosure from the partner. It would seem that a degree of honesty is taken as a sign of trust and encourages more trust in its turn. As Myers and Myers put it: 'a relationship develops only when you and the other person are willing to go through the mutual process of revealing yourself to each other. If you can't reveal yourself, then you can not be close. To be silent about yourself is to remain a stranger' (Myers and Myers 1992).

It is important to realize that self-disclosure cannot be used as a mere device to force the other person into a relationship. It is the kind of communication that works best a little at a time. It works when there is a degree of trust between the people concerned, when there are some nonverbal signs of approval that suggest that each person wants, experimentally, to try the first stages of a relationship. Telling someone your life story and your opinions within ten minutes of meeting them is not going to start a beautiful relationship. You have to be sensitive to the other person's needs and feelings, to be empathic. And once more, even if only a little, you have to take risks. In fact, most people, even if the relationship does not come to anything, will still respond to your trust with confidentiality.

The Johari window

One way of illustrating the hidden self and of showing the capacity of change in the Self through disclosure is seen in **the Johari window**, as shown in Figure 1.6 (Luft 1969). The four panes of the 'window' represent four areas of the Self that are defined in terms of what the person does and does not know about themselves, and in terms of what others do or do not know about that person.

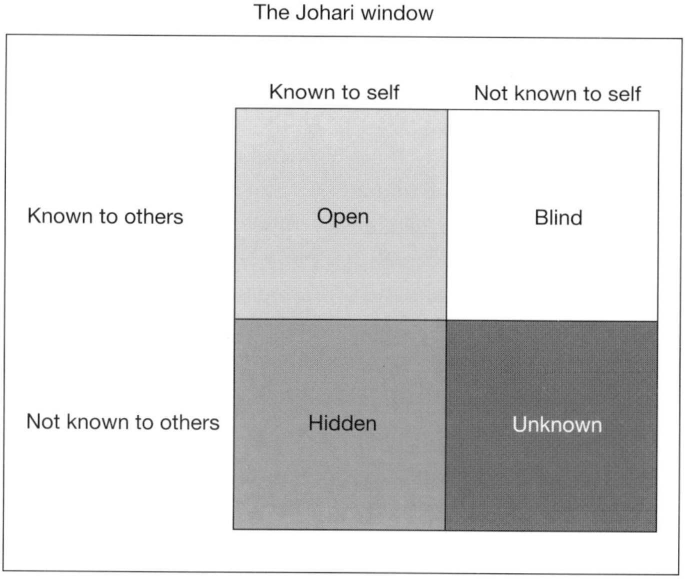

The Johari window

Fig. 1.6 Luft's model of the Johari window (Luft 1969)

- The *Open area* is the most public one, containing things that both you and others know about you – things such as your name, your job, and facts like these.

- The *Hidden area* is one where you keep things from others that you do not want them to know – perhaps a fear of black beetles, and certainly your personal fantasies about things like the man or woman of your dreams!

The other two panes are areas where you do not know yourself.

- The *Blind area* is one where, nevertheless, others do know things about you. They might see you as being very noisy or as using too strong a perfume – something like that which they do not tell you.

- And, lastly, there is the mystery area of the *Unknown*, known to no one, where the Self is buried in the subconscious and there are qualities waiting to be discovered.

One basic principle of the window is, 'change what is in one pane, and you change the rest'. If you ask for feedback then you may find out things you did not know about yourself from others, and shift them into the open area. If you give feedback to others then they will find out things about you, and again you will move information into the open area. In one sense, moving information about your Self into the open area means that you have more to share with others. Certainly to do this moving you have to communicate.

A process of self-disclosure

A sequence of actions in a **process of self-disclosure** (which will affect the window) may be described as: **disclosures – feedback – self-esteem**. That is to say, if one reveals something about oneself then others will react to this information, usually with reciprocated trust. This trust, sometimes shown in the form of further disclosure from the others, makes one feel better about oneself, and so develops self-esteem.

In this process of self-disclosure, communication becomes the means through which sharing takes place and mutual trust is developed. It is the means through which we make ourselves known to others and they to us. Sharing brings personal growth, defined as a growth in our knowledge of ourselves and of others, a growth in the bonding of our relationships and a growth in our sense of our own value. If communication can achieve this kind of growth then it is, indeed, worthwhile. We hope therefore that you will agree that this chapter has been concerned with very significant parts of our lives. This is why we have underlined the importance of understanding communication and of being able to use that understanding constructively and with respect for other people.

KEY QUESTION

The person and personal development

Look again at Fig. 1.6, the Johari window. Use this model to analyse a relationship between a person and her/his supervisor. Which areas of the Self is the employee *likely* to disclose *and* which to conceal?

1.9 Skills in intrapersonal communication

At its simplest, and yet at the same time its most complex, the overarching intrapersonal skill is **'to know thyself'**. Being able to recognize one's personal characteristics, strengths, weaknesses and effects on other people, and also to have a positive and accurate self-image can be described as intrapersonal skills.

Our ability to communicate with other people reflects our own ability at being able to be in touch with ourselves. We develop the skill of seeing ourselves as both subject (I) and object (me) – that is, we can both analyse our internal feelings and view them objectively in the way they are seen by others.

Intrapersonal communication skills are closely linked with interpersonal skills. Being able to express ourselves in words and in nonverbal behaviours to other people, and being able to recognize the effect we have on other people and to compare ourselves with others are all skills we can practise.

These general skills can be summarized in the following list of specific skills. Although, for convenience, we have presented them here as discrete skills, they do in fact interrelate:

- Skill of being **self-aware** so that we can try to see ourself as others see us.

- Skill of **accurately knowing our own body image** so that we can recognize how others see us. We also learn to change this as we go through life.

- Skill of **developing a positive self-esteem** so that we value ourselves and generally approve of the sort of person we believe we are. Our self-esteem may be low if we feel that we fall short of a 'self-ideal' that we set ourself.

- Skill of **developing a personal range of social roles** so that we can relate to other people in a variety of situations.

- Skill of **recognizing what needs and motives we have** so that we can seek to meet our own needs through our own interaction with others.

- Skill of **being aware of other people's reactions to us** so that we can adapt our behaviour.

- Skill of **taking control of our own thoughts and actions** so that we can take personal responsibility for ourselves, our attitudes and beliefs.

- Skill of **self-disclosure both to ourself and in appropriate ways to others** so that we can build relationships on openness and mutual trust. Intrapersonal communication is not confined to ourself. Internal processes of communication and the development of concept of Self (which we, in turn, present to others) are products of our relationships with others. The nature of these relationships, particularly in childhood, is very important to the development of Self.

Review

You should have learnt the following things from this chapter:

1.1 What is intrapersonal communication?

- What the term 'intrapersonal communication' means in terms of its main elements and activities.

1.2 Self-drives

- How we are motivated by various needs, the main ones of which are physical, personal and social.

1.3 Elements of the Self

- Self-image is an internalized view that we have of our Self.
- We have public and private Selves.
- Our self-image is composed of physical, intellectual and social attributes.
- We have both an ideal and a realistic self-image.
- There is something called the 'looking-glass self' — seeing ourselves reflected in the reactions of others.
- Our Self is also partly something that we imagine others see in us.
- Our Self contains ascribed and achieved roles.
- Self-esteem, or how we value ourselves, is the most important aspect of self-image. A lot of our self-esteem depends on getting positive feedback from others.
- It has been suggested that, at least in part, we construct our ideas of Self from our media experiences.
- Our Self contains attitudes, beliefs and values that influence all our judgements.
- We are all said to have certain personality traits, which are described in much the same way as attributes. Different traits are brought forward in different situations.
- We have something called an emotional Self, which we construct from observation of our own behaviour.
- Our Self includes a picture of our physical and social worlds.
- Most of us see the Self as being the source of decisions and actions.
- Most of us see the Self as having a moral dimension that affects how we view the world and how we deal with others.

1.4 The Self and identity

- The idea of 'identity' helps explain what we understand by 'Self'.

- Identity is bound up with our sense of where we come from, of our family history, of what we look like, of what group(s) we belong to – their history and beliefs – of our gender.
- Identity is also bound up with a sense of difference, which may be especially strong for subcultural groups.
- Our identity is produced and made real through our interactions with others.
- If identity is partly to do with beliefs, then it must also connect with ideology.
- Identity is about cultural belonging, not nationality, and may help define a sense of self for people on a global scale.

1.5 Maintenance and evaluation of Self

- The four key factors in creating a sense of the Self are: reactions of others, comparisons made with others, roles played and identifications made with others.
- There is tension in us between a desire to maintain the Self in a stable state and a desire to change the Self. We operate various self-maintenance strategies in an attempt to hold on to our view of Self once created.
- Communication from others is very important in confirming or disconfirming our view of Self.
- The most important other people who offer us feedback related to the Self are described as significant others, reference groups, role models.
- We attribute characteristics to our Self through a process of perception in the same way as we perceive others.
- The effect of cognitive dissonance is to cause us to revalue or change self-image.

1.6 Intrapersonal processing

- There are five main elements in the process: decoding or cognition, integration, memory, perceptual sets or schemata, and encoding.
- IRPC involves us in making sense of information with reference to what we have known (memory) and to frameworks we have built up for making sense of experience (schemata).

1.7 The Self to others

- Self-fulfilling prophecies are communication strategies through which we construct communication in order to get the response we want – to make our wishes come true.

- Saliency refers to the fact that some features of the Self become more important in certain situations than at other times.
- Self-presentation is about communicating a selective view of Self to others (further described in Chapter 5).

1.8 The person and personal development

- Knowledge of what we are and how we come to be this makes it possible for us to control our Self as it relates to others.
- We may deceive ourselves and conceal ourselves from others because we lack self-esteem and are not prepared to take risks.
- Self-disclosure, handled in the right way, enhances trust, improves relationships and helps the individual grow in various ways.
- There is a hidden Self that can be disclosed, described through the Johari window.

1.9 Skills in intrapersonal communication

- These may be summarized in terms of:

    - being self-aware
    - being honest in self-disclosure
    - being positive in one's view of oneself, and
    - applying these skills to one's own interpersonal behaviour.

Case situation: Know thyself

Read the extract below about an interchange between friends and answer the following questions:

What is illustrated about Steve and Louise's relationship?

How does Louise view herself?

How does Steve view her?

Louise Thorne felt despondent as she stirred her coffee and listened to the roar of the hot water filling yet another teapot at the counter of Meg's Caff. She was not a person much given to self-doubt, and not getting the job at Rayner's Shoes had actually surprised her. It wasn't the end of the world, of course. She would apply for other jobs. But as Saturday jobs went it would have been quite well paid, and Louise had already made plans how to spend her money. She looked out of the window, feeling almost cross now, and hardly reacted to the grinning face with spiky ginger hair pressed against the pane on the street side. 'Hi!' said Steve, taking the opposite seat. 'Mind if I share your cup?'

'Go buy your own, freckle face,' she said, almost automatically.

'This is not the girl we all know and love.' Her silence confirmed this. 'So, don't tell me, you didn't get it.'

'OK, I won't tell you.'

'Hmm – I think you should. Hang on a minute. I'll get you one of Meg's special greasy doughnuts' – which he did in less than a minute, and Louise was grateful to Steve even though she could feel every bite going straight to her waistline. She gave him a blow-by-blow account of the interview with the manageress.

'You know,' he said, poking at the sugar jar with his plastic stirrer, 'speaking as at least your third best friend, maybe you should think again about how you come across – you know, how they see you.'

'And what does that mean exactly?'

'It means that I don't see the point in giving you the "what bad luck routine". I guess I'm trying to be helpful. You know, before I got my weekend job at the hardware store my brother did the same for me – asked me to take a good look at myself, if you see what I mean.'

'Hey, I don't want some heavy analysis.' Steve said nothing. 'Anyway, I thought I was pretty positive, and spoke up for myself.'

'You probably did. But maybe she thought you were just too pushy.'

'You won't sell shoes by standing around with a silly smile on your face.'

'No, but you don't back the customer against the wall and shove the shoes up their nose either!' Steve stopped, looked embarrassed. The jukebox had stopped and his last words had come out loud, which caused a couple of people to look round. 'What I mean is you're very determined. You always have to get your own way. Not that you're nasty with it, Lou, but you do like to organize people and push them into agreeing with you. Some people don't like it, even when they do end up agreeing with you.' Louise was looking slightly stunned. 'Don't get me wrong, I like you. You know that. But you really know how to cut up people who won't go along with you. You're lots of fun. But it sort of swamps some people. They don't get a chance to put over their ideas. Be honest, it is always you that runs our group sessions and that sort of thing.' For once Louise had not been able to get a word in edgeways. 'So what I'm trying to say is, if you act like that at an interview, you'll come over as too much.'

For once Louise was lost for words. Steve sat uncomfortably as she looked out of the window, then at him, then out of the window again. Her smile was a small one.

'It's funny, isn't it,' she said at last. 'I don't see myself like that at all. I mean, I know I'm no shrinking violet. It's difficult to be that when you're my height! But I always thought I was just positive. I thought I was just being helpful in the group work. Actually, I always felt I was a bit nervous, really, so I ought to . . . give something. I thought I was a reasonable sort of person. I'm not really that clever, you know, so I suppose I see myself as a doer, not a thinker. And I do try to help people.' She sat back. 'Well, it's funny how wrong you can be about yourself.'

'I'm not saying you're wrong,' said Steve quietly. 'I'm only saying that other people don't see you quite the way you do.'

Suggested reading

There are many books that are relevant in parts to the material of this chapter. We have chosen just some that you can read selectively. It is also true that these books cover more than one chapter of this work, so you will find that many of them are more general use.

Barker, L., 1984, *Communication*, New Jersey: Prentice-Hall. (See Chapter 5.)

Butler-Bowden, T., 2003, *50 Self-help Classics*, London: Nicholas Brealey.

Ekman, P., 2003, *Emotions Revealed: Understanding Faces and Feelings*, London: Orion.

Gardner, H., 1993, *Frames of Mind: The Theory of Multiple Intelligences*, 2nd edn, London: Fontana.

Gardner, H., 1999, *Intelligence Reframed: Multiple Intelligences for the 21st century*, New York: Basic Books.

Gauntlett, D., 2002, *Media, Gender and Identity: An Introduction*, London: Routledge.

Gergen, K. and Gergen, M., 1986, *Social Psychology*, New York: Springer Verlag. (See Chapter 3.)

Glass, L., 1992, *He Says, She Says – Closing the Communication Gap between the Sexes*, London: Piatkus.

Goleman, D., 1995, *Emotional Intelligence: Why It Can Matter More Than IQ*, London: Bloomsbury.

Goleman, D., 1998, *Working with Emotional Intelligence*, London: Bloomsbury.

Hartley, P., 1999, *Interpersonal Communication*, 2nd edn, London: Routledge. (See Chapter 6, Social identity.)

Hodgkinson, L., 1987, *Smile Therapy: How Smiling and Laughing Can Change Your Life*, London: Optima.

Myers, G. and Myers, M., 1992, *The Dynamics of Human Communication*, New York: McGraw-Hill. (See Chapters 3 and 4.)

Persaud, R., 2001, *Staying Sane: How To Make Your Mind Work For You*, London: Bantam Press. (See Chapter 5.)

Persaud, R., 2005, *The Motivated Mind: How To Get What You Want From Life*, London: Bantam Press.

Reid, M. and Hammersley, R., 2000, *Communicating Successfully in Groups*, London: Routledge. (See Chapters 5 and 6.)

Rogers, C. R., 1990, *On Becoming a Person: A Therapist's View of Psychotherapy*, London: Constable. (See Chapter 1, 'This is me'.)

Stein, S. and Book, H., 2001, *The EQ Edge: Emotional Intelligence and Your Success*, London: Kogan Page.

The Mind Gym: Wake Your Mind Up, 2005, London: Time Warner.

Wheen, F., 2004, *How Mumbo-Jumbo Conquered the World*, London: HarperCollins.

Woodward, K., 2002, *Understanding Identity*, London: Arnold.

Zohar, D. and Marshall, I., 2000, *SQ – Spiritual Intelligence: The Ultimate Intelligence*, London: Bloomsbury.

Fig. 2.1 Perception of others – we are selective in what we observe and judge

Chapter 2

Perception of others

The perceptual process is more complex during interpersonal encounters. There are three forms of perception in social interaction: first, we perceive our own responses (we hear what we say and how we say it, and may be aware of our nonverbal behaviour); second, we perceive the responses of others; third, we enter the field of metaperception, wherein we attempt to perceive how the other person is perceiving us and to make judgements about how others think we are perceiving them.

(Hargie and Dickson 2004)

2.1 Introduction

Perception as communication

It is a truism to say that we perceive people as part of the communication process – a process within the process. But **this perception of other people is not**, begging a few questions, **a natural process**. The great weight of evidence shows that we learn to notice some things more than others about people, and that we learn to make sense of what we have learnt. So what follows is substantially a description of what we have learnt to do, why and with what effect.

It should be clear that **perception involves internal and external communication activities**.

- Internal activities (in which information is categorized and meanings about the other person are deduced) are, strictly, intrapersonal communication. This has been dealt with in Chapter 1, but will be expanded upon in this chapter to the extent that it relates to how we understand other people.

- External activities are the behaviours of the two people involved in an interaction. Most of these behaviours are verbal and nonverbal communication. When we perceive someone, these are what we note when looking for meanings.

The internal and the external communication coexist as one in the whole communication process.

The quotation above draws attention to the importance of communication activities. We are indebted to the work of social psychologists referred to in this chapter. All the same, it is true that much of their work is concerned with cognitive processes, with evaluation and judgement. We will look at these elements, but would also wish to see them as part of the whole process of communication. Ultimately, it is the acts of communication that count. Meaning is in the communication. Medium and message are intertwined. Perception cannot take place unless there is communication activity to assess.

Research into how people perceive others also depends on observing the communication of perceiver and perceived, and on asking perceivers to communicate about their perceptions of others. We would therefore ask you to remember that behind what follows is always the reality of active communication – a dynamic interplay of verbal and nonverbal signals that are the only hard evidence that perception and communication are taking place.

It is also worth remembering, without devaluing language, that **nonverbal signals are pre-eminent in perception**. We are talking about judgements made about other people's attitudes, personality and emotional state. There is every evidence that nonverbal behaviour dominantly carries messages about these three items. It has been shown that people read this behaviour even while, say, they are listening to a reasoned explanation. They will believe what nonverbal behaviour 'tells them', however much the speaker may be trying to use words that run counter to this.

Perception is not only about communication that is happening, it is also about communication that is about to happen. This is so because **we make perceptual judgements in order to anticipate the behaviour (including communication) of others, and in order to plan our own communication in the conversation as it unfolds**.

Perception of other people is obviously different from our perception of objects or the natural world. In this chapter we will explore ways of explaining how we perceive others as part of the process of interpersonal communication.

Before we embark on this, however, we want to emphasize that although perception of people is different from perception of things or animals, the personal mental and emotional processes are basically the same and consist of three principal stages:

- **Selection**: we select certain features or characteristics from all the possible ones for our attention.
- **Organization**: we seek to organize our sensory information into a meaningful whole.
- **Inference**: we form judgements based on previous experience, and so on, which may, for instance, lead us to stereotypical or erroneous conclusions.

We will explore these aspects of perception in the following sections of this chapter.

The internal perception processes of 'selection . . . organization . . . inference . . .' happen very fast unless we make deliberate efforts to control them. We can, of course, learn to handle our perception of others more consciously, but it is not easy:

Try as we might to avoid hasty judgements, at first meetings we assess people by how they look. Body shape, facial features, hairstyle, dress and adornment all influence our impression and affect the way we react. By influencing our assessment of personality and character, they may even affect the way we first interpret what the other person says and does.

We may find later, of course, that our first impressions were wrong – the apparently straight-laced matron might turn out to be a fun-loving lady with liberal attitudes, or the seemingly radical young man with long hair may be a trainee lawyer with quite conservative views.

But we deceive ourselves if we think we can postpone our opinions about others until all possible information is in, and we presume too much if we expect others to disregard our appearance . . .

This extract from *Eye to Eye: How People Interact* edited by Peter Marsh (1988) stresses that we inevitably make quick assessments of appearance, which lead to inferences about the Self within the appearance. Marsh's book is a comprehensive, easy-to-read and well-illustrated book that explores some of the ways we express ourselves and perceive other people. The point in the above extract (that perception between people meeting is *two-way)* is significant – the behaviour of the person you are looking at will change according to how she or he is reacting to you. Those reactions and interactions and the meanings that are placed on them are also very much culturally determined.

As the stereotypes noted in the extract above show, phases that come to mind like 'straight-laced' (with its Victorian corsetry resonances) and 'young man with long hair' (with its 1960s Beatles-inspired swinging Britain resonances) can determine how we view and categorize other people. There are cultural expectations that one can follow or flout, consciously or unconsciously. That is comparatively easy within the culture in which you have grown up and been 'socialized', where you know the expected codes of dress and appearance and nonverbal behaviour.

However, in intercultural meetings these first impressions can be very difficult for all involved. There are cultural differences of varying degrees in our behaviour patterns – and hence in our perceptual expectations– in personal appearance and personal expression, as well as social customs such as:

- Body language: for example, southern Italians use what seem to British people rather large gestures to illustrate their speech; or, as another example, comfortable distance in a conversation (what is called 'proxemics') varies between cultures, so that what seems the natural distance for a Latin American person may feel very close and intrusive to a North American.

- Facial expression: for example, although smiling or eyebrow raising may be universally used signs they will be controlled in different ways according to what is considered appropriate. Stereotypically, the British male will maintain a 'stiff upper lip' so as not to show either extreme of happiness or sadness, which perhaps reflects a cultural process that seeks to avoid extremes of emotion. The novelist E. M. Forster – who challenged some of these stereotypes in the early part of the twentieth century and explored cultural differences between Britain and India and Italy – quotes an Indian friend, who seemed to be showing an excess of emotion to British eyes, 'Is emotion like a sack of potatoes to be weighed out according to need?'

- Eye contact: for example, people from Arab or Latin American cultures will make, and expect, more direct eye contact than western Europeans, which can lead to inferences that the other person is either insulting or stand-offish.

- Contact: for example, touching is a powerful form of communication since it is used to express close personal affection. If the touching is considered too personal it can therefore feel threatening or harassing. We tend to talk about some cultures being a more 'contact culture' than others – one researcher observed 180 touches on average between pairs of acquaintances spending an hour together in Puerto Rico, and 110 in France; in Florida the average was less than 2 and in England it was nil.

With such differences, there is plenty of scope for misunderstanding when people from different cultures meet for the first time. Hence, there are training programmes for international visitors to learn how to cope with what has been called 'culture shock' – a state of shock resulting from different behaviour patterns and languages.

Issues raised

We wish to fasten on three issues before moving on to the main part of this chapter.

- One is concerned with the dynamic nature of communication and interaction. The issue is about the difficulty of dealing with perception of people – **when people are not actually fixed objects for our evaluation**. When one considers the shifts in attitude and feelings that people may experience during a conversation, the wonder is that another person is able to perceive them with any accuracy at all. As we will see, all of us do in fact make a lot of mistakes in evaluating others.

- Another issue concerns the evaluation itself. It is assumed that we are looking at perception as it reflects on a view of another person. But, in fact, **whatever judgements we may make of someone else also say something about ourselves**. They may say something about our personality and predispositions. The fact that we judge someone else to be happy or sad may just be a reflection of our own mood.

- The third issue concerns reality. We have already pointed out in Chapter 1 how physical and social reality are constructs in the mind, and are one element in a description of Self. The question is, 'What are we dealing with when we perceive others?' It could be said that we are dealing with social reality, not simply a process of making judgements. People and our relationships with them are the main part of our social world. So **perception is fundamental to the construction of social reality**.

KEY QUESTIONS

Perception as communication

Make a list of some of the intrapersonal and interpersonal communication processes that are likely to occur when you meet someone for the first time.

Look at the photographs on pages xvi and 60, Figures 1.1 and 2.1.From the appearance and expressions of those people in the photos, describe their personality attitudes, emotional attributes as you perceive them. Then, if possible, compare your description with someone else's who has done the same task.

How would you use this section on perception to influence your behaviour when you meet someone for the first time whom you wish to impress?

2.2 Why do we perceive others?

This question is not quite as naive as it seems. There are several answers to it. They emerge from the fact that perceiving other people is not a straightforward business of looking and understanding, nor is it a skill that one is born with. If one remembers that perception is about making judgements on the basis of sensory evidence about the other person, then it is *the reasons why* we feel the need to make these judgements that are significant. So here follows quite a long list of reasons.

To remember information

Perception is an active process. We remember experiences that we are actively engaged in, hence, the belief in learning by doing. But also (to anticipate section 2.4 of this chapter) it is clear that we organize the information that we trawl in. We organize it into units under headings, as it were. And there is some evidence (Markus 1977) that such organization does help us remember. So, we are perceiving in order to make sure that we remember what the other person has said and has nonverbalized.

To make sense of the other person's behaviour

It follows from the above that we are not only storing, but we are also categorizing. We are trying to deduce meaning from communication signs about what the other person may be thinking and feeling. In particular, as will be explained in more detail later, we are trying to make sense of the other person in terms of their emotional state, their personality and their attitudes towards us.

To organize social understanding

Because we perceive many people in our lives, we build up a sense not only of individuals whom we are dealing with, but also of people in general. This is not to say that the sense we make of people, of their behaviour, is always accurate. But, as far as it goes, this is our understanding of social relationships and of social behaviour. It helps us deal with people if we believe that we do understand them in terms of their motivation, their orientation towards ourselves, their likely behaviour. This understanding through perception depends not just on individual cues that others give us about what they are like. It depends on the organizing power of perception. We understand one communication sign in the context of others. We understand one trait of personality in the context of others perceived. We put traits together to make sense of them. We organize these traits and our understanding of them around certain key elements perceived, such as the degree of friendliness or hostility that the other person appears to feel towards us. So, as the seminal work of Asch (1946) suggests, our interpretation of friendly cues depends on many other cues perceived. For example, it might be that a person is understood to be rather hostile towards us. In this case, a sign of friendliness will be perceived as hypocritical, and will actually deepen our sense of that person's untrustworthiness.

To predict other's behaviour

We want to know what will happen next in any given interaction. We want to know how the other person may react to what we are going to say. Indeed, there is some evidence that people perceive others with rather more interest in predicting their behaviour than in explaining why they are behaving the way they do. So, there is a view that says that we perceive in **order to explain the behaviour of others**. But then one immediately asks, why do we want to explain the communicative actions of the other person? This leads us back to prediction and to the other answers that we are now giving.

To plan our own communication

If we believe that we understand the other person, and can predict how they will react to us, then it is possible to organize our own communication so that the interaction proceeds in the way we want it to. It is very likely that we will want a conversation to proceed in a friendly manner. So we believe that we can aid that smooth progress through careful perception. To this extent a subsidiary reason for perception is, indeed, **to help effective communication**. But do notice that this follows from the ability to predict.

You may notice here that this planning and conduct of the interaction is also to do with **feedback**. We may in fact give feedback to another person so that they will perceive us as we wish to be perceived, and so that the conversation will proceed satisfactorily for both people involved. It can thus be seen that perception is certainly not merely a 'watchful' activity in which one person pulls in information about the other person. It is part of communication as a dynamic activity. We are aware that others perceive us. There is, as it were, a dynamic exchange of perceptions in a conversation, where each person is continually monitoring the other and themselves, and continuously adjusting their communication according to social conventions and their own purposes.

To maintain our self, our reality

It needs to be remembered that there is self-perception as well as perception of others. And others are part of that world of social reality that is in ourselves and in our heads. So, by checking our understanding of other people we are also checking ourselves. We see ourselves in relation to others, so we have to check them to check ourselves.

To reduce anxiety

Putting it at its most basic, a world without structure is a world without meaning, and this is clearly disturbing. Communication, in general, helps order the world. The physical sciences, for example, make sense of the physical world by labelling, relating and explaining phenomena. We do the same thing when we perceive other people. We would be very anxious if we did not understand other people. It would be disturbing if their behaviour was apparently meaningless and unpredictable. This is why most of us find it unsettling to deal with people who are mentally disturbed, or drunk or drugged. We cannot make sense of their behaviour. They make us anxious. Most of the time we can, through perception, allay anxiety by categorizing the communicative behaviour of others. We can assume reasons for their behaviour. We can guess how it may affect us. As Gahagan says, 'We want to believe that we can understand others. This creates a stable and predicable view of the world. The fact that our understanding often proves to be inaccurate is another matter' (Gahagan 1984).

To satisfy needs

The motivating force of needs and their satisfaction is behind all communication. Needs have been discussed already in Chapter 1. In this case, one is concerned especially with human needs to relate to others and to be recognized by them. It is worth picking up the ideas of William Schultz (1958) with reference to interpersonal communication and looking at his description of three types of need.

Schultz: Three needs

The first need is described as **inclusion**. This refers to the idea of wanting to enter into relationships, of being interested in others. Clearly one cannot enter into a relationship without making some assessment of the other person so that one interacts with them appropriately. Perception becomes an essential activity if productive interaction is to take place.

The second need is to **control**. This is about being in control of oneself and being able to make decisions. It may lead to dominance in a relationship or to leadership behaviour. But it does not have to be about 'bossiness'. It includes the idea of also recognizing the other person's need to control. Unless perception takes place, such needs cannot be recognized, and balance in interaction or a relationship cannot be achieved. Both people have to represent their need and the fact that they are in control through communication.

Third, there is the need for **affection**. This is particularly about dyadic relationships in which a pair of people want to love and be loved. Whether one is talking about friendship or caring or loving, these terms and the need behind them have no basis in reality unless communication takes place. Whatever the faults of our perceptions, whatever the limitations of words and of nonverbal behaviour as means of conveying needs and feelings, they are all we have got. We have to signal affection through eye and body contact, or through statements about our feelings towards the other person, or they will never know that we care. **Perception (and the communication associated with it) is the bridge between one person and another**.

KEY QUESTION

Select three of the purposes listed above and give two examples of each to illustrate how it might work.

2.3 What do we perceive?

In the first place one should remember that perceiving is itself described through a number of other terms. Those are:

- **making evaluations**
- **passing judgements**
- **attributing cause and responsibility**
- **inferring personality traits**.

More will be said about inference and attribution in the next section.

These statements begin to answer the key question. But first we need to acknowledge **the double nature of perception, that is, the sensory and cognitive elements**. Perception is about absorbing information through the senses, on the one hand – whether the original stimulus is some verbal statement or a gesture from the other person – and, on the other hand, it is also about making sense of these stimuli. We tend to fuse these two activities, the interpersonal and intrapersonal, in our consciousness. When we fuse them, we tend to talk about someone's attitude towards us, as if this is as physically obvious as, say, the rude gesture that they are making. But it is not. The gesture as signifier may be there for all to see. But the signified, the meaning, depends on how we *choose to read* the gesture. There is a lot that we may take for granted about perception that we should not.

So the first answer to the key question is that **'we perceive verbal and nonverbal signs'**. The second answer is that 'we believe that **we perceive meanings in those signs'**. What follows is an elaboration of the second answer. These other answers are also best understood if one substitutes the word 'evaluate' for perceive. We are not seeing something that is given. We are weighing up qualities and motives in the other person that we think we see, but which, in effect, have been constructed in our heads.

Personality, attitude, emotion

We perceive and evaluate the following three key elements, which can be described as three dimensions of the other person.

Personality

Personality is usually referred to in terms of traits. These may themselves be described in opposing pairs such as generous–mean, dominant–submissive, and so on. Personality is inferred not only from behaviour, but also from physical characteristics over which we have little or no control. So, females with full lips are thought to be warm-hearted and generous; tall people may be assumed to have more status or dominance. These assumptions are based on readings that are usually culture-specific. They are also affected by other characteristics and by the time over which perception takes place. So, given time, we may modify judgements. However, the importance of such judgements lies in the fact that we do not always have the time to make corrections (job interviews), and the fact that there is, nevertheless, evidence of a tendency for first impressions to stick to some degree. We will say more about this in the next three sections.

Attitude

Attitude is defined in terms of our orientation towards the other person: what we feel about them. Crucial dimensions of attitude are the hostile–friendly pairing, which has obvious significance in primitive survival situations where one wishes to know if the other animal is for us or against us. Again, relevant nonverbal behaviour is often culture specific, and may be represented through unconscious habits that we pick up in early years, for all kinds of reasons. For example, someone who stands relatively close to others and orientates his body directly towards them may do this because he comes from a Middle Eastern culture where, by convention, this is acceptable. In North Europe and North America this will be seen as aggressive and intimidating to a degree. It is the kind of behaviour that someone may even have learnt to adopt simply because it satisfies their power needs and has been found by them to help in winning arguments and generally getting what they want. This will not make such a stance any the more agreeable for those who have to deal with it, and this person will still be perceived as hostile, aggressive or pushy.

Emotion

Emotion is very difficult to describe, however sure we all think we are about what words such as sad, joyful, excited or depressed mean. It seems to be something like **a state of high or low arousal, in which we are positively or negatively orientated towards ourselves**. What evidence there is suggests that we define emotion in others by defining it in ourselves. That is to say, we perceive ourselves as offering certain nonverbal cues when we are experiencing an inward state that we have learnt to label jealousy or love. We assume that when others are offering the same cues these mean the same thing for them. This is not necessarily so. Once more, there is the same possibility of inferring emotional states in others from cues over which they have relatively little control. You may have heard someone described as a 'miserable-looking devil'. What the speaker may mean is that the other person has been born with downward tucks at the side of the mouth. By the same token, someone may have strong eyebrows that meet in the middle and which are taken to signify ill temper. So, with respect to emotion, as with other elements that we evaluate, there is room for a deal of error.

Attributes

This term can be confusing in the various ways that it is actually used by commentators. Since, strictly, it refers to anything that we attribute to the other person, it could be taken to refer to personality traits or any of the other items in the previous section. But there are also elements that the previous headings do not properly cover, such as cleverness–stupidity or wealthy–poor, all of which are things we do perceive in others. Here, too, nonverbal cues can be crucial. Assumptions are made that a natural characteristic such as a high forehead signifies intelligence.

Abilities and habits

The term attributes may also be taken to cover items such as **abilities or habits**, which we also like to infer from the appearance and behaviour of others. Habits are, of course, repetitive communication behaviours that become characteristic of the person perceived. They can be verbal, such as saying as things like 'sort of', or nonverbal, such as sneering. Abilities might be exemplified by a judgement that a person is articulate or artistic. Being articulate is clearly shown through communication activity. However, one might make an inference that someone is artistic from the appearance of their hands (long, slender hands often being regarded as being artistic) and how someone uses them to make gestures when making conversation.

Roles

We also evaluate people's roles. We try to work out what kind of person we are dealing with in social terms. In effect, **we are trying to read items that have to do with class, status, occupation, family position, social grouping and the like**. Roles imply categories in themselves, and the perception is all about categorizing people. Role has attached to it not only the notion of a certain social slot and a certain kind of social relationship with other people, but also the assumption of certain behaviours. Once we have categorized someone in this way and have made all these associations, we are in a good position to plan our interaction with them. Sometimes this planning may be rapid and nearly reflexive, sometimes there may be a degree of consciousness about it. To take one instance, it might be that a female at some social gathering initiates conversation with a male. But, as with all male–female encounters, both people want to know about the roles and social orientation. So the woman will notice communication behaviour that might, for example, cause her to assign the role of husband to the male. Obvious signs could be the wearing of a ring, or references to family life. Less obviously, she may attribute the role on the basis of apparent age, combined with dress, combined with a degree of restraint in body language. Once she has categorized the male role, she will feel able to organize her own communication accordingly, and, indeed, will feel happier about the whole interaction.

Social reality

It also follows from the last paragraph that, in a broad sense, we are evaluating social reality when we perceive people. Our collective perception of people adds up to making a map of social relationships, bound by beliefs about those relationships. Certain individuals – family and friends – figure largely in our map of social reality. Communication with them, perception of them, is a way of checking and updating that map. The importance of this cannot be overemphasized, because this internalized view of reality is the only reality we have. Perception and its associated communication activities do, as it were, mediate between this internal reality and whatever is going on externally.

Cause and motive

When perceiving others we try to evaluate the true causes of their behaviour. If someone shows friendliness towards us not only do we have to perceive their communication as being friendly, but we then have to decide what this tells us about them. We may not take this behaviour at face value. We may not make the assumption, friendly face equals friendly attitude. If we do assume that we are looking at a friendly face, and that this stands for a friendly attitude within the person, then we are making an **internal attribution** of motive. But if we have other information that suggests that this person is being friendly because they have been told to be pleasant to us by a friend (perhaps because things have been going badly for us), then we will make an **external attribution**. We will assume that the cause of the communication is outside that person rather than inside. We may feel unable to attribute genuine friendliness to that other person.

This example effectively reminds us that the construction of meaning through communication depends on a great number of factors apart from the immediate signs of communication being offered. It depends on such factors as context and previous knowledge of the person whom we are dealing with.

The unexpected – predictability

There is evidence (Weiner 1985) that **what we choose to perceive is often the unexpected** – and here, again, we then look for causes. So, if we have just started a conversation with someone at a social gathering and they suddenly look round and walk away, we will look for the cause of this unexpected behaviour. It may well be that we will perceive them as lacking in proper social orientation and social skills. In 'explaining' their behaviour we have accommodated it within our view of social reality. We have 'made sense of it'. We have made an attribution that does, as it were, restore the status quo. Eiser refers to this behaviour and quotes Heider (1958): 'Attribution serves the attainment of a stable and consistent environment . . . and determines what we expect will occur and what we should do about it'. This quotation also implies that what we look for in perception is predictability or lack of it. In this case, referring back to the last section, we are not only looking for explanations of what someone may be saying to us, but also for ideas about what they will say and do in the future. The person who walked away from us may be perceived as eccentric and unreliable, and we may feel that we cannot rely on what they will say or do in the future.

KEY QUESTION

Describe some of the verbal and nonverbal signs that are used to reveal our attitude to someone else.

2.4 Perceiving and communicating

Introduction

Having tried to sort out the purpose and the object of perception, we will now look at the process itself. Social interaction, communication, perception are all activities. The question is, 'What specific activities are involved in perception?' If we isolate perception from our external communication activity, then it seems that the emphasis must be on reception, decoding and cognitive activities. At the same time, it needs to be remembered that this isolation is very artificial, a matter of intellectual convenience before we look at complete social interaction in the next chapter. So, do bear in mind what we have already pointed out – that one reason for perceiving others is to adjust our communication. **Perception leads to external communication activity when we interact with others, as well as to the cognition behind these actions.** The analysis and description in this chapter is like dealing with the process in slow motion. In real life the interplay is very rapid, and the judgements that we make of the other person, and how to proceed with interaction, occur as rapidly as the verbal and nonverbal behaviours. It has been found that expression can shift up to five times a second, and all those shifts will be perceived and assessed, however much at a subconscious level. We make 'inferences about another person based on visible or audible behaviour' (Argyle 1973).

First impressions

These are perceptions that occur at the beginning of an interaction. There is inconsistent evidence about the importance of these, in terms of fixing judgements about the other person. It is true that some people talk firmly about the importance of such impressions, and actually boast of their ability to perceive people accurately and quickly (though there is also every evidence that we are not good at doing this!). Some research throws up evidence of a four-minute period in which judgements are made that are then hard to eradicate. Equally, it is true that extended interaction does allow first impressions to be modified.

But one also needs to bear in mind that in many situations there is not the opportunity to spend more than a short period of time perceiving the other person. For example, some job interviews last only 20 minutes, as may interviews for undergraduate places. So there can be important outcomes from first impressions. Berger (1974) says:

We believe that the first few minutes of verbal and nonverbal communication between strangers may determine, at least under some conditions, whether persons will be attracted to each other, and by implication, whether the persons in the interaction will attempt to communicate at a future time.

There are many other examples of social and work situations in which we have to form judgements rapidly, from limited information. We are very prepared to do this, even if we do not know what that person's 'normal' behaviour is like. So a salesperson may be taken at 'face value' in a brief encounter, even though we do not really know how honest or capable they are.

Although we may all agree with the old adage 'you can't judge a book by its cover', we do tend to judge other people by their appearance – especially when we first meet them.

Symbolic interaction

We communicate through signs and symbols. Perception, as part of communication in social interaction, depends on identification of signs and on the manufacture of meaning from a combination of signs so identified. Speech is a sequence of phonemes, and gesture is a sequence of arm movements, and they are no more than that until sense is made of the elements (and, indeed, until the sequence itself is recognized). But if we are talking about perception as a process, and a process in which the participants interact through an exchange of symbols, then it is also true that the meanings constructed through perception come indirectly. Directly we may apprehend the tightening of mouth muscles that we are going to label 'smile'. The cues given by the other person are part of the process. But the sense and meaning of these muscular changes happens indirectly through cognitive processes, once the message has been internalized. There is no truth or reality out there. It is manufactured in our heads. **People are joined by symbols and made real in their minds**.

Cognitive process

We have already discussed cognition in the first chapter, with reference to intrapersonal communication. So it will be enough to say here that clearly **perception involves a cognitive process in which data received from the other person is combined with data already held about the person or about communicative behaviour in general**. There must be a 'search' element when dealing with the data coming in, in order to find something already held in memory that can be related to that data. What is selected from the data coming in depends on factors such as *saliency*. *How* these data are organized in the mind may be in terms of structures labelled *schemata*. We will discuss both these terms in a later subsection, once we have looked at overall notions of what the process is about.

Data and generalizations

From one point of view, perception is all about information handling. The data is dominantly about the behaviour of the other person (communication) and about the social and physical context (environment) in which the interaction takes place. From the data the perceiver makes inferences and predictions. In making these, the perceiver decides that the behaviour of the other person is produced either by external forces (context) or by internal forces (personality, emotion, attitude, attributes). For example, if you have invited friends round to your house, there might be a couple leaving and one of the two might say how much they had enjoyed themselves, then thank you and smile. You might take in the words and nonverbal behaviour, and you would also take account of the fact that they are saying this after attending your party and while on your doorstep. But then, as you rapidly reflect on the words and smiles (and check that one of the couple was not prompting the other to say this!), you might compare this information with what you already knew about them. Then you might say to yourself, 'Okay, from what I can see and hear, and from what I know, I perceive these people as being grateful and friendly: that's fine – I'll be friendly in return.' Data in, data out, and they, in their turn, will be perceiving you.

Generalizations – Perceptual sets

In handling this information we make generalizations. The generalizations are about what other types of information to attach the new data to, and about how these groups of data hang together. Stereotyping is a kind of gross generalization in which we might see a man sitting in a café wearing paint-stained overalls, and immediately make assumptions about his occupation, class, interests, and so on. It is also the case that we appear to have a type of cognitive structure called 'perceptual sets'. These sets are kinds of pre-formed patterns in the mind that incline us to handle information in certain ways. In the case of our man at the café, it would be the sets for 'clothes' and for 'male' that would be the reference points for dealing with the data that was there, and also for guessing at information that was not there. The guesses are assumptions. Sometimes they are right, sometimes wrong. It is very useful to be able to make generalizations – it is helpful to be able to predict. But it can also cause us to fall into all kinds of errors.

Redundancy

This guessing illustrates that principle of **redundancy**. Sometimes information is redundant (or we believe it to be redundant). We can make guesses from the information that we do have. We can fill in gaps in our knowledge. This is the principle behind those aptitude tests that you may have taken years ago, where you had to fill in the missing numbers in a series, to see if you could perceive the numerical pattern. Unfortunately, people do not behave with the regularity of numbers. For example, parents may sometimes be guilty of saying things like, 'I don't want to hear any more excuses about that broken window. It's clear what happened. You look as guilty as hell!' The unfortunate child might not in fact have broken the window!

Distinctiveness, consistency, consensus

It has been suggested, by Kelley in particular (1967, 1971), that when we are handling data **in perception we are actually looking for ways in which that person's behaviour does, or does not, stand out in some way**. In the first place, what they say and do may be seen as either distinctive or not. If not, we may describe it as fitting a consensus, an agreement with the way that person or others usually behave in that situation.

Consistency can be judged in three ways:

- in terms of the consistency of someone's behaviour over a period of time
- in terms of the consistency of their behaviour in similar situations
- in terms of the consistency of their behaviour when compared with others in similar situations.

So if someone says to you, 'Oh, do shut up!' you will have to decide if this is:

- consistent with the way they usually talk, or
- consistent with the way they have responded before when, perhaps, you have tried to provoke them, or
- consistent with the way other people respond at times of provocation.

McArthur (1972) suggests that if such an utterance is not very distinctive and is consistent in one of the three ways given above, then you will put it down to an internal condition, and probably say to yourself that the person is just feeling irritable. But if that phrase was distinctive, then you might look for external causes, and might perceive that person as, perhaps, 'having problems'.

Validation of perception

Myers and Myers (1992) **refer more or less to the ideas of consistency** and consensus when they define five ways in which we check data for validity (and, by implication, for meaning and action). Their list is useful and self-explanatory.

Validation type method

- Consensual   By checking with other people.
- Repetitive   By checking with yourself by repeating the observations.
- Multisensory   By checking with yourself by using other senses.
- Comparative   By checking your past experiences with similar but not necessarily identical perceptions.
- Experimental   By acting on the basis of your perceptual theories as if they were correct and checking the consequences of your actions by comparing them with what you guessed would happen.

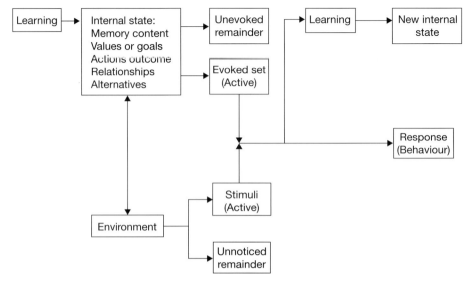

Fig. 2.2 March and Simon's model of perception in terms of behaviour (March and Simon 1958)

Perception as stimulus–response (S–R)

A classic behavioural model to explain perception would see it as a way of responding to external stimuli. March and Simon's (1958) model (see Fig. 2.2) would regard the communicative behaviour of the person and the context as providing the stimuli. These stimuli are dealt with internally. Within the Self are internal states that have been learnt. In particular, there is the content of the memory, which includes values, relationships and remembered outcomes of previous interactions. This information in the memory is accessed through sets, which are evoked when we try to deal with stimuli internally. Dealing with the stimuli, the new data, results in two things. Internally, we have learnt something from the encounter so our internal states are changed, however infinitesimally, every time we talk to someone. Externally, we make a behavioural response – we reply to what that other person has said.

Two other elements in this model are identified as:

- what is unnoticed in the environment, and
- what is unevoked in the mind.

These phases also relate to the idea of **selective attention**. With regard to the internal state, it does not appear that we evoke some sets as means of structuring information, and leave others dormant. With regard to the external stimuli one needs to question the word 'unnoticed'. We 'notice' everything within the scope of our senses. Whether or not it then gets filtered out through the process of perception is another matter. Clear evidence of this filtering is provided by the way in which one is capable of tuning in and out conversations overheard in some public place.

The problem with S–R theory is that it is rarely as predictive as it would like to be. The number of variables in a given situation, in the communication of the one who is perceived, and in the internal states of the perceiver, are so great that one cannot often be sure of response. Only in ritual situations and those involving redundancy, where there are powerful conventions, does one easily see S–R operating at all clearly. In the region familiar to the authors (and possibly in your own region, too), the stimulus 'How're you doing, then?' will almost invariably meet with the response, 'Not so bad, thanks. And you?'

Attribution

Attribution theory is well established with relation to perception and cognition. It is much based on the work of Heider, and **assumes that people are inclined to see their environment as predictable and controllable**. Predictability depends on identifying causes of events or behaviour. Some causes may be external to the other person, existing within the social and physical context. Some causes may be internal, lying within the person or people perceived. By reading people's behaviour we may be able to infer what it is in them that has caused that behaviour. And so one returns to the point that what is attributed may be described as personality traits, for example. Heider says, 'Attributions in terms of impersonal and personal causes, and with the latter, in terms of intent, are everyday occurrences that determine much of understanding of and reaction to our surroundings' (Heider 1958).

Intentionality

The problem of intentionality is a knotty one. We have already explained that, given the correct information, we may perceive someone's communication and actions as being caused by their environment. Someone who is under stress and snaps at us may be judged relatively favourably because of known conditions that are creating that stress. But it is not possible to make a glib distinction between internal and external attributions. We may just as easily say of someone who gives us a hard time at work or college 'I know he's been under a lot of strain lately, but all the same, there's no excuse for him being so irritable'. In other words, we are attributing at least some blame internally. We are inferring that the person does have the trait of being bad-tempered.

There are also instances in which we will not know of external factors that have affected someone's behaviour. There will be nonverbal behaviours, in particular, that the other person will not be aware of, that will not be conscious and intentional. But if the behaviour is there to be perceived then we can and will still make attributions. The Self that is hidden from the speaker may not be hidden from others. So it could be that someone offers signs of displaced anxiety, such as repetitive touching of their face or pulling of their hair, that they are not aware of. The perceiver can still attribute anxiety to that person.

Information and discrimination

Accurate perception and sound inferences depend on sound information and good discrimination. If we know people well and know a lot about their background, then we are more likely to make accurate judgements than if we do not know such details. If we check information about the other person (perhaps through reflective listening) and question the validity of what we perceive, then again we are more likely to make accurate inferences. **Rapid assumptions based on limited information are the least reliable acts of perception**. If you encourage someone to talk, and listen and watch them carefully, then you are more likely to get a better picture of their attitudes, beliefs and emotions than if you do all the talking.

Deception

Attribution is also complicated by the fact that **people may wish you to perceive them in a certain way** (see Chapter 5 on Self-presentation). For example, in public and social situations people may be quite good at keeping up their mask. They will wish to be perceived as cheerful, sociable and attractive. In other situations they may be different. Girl may perceive boy as humorous, considerate and cheerful when they go out together. Whether he is like this all the time is another matter.

Stable attributes

Argyle and Trower (1979) refer to **stable attributes** and remind us that our inferences may be about stable, long-term characteristics of, say, belief or ability, but they could also be about temporary conditions. Again, unless we perceive the other person over a period of time, we have no way of knowing if our inference about stable attributes is in fact correct. If we first meet someone who appears to be depressed, we have no means of knowing whether or not they are usually optimistic and cheerful. This provides yet another argument for reserving judgement as long as possible.

Influence of Self

Then there is the question of Self and **the influence of Self on attribution**. When we perceive others we are not just some kind of analytical machine. We are human, dealing with other humans. **Our own moods, experiences and values may predispose us to make selective inferences about others**. Indeed, as we will explain in the last section of this chapter, we are too often inclined to assume that others think and feel as we do. The process of perception, the act of attribution, occurs in a complex interplay between participants in the interaction and their environment. For the other person being perceived, we are part of their social environment. How we behave affects them. If we were to perceive someone as being relatively unfriendly, it might be that our own communication behaviour is the real cause of theirs. The interviewer who asks the interviewee to enter with a curt 'Come in' and a preoccupied frown (first impressions!) may cause that person to respond at least with restraint. Perhaps the interviewer will end up with notes reading, 'Rather nervous. Not very friendly. Not likely to impress our clients if employed.' Apart from offering inappropriate communication, this interviewer has made false attributions on the basis of poor perception. To this extent, you get what you give.

Conclusion

Attribution theory tries to take a logical, structured approach to the making of inferences about other people. Put simply (see Fig. 2.3), it assumes that one sees behaviour as effect, and external conditions and internal states as causes. These causes are inferred with relation to the perceiver's own knowledge and experience, especially knowledge about the person perceived. What is perceived may depend on how distinctive or consistent the behaviour of the other person seems to be.

Schemata, categories, sets

There is general agreement that as we perceive people and make inferences there is, in the internalized part of the communication process, reference made to **cognitive structures**

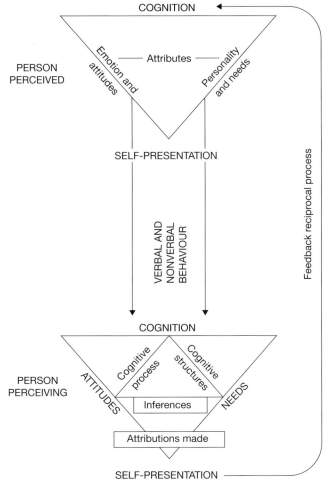

Fig. 2.3 A model for the process of perception

that help organize understanding (see Fig. 2.3). These structures are, it can be supposed, rather like collections of information placed under headings. They help organize the information that the other person is giving us through their communication. We can check that information against the collections, and so look for similarity or difference when making comparisons with previous communication. We can assign that information to one of these collections so that we have more to refer to next time. We can pull out information and combine it with what we are being told (assimilation).

The three terms of this subheading bear a close relationship to one another. We have already described perceptual sets as patterns that incline us to associate one piece of information with another and to use it in certain ways.

There is little effective difference between this and the idea of categories and categorizing. Tajfel and Fraser (1986) argue that having categories and being able to categorize is 'crucial to the general study of perception'. There are many categories that we may hold in our heads, and even categories within categories. One example that is often discussed, because it relates to stereotyping, is the category of race. Within this are categories of various races and their attributes, as we have defined and stored them. **Categories also have social values attached to them**. In other words, it may be more desirable or attractive to be placed within one category than in another. In terms of occupational categories, for instance, there is value attached to being a doctor that is not attached to being a boiler-room attendant. So, discrimination between categories is not just based on, for example, physical differences; it is based on notions of worth as well.

Basic perceptual activities

Tajfel and Fraser (1986) describe **basic perceptual activities** that will serve as another useful account of process – the process of categorizing as part of the process of perception, which itself is part of the process of communication. These are:

- selecting for closer attention certain aspects of the environment
- identifying a stimulus, an object or an event for 'what it is'
- accentuating certain of its features so that it 'fits' in some important ways one category or another
- neglecting other features which are less important for the 'fit'
- recognizing a familiar object or event on the basis of partial information
- discriminating between objects, again on the basis of partial information; so that appropriate distinctions of category membership can be made between them.

It will be seen that some emphasis is placed on the fact **that categorizing necessarily means 'distorting' to some degree**. Categories are useful in one sense. But, in another sense, their presence causes us to exaggerate or miss out some of the things that we perceive, just so that we can make the categories work. For example, someone may criticize a piece of work that we have done. Their verbal and nonverbal phrasing indicates disagreement and disapproval. In fact, their remarks may be well founded. But they have criticized our work before, and that of other people we know. Because of this, we not only categorize them in terms of 'orientation' as being hostile, but also we may perceive them as being 'overcritical'. If at the end of their analysis they mention some positive features and offer encouragement, we may ignore these comments because they do not fit the attribution made.

Two more points may be drawn from this. One is that perception is continuous, and that we do not wait until the end of an interaction before forming judgements. So, categorising will happen early on. It cannot be stopped, only modified in the light of later information.

The other point has to do with negative assignment in categories. In the example given it may well be that because we have already had 'bad experiences' with this supervisor or tutor we are already prejudiced towards them. This will incline us to make negative assignments. A number of researchers, including Tajfel (1969), have demonstrated the existence of negative predispositions that cause subjects, for example, to assign people wrongly to negatively valued racial groups.

Schemata

As we have said earlier, the notion of a **schema** is fundamentally the same as the idea of categories. If there is any distinction to be made it is that a schema not only describes a collection of attributes, it also **describes the basis of relationship between those attributes**. It does not just assume a list with a heading. However, when you come across the terms in other books you should bring them together in your mind. Gergen and Gergen (1986) describe a schema as 'cognitive organization of knowledge about a given person, object or stimulus'. A schema includes, in effect, beliefs about what binds the attributes within it.

Schemata actively help us select from and arrange the information that we are taking in about the other person. We will extend schemata when making inferences, often in terms of reaching a positive or negative evaluation of the other person. Because schemata aid prediction of behaviour there is, once more, a tendency to look for information that confirms our view of that person. If we concentrate on the idea of a schema being a kind of plan for making sense of the other person, then there are some remarks we can add to those already made.

One is that there are schemata for people in general, and schemata for types of people, as well as schemata for specific people whom we know. The **schema is both a kind of proposition about people and a predisposition towards them**. In the first case we can check the validity of our proposition: 'Is Becky as bouncy as ever today?' 'Oh, yes, she's as cheerful as ever – there's the big smile and the loud "good morning".' In the second case we want to confirm the predisposition within our schema: 'There's Becky – hmm, rather a wan smile, but she said "good morning". Oh well, she's probably quiet because it's the tenth time she's said it this morning – oh yes, she's as cheerful as ever.'

Gahagan (1984) refers to **schemata as implicit theories of personality**. She suggests that we all carry these theories in our heads and that evidence of them can be obtained from analysis of people's communication. She refers to an unusual piece of research in which Rosenberg and Jones (1972) analysed character descriptions written by the American novelist Theodore Dreiser in one of his books. They concluded that Dreiser was most concerned with whether or not people were male or female, conventional or unconventional. We might then conclude that these pairs of factors would predominate in Dreiser's schemata. So Dreiser might have a set of behaviours seen as unconventional. He might also have a set of types of occupation that would be tied to the criteria of conventionality or unconventionality. The principle of having schemata operating within perception as communication takes place remains valid for dealing with real people as much as with fictional characters.

Whether one talks about schemata or categories, it seems possible that they may be tied to key concepts. We have to refer to these words on the page, but do remember, as competent communication students, that really it is only the idea behind the word that exists in our minds. The word itself is merely a sound-symbol that calls up the concept.

The classic experiment in terms of organization of perception around key concepts was conducted by Asch (1946), in which he found that the terms 'warm' and 'cold' appeared to be crucial when included in a list of personality traits used to describe people. These two words seemed to attract attention and to bias further description of a hypothetical person positively or negatively. As we say, it is not that the words 'warm' and 'cold' exist in the mind, but their meanings do. It is these meanings and their associations that would seem to be important in perception. Certainly the warm–cold opposition would fit with the kind of attitude model proposed by Argyle and others, in which one axis is defined in terms of hostility–friendliness.

Although it may seem that some concepts are more important than others, it is still not possible to identify a definitive list of priority terms, let alone relate them within some structure. The principle of having and using categories would seem to be acceptable. It is possible to agree about certain main categories such as male–female. But it is not possible to produce a neatly packaged list of everyone's categories and of terms within these, that act as consistent points of reference.

Stereotypes

This word identifies **a category that we refer to when making inferences about items such as attitude, role, emotion, motive**. The word is often used in an adverse sense, and in fact we will return to it used in this way in the last section. But you should realize that, in principle, stereotypes need not be a bad thing. They do act as a point of reference, somewhere to start when trying to make sense of people. **They represent especially dominant or important categories with strongly associated elements.** They offer generalizations about a group of traits or attributes – in fact, they create the idea of the group being a group. It is the degree of exaggeration and simplification that we will criticize later. But again, commentators such as Brigham (1971) have argued that, nevertheless, stereotypes of people do have some basis in fact. This is not to defend the intellectually and morally bankrupt uses to which stereotyping is put (you can find examples in the media). But it is to recognize the positive use of associating information and experience when trying to make sense of other people. For example, a stereotype of old people might include the attributes of being doddery and grey-haired. Now, if you actually dealt with people over the age of seventy you might find it very arguable as to how doddery they are. But it is likely that a considerable number will in fact be grey-haired. And, in terms of media stereotyping, it can be pointed out that the elderly Miss Marple character created by Agatha Christie in detective fiction runs counter to typing of both old people and of women as being woolly-headed and intellectually incompetent. Her perceptions are very acute!

So stereotypes are not bad in principle. They are **salient categories with a high degree of cohesion, and represent powerful cognitive structures** within the process of perception. It is the social values attached to categories and stereotypes in particular that cause one to pass judgement on their uses. The values themselves represent a kind of pre-judgement. Making pre-judgements is dangerous – they are assumptions until proved, and may be proved wrong.

Conclusion

So, it is clear that **perception is a process operating as part of communication when we interact with others**. It contains at least two major points of reference:

- the verbal and nonverbal signs offered by the person perceived
- the categories within the mind of perceiver.

These categories may also be called sets or schemata or stereotypes. These points of reference have to be used by the perceiver. Types of use, or perceptual activity, have been described above. They include selecting, assigning, comparing, integrating. Another common word for describing perception and making sense of others' behaviour is 'attribution'.

The categories we refer to are useful for making rapid judgements and for calling up related pieces of information. But they may also lead to bias in the sense that they represent assumptions about what piece of information is connected with what other piece of information. They enable us to make guesses about the internal state of the other person, and to make predictions about how they will continue to behave and communicate. But they also enable us to be lazy. It is easy to make generalizations. There is a certain pressure on us to do this when we are meeting someone for the first time, and we need to make decisions about them quite quickly if we are to carry on interacting successfully. There is another kind of pressure in that communication is dynamic, can proceed rapidly and offers a great deal of information. It is sometimes difficult to digest the full meaning of what someone has said when they are waiting for a reply, and when both people want to get on with the conversation. Nevertheless, **it is within our powers to reserve judgement and not to jump to conclusions**. If we wish, **we can consciously pay closer attention to what people are saying**. You should refer forward to the section on perceptual skills for a summary of the view that, to a degree, perception is controllable.

KEY QUESTION

Using the model on page 79, Fig. 2.3, explain the process of perception of a person who is watching people in the following situations and roles:

1. a model displaying haute-couture fashions
2. a teacher in a school class, and
3. a salesperson in an electrical goods shop.

2.5 What affects perception?

This section will look at the main elements that affect how we perceive other people. Some of these ideas have already been referred to because they also relate to earlier topics.

We will look at these factors in terms of:

- **context** – the physical and social environment
- **physiology** – the physical competence of participants in the interaction; and
- **psychology** – mental competence and activity.

It is worth remembering that one always comes back to psychological factors because sense and meaning are constructed in the mind.

Contextual factors

Physical context

We will break these down into three kinds: physical context, social context and spatial position.

Physical context facts may be entirely physical. For example, if we go to visit someone not known to us and see in their house various expensive possessions, then we may be inclined to attribute wealthiness to them. There are a great number of possible examples in which physical context is read in terms of cultural symbols. To take one more instance, if one was interviewed for a job in an office that contained little furniture but did have telex links and a desktop computer, then one might make inferences about the traits of the interviewer. That person might be seen as being severely practical, competent in use of technology, and so on. We assume that people create a physical environment around them that is an extension of their personality and their beliefs.

Social context

In the second place, there is the social context. If one has been invited over to someone's house in order to socialize, then in this situation people obey certain conventions of social behaviour. They assume that social rules include making an effort to get to know people and being pleasant towards them. If people do behave like this then they are more likely to be perceived as friendly than they might be at, say, a business meeting.

Spatial positioning

Perception is also affected by where people place themselves in relation to one another. This aspect of context is known as **spatial positioning**. There may, in fact, be cultural factors that will affect where people stand or sit. To sit directly opposite someone can be taken as a sign of aggression or confrontation. For a woman to sit close beside a man may be taken as a sign of invitation. But clearly there are also practical considerations in positioning. If you sit right beside someone it is actually rather difficult to see them. People forced into this situation end up twisting round in their seats to get a better look. So people who are seated perceive and communicate most effectively when they are at an angle of about 90 degrees to one another. When standing, an angle of about 45 degrees is the norm.

Physiological factors

These refer to the physical characteristics of the people involved.

- In the first place these may affect perception in a mechanical sense. If one person is deaf, then they will be denied one channel of communication through which perception takes place. This limits the amount of information that they can receive.

- Second, one could be talking about the inherited physical appearance of the person being perceived. People who fit culturally acquired ideals of beauty are seen as more attractive, and are therefore perceived more favourably than those who do not. This fact is implicit in the efforts that some people make to change their appearance so that they become more attractive to others. Hence the many occupations and industries such as those of beautician or even plastic surgeon, which are geared to making such physical changes.

The interpretation that we make of physiological factors leads to attribution. There are a great number of studies showing that various physical characteristics lead to particular judgements. For example, dark-skinned people tend to be assigned negative attributes by fair-skinned people – such as unfriendliness or lack of humour.

Together with physiological factors, one might also consider **dress and display signs**. We read things into what people wear. Males who wear dark, plain suits are perceived as being more authoritative and reliable than those who do not. Women who wear large or colourful jewellery will be perceived as being more extrovert (and even more 'feminine') then those who do not.

There is a considerable literature on nonverbal communication that you can read in order to extend these examples.

The fact that these signs appear to 'stand out' as being important is discussed below with reference to saliency.

Psychological factors

Motivation and predisposition

These factors work in conjunction with those described above. For example, the **degree of motivation** that we feel in conducting an interaction will affect how careful or how selective our perception is. This has to do with self-gratification and our personal needs. So, if you are taking a college course that you very much want to pass, you will tend to pay good attention to what is being said by the teachers. If you want to develop a relationship with someone else, you are likely to perceive their communication, especially in response to your own, with some care.

Unfortunately this will not stop you also having **predispositions**. These are pre-formed ideas about your Self and about others. These are incorporated within the schemata already referred to. So **perceptual sets** (also already explained) will operate with the effect of predisposing you to read things into the other person's behaviour. A simple example would be where, as a man, you have a set that incorporates favourable attitudes towards women with dark hair and a sense of humour. When you meet a dark-haired woman who laughs a lot, you may then have a predisposition to like her.

Attraction

This is closely linked with the idea that attraction is an influential factor in perception. If, for the reasons just given, you are attracted towards someone then you are more likely to perceive them favourably than not.

Past experience and resemblance

The factor of **past experience** is also bound up with attraction, sets and predispositions. For instance, if you were looking for someone to share an apartment with, then you would probably look for a person who had similar attributes to those of a known friend. If you met someone like this, you would be predisposed to believe that you would get on with them. You would make certain attributions, including those all-important predictions. The phrase **resemblance criteria** is also sometimes used to describe details of behaviour and appearance that remind one of some previous experience. If you visit a new dentist and he or she reminds you of one visited in childhood when you had a painful extraction, then you might perceive this dentist unfavourably.

Open and closed minds

It is possible to see **open- and closed-mindedness** as factors that affect perception. Basically, these are about Self – the kind of person you are. If you are very concerned to maintain your view of your Self, then you will be inclined to perceive others only in terms of preserving your self-image. So you might edit out the full effect of critical remarks someone was making about you because this threatened your self-image. This would also be an example of ineffective listening. Equally, if you have a secure self-image then you may be more honest in your assessment of what someone else is saying because you can cope with criticism and can accept praise without becoming arrogant.

Role relations

Role relations will affect perception for the obvious reason that there are schemata associated with role. If you have to deal with your supervisor at work, you will see them in a certain light just because they are your supervisor. You will expect to see certain attributes and behaviours associated with that role. The supervisor might be the same age as yourself, possibly known to have similar interests. But you still would not perceive that person as a potential friend, because you would also have perceived attributes of status and power that you would not associate with friendship.

Saliency

Saliency describes distinctive characteristics of the other person that will bias the way we collect information about them and the way that we form our judgements. What we consider to be salient depends on the situation and on what we have learnt to consider 'normal' (to be part of the social consensus). The fact remains that we do tend to notice salient features, and that thereafter they incline us to perceive the person in a certain way. For example, it could be that we believe that a beard is a salient feature when perceiving a male. It may be that we have a set with regard to beards, that we make associations with beards. If so, then the recognition of that beard will certainly influence our assessment of that male. Similarly, if someone starts shouting in a business meeting, this may well be perceived as salient communication behaviour. Judgements made by others at the meeting will be dominated by the fact that this person behaved unexpectedly. This also makes the point that unconventional behaviour automatically achieves saliency.

Social values

Finally, we consider **social values** as influential factors. We might also say that it is a matter of convention that some behaviours are preferred to others. Values are indeed about preferences, likes, dislikes, aversions. For instance, someone might converse in what they perceive to be a positive, firm manner. But we might see it as being overbearing. Specifically, we might observe a loud voice, close body proximity, emphatic delivery, assertive gestures. There is a close relationship between the social value placed on such behaviour and the inferences that we will make. If we believe that it is socially inappropriate, this is much the same as saying that it is not valued socially. Because it is not valued socially – as well as because it may seem threatening to ourself – we dislike this style of communication and perceive the person unfavourably.

   As we approach the end of this chapter, you may think that we have said much that is critical of the way that we perceive others. There does seem to be much room for error and misunderstanding. We shall go on to look at these errors in the next section.

KEY QUESTION

Compare the importance of context, physiology and psychology as factors affecting interpersonal perception in the following situations:

- between friends meeting for an evening out
- between work colleagues
- between doctor and patient in the surgery.

2.6 Errors in perception

The list of errors that we may make in perceiving others is formidable! So much so, that it is almost a relief to remember that people do actually manage to communicate successfully with one another in spite of their mistakes. Of necessity, we have already referred, as least in passing, to the various kinds of error that we can perpetrate. Basically, one can say that we do one of four things, separately or in combination.

- We miss out some piece of information.
- We make too much of something.
- We make false connections between one thing and another.
- We guess wrongly about the other person by making false association of traits or of experience.

Most errors in perception can simply be described as false assumptions, as will be seen from what follows. It can also be argued that if perception involves the use of 'labels' and categories, then error is built into the system. Labelling an example of communication behaviour as meaning one thing tends to exclude it from meaning another. The categories we use may be incomplete. By including some information within a category we are presumably excluding other information.

Fundamental attribution error

This phrase, first used by Ross (1977), refers to **the tendency to attribute cause and blame to people rather than to circumstances**. It means that we really ought to find out about circumstances before forming judgements from what people tell us. Look and listen before jumping to conclusions.

False consensus

This error was also tested by Ross (1977) and comes down to **a tendency to assume that other people agree with our own views**. It is part of a general tendency to suppose that others see the world as we do. This kind of perceptual filter is sometimes described as **projection** – the mistaken projection of one's own values and beliefs onto other people.

False consistency

In this case **we tend to assume that the behaviour of other people is more consistent than it is**. It makes it easier to deal with them, easier to predict what they will say and do next if we believe that they are consistent (see Nisbett and Ross 1980).

Primacy effect

This refers to a tendency to fix first impressions and to build on these, rather than be open to changing our views of others. There is much evidence of this effect, built on the work of Asch in the 1940s. It has been suggested (Wyer and Srull 1980) that this effect can be so strong that general impressions of others persist even when we cannot remember what led to the formation of these impressions in the first place. It appears that this effect may result from our desire to create a schema for another person and then to look for information that builds upon it. This initial creation of a schema may also be described as a **priming effect**. Hodges (1974) draws attention to the fact that negative first impressions seem to be stronger than positive ones, harder to get rid of or modify. This has some relationship to the strength of norms and values – someone whose behaviour is distinctly antisocial or unfitting to an occasion really sticks in our minds. Once more, the lesson seems to be that one should hold back from making snap judgements, and consciously look for information to modify first impressions.

Halo effect

This bears close comparison with the primacy effect. It describes a **tendency to privilege one piece of information above others when forming an impression of someone**. The curious thing is that in some ways it seems to work the other way from the primacy effect in that in this case it is a positive factor that is sociably desirable that creates the halo and blots out clear judgement of other elements of behaviour. For example, if one perceives a member of the opposite sex to have looks, possessions or even something as specific as a hairstyle that the perceiver believes is socially desirable, then this will cloud perception and influence judgement of other characteristics. Other elements will be ignored or reinterpreted in the light of what is seen immediately to be an attractive and dominant feature. Again, there seems to be a dangerous tendency to see what one wants to see, rather than what is actually there.

Recency effect

This bears some comparison with the primacy effect. Simply, this describes the alternative **tendency for people to perceive others in terms of the last thing that they have said or done**. Perhaps at the end of an argument the other person will say to you, 'and I don't want to talk to you again unless you are prepared to apologize'. This last sentence may well prey on your mind. The issue of apology will be the one that dominates your perception of what the argument was about. It is well known in terms of communication practice that people tend to remember best information that comes at the beginning and at the end of the communication.

Preconceptions and predispositions

Although we have described these already, **the effect of our internal states** is so powerful that it bears repetition and expansion. For instance, even while we may be perceiving the **emotional state** of the other person, we ourselves will be in a certain emotional state. Moods of elation or depression will certainly affect how we interpret the cues given off by the other person. If we are much obsessed with how we feel then this will cause us to screen out cues from the other person. In colloquial terms, if we are feeling very sorry for ourselves then we may not be perceptive enough to see why we should feel sorry for someone else.

Cultural bias is another kind of preconception. We grow up within a culture and perhaps within a subculture in which certain kinds of behaviour are considered 'normal'. Normality is relative. Our idea of social reality is relative to our upbringing. It is notorious that the English are perceived as being 'cold' people, and that they perceive many other cultures (Italians, for example) as being noisy and excitable. It has been demonstrated that, indeed, the English specifically gesture less than the Italians and offer far less body contact. This does not make one or the other kind of communication behaviour right or wrong. But it does explain how culture can distort perception if one is not aware of what is happening and does not consciously try to modify one's judgements. In these cases one should not fall into the trap of seeing what are only conventions of communication as reality. **The conventions of behaviour change from culture to culture**.

We will also have **pre-formed attitudes** as part of our schemata (discussed above). These cause us to interpret the other person's words and actions according to the beliefs and values that are associated with these attitudes. Attitudes can be triggered even by small details of behaviour and, like all predispositions, may be associated with stereotyping. For example, someone may have a habit of tapping their teeth with a pencil while they are trying to work out a problem. This repetitive behaviour causes you irritation because it breaks concentration. Your reaction may be summed up as, 'I can't stand people who tap their teeth like that' – and then you begin to look for other things that you do not like about that person!

Self-fulfilling prophecy

You will remember that we have already referred to this in Chapter 1. But it is worth reminding yourself that this is very much an example of communication in action. It describes what happens when we act on our perceptions. If we perceive someone to be pleasant and friendly, then we treat them accordingly. This means that they, in turn, get positive feedback from us. So they are even more inclined to be pleasant and friendly. If they do behave like this then our original assessment is confirmed – what we prophesied has been fulfilled.

Stereotyping

You can also refer back to the last section for other information on this way of making some categories more dominant than others. Stereotypes are quick, simple ways of classifying people. They are harmless if used only as a temporary rule of thumb, but lethal if taken as the last word on another person. Stereotyping usually starts with identification of a few salient nonverbal signs such as dress or expression. Then, by rapid association within the category, judgement passes on to make assumptions about that person's attributes and beliefs. Common stereotypical categories are those of race, age, gender, class. **What is lethal about stereotyping is the speed and intensity of the assumptions and predictions that are made about the other person on a slender basis**. These assumptions and predictions are also too often critical of that person. The associative power of stereotypes is such that we 'know' that women are no good with technology, that Russians are out to take over the world, and so on. Of course, we do not know anything of the sort. But an associated problem is that of the self-fulfilling prophecy, because if women are treated as if they are incompetent at handling technology then they will perceive themselves as being like that. A rather neat vicious circle!

Stereotypes are such extreme generalizations about people that they miss out the individual variations – they ignore the gradation of attributes. One example of such simplistic judgements was seen by the authors recently in an English pub, where a notice said, 'Hippies cannot be served here'. We never did find out what it was that made the owner feel unable to serve the people so labelled, but we could make our own assumptions!

In some ways it could be said that stereotyping is the lazy person's perception. It means that they do not have to concentrate in order to distinguish features. Anyway, if a stereotype is assumed in order to criticize some group of people, then there is an assumed corollary that somehow the perceiver is better than the person stereotyped. In other words, the stereotype can have the pay-off that one feels better about oneself – a cheap way to achieve self-esteem.

This bias in perception based on a desire to bolster one's self-esteem has been described by Argyle (1994) and others as a type of communication barrier separate from stereotyping. In this case one would be looking for the cause of the bias, as much as the way that it operates. The cause is to be found in our motivation. We have needs to see people in a certain way, **so we adjust the facts until they fit**.

Stereotyping has been described as **illusory correlation** (Hamilton 1976). In other words, the categories include associations between attributes that are not necessarily true.

It has been suggested that there are two kinds of bias at work in stereotyping:

- One is where **we simply make things up** – again, perhaps because of personal needs.
- The other is where **we exaggerate traits** that actually do exist.

Another reason for making these distorted judgements may have something to do with our membership of groups. We tend to want to see our group as being better than the other lot, so we exaggerate or make up derogatory things about the other group, and make up flattering things about our own group.

This can be seen in national stereotypes. There is a fund of jokes by the English about the stinginess of the Scots or the illogicality of the Irish – and, of course, vice versa. There is a fund of jokes by the French about the Belgians, by the Russians about the Polish, and so on. These jokes can lead, in turn, to people perceiving particular nationalities or groups in terms of those stereotypes.

This can also be seen in subcultural groupings, such as social or professional groups, or in gender-based stereotypes. People with black leather outfits, tattoos and motorbikes are proclaiming their membership of the group; they may also wish to impress people outside the group. Outsiders may despise them or fear them or simply draw mistaken conclusions about them from their different dress codes. There are, for instance, groups of bikers who are professed Christians who seek to do 'good works'.

Accountants or lawyers who tend to dress soberly and adopt a serious demeanour while at work also get labelled stereotypically as dull and conservative. Again, jokes are used to reinforce these outsiders' views – 'Auditors are accountants who found accountancy too exciting . . .'

Stereotypes of male and female, men and women have been discussed and challenged in all quarters. There is now a large body of literature on the communication patterns of men and women, which serves to understand and change these stereotypes. Some of these books are listed in the Suggested reading at the end of this chapter. For effective perception of others we obviously need to guard against such stereotypical labelling.

KEY QUESTION

Describe three different situations in which you feel you have fallen into one or more of the errors of perception listed here. If you cannot think of real situations, imagine situations in which you might make one of these errors.

Conclusion

As we have said, all this adds up to a long and dismal list of errors. Clearly our judgements on other people may be more fallible than we realize. What is significant is how these judgements affect our relationships with others because they affect the way we interact with them. We are going to look at social interaction in more detail in the next chapter.

As a matter of terminology you should also note that these errors in perception are sometimes called **perceptual filters**, and are a major part of what we have described elsewhere as **psychological barriers** to communication.

But we would like to end this chapter on a more positive note, believing that recognition of these barriers is halfway to doing something about them. Communication theory should lead to communication practice. So now let us look at perceptual skills.

2.7 Skills in perceiving other people

In this chapter, Perception of others, we have dealt with the processes we use in perceiving other people. We have not sought to provide a general treatment of psychological theories and physiological experiments that seek to explain all the ways in which we perceive and make sense of the world around us. However, we have used the idea that all perceptual processes can be described in three stages: **selecting, organizing and inferring**. These can be seen as three general perceptual skills that we use when perceiving other people:

- Selecting: we have to choose certain features from all the possible sensory inputs – sight, hearing, smell, touch and general impressions – from another person. That choosing will depend on our own attention and the context and purpose of our encounter or interaction. If you and a friend meet a stranger and afterwards try to describe the stranger to each other you are likely to have selected different features about that person. It is a perceptual skill to make this selection process more conscious. At this stage we can imagine we are perceiving another person as a 'physical object'.

- Organizing: the features we have chosen to notice will then be arranged within our own cognitive processes to enable us to make sense of the other person. We are likely to categorize them and need to use skill to avoid stereotyped categories as we place them into a particular group identity of gender, race, social class, occupation, nation, and so on.

- Inferring: we will then draw conclusions about the person, for example, we might categorize them within opposites such as like me/not like me, friendly/not friendly, honest/dishonest, trustworthy/untrustworthy, confident/not confident, and other less personal inferences as wealthy/not wealthy, up to date/old-fashioned. It is a perceptual skill to be aware of the evidence that leads us to such inferences. At this stage the other person becomes a 'psychological entity', with feelings, motives, personality traits, and so on, and not just a physical object.

These processes can lead us into errors of:

- selecting (e.g. giving one characteristic attention above all others)

- organizing (e.g. failing to allow for cultural differences or our own emotional state), or

- inferring (e.g. forming a judgement based on factors that are not to do with the other person).

We should watch out for the traps described in Section 2.6 above. The main thing to realize is that perception requires a positive act of attention and the reserving of judgement as we categorize the noted features. The first rule is recognize the inferences you are making and avoid unfounded assumptions; the second is not to jump to conclusions and thus create fixed, unchangeable perceptions.

The following list of skills should help in making more accurate perceptions of other people.

Attending to detail

This refers to making a conscious effort **to notice verbal and nonverbal clues that may provide information** about the internal states of the other person.

Withholding judgement

This refers to reserving one's opinions and decisions about the other person for as long as possible, so that a proper range of information about them may be acquired.

Modifying assessments

This refers to being prepared to change one's view of the other person when you find out more about them.

Checking evidence

This refers to continually **checking speech and actions of the perceived to match these against opinions already formed**. This, in turn, suggests that you are always ready to modify your assessment of that person.

Comparing information in different ways

This refers to **cross-referring various details** noticed in different ways in order to avoid stereotyping. If one tries various associations of information then one may either change judgements or perceive alternative judgements.

Looking for alternative causes

This refers to **consciously seeking different reasons for people's behaviour**. This kind of skill is about a deliberate attempt to explain why people talk and behave as they do in more ways than seem immediately obvious. This includes looking for cause and blame in situations as much as in people themselves.

Seeking further information

This refers to **a search for more information in what people say and do**, in order to support or reject opinions already formed.

Empathizing

This refers to **sympathetic projection of one's awareness and perceptions into the viewpoint of the other person**. This skill is about trying to understand the other person's point of view, and about trying to see the world as they see it. This must lead to a more honest perception of that person. It also counteracts our tendency to see the world only from our own point of view, and to become victims of our own preconceptions.

Practice and use of these skills has more to do with consciousness of Self and of the other person than anything else. They may be described as kinds of social skill (see next chapter). They are skills that may be developed with some mental effort and through awareness of what is happening when we perceive others and when we communicate with them. They are about consciousness of Self, not self-consciousness. Too much deliberation leads to artificiality. But equally there is an effort that can be made, and which counteracts our tendency to 'naturalize' perception. That is to say, we tend to see the way we perceive people as something naturally acquired, and practised equally and accurately by everyone. This is not so. **It is possible to learn more about how to perceive, and more about forming more accurate perceptions of others**.

Review

You should have learnt the following things from this chapter:

- What the term 'perception' means and how it fits within the process of communication.
- How it affects interaction with others.

2.1 Introduction

- Perception of others is defined as assessment of others – of their verbal and nonverbal communication – for our own purposes.
- Perception predicts how we will carry on communication with others.
- Perception is about creating social reality in our minds.

2.2 Why do we perceive others?

- to remember information
- to make sense of the other person's behaviour
- to organize social understanding
- to predict the behaviour of others
- to plan our own communication
- to maintain our Self and our view of reality
- to reduce anxiety
- to satisfy our needs.

2.3 What do we perceive?

- the personality, attitudes and emotions of the other person
- attributes of the other person
- people's roles
- social reality
- presumed causes of behaviour and the motivation of the other person
- unexpected and predictable behaviour
- purpose – what we look for changes according to the purpose that we have in communicating with the other person.

2.4 Perceiving and communicating

- All perception and communication must take place through the senses.
- We do form first impressions when perceiving. These need to be modified through further perception, but many examples of interaction do not allow time for this further perception.
- Perception and communication take place through the exchange of symbols.
- There are cognitive processes that carry out the assessment in perception.
- Perception involves acquiring data or information about the other person. We tend to make dangerous generalizations from this data.
- In handling data we look for: distinctiveness, consistency and consensus.
- There are five types of validation used when checking this information: consensual, repetitive, multisensory, comparative and experimental.
- Perception can be described as stimulus–response behaviour up to a point.
- Attribution theory describes perception as a process of looking for reasons behind the way people communicate. We build up a view of what the other person is like as a way of explaining why they behave as they do.
- We have schemata, categories and sets in our minds which we refer to when trying to form these explanations. These are pre-formed groupings that associate traits and place values on them. We can describe six kinds of perceptual activity that take place.
- One dominant type of category used is also described as a stereotype.

2.5 What affects perception?

- physical and social context; spatial positioning
- physiological factors relating to the person perceived
- psychological factors within ourselves: our motivation, perceptual sets, predispositions, attraction to the other person, past experience, resemblance criteria, open- and closed-mindedness, role relations, saliency, social values.

2.6 Errors in perception

These can be summarized as:

- the fundamental attribution error
- false consensus
- false consistency
- the primacy effect
- the halo effect
- the recency effect
- preconceptions
- self-fulfilling prophecies
- stereotyping.

2.7 Skills in perceiving other people

These can be summarized as:

- attending to detail
- withholding judgement
- modifying assessments
- checking evidence
- comparing information in different ways
- looking for alternative causes
- seeking further information
- empathizing.

Case situation: The wrong message

Using the extract below, answer the following questions:

- Describe what Carl was trying to present about himself and how he tried to achieve it.
- Describe what Jennifer actually perceived about Carl.

> What would you say to Carl to help him create the impression he wants next time he meets a woman?

Carl is an extraordinarily handsome, well-built, 38-year-old lawyer who hates going to parties or social activities. Even though he seems to have it all – a nice home, a smart car and financial security – he doesn't seem to have any 'luck' with women, as he puts it. After much coercion by Michael, a colleague at his law firm, Carl relented and attended Michael's party after being assured that a lot of attractive single women would be there. Even though he felt uncomfortable, he was glad he had accepted the invitation as he noticed across the room a woman to whom he was immediately drawn.

He observed that she was vivacious and seemed to talk to everyone around her. She had a big radiant smile and appeared open and warm. Carl immediately went over to her and said, 'Hi, I've been noticing you from across the room, and you have a gorgeous smile.' The woman beamed and thanked him. He then noticed that she kept smiling and looking at him, which suddenly made him feel uncomfortable and self-conscious. Even though he started feeling awkward, he forced himself to shake hands with her and introduced himself. 'I'm Carl Templer,' he said, as his eyes shifted downwards, reaching out his hand. He still kept looking downward until the woman introduced herself as Jennifer Dalton. Then his eyes began darting everywhere. Since they were standing near a sofa, Carl said, 'Sit down. Let's talk.' The woman agreed, and continued smiling at Carl. When they were seated, Carl seemed to be taking up the entire sofa: his arms were spread out around the back, his legs jutted out in front, and he had adopted a semi-reclining position.

As he talked about himself and what he did for a living, he kept fidgeting and moving around. This made him appear uncomfortable. His gestures were broad and sweeping when he spoke, which made him seem overbearing. As he continued to talk to Jennifer, he hardly looked at her. Instead, he kept looking off to the side – which made him appear as though he was more interested in the other people at the party. He hardly looked at Jennifer's face when he talked to her, and whenever he did manage to look at her his eyes moved down and seemed to lock in on her breasts. When she asked him a question, he ignored it and kept on talking about himself and other subjects. Jennifer began to feel as though Carl was having a one-way conversation – with himself. Her presence didn't seem to matter. Eventually, she decided she had had enough.

She strained a phoney smile, got up and said that she would be right back. While making her way to the other side of the room she ran into her girlfriend, Cathy, with whom she had come to the party. This was their conversation:

Cathy	Wow! You lucked out! Who was that gorgeous hunk you were talking to?
Jennifer	Gorgeous hunk? Asshole is more like it!
Cathy	Are you serious? What did he do?
Jennifer	First of all the jerk orders me to sit down like a dog and then he kept talking to my boobs the whole time – not even looking up at me. Then, when he did manage to break away from them, he'd look to see who else was coming in the room. He had a cocky air about him and

	acted like he was so great. It was like he was looking down at me and judging me. What a snot! Then, all he kept talking about was himself, his stupid cases and his stupid car. Ugh! Forget it!
Cathy	Oh, no! What a geek! And to think I thought he was cute!

After realizing that Jennifer was not going to come back, Carl went to find Michael. When he found him, this was their conversation.

Michael	*(all smiles, patting Carl on the back)* See, I told you you'd meet some nice-looking babes here. Aren't you glad you came?
Carl	No, not really! That chick I was talking to . . .
Michael	Yeah. Boy, did she have a nice pair!
Carl	I guess. But what a bitch! Here I was being my nice-guy self, telling her all about what I do – and then she splits, like she couldn't care less. She probably figured out that I wasn't a partner yet and wasn't a millionaire. I probably didn't have enough money for her.
Michael	Don't lose any sleep over *her*. It's good you found out now. You wouldn't have wanted her anyway!

From *He Says, She Says – Closing the Communication Gap Between the Sexes* (Glass 1992).

Suggested reading

There are many books that are relevant in parts to the material of this chapter. We have chosen just four that you can read selectively. In fact, these books cover more than one chapter of this work so you will find that they do actually have a more general use.

Argyle, M., 1973, *Social Interaction*, London: Tavistock. (See Chapter 4.)

Gahagan, J., 1984, *Social Interaction and Its Management*, London: Methuen. (See Chapters 4, 5, 6.)

Gross, R. D., 1992, *Psychology: The Science of Mind and Behaviour*, London: Hodder & Stoughton. (See Chapter 17.)

Patton, R. and Griffin, K., 1981, *Interpersonal Communication in Action*, New York: Harper & Row. (See Chapter 3.)

Fig. 3.1 Social interaction – social skills in operation

Chapter 3

Social interaction and social skills

When you were growing up, adults taught you how to read, write, add and subtract. Conversational skills were another matter. You were taught how to pronounce words and to organize those words into sentences, but nobody ever taught you how to communicate effectively with other people.

(Pease with Garner 1989)

3.1 Introduction

Many of us spend almost all of our time interacting with other people: think back over your last week, how many of your waking hours have you spent completely alone? Perhaps at some of those times when you were alone, you were reading or listening to the radio and hence involved in indirect interaction with others. **This chapter is concerned with face-to-face interaction – how we communicate with other people**. We shall mostly concentrate on one-to-one relationships here, since in Chapter 6 we deal with communication in groups.

A great deal of time in schools and colleges is spent on developing language skills, even for those who are naturally fluent and precise in their use of spoken and written language. Less time is spent on consciously developing the languages of social interaction, which include a range of nonverbal and social skills such as:

- effective self-presentation
- accurate perception of others
- building of relationships and
- managing a sequence of interactions (speaking, listening, eye contact, facial expressions and gestures, questioning, and so on).

Making our knowledge of interactions and our behavioural patterns more conscious can certainly result in our being better able to express our feelings and achieve our personal aims (most of which can only be achieved through other people) and to understand other people and their needs and feelings more fully.

It has been suggested that 'All communication consists of reaction and counter-reaction' (Markham 1993). Hence, closely observing our own and other people's reactions to each word and action and the context in which they happen can help us to manage those 'inter-reactions' more effectively. There is nothing inevitable about our responses to other people, and their responses to us.

You may have heard people say things like, 'He and I just don't get on, there's a personality clash.' It is true that the people involved may have different personal characteristics and different views of the world, but if they can develop techniques to manage their interactions, their 'clash' could be developed into a greater level of mutual understanding, even if it serves to recognize the nature of their differences.

3.2 What is social interaction?

Quite simply, it is everyday encounters with other people. Erving Goffman (1968), whose work we shall be looking at more closely in Chapter 5, suggests that social interaction is: 'that class of events which occurs during co-presence and by virtue of co-presence. The ultimate behavioural materials are the glances, gestures, positionings and verbal statements that people feed into the situation, whether intended or not'.

There are several elements here that we wish to highlight:

- First, that social interaction consists of 'events', a sequence of happenings between two or more people when they meet face to face.

- Second, that it consists of physical behaviour – we make sounds and give visual signs to express our meanings to other people.

- Third, that these signs may or may not have been 'intended'. We may deliberately formulate our verbal statements to elicit a required response, but we may not be so conscious of the nonverbal statements we make that are picked up by the other person. As we shall see later in this chapter, social skills training is concerned with making our verbal and nonverbal behaviour more conscious, and with developing patterns of behaviour that, in turn, become unconscious. A parallel has often been made with driving a car: when we learn to drive we are conscious of all the behavioural sequences we employ, but when we are experienced drivers we perform these behaviours unconsciously.

Goffman (1963) draws a distinction between:

- on the one hand, social interaction as 'co-presence' (for example, a group of people in a bus or in a waiting room are aware of each other, but not necessarily involved with each other); and

- on the other hand, 'focused interaction', in which two or more people are actually giving full attention to each other and developing a relationship built on verbal and nonverbal exchanges.

It is useful at this point to introduce the concept of a **'transaction'**, which indicates where an interaction is more than just awareness of each other and becomes a main focus of exchange and negotiation. At its simplest, this can be built on a model of stimulus and response and we shall see how these notions are employed in the later chapter on transactional analysis.

Myers and Myers (1992) suggest that there are three components of a transaction: a transaction can be defined as:

'two or more people who mutually and simultaneously

- take one another into account
- figure out their roles, and
- conduct their interaction by a set of rules.'

The crucial issue in a transaction is that it consists of a two-way flow of messages and influence – of action and reaction that changes and develops the relationship. It can be visualized as a series of verbal and nonverbal statements and feedback loops that spiral forward in time.

There are, of course, an infinite number of possible occasions for private and public social interactions and transactions. During the course of one day we, your authors, found ourselves in encounters with other people such as at home with wife, son and daughter; in the car, bus or train with neighbours, acquaintances and strangers; at work with colleagues, both managers and peers; in the classroom with colleagues and students; at lunch with friends; at a meeting with industrialists or other employers; at a public function with groups of people, and so on. You might like to review your typical day's interactions with other people.

The concept of social interaction has been so frequently studied and discussed that it has developed complex layers of meanings and associations. O'Sullivan et al. (1994), in their *Key Concepts in Communication and Cultural Studies*, define it more fully: 'The exchange and negotiation of meaning between two or more participants located within social contexts'.

We wish to investigate briefly the four main components of this definition:

1. At the heart of the notion of interaction is exchange or negotiation, that is, two or more people must be engaged together, aware of each other and giving and receiving messages that are decoded. Interaction presupposes two or more people to interact.

2. The participants have separate existences before and after any particular moment of interaction and meet in a specific social context, which influences the nature of their interaction – whether they meet at an informal party, a street demo or a job interview. The personality and temperaments of the participants also influence the interaction, but recent research suggests that the situation has more effect than the individual personalities. Patterns of behaviour are a result of the interaction between a particular social situation and the personalities of the participants. Also, the participants will relate to each other according to how they perceive themselves (self-concept), how they wish to present themselves and what roles they adopt in relation to each other (for example, submissive–dominant, friendly–hostile, formal–informal, and so on). These roles may be determined by the social context and its cultural expectations – for example, if the participants are father/daughter in a family, or teacher/pupil in a school, or doctor/patient in a surgery.

3. Additionally, this definition stresses a location in a social context – interaction cannot

take place in a social vacuum. Inevitably an interaction exists in a particular situation that may be familiar or unfamiliar. The situation may have clear, culturally prescribed expectations – for example, a church service or a school class – or it may be informal and open – for example, a party among friends. In any case, the participants are free to some degree to define the situation for themselves: an atmosphere can be created to fulfil their needs – for example, a coffee morning can suggest certain expectations of appropriate clothing and behaviour, but participants can redefine this as more or less informal, more or less personal, and so on.

4. The fourth element in this definition is meaning. This is the element we shall be particularly concerned with, since the creation and generation of meaning from the exchange of verbal and nonverbal behaviours dictates the outcome of all interactions. The message of an interaction is what the participants perceive to have happened between them. If communication has been effective, then each participant will have closely similar perceptions of what took place.

We manage our social interactions and negotiate meanings between each other through a combination of the following:

- language – words in sequences
- paralanguage – the ways in which words are spoken, for example, use of different tone, pace, volume, pitch, accent or emphasis
- nonverbal behaviour – posture, proximity and use of space, facial expression, gaze and eye contact, gestures and body movement, bodily contact, clothes and appearance, physical objects
- relationship of participants – adopted roles and attitudes to each other, mutual perceptions (see Chapter 2)
- social context – physical place, atmosphere, cultural expectations, definition of the situation.

We will now investigate these separately. It is important to keep in mind that for purposes of analysis and explanation we need to separate these, but in practice they all interrelate and overlap – for example, the expectations about the context will influence the words considered appropriate and the words used will determine the warmth of the relationship, and so on.

KEY QUESTIONS

Using the four main numbered components of a social interaction described in Section 3.2 above, analyse the following specific examples of interactions:

- patient/doctor
- customer/salesperson

- prisoner/prison officer
- mother/son, or father/daughter
- child/teacher.

3.3 Language and social interaction

Uses of language

There are many ways of approaching a description of human language: what it is, how we use it and why we use it. **Use of language and speech are the primary distinctions between humans and other animals**. Language is our most sophisticated symbol system, consisting of a vocabulary and structures (syntax and grammar). **We use it for:**

- **generating meaning**
- **handling our experiences**
- **expressing our ideas, opinions and feelings**
- **thinking**
- **controlling other people, and**
- **communicating with each other**.

Aitchison (1976) (after Charles Hockett) has developed a list of design features that characterize the nature of language. The key elements of these are as follows.

Use of vocal auditory channel

In social interaction **language is essentially a system of organized sounds**. Our individual patterns of speaking are personal to us and yet also share a common cultural and social inheritance.

Arbitrariness

Both sound and written forms of language are neutral symbols that have no connection with the objects or ideas they symbolize. We agree within a particular culture to invest specific sounds and patterns on the page with agreed meanings. Although we agree about these meanings, each symbol represents for us slightly different meanings, according to our level of experience, knowledge and range of attitudes.

Semanticity

We use these arbitrary sound symbols to mean, or refer to, objects, actions or ideas. In social interaction, language is the prime carrier and creator of our meanings – this is

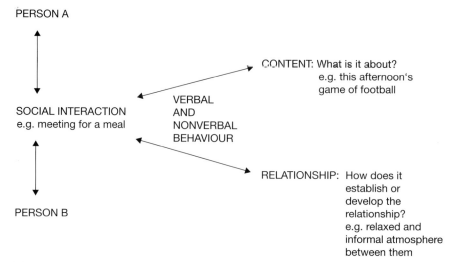

Fig. 3.2 A model for social interaction

sometimes referred to as an **ideational function**; it is also used to carry and create the meanings of our relationship between the participants – **our choice of words reflects the nature of the relationship we wish to create and this can be referred to as an 'interpersonal function'**.

A sequence of social interaction can be analysed on at least two levels of meaning:

- one is the content of the interaction, what it refers to outside the situation; and

- the other is the actual relationship between the participants.

We can perhaps visualize this in a simple diagram (see Fig. 3.2).

Another significant aspect of semanticity is that we invest words and structures with layers of meaning. We certainly do not have a language that exists as one word having one meaning. Even the simplest word, such as bird, will denote a basic meaning, but will also connote a range of cultural and personal associations. These personal associations are often charged with an emotional response, for example, one could take words such as 'dead animals', 'money' or 'marriage' and illustrate their denotative and connotative meanings, as has been done in Fig. 3.3.

Words are repositories of personal perceptions and experiences – hence we talk about exchanging and negotiating meaning between each other. The same is true of nonverbal signs and symbols – they do not exist simply in terms of 'one sign has one meaning'. We invest them with different meanings, according to our personal experience and the social and cultural context.

While discussing some aspects of semantics, we wish to spend a moment on what has been called 'metalanguage', which refers to the way in which words can be used so that the meaning goes beyond, or is hidden within, the accepted literal meaning of the words. Commercial transactions and advertising are a rich source of metalanguage examples, and,

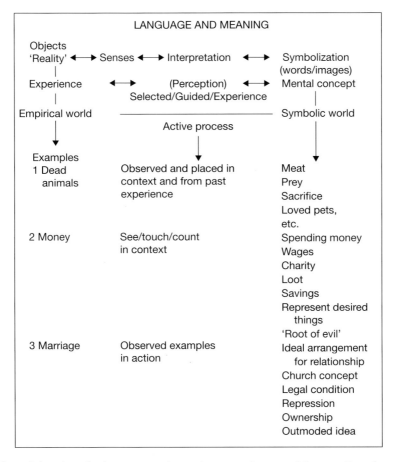

Fig. 3.3 A model to describe language and meaning, experience and the creation of symbols

in particular, estate agents have developed a metalanguage of their own which an experienced purchaser will have learnt to decode.

Pease and Garner (1989) have provided some amusing examples of this:

Metalanguage	*Translation*
Unique opportunity to purchase	We are having difficulty selling
Compact	Very small
Residence with great potential	Fallen-down dump
In an exclusive quiet area	A long way from shops and schools
Ideal for the handyman	Will cost a fortune to renovate

In metalanguage the words take on specific contextual meaning. It is worth differentiating this from 'paralanguage', which refers not to the words themselves but to how they are said, including stress, intonation, loudness, warmth, and so on.

Cultural transmission or tradition

People hand down language from generation to generation, and a major role of schooling is to enable young people to develop language skills. **The language also becomes a vehicle for containing cultural values and experiences and shapes people's thoughts into the ways of that culture**. A particular view of this process can be found in Dale Spender's book *Man-made Language* (1980), which provides examples of how the vocabulary, structure and conversational use of language reflects a primarily male-dominated (man-made) view of the world.

Duality or double articulation

This refers to the fact that **language is organized into two layers**. The basic sound units (e.g. *c, a, t*), which are meaningless by themselves, become meaningful when combined into a sound sequence (e.g. *cat*).

Displacement

We use language to refer to things far removed in time and place. The words we use in social interaction are an important element of the actual relationship at that moment, as noted above. But they can also refer to events of thousands of years ago, or create imagined worlds in far-distant futures.

Structure dependence

We recognize the patterned nature of language, and group sounds and words into meaningful structures. We have a notion of sentence structures, so that during a conversation even hints given by an unfinished sentence can be sufficient to convey meaning. For example, a transcript of a phone call might look like this:

Receptionist:	Hello
	Curl up and dye
Caller:	Oh, hello
	Hello, this is Sarah Johnson.
Receptionist:	Hi, how are you?
	Long time no . . .
Caller:	Is that you Jane?
	Hi, no. I've been away for a month
Receptionist:	Where did you go?
	Was it Portugal, did you say?
Caller:	Yes, it was great, beautiful beaches, hot weather, and the hotel was good. Got a gorgeous tan. We didn't want to come . . .
Receptionist:	*No, I* know.
	It always goes so quick . . .

> I'm off next week – can't wait . . .
> I'd like to hear about it. We fancy Algarve next year.

Caller: Yeah, OK
> Well I can tell you when I come in.
> I wondered if I could come in on Saturday. Have you got a gap? Just a cut and dry . . .

Receptionist: Um, well. I think so. Let me see, a bit busy. But yeah, how about 1.30?

Caller: Fine. I'll see you then.

Receptionist: OK, so half-past one on Saturday. See you then.

In reviewing this dialogue, you can see how rarely in a conversation do we use complete, structured sentences. Also, you might like to decide how much of the interaction was 'ideational' (the purpose of the call was to make an appointment for a haircut) and how much 'interpersonal' (about the relationship between the participants).

Creativity

Finally, the most important and interesting characteristic of language is its creativity. We can talk about anything we like in any way we like. The phone call we just looked at was in some ways unpredictable and went beyond its simple, predetermined aim. However, creativity does not mean completely open licence, since if we wish to communicate with each other we depend on a level of orderly predictability. **We are creative within limits that we learn. These limits are both those of linguistic structures and of culturally learnt relationships**.

Having reviewed the characteristics of language in a rather abstract way, we now wish to concentrate on three uses of language that are important for understanding the use of language in social interaction:

- controlling a conversation
- influencing a relationship
- expressing a personal identity.

Language and controlling interaction

One of the prime areas of research in social interaction has been into how we initiate, maintain and close a face-to-face encounter. These are conscious, deliberate elements in an interaction and much of the overt communication in interactions is carried by our use of words. But, as we shall see later in this chapter, nonverbal signals are also used to reinforce our verbal messages.

Peter Honey, in his book *Face to Face* (1988), sought to help managers develop their skills in achieving objectives through face-to-face interaction. He stresses the need to establish clear objectives for any interview or meeting and to use verbal and nonverbal means to keep the total personal behaviour in step with those objectives. He uses transcripts and case studies to illustrate how effectively, or ineffectively, people manage their interactions at work. **Critical points in any interaction are the opening and closing moments**.

Typically, the opening sequence builds the relationship and clears the channels for communication:

– Hello

– Hello

– Nice morning

– Yes, better than yesterday

– Yes, we all feel better when the sun shines. Well, I thought we ought to meet today to . . .

These opening moments, in terms of the task in hand, are redundant. But they are also vital for establishing contact and for setting the mood and atmosphere for the interaction. At the outset we can determine how formal/informal, positive/negative, friendly/hostile the interaction is going to be. Notice, also, how the phase of opening remarks is neatly turned to the main business by the use of the word 'well' (other often used words for this are 'right', 'OK', 'now', 'anyway'). When you are next speaking on the phone, consciously listen for when either you or your caller use one of these words to mark the shift from one part of the interaction to the next. We all use these language markers to identify the boundaries. As we come to the end of an interaction and one of the participants wants to wind up, the same device will normally be used:

– OK then. We seem to be agreed.

– Well, not really. I'm not clear about who . . .

– Right. I thought we agreed that you would . . . and I would . . . Anyway, we need to sort it out now.

– But surely we still need to . . .

We use speech as a cue or regulator of our interactions. In the extract here, one speaker is clear that he or she wants to close the interaction; but there is reluctance to do so on the part of the other – language cues usually make participants' views unambiguous. If the point is not taken then gestures or eye contact can be used to reinforce the point. Often before the commitment of 'anyway' or 'OK' to signal a shift in the interaction, some more ambiguous nonverbal cues might have been used (for example, shuffling documents, seeking eye contact, shifting on a chair).

Language influencing relationships

We use speech as the main vehicle for referring to the task or topic in hand. We might, of course, also be using some written material or a picture or plans to focus the topic as well. We also use speech for controlling the stages of development of the interaction, from the opening through the main business and to the closing. In addition, we choose our words as a means of influencing the nature of the relationship and the roles we adopt with each other.

As we have suggested, one characteristic of language is its creativity. We have a wide choice in any utterance of the vocabulary and structure we use. For example, we could greet the same person in any of several ways:

1. 'Hiya, Nobby, how's tricks?'

2. 'Hello, Bob, how are things?'

3. 'Good morning, Mr Clarke. How are you?'

These three questions all carry the same information, but you would choose the more appropriate one according to the context and your previous relationship with the other person. You would not expect your doctor to speak to you in the surgery as in (1), but she might speak to you in the pub as in (2).

We use these different registers of speech according to how we perceive the situation and how we wish to relate to other people. One of our social skills is to be able to shift our language registers. Sometimes it is necessary to use a formal vocabulary and structure (for example, in a court), but at other times such a register would be quite inappropriate (for example, in a football crowd).

Language and self-presentation

Finally, in this section, we want to draw attention to how we use speech as a way of presenting ourselves. Register is not only chosen as a result of the situation, social context and the other person, but also as a personal choice – to reveal ourselves. We each have an individual language capacity resulting from our experience, upbringing, education, and so on, which can be called our **idiolect**. We might be conscious of how we choose and pronounce our words, but may not also be conscious of our own particular word usage and accent until we receive feedback from other people or listen to a tape-recording of ourselves.

We develop a personal communication style that consists of a repertoire of behaviour patterns including verbal and nonverbal elements. As we shall see in the next chapter, this notion of self-presentation has been described in terms of a performance. **We play roles that we believe are appropriate for a particular situation and relationship**.

In face-to-face interactions, however, the language we use exists alongside a whole range of nonverbal features. Words are only one channel of communication and, it has been claimed, not the most important channel. For example, Bandler and Grinder (1979), in a book that is a transcript from their seminars, quite baldly state:

> and while the record that follows may have contained enough clues for the participant in the seminar, only the more astute reader will succeed in fully reconstructing the earlier events. As we state explicitly in this book, the verbal component is the least interesting and least influential part of communication.

As we shall see in a later section, Bandler and Grinder provide useful information and theories about how to be more sensitive to people's nonverbal feedback. However, for conscious sharing of ideas and information with each other, rather than attitudes and emotions, spoken language remains a primary means of communication.

3.4 Nonverbal communication and social interaction

So far in this section on how we manage social interactions we have mainly concentrated on verbal language – the use of words. However, as mentioned elsewhere, nonverbal 'language' is always present in interpersonal interaction. In fact, it has been suggested by many researchers that nonverbal dimensions account for 80 per cent of the 'content' or meanings that are conveyed in face-to-face interactions.

Later in this chapter we describe some aspects of social skills that we develop more or less consciously and effectively. At this stage it is useful to draw a distinction between 'linguistic competence' and the wider concept of 'communicative competence'.

- **Linguistic competence** refers to our ability to speak, read and write at least one language, with understanding of accepted word meanings and with a knowledge of accepted grammatical forms. There seems to be continual debate in Britain about Standard English and the 'correct' use of grammar and spelling and also about the matter of Standard Pronunciation, which is sometimes referred to as 'Received Pronunciation'. From a communication point of view, these forms of language are just part of a range of forms and styles that are needed for linguistic competence since non-standard forms may also be appropriate in some contexts.

- **Communicative competence** refers to our ability to use forms of verbal and nonverbal languages in ways that are appropriate to different situations and with an awareness of social and cultural expectations. Appropriateness is a key concept here – although someone with such competence could choose to challenge what may have become norms of cultural appropriateness, in the same way that a poet may challenge accepted forms of written language. The different ways of greeting Nobby Clarke illustrated above demonstrate verbal forms that reflect ideas of appropriateness in different social contexts and different interpersonal relationships.

In the last thirty years much has been revealed about nonverbal communication in academic and popular publications. The term 'body language' has become familiar enough to feature regularly in magazine articles and advertising.

The description and analysis of nonverbal behaviour in social interaction are some of the main reasons why notions of social skills and of social skills training (SST) have developed. One simple measure of this growth of knowledge is to compare the first edition of Michael Argyle's *Psychology of Interpersonal Communication* (1967) with the fifth edition (1994).

In this section we outline briefly what are now considered to be the main functions of nonverbal communication and then focus on some aspects of nonverbal communication and its place in regulating social interaction.

The **principal functions of nonverbal communication** in social interactions can be categorized as follows.

To convey our attitudes and emotions

This can be deliberate as, for example, when we use gaze or physical proximity to indicate our feelings towards someone else. However, it may not be deliberate, as, for example, a reluctance on our part to be close to someone or to make eye contact with them may give the other person the impression that we do not like them, which may not actually have been our intention. **The notion of nonverbal communication presupposes some intention to communicate. It is useful to distinguish this from nonverbal** *behaviour,* **which may cause other people to decode messages that we did not deliberately or consciously encode**. Another way of describing this is to distinguish between communication (as a deliberate sharing of meaning with someone else) and information (as a message that is picked up by someone else). Another term that is useful here is **leakage**. This describes the way in which we might be aware of deliberately controlling our facial expression and hand movements to hide our nervousness in a situation, but be given away by leaked messages from our strained voice or shaking knees.

To support our verbal communication

We are quite often aware of using facial expressions or gestures deliberately to reinforce or complete what we are saying. In fact, analysis of social interactions by video recordings and close observation shows that the whole body is engaged while speaking and listening. This was well expressed by Abercrombie (1968) in an article on **paralanguage** when he said, 'we speak with our vocal organs, but we converse with the whole body'.

Pioneering work on body movements in social interactions, which he named kinesics, was done by Ray L. Birdwhistell (1968), who sought to break down movements, gestures and facial expressions into their component parts (kinemes). Birdwhistell analysed body movements as a series of structures, comparable with analysis of language as a series of structures building from basic sounds (phonemes) that are built into sequences and paragraphs. He pointed out that nonverbal behaviour constantly takes place, both during speech and during silence.

Kinesics is the science of body behavioural communication. Any person who has learned the right way to behave in public and is at all aware of his or her own response to the awkward or inappropriate behaviour of others recognizes the importance of body-motion behaviour to social interaction. However, it is more difficult to conceive that body motion and facial expression belong to a learned, coded system and that there is a 'language' of movement comparable to spoken language, both in its structure and in its contribution to a systematically ordered communicative system.

In describing social interaction we still tend to assume that speech is the prime channel of communication, and that nonverbal behaviour supports speech. It is important to remind ourselves that **in some circumstances, especially of intimacy or hostility, speech is replaced by nonverbal communication**. It has also been suggested by Mehrabian (1971) that of the messages received in a conversation, 7 per cent are verbal, 38 per cent are vocal (paralanguage) and 55 per cent are facial and nonverbal.

To present yourself

In discussing language earlier in this chapter, we referred to speech as a way of presenting oneself. But also very significant in self-presentation are our choice of clothes, bodily adornment (hairstyle, make-up, jewellery), the objects we surround ourselves with and our general styles of behaviour. We choose to present ourselves through a variety of roles, and this theatrical metaphor of self-presentation will be explored more fully in the next chapter.

To regulate social interaction and to provide feedback

As we saw above, we use speech to regulate and guide a conversation, especially in the opening and closing phases. However, in many situations, even before we speak, we need to catch someone's eye before we can begin the interaction. For example, in public places such as restaurants or shops we have to gain attention, usually nonverbally. Nonverbal cues are also crucial to the smooth management of interaction.

We signal our desire to speak by mutual eye contact. Having got the floor, the speaker will not maintain the gaze, but the listener will tend to keep looking at the speaker. The speaker will then make eye contact as a signal that he or she is about to stop and pass over to the other. These turn-taking signals are mostly nonverbal. While listening, the listener will provide feedback through head-nods or murmurings to acknowledge agreement or to encourage the speaker to continue. Alternatively, frowns or seeking eye contact or murmuring 'yes, but . . .' indicate a desire to take the floor.

In addition to using nonverbal signals to help turn-taking, we also use nonverbal feedback signals to indicate the status relationship of the participants. The clearest examples of this are the use of physical space and proximity, and paralanguage (especially the tone of the voice). The positioning of participants in a room – who stands, who sits, their orientation to each other, how far apart they are – indicates the power relationships. Similarly, bodily posture and body tension are signals of the interpersonal relationship. Blushing can also be an example of leakage rather than communication.

The regulation of interaction is often tentative – that is, one person is not necessarily in a clearly dominant power position, and so it is an asset to use nonverbal rather than verbal signals. Nonverbal signals often work by hints or innuendo and are therefore ambiguous. It is possible to retreat from a nonverbal message by saying, 'Oh, I never intended you to get that impression', but a consciously expressed spoken utterance is less easy to withdraw. For example, it is unlikely that you will say, 'Will you come to the party with me on Saturday?' unless you are fairly confident from nonverbal messages that have been exchanged that the answer is likely to be yes. Openly asking someone for a favour and openly being rejected is more difficult to cope with and more embarrassing than hinting at such things nonverbally.

KEY QUESTIONS

Make a recording on video of someone speaking.

Then watch the recording and write down details of the nonverbal behaviour used with speech. Comment on how these details affect your understanding of what is said.

3.5 Making conversation

- Where have you been?

- Out.

- What did you do?

- Nothing.

We learn, and are taught, how to talk to other people from an early age so that 'making conversation' comes to seem as 'natural' for most people as walking on two legs. We may also, as in the above quotation, practise the art of not making a conversation!

However, we recognize that the 'art of conversation' is a highly complex set of conventions, skills and attitudes when we find ourselves floundering as we try to talk to someone, or when we occasionally hear someone suggest that the art of conversation is dead, or when we become very conscious of our need to interact with someone to get something we want. In a conversation lots of things are going on all at the same time. To put it more precisely:

> But conversation is more than a co-operative form of verbal interaction rooted in a huge reservoir of background knowledge and assumptions, it is also the context in which multifarious channels of human communication operate and interact. (Ellis and Beattie 1986)

The cooperative nature of conversation is fundamental. Two or more people use verbal and nonverbal signals to share something of themselves. The exchange given at the start of this section indicates a lack of cooperation on one side. One can easily imagine the nonverbal and paralinguistic signals accompanying those words. It is an everyday sort of exchange and is located in Argyle and Henderson (1985) as an exchange between 'parent' and 'adolescent'.

In the past three hundred or so years, there has been a great deal of research into how people interact verbally and nonverbally. Techniques of observing, analysing and recording interactional sequences (especially using video equipment) have been systematized. What has previously only been intuitively felt can now be more scientifically described. Atkinson and Heritage (1987) observe that:

> Conversation analytic studies are thus designed to achieve systematic analyses of what, at best, is intuitively known, and more commonly, is tacitly orientated to in ordinary conduct. In this context, nothing that occurs in interaction can be ruled out, *a priori*, as random, insignificant, or irrelevant.

115

Every flicker of an eyelid can count in a conversation.

It is beyond the scope of this book to summarize all the findings of recent research in conversation analysis and sequential analysis of interactions, but the brief reading list at the end of this chapter offers further sources of information. There are now conventions for transcribing elements of conversation such as:

- simultaneous or overlapping utterances
- intervals between and within utterances
- characteristics of speech delivery (for example, falling or rising tone, animated tone, emphasis, quieter or louder volume, faster or slower pace, gaze direction, head nods, applause).

For details of these, see Atkinson and Heritage (1987).

We will now discuss seven significant elements of conversation making:

- openings
- turn-taking
- closings
- questioning
- listening
- using nonverbal communication, and
- recognizing feedback.

As a background to these specific elements, it is important to remember that social interactions are carried out using various communication channels within a range of contexts and relationships (see Section 3). They often also accompany other activities such as eating, dealing with children, mending a car, and so on.

Openings

In the case situation at the end of this chapter, we have an imaginary situation in which two people find it difficult to open an interaction. The opening moments of an encounter are commonly accepted as being very important. In advice for people attending interviews it is often suggested that 'You don't get a second chance to make a first impression'. However, such advice may serve only to make the opening moments more nerve-racking.

We easily recognize that some of our conversational openings are difficult, but it is less easy to recognize how such openings are successfully negotiated. What skills are required to open a conversation?

Christine Saunders in Hargie (1986) defines openings as:

the interactors' initial strategy at both personal and environmental level, utilized to achieve good social relationships, and at the same time establish a frame of reference deliberately designed to facilitate the development of a communication link between the expectations of the participants and the realities of the situation.

This definition highlights a number of points:

- openings should be consciously managed
- at a personal and at a context level, the scene must be set
- the appropriate relationship must be established
- the expectations of the people and the task in hand must be kept in focus.

The essential move is to open contact and to greet each other. This is done nonverbally through eye contact, eyebrow flash, open smiling expression, touch, handshake, embrace, kiss or simply beckoning, welcoming tone of voice and body proximity. Verbally, there are standard greetings, of course – 'Good morning', 'Hello', 'Hi', 'How are you?' The choice of vocabulary will reflect the relationships, personalities, moods and context. One needs to set the tone for the rest of the interaction – and, indeed, perhaps for a continuing relationship. Fig. 3.4 summarizes these verbal and nonverbal components.

If the encounter is to be friendly and warm then a series of 'phatic' remarks might be exchanged on subjects such as the weather or controversial current events. If the encounter is to be cool and more hostile, then the opening can lead straight to the task or issue. 'I asked you to come to see me because . . .'. The choice of where you meet, whether you are sitting or standing, when you meet, and so on, will all contribute to creating a mood and relationship.

If you know why you wish to open a particular interaction then all you do and say should contribute to the relationship you want to establish and to the task you want to achieve. If you are the recipient, rather than the initiator of this opening, then you still have the opportunity to influence the situation through your verbal and nonverbal contribution.

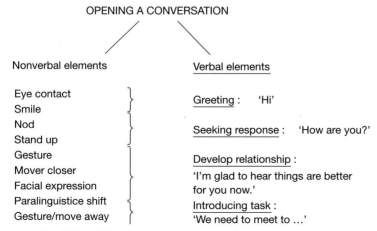

Fig. 3.4 A model describing skills in opening a conversation

Taking turns

A successful conversation is neither a monologue nor a confused babble of voices. Somehow, almost mysteriously, we take turns to speak and maintain a continuous nonverbal dialogue. In general, we take turns to hold the floor; one person speaks at a time; we do not talk simultaneously for any length of time; we manage transitions from person to person quite smoothly. Most of us succeed in this through a system of verbal and nonverbal 'cues' that regulate interaction.

In this section we shall briefly review some of the research that has been done into how we take turns in conversation. Such knowledge represents an important communication skill in managing conversations.

There are two main research traditions in studying turn-taking:

- First, that we use *rules* in what we say and how we say it in order to manage the transitions from person to person.
- Second, that we use *signals*, especially nonverbal ones, to manage transitions. In practice, we intuitively use both rules and signals.

The **rule-based emphasis** suggests that we use particular units of speech to indicate possible completion points for another person to come in. Clear examples of this are to be seen in questions that invite a response from another person. These may be specifically addressed:

— 'Bill, what do you think?'

or they may require self-selection by the next turn-taker in a group:

— 'Who can tell me why it happened?'

Such turns may not be so directly signalled by questions, but may hint at a relevant point for transition. This can be done through treatment of the topic and through use of words such as 'Anyway', 'OK', 'Anything else'. Conversation analysis indicates that we move the topic forward, sideways or backwards by a series of small steps and mark the boundaries of topics with transitional markers.

The 'next turn' indicates to the previous speaker what the recipient has understood and how he or she is guiding the topic. For example:

A: It's hot tonight.
B: I'll open the window.

This indicates that person B took the initial statement to mean a specific thing, which was not necessarily what was intended.

When analysing naturally occurring conversations we find that they take a number of unpredictable turns. Studies in conversation analysis aim to expose what Harvey Sacks called 'the technology of conversation' (Atkinson and Heritage, 1987). You can listen to conversations to identify how the interactants move from topic to topic, turn to turn.

The **signal-based emphasis** on turn-taking in conversation stresses the nonverbal cues that lead people to 'take the floor'. A good deal of research has been done on the use of gaze and eye contact as signalling mechanisms. In general, the speaker does not maintain eye contact throughout his/her turn, but signals the final moments of the turn by making eye contact for the next speaker to come in. A deficiency in some of this research has been the concentration on one type of nonverbal signal without attention to the context of other nonverbal channels, and verbal and paralinguistic channels. Duncan (1972) listed the following behaviours as 'turn yielding signals' to act as 'cues' for the next speaker to take the floor:

- Intonation: the use of any rising or falling intonation contour.
- Drawl on the final syllable, or on the stressed syllable of a terminal clause.
- Sociocentric sequences: the use of one of several stereotyped expressions, typically following a substantive statement, for example, 'or something', 'you know', etc.
- Pitch/loudness: a drop in pitch and/or loudness in association with a sociocentric sequence.
- Syntax: the completion of a syntactic clause involving a subject-predicate combination (that is, a completed statement).
- Gesture: the termination of any hand gesticulation or the relaxation of a tensed hand position.

Thus, we can see that there is a range of signals to indicate that you are handing over to the next speaker. We can, of course, accidentally or deliberately misread these signals. But the give and take of conversation will make it flow if all participants want it to continue.

As with all social interaction, we manage this flow through a combination of attending to:

- the topic, task, context
- the relationship
- the verbal channels
- the nonverbal channels.

Closing

We do not usually simply end a conversation by stopping our talk and our listening. If we were to do this, then we would give off rather a brusque and rude impression. Quite often it is difficult to make a smooth transition to close an interaction. We can occasionally simply say, 'Well, that's it. We've finished now', or we may look at a clock and stand up to indicate that we have to be elsewhere. The nature of the relationship and of the context will dictate suitable closing strategies. There may, however, be tensions between needing to leave and not wanting to separate.

As with turn-taking, it is possible to observe verbal, topic-based conventions and also nonverbal, relationship-based signals for disengaging from an interaction. Verbally, the participants can summarize the encounter or look forward to future actions and thus show that the conversation is coming to an end. There will then be formal exchanges, such as:

– Fine, OK. That's it then.

– See you next week when we'll check how it's going.

– Bye, see you.

– Bye, see you.

A conversation needs to be concluded in the appropriate mood for future contact, or for future non-contact.

Nonverbally, there are a range of closing conventions. These include:

• breaking of eye contact

• clearing up papers

• standing up

• straightening clothes, hair, and so on, ready for departure

• smiling

• shaking hands, and so on.

Early signals to end may be given and then, depending on the response, they can be adjusted to prolong the encounter, or may be continued in order to close it.

In long-standing relationships, as opposed to one-off encounters, the closing strategies are important moments not only to end the face-to-face contact, but also to set the tone for the next encounter. With someone close to you, there may be a bitter feeling on either side if one of the partners leaves without the ritual hug and kiss. With a working colleague, there would be uneasiness if you simply walked out without jointly signalling the close of the conversation.

Questioning

This is an essential skill for any type of interaction. Questions are used to obtain different sorts of information (the task) and to keep the interaction moving forward (maintaining the relationship).

As with many social skills, we may feel we know how to ask questions because we have been doing so since we could first talk. However, it is possible to refine these skills – especially for particular purposes, whether interviewing, teaching, market surveys, counselling, interrogating or social conversation.

There are a variety of forms of questions, such as:

• open questions ('What were you doing last night?')

• closed questions ('Did you stay at home last night?')

• leading questions ('Isn't it true to say that last night you were at that party?')

• recall questions ('Were you at the party at 8.00 pm?')

- process questions ('How could you have improved the party last night?')
- affective questions ('Do you feel embarrassed about talking about last night?').

It can be easy to assume that because a question has been asked there must be an answer. However, in their useful textbook on communication, Myers and Myers (1992) suggest that there are 'unanswerable' questions. As examples, they cite two types of question:

- First, a question like 'Is photography an art?', to which there is no definite answer, and for which the response is simply a matter of semantic definition.
- Second, a question like 'Does God exist?', to which, again, there is no definite answer and for which the response depends on personal values and beliefs.

Listening

As with questioning, we may well believe that we have been listening successfully to other people all our lives. However, we might also accept that often we *hear* other people talking, but we do not always *listen* to what they are saying. In recent years several large business organizations in the UK have made listening a theme in their advertising campaigns. For example, we are told that one of the major British banks is 'the listening bank'. The implication is that if the bank listens to its customers it shows that it takes its customers seriously.

Listening, like all acts of perception, is an active, not a passive process. We need to attend to what is being said, select from it and then interpret it for ourselves.

Common **problems of listening** come from:

- merely taking note of the information and content and not taking note of the context and feeling behind it
- allowing ourselves to be distracted and sidetracked into our own interests, which often leads us to hearing only what we want to hear
- being put off by the context or by the speaker
- preparing our response before the speaker has finished
- not looking as if we are listening – that is, failing to give verbal and nonverbal feedback to the speaker.

A useful discipline to develop our listening skills was devised by Carl Rogers, the psychotherapist and counsellor who developed the client-centred therapy method. At the heart of this therapeutic method Carl Rogers stressed the need to listen to what his clients were really saying through their verbal and nonverbal messages. To be able to do this he believes you must really empathize with the other person – that is, you must imagine how it would make sense to say what the other person is saying without filtering it through your own beliefs and experiences. In order to develop this skill he suggests that before you reply to a speaker you repeat in your own words what the speaker has just said to the speaker's satisfaction. This method certainly slows up a conversation or a meeting. But if you try it, you will find that it does make you listen – and shows that most of the time we do not listen to what other people are really saying.

As well as this technique of 'reflecting' or mirroring back what you have just listened to, an active listener will also be giving verbal and nonverbal feedback to show that she/he is listening to the other person. This can be positive head nodding or smiling, or saying 'Yes, I see' at appropriate points.

Like all other activities that are part of interaction, listening is a mutual activity – all parties need to display the skills of listening. A conversation comes to an end if either partner stops listening. A good conversationalist spends more time listening than speaking and concentrates on what the other person says rather that what she/he will say next. An exercise in listening skill is to listen to a radio news broadcast with full attention and monitor the stories without taking notes. When it is finished, write down as much as you can remember. You can then gauge for yourself how fully you normally give your complete attention and listen actively without wandering into your own intrapersonal distractions.

Using nonverbal communication

The clearest example of conscious learning of the social skills of nonverbal behaviour is in the training of an actor: the most important way of revealing a character on stage, film or TV is through nonverbal cues. Hence, an effective way in which you can observe nonverbal behaviour (especially facial expression, body movements and gestures) is to watch a TV drama with the sound turned off. As you would expect, the effect is generally more obvious and larger than real life and it is interesting to contrast such conscious acting of a part with the silent 'performances' of people in a factual piece of television such as a documentary, or news. In these ways we can analyse other people's nonverbal behaviour, consider how we normally 'read' people's behaviour in daily life, and compare our own use of NVB. It is also possible using a video recorder to review a sequence of social interaction several times and to concentrate on specific elements each time – for example, gaze and eye contact, gestures, facial expressions, and so on.

Another interesting and accessible way of developing increased sensitivity to one specific type of nonverbal behaviour is by recording from the radio. This medium, of course, has no nonverbal channel except paralanguage and the occasional 'sound effect' or 'background noise'. However, when listening to radio drama you can concentrate on how a character and relationships are developed without any visual observation of nonverbal behaviour. And, by way of comparison, you can also listen to factual radio programmes: at the very least this heightens one's awareness of how we place people through their use of language and paralanguage (that is, in terms of age, gender, nationality, social class, temperament and even personal appearance). To do this we attend to such things as their accent, tone, speed of speech, volume and pitch. We characterize a voice as friendly/unfriendly, cold/warm, educated/uneducated, young/old, all from aspects of paralanguage.

As students of communication we can engage in field observation of social interaction – whether in shops, streets, waiting rooms, sports activities, schools, cafés, pubs, and so on, all of which provide rich data for analysing nonverbal behaviour. How do customers and salespeople negotiate nonverbally? How do couples or groups in a café interact nonverbally? You can try to draw conclusions about people's attitudes and relationships from their nonverbal behaviour – who's trying to impress whom? who's dominant? who's nervous? and so on.

As well as observing others, try some experiments with your own nonverbal social skills by breaking conventions, for example, while speaking to a friend maintain eye contact or avoid any eye contact. Try to note what is your 'normal' use of eye contact.

Recognizing feedback

Finally, we want to illustrate the **social communication skill of being sensitive to feedback from other people**. Listening to words spoken and being sensitive to nonverbal responses are essential elements in effectively managing our social encounters. Here we are going to review briefly two important concepts from **neurolinguistic programming (NLP)**, a therapeutic counselling method developed in the USA. We also look again at NLP in another context this later in this chapter.

Practitioners of NLP seek to develop increased awareness of the nonverbal messages that people give off and receive. It is based on the idea that each of us has internalized from our life experience, perceptions and thinking, a particular pattern of language use and physical, neurological reactions. We have each processed our perceptions in a specifically personal way that is labelled 'neurolinguistically programmed'. To understand someone and their deepest feelings and fears, NLP practitioners argue, we need to be able to see how they have 'programmed' their past experience. NLP practitioners claim to be able to detect people's emotional experience and world view through sensitivity to their verbal and bodily responses. It is the nonverbal feedback that is really crucial. Bandler and Grinder (1979) stress that most of the time we are not aware of the physiological responses people are giving off. Let us look at two examples.

First, language: Bandler and Grinder (1979) suggest that our selection of words reveals how we think and feel. For example,

> I might 'naturally' say, 'I hear what you're saying', or 'that rings a bell'. You might naturally say, 'I see what you mean', or 'I can picture it now'. Someone else might say, 'Ah, I can grasp it now', or 'I get the feel of it'.

Bandler and Grinder suggest that these choices of words, which are all intended to convey the same meaning, represent different people's different ways of programming their experience.

In the quotations above:

- the first person is using an **auditory mode**
- the second person is using a **visual mode**, and
- the third person is using a **kinaesthetic mode**.

Neurolinguistic programming hypothesizes that when we make initial contact with a person, he or she will probably be thinking in one of these three main representational systems.

Fig. 3.5 Sometimes the meanings of nonverbal communication seem to be easy to decode

Internally, he or she will either be generating visual images (visual mode), having feelings (kinaesthetic mode) or talking to themselves and hearing sounds (auditory). By being aware of this, it is claimed, we can understand each other more fully since we can recognize how people access their own meanings through a particular choice of words. If we listen carefully to the words and recognize how they represent other people's feelings and personal histories, then we can understand them more clearly.

A repeated theme of this book is that we are constantly generating meanings and negotiating or sharing these meanings with other people. These meanings, as we saw in Chapter 2, result from our processes of perception – that is, the selective attention we give to our experience, the interpretations we put on our sensory experiences and the categorizing and labelling of these.

Bandler and Grinder (1979) stress that,

in order for you to understand what I am saying to you, you have to take the words – which are nothing more than arbitrary labels for parts of your personal history – and access the meaning, namely, some set of images, some set of feelings, or some set of sounds which are for you the meaning of the word you chose. Words are triggers that tend to bring into your consciousness certain parts of your experience and not other parts.

The second example of feedback is nonverbal behaviour. Another repeated theme of this book is that **much of our communication in face-to-face interaction is not intentional**. People read messages into our unconscious body language. This idea of unintended physiological feedback and how to be aware of it is the second interesting strategy of NLP.

The example from Bandler and Grinder that we will use here is that of eye movement. Bandler and Grinder suggest you can ask a set of questions about:

- visually remembered experience (for example, 'What colour is the floor of your living room?')
- visually imagined experience (for example, 'What would you look like with blue hair?')
- aurally remembered experience (for example, 'What does your mother's voice sound like?')
- aurally constructed experience (for example, 'What would your favourite piece of music sound like played on a harp?')
- kinaesthetic feelings (for example, smell, taste) that are remembered (for example, 'What do onions smell like when they are frying?')
- kinaesthetically imagined experience (for example, 'How would it feel to plunge into ice-cold water?'). (Bandler and Grindler 1979)

If the person who is answering these questions does not verbalize his/her response, but merely thinks/feels the response, it will still be possible to observe some sort of physiological feedback – especially in terms of eye movement, facial expression or body movement (for example, the cold water plunge is likely to evoke a fast physical reaction).

Practitioners of neurolinguistic programming further suggest that a right-handed person is likely to access their remembered or imagined experiences with a regular pattern of eye movements. Eyes are likely to go up to their left for remembered visual experience, up to their right for constructed visual experience; eyes defocused or moving also indicate visual accessing; for kinaesthetic experience eyes are likely to go down to their right.

We suggest that you could test out this theory in an experiment on some friends. Observe their nonverbal feedback to your questions. There is nothing magic about this. What NLP and its strategies show is that most of the time we are not really observing the responses that people make. This is neatly expressed as follows:

you will always get answers to your questions in so far as you have the sensory apparatus to notice the responses. And rarely will the verbal or conscious part of the response be relevant. (Bandler and Grinder 1979)

As we shall see in the next chapter, presenting ourselves to other people is about 'defining the situation' for other people and managing the impression that other people get of us. **Effective communication is about gaining the desired response from someone else**. Once again, Bandler and Grinder neatly sum up this idea:

> The meaning of your communication is the response that you get. If you can notice that you're not getting what you want, change what you're doing.
> (Bandler and Grinder 1979)

If we can see and feel the way another person is handling their experience, how they really feel, and if we can reflect that back to them through mirroring their use of words and nonverbal communication, then we will build an effective relationship for interactions.

Assertiveness

Assertiveness training has gradually become a common phenomenon over the past forty years. It is very likely now to be available as an evening class at your local college. Many people believe that these courses are aimed at women who, stereotypically, are portrayed as submissive as compared with the stereotypically aggressive male. Several books listed at the end of this chapter deal with male and female socialization, which tends to create different linguistic and communicative behaviour for men and women. We also discuss gendered communication in Chapter 4.

However, the need for assertiveness as a communication skill applies to everyone. It is likely that every reader of this book has at some time or other dreaded or sought to put off an awkward meeting with someone, or dreaded making a complaint about something even though they felt it was justified. Similarly, many of us find it difficult to say 'no' when we are asked to do something by our partner or boss, even though we do not want to do it. We also refer briefly to assertiveness under the section about social skills, on page 134.

Being assertive is not the same as being aggressive. Assertiveness enables you to express your view in a clear and confident way without putting down the other person. Dickson (1988) draws the distinction between aggression and assertion very clearly:

> Aggressive behaviour is competitive, overriding, always lacking in regard for the other. It means winning at someone else's expense. Assertion is based on equality not superiority, co-operation not competition, honest and appropriate expression of feelings instead of ruthless expression of them . . .

All the elements of interaction and social skill we have discussed here can be used to create encounters that are mutually assertive, in which people express themselves and are accepted as themselves. But, how do we deal with difficult people?

Ursula Markham, in her book, *How To Deal With Difficult People* (1993), gives a great deal of useful advice and applies many of the skills outlined here. In particular, she roots the notion of assertiveness in terms of 'rights'. As an assertive person you have certain rights:

- 'You are entitled to ask for what you want – but you also have to remember that the other person is entitled to say no.

- You are entitled to make decisions and choices for yourself.

- You are entitled to your own opinions and feelings, to acknowledge them to yourself and to express them to other people.

- You are entitled to make mistakes, bearing in mind that others must be allowed to make mistakes, too.

- You are entitled not to know everything.

- You are entitled to decide whether you want to become involved in someone else's problems.

- You are entitled to change your mind.

- You are entitled to privacy.

- You are entitled to achieve.

- You are entitled to alter yourself in any way you choose – granting the same right to other people.' (Markham 1993)

Of course, one has to understand that these notions of assertiveness are culturally relative.

> each culture, however, should be understood from its own frame of reference: from its ecological, historical and cultural context. (Miyahara, in Jandt 2004)

This writer points out that qualities that are valued in Japanese culture – not 'standing out', and not stating one's intentions directly – contradict what is valued in our western notions of assertiveness. The Japanese, like a number of other cultures, are collectivist rather than individualist. Both cultures might agree that a 'mature personality' should be 'finely attuned to the expectations of others' (Jandt 2004). But the Japanese do not value or practise what we would describe as 'being frank and straightforward'.

In spite of its popularity, one should not assume that all assertiveness training or ideas about assertiveness are endorsed by all commentators, including those within the feminist camp.

Crawford (1995) questions the assumptions behind assertiveness as suggesting that women have some kind of deficiency that needs remedying, when, in fact, it may be males who need sorting out: 'if women need assertiveness training to counter socialised passivity, men need to counter socialised aggressiveness and insensitivity'. She also criticises the individualistic assumptions behind assertiveness, which emphasise an 'I' or 'Me' outlook, and which avoid giving reasons for needs expressed. She argues that assertiveness training could be seen as being about taking on a masculine style.

She also argues that other commentators' remarks about male–female differences in communication behaviour contain as many assumptions as demonstrated truths. She states that research indicates that factors such as age make a difference to communication styles, but that in observation of real-life situations there is no discernible difference overall between male and female behaviours. She points out that, while there may be assertive behaviour, there are no assertive people as such. This links back to our own points made earlier about the way in which theories of personality contain assumptions, and that all that can be observed is behaviour itself. Crawford points out that being non-assertive is not necessarily a bad thing – 'a positive and adaptive strategy for women' – but that one should not assume that being male and assertive is necessarily a good thing. We would counter-argue that 'the problem' is that men are often not assertive as such, but simply aggressive and bullying.

Nevertheless, it is right that Crawford points out a number of problems with research and the conclusions drawn from this. Notions of rudeness and politeness are culturally relative. Much research fails to deal with factors such as class, race and status. Too much research depends on using college students – a selective group within the population. Research does not take sufficient account of contextual factors.

3.6 Communication and relationships

Any relationship is conceived, affirmed, conducted and, even, broken by the use of communication. People build or destroy bridges between one another, and those bridges are built through communication. However, if communication is a bridge then in relationships it is one that carries an immensely complex traffic of meanings. These meanings are about nuances of feelings in a relationship, about its condition, about where it is going. There is a great deal of nonverbal traffic that travels across with deceptively simple phrases such as 'I really like you'. The communication style of a given relationship is peculiar to its participants. Therefore it is not possible to prescribe what would be 'good communication' for all relationships, although in what follows you will find references of ways of talking that are more likely to lead to 'success' than others are.

Establishing relationships

Obviously relationships are established when people make various kinds of communicative contact – eye contact, greetings and the like. Given different social conventions and situations, people have different expectations of the kind of relationship that they want to establish. Examples of possible relationships are:

- the birth relationship of parents and child
- the business relationship of worker and client
- the personal relationship of one adult loving another.

It is this last from which we will tend to draw examples in this section.

The social exchange theory suggests that people form relationships on the basis of rewards and gain. They will use communication to establish a bond with one or more other people because they see some rewards in it for them, and they believe that they will gain something. Deaux and Wrightsman (1984) also point out that 'people may measure the gains in a relationship against some baseline that they have come to expect'. This would support a view that people can find it more difficult to establish relationships as they get older; they have changed their 'baselines' as they get older, and have become more particular about the rewards they expect.

We have all heard of 'love at first sight'. Certainly, passionate relationships can develop very quickly. Unfortunately the evidence is that this is an indicator that such relationships will be short term. Also, the cues for initial attraction between people do not of themselves predict long-term stability in the relationship. There is also evidence that the 'arranged marriage' is not a bad way of establishing a relationship. This evidence comes from research that makes it clear that in many cases similarities of age, education, intelligence and attractiveness are good predictors of the survival of a pair bond. It has also been found that common interests, common values and similar personalities are a fair predictor of success in forming a relationship. The work of dating agencies confirms this. In fact, many people do use their perceptual skills to search out similarities. People have a 'preference for the familiar over the unfamiliar' (Duck 1993).

Developing and maintaining relationships

The quality of any relationship depends on the positive use of social and perceptual skills. People who try to empathize with one another are likely to relate successfully. By the same token, people who play games with one another are likely to destroy a relationship in the end. To link back to earlier in this chapter, assertiveness within a relationship should be a healthy thing because it includes the honest expression of feelings and needs. Of course, this may not work if one partner has a poor sense of self-esteem and sees the assertiveness as being threatening.

Poor perception of others is broadly based on false assumptions. Such assumptions are likely to be dangerous and even prevalent in the early stages of a romantic relationship because of the force of attraction. We can project on to others, we can believe that the other person has the same attitudes and values, likes and dislikes as ourselves because we want to believe it. These assumptions actually lead to a lack of communication. Hence the finding that many married couples have never clearly discussed intimate matters such as whether or not to start a family, let alone when and how many children they would like to have. However, once a relationship and communication is well established between a couple then a degree of assumption may not be a bad thing. Being able to be quiet with a partner does not mean that feelings do not exist. Older couples may justifiably make some assumptions and communicate accordingly, precisely because they have done a lot of careful perceiving. But again, **it is the quality of communication in the early stages that establishes the quality of a relationship in the long term**. Even a long-term relationship lacks quality if it is, in fact, based on long-term false assumptions.

In one sense a relationship is developed by using communication to establish information about the other person, which reduces uncertainty. The more one is sure about another person's background, activities, beliefs, the more one is able to be sure that the relationship is or is not likely to develop. It has been observed that couples will often 'test' one another to try to sort each other out or to sort out which stage of the relationship they are at. Testing might involve using words to provoke statements of belief, or might be about intimate gestures used to test the 'trust' and 'liking' stage of the relationship as far as the other person is concerned. Relationships are always developed through degrees of self-disclosure in which the participants gradually reveal information, feelings and attitudes to each other through their communication. As mentioned earlier, self-disclosure by definition involves trusting the other person, and when such trust is reciprocated then one feels that much more intimate with, and bonded with, the other person.

Duck (1993) says that 'interdependence of the two individuals in a relationship is an essential element to relationships and to relationship development'. He also refers to Hinde's ideas about the features of a developing relationship. These are:

- 'The content of interactions – what people talk about. The more a relationship develops, the more personal is likely to be the subject matter.

- Diversity of interactions – different kinds of situation and communication between people. The more activities a couple share the better they are likely to "get to know" one another.

- Qualities of interactions – the style of talk. Words whispered into someone's ear betoken a kind of trust different from the same words spoken across usual body space.

- Frequency and patterning of interactions – how often we communicate. A lot of interaction and communication that is patterned according to the needs of both partners signifies a positive relationship.

- Reciprocity and complementarity – whether people respond as they are expected to socially or whether they respond in a way that matches the other person's need. Those who respond in a complementary way are more obviously considering their partner and are signifying a degree of intimacy in their relationship.

- Intimacy – the personal closeness of communication actions. There is well-established work on the significance of intimate touching in relationships.

- Interpersonal perception – mutual judgements and self knowledge. Successful relationships include the ability to have an accurate view of how one is seen by one's partner.

- Commitment – the degree of time and trouble that one is prepared to go to for the other person. Commitment includes sexual exclusivity with a partner, but more generally is about putting the needs and interests of the other person before one's own.' (Hinde, quoted in Duck 1993)

In terms of the **continuation of a relationship** there are a number of factors that will affect this, not the least of which is the partners' relationship to others. Duck talks about 'ways in which interior aspects of relationships are communicated to others'. It is also true that how others communicate their view of a relationship will affect its stability. A relationship may not even progress if, for example, parents express strong opposition to a couple getting together. On the other hand, just the act of talking about the relationship with other people helps validate the relationship. But that talk must be a positive experience. Public disagreements and negative feedback can be as damaging to a relationship as private quarrels. Connected with this is the idea that having a variety of activities, having friends and exchanging activities is a positive thing. It seems that social experience for couples is on the whole concerned with kinds of play and is helpful. Private experience – running a home and so on – can be pretty much routine, and does not do much to make life exciting. At the same time, sorting out roles and responsibilities through which to run a relationship does seem to be important to its survival.

In fact, Argyle and Dean (1965) proposed an **equilibrium model** for relationships. This would seem to be a development of Heider's earlier theory in which people balance liking and disliking in their evaluation of others. The equilibrium model is about the balance between wanting to approach people and wanting to avoid pressures from others; about needing relationships but fearing rejection. In particular, they proposed that often the balancing was carried out by using nonverbal behaviour to 'compensate' for what was said. One person might suggest a meeting with another using words. The other person does not want this closeness, and balances the relationship by making nonverbal signs to indicate 'distance'.

It has been found that some couples maintain their relationship by using avoidance techniques, for example, there are things that they do not talk about, by tacit agreement. On the other hand, some couples work successfully together by being very direct and always talking about issues and feelings. Equally, being direct or honest can become a kind of obsession and fail to take account of sensitivities. In general, it would seem that directness, disclosure and openness are more likely to maintain than are other ways of using communication.

Howitt et al. (1989) talk about an attraction–dependency theory. They see attraction as being about qualities that make a current relationship better than anything that has gone before. Dependence they see as identifying the fact that our present relationship is better than anything else that is possible. One consequence could be that if the quality of the relationship drops below previous experience, or if a better relationship becomes possible, then the existing one is threatened and may not be maintained.

Ending relationships

In one sense, what has been said so far explains why and how communication may end. A lack of social skills, a lack of equilibrium and a lack of social networking are all factors that may well lead to the break-up of a relationship. One never knows for sure. Sometimes relationships are maintained (but without much quality to them) when people stick together simply because the alternatives are uncomfortable. This is especially true of marriages, where the economic and social interdependency of a couple is such that splitting up would cause huge practical problems as well as personal discomfort.

Relationships may break up before they are well established because partners are aware of a lack of development – it was not going anywhere. It has also been found that men tend to have greater needs for power in a relationship than do women. In fact, there is a correlation between the degree of male power demanded and expressed and the likelihood of the relationship breaking down. Also, women are more likely to actually end the relationship than are men.

Research carried out by Noller (1980) also suggests gender differences in terms of effective communication. This indicates that men are less effective than women in sending clear messages and have a tendency to interpret the female partner's communication adversely in some way, when this was not the intention. It is not surprising that one can then argue that poor married relationships are about poor communication. However, there is also an argument about symptom and cause. One view is that failures of communication are symptoms of underlying causes. On the other hand, one needs to bear in mind the view that one does not actually know anything about the other person other than through their communication. So, in a sense, it is pointless talking about hidden feelings or attitudes that may be relevant. They remain hidden precisely because either one partner does not express themselves clearly or because the other partner is incompetent at picking up relevant signs of communication.

Baxter (1986) describes **eight elements of a relationship that partners value**. The loss or absence of one or more of these elements tends to predict the breakdown of the relationship – though this can only be a generalization. The elements are:

- a degree of autonomy (personal freedom)
- a certain amount of similarity (in views, interests, likes)
- mutual support
- loyalty and good faith
- honesty
- time together (both private and public)
- fair sharing of efforts and resources (goods, time, money)
- a sense of something special between them.

Duck (1993) recognizes **four phases in the dissolution of a relationship**, all of which can be seen as being very much about communication.

- Intrapsychic phase: in which one or both partners have intrapersonal reflections on the other, on the negative aspects of the relationship, on the possibility of breaking it up.
- Dyadic phase: in which there is talk between the two people about what is wrong and what might happen. The relationship can be repaired at this stage. But a lot depends on how open and constructive the talk is.
- Social phase: in which the partners actually talk to each other about breaking up with each other and about the realities of this, in which they begin to reorganize things in their heads to make themselves feel better about it all.
- Grave dressing phase: in which the break-up has occurred or is about to, and communication is all about getting over it and about public versions of what has happened and why.

The essence of our social experience is the relationships that bind us to other people. The life cycle of human beings all over the world is bound up with the formation of pair bonds. These relationships happen because of communication. The nature of that communication defines the nature of the relationship, its qualities, its continuance or, indeed, its collapse.

KEY QUESTION

Describe (with examples) the kind of communication that would be good in keeping a relationship going.

NLP and relationships

We have already explained earlier in the chapter some basic points about neurolinguistic programming, especially as it relates to giving and receiving feedback. Now we want to briefly relate NLP to ideas about relationships, drawing heavily on ideas from Prior and O'Connor (2000). These writers do, in fact, also have a lot to say about the importance of recognizing and carefully interpreting feedback, and how this can affect relationships. They refer to specific signs, such as the lowered eye position, which they point out has to do with reflection and consideration. They comment on the way in which this signal can be misinterpreted as evasiveness, giving rise to suspicion and misunderstanding in a relationship.

Specific to relationships, however, they propose that our interactions are driven by what they call 'three voices' within us:

- the **instinctive voice**, which is genetically driven, and relates, for instance, to sexual attraction to others.
- the **conditioned voice**, which is driven by social conditioning and is dominated by experience of our parents, which we imitate. This affects how we behave in developing and maintaining a relationship and is also affected by cultural beliefs and by significant others in our life's experience.
- the **civilised voice**, which is an intellectual construct that we develop apart from the other two, a kind of voice of reason.

We would suggest that these voices bear a close resemblance to ideas in transactional analysis (TA), which is a theory that we explore in Chapter 6. TA proposes a notion of our responding from different positions: as the child, the parent and the adult:

- The 'child' corresponds to the instinctive voice above and wants 'it' now, and would seek a relationship with another on the basis of biological drives, regardless of other factors.
- The 'parent' corresponds to the conditioned voice, which would try to conduct that relationship in ways that the real parent had done, seeking perhaps to dominate a partner in a wholly inappropriate manner.

- The 'adult' corresponds to the civilized voice, which would be more ready to recognize context and the needs of the other in the conduct of a relationship.

Once more, we see a view of relationships in which being self-aware and self-critical, as well as recognizing the other person, are factors essential to a healthy relationship. In some cases Prior and O'Connor seem to be assuming heterosexual relationships in that they talk, for instance, about their view of differences, such as a male tendency to prioritize rights compared with a female tendency to prioritise responsibilities. However, other points, such as reading and understanding the other person in relation to 'trust', are not gender-oriented. They argue that trust does not have to include unconditional belief in the other person, but it does have to include being open about expressing feelings. Negative relationships are exemplified by those that are based on blame; positive ones are based on shared and articulated goals.

Prior and O'Connor argue that maintaining a balance between the 'voices', and listening to them, is a basis for a positive personality and constructive relationships. Imbalance is destructive – for example, trying to 'turn' one's partner into a parent in order to answer the conditioned voice is destructive to sexual relations (not least because of prohibitions against having sex with a parent). Similarly, people have to manage their instinctive genetic voice as they get older, when the idea of having a relationship with a biologically attractive but much younger partner becomes less and less appropriate.

Prior and O'Connor (2000) suggest that:

Communication is sharing something and involves much more than just an exchange of facts.
Communication is how you build your relationship or you destroy it.
. . . good communication means doing two things:

1. Sharing your expectations, beliefs and values, and explaining your experience so your partner can understand it. We all expect others to navigate our world, but often keep the map locked behind our eyebrows.
2. Asking questions so you can understand your partner's expectations and values, so you can get a glimpse of their map and not have to travel blindly through their world.

3.7 Social skills

Social skill is the sum total of our ability to interact with other people. It is the ability to take appropriate social initiatives, and understand people's reactions to them and respond accordingly . . . Individual social skills include all of the various components of the behaviour we use in these social interactions – the right patterns of eye contact, the right facial expressions, gestures and tone of voice, saying the right thing, using humour and so on. Like any skill, we can learn these and get better at them with practice.

The above extract from *Eye to Eye: How People Interact*, edited by Peter Marsh (1988), neatly sums up the idea of social skill:

- it is the result of learned patterns of behaviour, and
- consists of verbal, nonverbal elements and responses to and from other people.

If we had written something similar ourselves in this book, we would have probably avoided using the adjective 'right', since there is no absolutely right behaviour, but rather behaviour that is considered mutually appropriate and effective in enabling people to share meaning.

In essence, **interpersonal social skills are the range of verbal and nonverbal behaviour patterns we have learnt that enable us to manage our encounters with other people**. It is possible to refine and analyse these behaviour patterns down to minute moments of action and reaction.

In this section we wish to provide an overview and a variety of perspectives on social skills. In the reading list at the end of this chapter you will find references to further sources of more detailed information.

However one tries to describe interpersonal skills, any social skill is, we would stress, more than a sequence of 'right' actions. A person-to-person interaction is rooted in the relationship that is built between those people; it is not the same as a person-to-machine relationship. This relational aspect has been stressed by us elsewhere and sets a context for this section:

Interpersonal communication skills are also social skills that are used in various social relationships:

- Social skills can make communication with others effective and satisfying. It is a skill to make sense of others' feedback and to make appropriate responses. Key social skills are: to show approval to others, to empathize with others, to listen effectively, to present oneself appropriately, to perceive ourselves and others accurately, to control verbal and nonverbal behaviour to good effect.
- Listening skills use nonverbal communication.

Key listening skills in social situations are: to acknowledge the person who is talking, to maintain the conversation effectively, to show approval of the other person.

- Perceptual skills are present in three stages of perception – recognizing, reflecting, and acting.

Key perceptual skills are: to make accurate observations of the other person, to avoid jumping to conclusions, to make careful judgements, to make appropriate responses to what is perceived about the other person. (Dimbleby and Burton 1992)

A more comprehensive and detailed list of 'core social skills' can be found in *A Handbook of Communication Skills*, edited by Hargie (1986). These are as follows:

Nonverbal communication

Research usually divides nonverbal behaviour into seven dimensions or categories:

- **Kinesics**, which embraces all body movements, such as hand, arm, head, foot, leg posture, gesture, eye movement and facial expression. The term body language is also often used for this.

- **Paralanguage**, which includes all sound patterns that are content free – that is, the way words are spoken as well as pauses and speed.

- **Physical contact**, which ranges from touching to embracing.

- **Proxemics**, which describes space and distance between people and also the setting of territory.

- **Physical characteristics of people**, including skin colour, body shape, physique and judgements such as attractiveness.

- **Personal adornment**, such as perfume, clothes, jewellery, make-up and hairstyle.

- **Environmental factors** that come from the physical setting in which the behaviour occurs, such as indoor or outdoor, type of room and how it is designed and decorated – an office is not usually also a kitchen.

A skilled communicator will use all these in presenting themselves and in perceiving and responding to other people. An unskilled, or unaware, communicator will take all these factors for granted and not use a range of choices in their use. There are obviously degrees of sensitivity to these factors – someone who stands very close, shouting and poking their finger at another person, is clearly using deliberately staged nonverbal behaviour to reinforce their words.

Questioning

Everyone knows how to ask a question, but asking questions that obtain the answers you want or gain the effect on other people that you want is a question of knowledge and skill.

There are clearly professions, such as teaching, the law, personnel management, selling or social work, where the effective use of question techniques is essential. In teaching, for example, questions may be used to check students' memory recall, to elicit knowledge, to solve problems, to speculate on the unknown, and so on. A factual question is likely to be a closed question – 'When did Columbus discover America?' – and expects a known answer. A speculative question is likely to be an open question – 'Why do you think there is life after death?' – and expects a range of possible responses.

The context of interpersonal communication will strongly influence the appropriateness of questions. For example, a doctor or nurse while on duty can ask personal and private questions that would be socially unexpected, or unacceptable, in any other context.

Questions are also the energy that maintains, or extinguishes, a conversation. They are your means of showing interest and empathy. However, Pease (1992) notes that starting with a 'difficult question' can ensure that the communication process never flows easily:

> A real estate agent once revealed this trick of the trade. 'When a potential client walks in the door, I don't ask him what he has in mind. That's too hard a question to start out with. He'd become nervous and withdrawn. And if I pressed him, he would probably withdraw all the way out of the door. Instead I ask him what type of home he's living in right now. That puts him at ease, gets him feeling comfortable around me. After a while, either he or I will shift the conversation around to what he's got in mind'.

Pease comments, 'This advice also applies to social occasions. It's usually best to start with simple questions about topics in which others are likely to be interested . . .'

This questioning technique is likely to show another person that you have empathy for them and to help the interaction along. But there is a general issue here about the whole notion of social skills. The estate agent's 'trick of the trade' suggests the use of a skill to give yourself a manipulative power over others – in the tradition of which Dale Carnegie's classic work, *How to Win Friends and Influence People* is the best-known example (Carnegie 1938). We will leave you to recognize such manipulations in your own or other people's behaviour and to be aware of the difference between a genuine interest in the answer to your question and a question that is purely manipulative. However, there are shades across this spectrum: is the defence lawyer questioning the prosecution witness in order to seek the truth about an incident, or seeking to prove his/her client's innocence regardless of what actually happened? The nature of the questions is likely to reveal the motives.

Reinforcement

An effective communicator 'naturally' gives feedback to the person or people she/he is interacting with – this acts as reinforcement to the other person to keep on as they are, or, if it is 'negative reinforcement', to ease off from what they are doing. Such feedback may be verbal or nonverbal – a gesture to carry on, a smile of encouragement, a maintaining of eye contact, nodding of the head or use of questions to maintain the flow, and so on. Such techniques are important in maintaining an encounter with someone else, and in building a relationship.

Reflecting

Elsewhere we have referred to the work of American psychotherapist Carl Rogers, who is credited with coining the term 'reflecting' to refer to the action of paraphrasing what has been said by the other person in your own words. At its crudest, this is simply a repetition of the other person's words, but the purpose of this is to seek to ensure a genuine empathy with the other person by seeking to reflect his/her feelings as they have just been expressed. It is also a technique to aid active and careful listening of what the other person has actually said.

To conduct an interaction such as an interview using this technique all the time could be very tedious; however, it is very effective in a counselling session. Used occasionally in other situations, it can also be very effective in establishing a genuine understanding of the other person's views.

Opening and closing sequences

These are important moments in any interaction for establishing the social relationship and for introducing the content or purpose of the interaction. In some cultures there can be elaborate greeting or parting routines that are expected.

Explaining

The ability to make something plain to someone else is clearly an important communication skill. Someone who has a passionate interest and knowledge of a topic can often find it difficult to explain that knowledge to others who do not share the passion. This skill depends on careful choice of words and linking of ideas, but also an empathy with the other person and a means of recognizing levels of interest and understanding – for example, through feedback.

Self-disclosure

We have described this skill in Chapter 1 (see page 50). In an interaction the levels of self-disclosure will reflect and determine the nature of the relationship:

- In an intimate relationship self-disclosure of experience and feelings as well as opinions and ideas is a key factor.
- In a professional relationship levels of personal disclosure will be less.

In the caring and medical professions the skill of one-sided disclosure built on professional trust has been well developed. Such self-description may lead to the carer having more extensive knowledge or theories about the client than the client him or herself.

Listening

Listening is more than hearing. It is an active process of deliberately attaching meanings to sounds, and calls for high levels of attention and concentration to interpret what is actually being said by the other person. It is easy to hear what you think was said rather than what was actually said.

Assertiveness

As this skill was discussed fully earlier in this chapter, here we want simply to stress the link between assertiveness and self-esteem (see page 13) and the differentiation of assertion from aggression. In her book *A Woman in Your Own Right – Assertiveness and You* (1988), Dickson caricatures four stereotypical women (who could also be men) who are either aggressive, passive, manipulative or assertive. Each of us exhibits these behaviour patterns in different situations. The assertive type of behaviour is described as follows:

> And so to Selma, the assertive woman. Selma respects herself and the people she is dealing with. She is able to accept her own positive and negative qualities and, in so doing, is able to be more authentic in her acceptance of others. She does not need to put others down in order to feel comfortable in herself. She does not believe that others are responsible for what happens to her. She acknowledges that she is in charge of her actions, her choices and her life. She does not need to make others feel guilty for not recognising her needs. She can recognise her needs and ask openly and directly – even though she risks refusal. If she is refused, she may feel rejected – but she is not totally demolished by rejection. Her self-esteem is anchored deeply within herself; she is not dependent on the approval of those around her. From this position of strength, she is able to respond sincerely to others, giving herself credit for what she understands and feels.

Such a feeling of self-confidence enables one more easily to develop the range of social skills we are describing here, neither to manipulate or be manipulated but to encounter people with mutual respect.

Assertiveness is the last in this list of the core interpersonal communication skills. In addition to these skills, Hargie (1986) also goes on to discuss other skills that reflect the types of skilled attainment and competence a professional such as a teacher, social worker, nurse, doctor, salesperson or counsellor will seek, such as:

- interacting in groups (see Chapter 6)
- chairmanship (*sic*)
- negotiating and bargaining
- making presentations
- humour and laughter
- handling strong emotions and
- showing warmth and empathy.

In recent years, it has become accepted that people who are involved in interpersonal interactions as part of their professional life need some kind of social skills training (SST). SST usually focuses on the coding and decoding of nonverbal behaviour. If we want to be able to express ourselves, present ourselves favourably and understand other people sensitively, then we need a clear understanding of how nonverbal behaviour is central to all social interactions.

At its most general, we can describe social skill in terms of having the ability to control and monitor the information we give off to others and to read the information others give off to us. If we are more socially skilled we should be able to manage our encounters with other people more positively. These social skills can be of general use to enable us to cope with a range of life encounters with friends, with family, at work, formal and informal, friendly and hostile, and so on.

The term 'skill' in the context of human relationships may seem rather off-putting since it has connotations of a mechanistic process. Argyle (1973), and others, has compared a social skill to a motor skill, such as riding a bicycle, in that both have:

- 'Specific aims and definite goals: for example, in social interaction we might wish to
  - convey knowledge, information or understanding
  - obtain information
  - change attitudes, behaviour, or beliefs
  - change the emotional state of someone else
  - influence another person's personality or temperament
  - work at a co-operative task
  - supervise another person's activities, or
  - supervise and co-ordinate a group task.
- Hierarchical structure: small units of skill are built up into broader units, for example, being able to ask questions, to listen and to provide feedback are all specific skills that need to be combined in order to conduct an interview or to carry on a conversation.
- Perception of others' reactions: reading cues and monitoring feedback are both essential to social skills and for performing a physical action.
- Timing of responses to synchronize a smooth operation.' (Argyle 1973)

However, there are also fundamental differences between social skills and motor skills:

- 'Dealing with other people and their idiosyncrasies and changes is different from dealing with a mechanism.
- Empathizing with the other person to try to imagine how she or he feels is never necessary with a machine.
- Presenting yourself to another person is a dynamic process. Both they and the relationship are changing whilst a machine is a static object.
- Rules of social behaviour are not as rigid as the rules of a game or the rules for operating a machine.' (Argyle 1973)

We take the view that social communication skills are not the same as mechanical motor skills because:

- 'they are people-based (predictable and unpredictable)
- they are dynamic (changing personalities and relationships) and
- they exist at various levels (conscious/unconscious, overt/covert).' (Argyle 1973)

At the heart of social skills is a conscious sensitivity to our own and to other people's intentions, emotions, experience and verbal and nonverbal behaviours. Understanding of our social skills also depends on our paying attention to various theoretical analyses and practical explanations of interactions, such as those of Eric Berne and his notions of games (see Chapter 6), or those of Erving Goffman and his notion of public performance (see Chapter 5).

We end with a checklist that summarises the main skills we have looked at in this chapter.

Social interaction – a skills checklist

Verbal skills

- Are you speaking too loudly or softly for the situation?
- Are you varying your tone, pace, and so on?
- Are you pitching your voice too high or low?
- Are you speaking clearly and aware of whom you are talking to?

Nonverbal skills

- Are you standing too close or too far away for the situation?
- Are you showing your attention to the other person?
- Is there any way in which your appearance may be inappropriate for the situation?
- Are you using facial expressions to express interest and provide feedback?
- Are you catching the other person's eye too much or too little?
- Is your posture too relaxed or too rigid?
- Are you using appropriate gestures?
- Does your body language match what you are saying?

Social skills

- Is your speech too formal or relaxed for the situation?
- Do you give and receive feedback?
- Are you using appropriate questions to maintain the interaction?
- Do you show that you are interested and listening?
- Do you spend the appropriate time on opening and closing the interaction?

Review

You should have learnt the following things from this chapter:

3.1 Introduction

- Patterns of social interaction are learnt.

3.2 What is social interaction?

- The ability to interact with other people is an essential everyday skill.
- The main aspects of social interaction are:

  - negotiation and generation of meanings
  - self-presentation and use of communication channels
  - creation of a relationship in a social context.

3.3 Language and social interaction

People in each culture have developed a language system that has a number of identifying features:

- use of vocal auditory channels
- neutral symbols
- meanings attached to sounds
- cultural tradition
- structures of sounds
- ability to refer to concepts, ideas and things that are far removed, dependence on conventions of use
- creativity.

- **Language and controlling interaction:** We use language to control face-to-face encounters and to influence the relationships we wish to develop and to affect the ways we want to present ourselves.
- **Language influencing relationship:** We use language (vocabulary, structure, register) to influence the nature of our relationship and the roles that we adopt.
- **Language and self-presentation:** We use language to present ourselves in different ways in different contexts to different people, with the intention of affecting how we are 'seen' by others.

3.4 Nonverbal communications and social interaction

- When in the presence of others our body language never stops.

- This nonverbal activity may be conscious, deliberate communication or it may be unconscious giving off of information.
- It fulfils several functions:

  - conveys attitudes and emotions
  - supports (or denies) or replaces verbal communication
  - presents ourself to others
  - regulates interaction through cues and provides feedback.

3.5 Making conversation

- We take conversation for granted but it is, in fact, a highly complex interaction between people.
- Openings to conversations are about making first impressions and offering greetings.
- These are often represented through a conventional set of verbal and nonverbal utterances.
- Turn-taking in conversation is seen as being rule-based and signal-based. Proper use of these rules and signals allows the interaction to flow smoothly.
- Closing conversations also obeys conventions, has to recognize the relationship of the participants and may predict later interactions.
- Questions in conversation are used to obtain information and to develop the interaction. They questions can be described as: open, closed, leading, recall, process, affective.
- Listening is an active process and is often helped by 'reflecting' back phrases used by the speaker.
- Being sensitive to feedback from other people is a social communication skill. Neurolinguistic programming theory suggests this involves noticing minute nonverbal signs that are given off unintentionally. NLP supposes that we deal with experience in three modes: auditory, visual, kinaesthetic.
- Assertiveness is about saying what you feel and what you want, but with consideration for others. Assertiveness is not about being aggressive. The idea of what is assertive is culturally relative.

3.6 Communication and relationships

- Communication is crucial to the establishment, maintenance of and ending of relationships.
- Interpersonal skills are important to good relationships.

- Good relationships depend on elements such as trust and self-disclosure.

3.7 Social skills

- Social skills involve the use of appropriate verbal and nonverbal behaviours to carry on an interaction that is successful for the people involved.
- Social skills include the controlled and sensitive use of nonverbal communication, questioning, reinforcement, reflection, explanation, self-disclosure, listening and assertiveness.
- Social skills are not as 'cut and dried' as manual skills.

Case situation: Getting started

Read the following short extract, then either:

- Write approximately 200 more words of the conversation, including his intra-personal dialogue and their nonverbal behaviour.
- Write the same situation from the woman's point of view.

It wasn't the first time she'd ignored him.

He first saw her when they were queuing for their loan cheques. He was in the A–L queue and she was next door in the M–Z. She looked just his type: tall, slim, short cropped hair – brown gently streaked blond, bead earrings, subtle make-up, student clothes. He'd tried to engage her in a smile. She resolutely avoided seeing him, but he knew that she knew that he was giving her the eye. She had that self-conscious, avoiding-seeing him look – she held her head just a little bit higher, she laughed to her friends just a little bit louder.

Now it's getting silly. Every time I see her she knows I'm looking but she doesn't look at me . . . It was twice yesterday. Three times the day before. I don't yet even know what course she's on.

Next time, I'll speak to her.

OK. This is it. There she is, at the bar with the same girl she was with yesterday.

Walk, purposefully but casually, next to her, money out to attract the barman. Not to be seen to be deliberately moving over to her. Now, half turning, obviously seeking the barman, but really just catching her eye – got it!

'Hi. Can I get you a drink?'

She turns, looks, half smiles, 'I don't know, can you?' (Oh no! Bloody clever. She's probably doing the English course.)

'I haven't managed it yet, and I've been here for ages', she smiled and lifted her eyebrows. (Oh, oh, not putting me down, but ready to talk.)

'I don't expect so then. If he didn't notice you, he won't notice me,' mutually gazing.

(Blimey, did I really say that? Puke. Obvious flattery – probably put her off. You've gone too far, no, she's smiled, she's accepted it. Keep calm. The barman's seen us, he's coming over.)

'What do you want?' 'Half a lager, please.'

'Two halves of lager, please, and . . .' leaning over her to see her friend, '. . . what do you want?'

'Gin and tonic. Thanks.' (Oh, my God – glad I like the lager girl. Good thing my loan cheque came last week.) 'And a gin and tonic.'

'Thanks.' Pay money. (Now what next? Keep calm.) Casually, my arm brushing hers, 'I saw you in the loan queue last week.'

'Yeah, I saw you too.'

Suggested reading

Argyle, M., 1973, *Social Encounters*, Harmondsworth: Pelican.

Argyle, M., 1983, *The Psychology of Interpersonal Communication*, 4th edn, Harmondsworth: Penguin.

Argyle, M., 1988, *Bodily Communication*, 2nd edn, London: Methuen.

Atkinson, J. M. and Heritage, J., 1987, *Structures of Social Action: Studies in Conversation Analysis*, Cambridge: Cambridge University Press.

Bolton, R., 1986, *People Skills – How to Assert Yourself, Listen to Others and Resolve Conflicts*, Sydney: Prentice-Hall.

Coates, J., 1991, *Women, Men and Language: A Sociolinguistic Account of Sex Differences in Language*, London: Longman.

Dickson, A., 1988, *A Woman in Your Own Right – Assertiveness and You*, London: Quartet.

Dimbleby, R. and Burton, G., 1992, *More Than Words: An Introduction to Communication Studies*, 2nd edn, London: Routledge.

Ellis, A. and Beattie, G., 1986, *The Psychology of Language and Communication*, London: Weidenfeld & Nicolson.

Gahagan, J., 1984, *Social Interaction and Its Management*, London: Methuen.

Glass, L., 1992, *He Says, She Says – Closing the Communication Gap Between the Sexes*, London: Piatkus.

Hargie, O. (ed.), 1986, A *Handbook of Communication Skills*, Beckenham: Croom Helm.

Markham, U., 1993, *How to Deal with Difficult People*, London: Thorsons.

Marsh, P. (ed.), 1988, *Eye to Eye: How People Interact*, London: Sidgwick & Jackson.

Montgomery, M., 1986, *An Introduction to Language and Society*, London: Methuen.

Myers, G. and Myers, M., 1992, *The Dynamics of Human Communication*, 6th edn, New York: McGraw-Hill.

O'Sullivan, T., Hartley, J., Saunders, D., Montgomery, M. and Fiske, J., 1994, *Key Concepts in Communication and Cultural Studies*, 2nd edn, London: Routledge.

Pease, A. with Garner, A., 1989, *Talk Language: How to Use Conversation for Profit and Pleasure*, London: Simon and Schuster.

Prior, R. and O'Connor, J., 2000, *NLP and Relationships*, London: HarperCollins.

Scollon, R. and Scollon, S. W., 1995, *Intercultural Communication: A Discourse Approach*, Oxford: Blackwell.

Tannen, D., 1991, *You Just Don't Understand: Women and Men in Conversation*, London: Virago.

Tannen, D., 1992, *That's Not What I Meant. How Conversational Style Makes or Breaks Your Relations With Others*, London: Virago.

Fig. 4.1 Communication across culture can be affected by details of interpersonal behaviour

Chapter 4

Culture and communication

And as a black child growing up in London I was baffled by the frequency and the poignancy of my father's complaints that I and my brother had no 'respect'. It took thirty years and the chance to visit and observe the rural Jamaica where he grew up for it to dawn on me what cultural and social resonance the word had for him and why it mattered.

(Foreword by Diane Abbott in d'Ardenne and Mahtani 1992)

4.1 Introduction

Throughout this book so far we have made reference to the importance of 'culture':

- as a factor in the development of the self
- as affecting the ways we use language and nonverbal communication
- as the determinant of the world view we each develop.

In this chapter we now explore in more detail cultural issues and aspects of communication between people from different cultural backgrounds. These differences exist within what we tend to think of as coherent cultures, as well as across obvious cultural groups. So, we would argue that communication between subcultures within Britain is as much intercultural as communication between the British and the Japanese. Obviously there are significant variations in degree of the differences. But they are there, and perhaps dangerously ignored because of assumptions made about their being a single identity on the grounds of geographical and national coherence. Like many nations, Britain is a multicultural society and so we will be looking briefly at subcultures, while giving more space to the larger scope of cross-cultural communication that happens on a global scale.

There can be problems here to do with the words used to define things. One way to deal with this is to describe communication between subcultures (and dominant cultures) as being 'intracultural', while reserving the term 'cross-cultural' to describe communication between larger cultural groups.

In the case of subcultures, there is also an argument for seeing gendered communication as taking place between different cultures. Without having to agree with this view, we think it appropriate to take a look at female-gendered communication within this chapter.

We will also be considering the relationship between recently developed technologies and human communication. We would argue that technology can be seen as a manifestation of culture, and furthermore that the ability to use it is affecting both how we communicate and cultural identities.

Another issue that needs considering is the extent to which, and the ways in which, we empower or disempower social groups by communicating with them or about them in particular ways.

In this chapter we will also revisit concepts such as discourse, and ways in which selective uses of language create meanings about manifestations of culture (the Arts) as well as meanings about cultural identities (for and about Muslims). Discourses are integral to the production of culture and cultural difference: for example, in what ways do the British talk about 'the environment' that are different to the way North Americans do, and why?

We need to take account of how ideology and its discourses naturalize those meanings which seem true for any culture: meanings which include values: meanings which encompass status and difference, not to mention cultural institutions such as religions.

It is also important to be aware of phenomena such as globalization, in all its economic, political and commercial aspects. This is throwing cultures together but not necessarily producing understanding. It is also changing nations like China, where materialism and commodification are now driving and changing the nature of Chinese culture.

We also need to think about the fact that communication covers a wide range of cultural performances, including public rituals such as those that remember the dead. And these performances, all of which are social practices, take place in contexts that may also be full of cultural significance: ceremonies in the Red Square for Russians on one level, but also talk in shopping malls on another level.

Clearly we cannot do justice to all these dimensions of culture within the space we have. However, we do want to raise these as issues and questions, while choosing to concentrate on interpersonal communication.

4.2 Interpersonal communication and questions of culture

Language has a key role in our interpretation of the world, although sharing a language does not necessarily involve sharing a culture. (Woodward 2002)

We can summarize the key elements of interpersonal communication (IPC) as we have explored them so far:

- Our concept of Self is the product of socialization and enculturation processes throughout our life. These processes can be explored through studies in social psychology, anthropology, sociology and media studies.

- This Self uses various forms of communication – language, nonverbal behaviour, personal resources and skills – to share meanings with other people. We use the word 'meaning' to indicate that what is shared is based on inferences and judgements and is not simply information or fact. There are always degrees of ambiguity and subjectivity and levels of meaning, from simple denotation to personal and cultural connotations. For example, if someone says 'I'll see you soon', the meaning and implication of that statement would vary according to the way it was said, the context in which it was said and, above all, the culture within which it was said.

- The forms of communication we use are both the creators of, and the product of, relationships between individuals. As children we learn and experiment with them and go on exploring them more or less consciously throughout our life.

- Personal relationships are, in turn, part of wider life experiences that both create, and are the products of, the particular culture in which we operate. We experience this culture directly through personal contact and indirectly through the media, as well as other processes of socialization such as family talk.

Our culture gives us a context and a history within which that communication takes place. It shapes the forms of communication that we use. These forms incorporate symbols that stand for ideas belonging to the culture and its values. Symbols range from the formal signs of writing, which create words and their ideas, to the more material signs of, say, kinds of headdress. These may stand for religious belief, gender identity, social status, and so on.

Cultural context provides points of reference within which IPC might take place (public eating places, for instance), which in different cultures, in different ways, according to different conventions, shape how communication is carried on.

Communication is about the production of meaning. Meanings about our identities, about how we see another person, about what we think is important, about what we may be trying to get across to another person, are all touched by culture and framed within it.

We would argue that **culture is a total experience, and communication is part of that experience**. One needs to recognize this in order to appreciate the extent of difference between cultures, and the problems of communication across cultures. This total experience is about values and attitudes, emotions, forms of behaviour and social practices, uses of verbal and nonverbal communication.

The tight lock between beliefs, behaviours, histories and geographies of a given culture gives strength to members of the relevant culture, but can also make them inward looking. Cultures tend to believe that *their* norms are correct, and that, by inference, those of others are somehow wrong. They see their lifestyles and social practices as being natural, and their own way of life as having a universal truth about it. At the core of most cultures is a particular view of the world, and, often, a specific set of religious beliefs. To criticize such views raises problems of a very deep-rooted ethical and social nature. For example, just as it is not okay to regard one's own cultural position as being universally correct, one does not have to regard it as being all wrong either. And although we have put forward arguments about the value of empathy and recognizing the validity of other cultures' beliefs, this does not mean that everything and anything about another culture is okay either.

This is where cross-cultural communication becomes so important, not least in the context of globalization. We have to interrogate our own values and attitudes, as we deal with other cultures in the spheres of work, leisure and politics. But, then, so should they. The world is full of flashpoints as cultures meet, each convinced of their 'rightness'. There is the outrage of religious groups in France, now subject to a law banning the wearing of symbolic and distinctive clothing – enacted ironically to reduce cultural conflict. There is the conflict within US society between creationists and others. Everywhere one sees evidence of cultures trying to assert their distinctiveness – but dangers arise when assertion becomes mere aggression. Cultures may seek cooperation with one another – but this is not to be confused with submission. And there is the 'bottomline problem' if a culture reaches the point of feeling that compromise is no longer possible. In what ways can New Zealand Maoris, for example, deal with the dominant white culture if they feel that their identity is being annihilated? How do other groups deal with religions that flatly deny notions of 'science' and 'evidence' and assert, for example, that the world was created four thousand years ago? Avoidance strategies and isolationism offer one kind of solution. But we would argue that communication and negotiation offer another. As Levi-Strauss said: 'The one fatal flaw which can afflict a human group and prevent it from achieving fulfilment is to be alone' (in Jandt 2004).

Guirdham (1999) discusses the influence of culture on communication strategies and produces a useful set of points, now adapted below:

- communication is goal driven, but those communicating are not always conscious of what these goals are

- culture defines the logic of communication – the way we deal with others always seems the 'right' way

- the cultural rules of communication are learnt through socialization

- different cultures value different communication goals and different ways of achieving those goals

- cultural influence is strongest in formal and planned situations; but in informal encounters people are more flexible.

KEY QUESTIONS

In the quote at the beginning of Section 4.2, what does Woodward mean when she says that sharing a language is not necessarily the same as sharing a culture?

In what ways does your family history influence the ways that you talk to others?

Try to think of examples of the 'formal and planned situations' that Guirdham talks about, where you can see a strong cultural influence on the way that communication is carried on.

4.3 What is culture?

It is important at this point that we briefly make explicit what we understand by the term 'culture' and the way we are using the term here. Williams (1983) considered that 'culture is one of the two or three most complicated words in the English Language'. It has been invested with layers of meaning well beyond its original meaning of 'growing process' (a sense in which it is still used in the phrase 'a test-tube culture').

Jenks (1993) describes the genesis of our concept of 'culture' through four sources:

- Culture as a cerebral, or certainly cognitive, category which is a general state of mind. It carries with it the idea of perfection, a goal or an aspiration of individual human achievement. We sometimes speak of a 'cultured person'.

- Culture as a more embodied and collective category which reflects a state of intellectual and/or moral development in society. In this sense culture is linked with notions of 'civilization'.

- Culture as a descriptive and concrete category, viewed as the collective body of arts and intellectual work within any one society. This is probably the meaning of the word in everyday language – and sometimes it is given a capital letter: Culture.

- Culture as a social category; culture regarded as the whole way of life of a people: this is the pluralist and potentially democratic sense of the concept that has come to be the zone of concern within sociology and anthropology and latterly, within a more localized sense, cultural studies.

Here, in the context of communication studies, we are using the term culture primarily in the fourth type in the above list of Jenks' points: 'the whole way of life of a people'. Hence, if you are communicating with someone who is in their whole way of life part of a different set of people, then the forms of communication used, the expected relationships achieved and the world view expressed are also likely to be different to our own.

To this extent it is hard to avoid some emphasis in the following sections on the differences between cultural groups, and on the difficulties of communication. One also needs to avoid some common errors in conflating the word 'culture' with other terms:

- Culture is not the same as nation – this is essentially a political notion. Cultures exist within national boundaries and they cross them.

- Culture is not the same as race – this is a broad anthropological notion. Caucasian peoples encompass many cultures.

- Culture is not the same as ethnicity – ethnic groups may share a culture or be identified as a subculture in some degree. South Africa contains a variety of ethnic groups with skins of many colours, who all feel that they are African and feel nothing in common with the cultures of, say, Britain or India, which places define their ethnic origins.

Guirdham (1999) provides a set of ideas about culture (after Kroeber and Kluckhohn):

- the members of a culture system share a set of ideas, and, especially, values
- these are transmitted (particularly from one generation to another) by symbols
- culture is produced by the past actions of a group and its members.

Clearly, sharing, transmitting and the production of culture involves communication.

Hofstede (1981) identifies four key elements to a given culture: symbols, heroes, rituals and values:

- Under symbols he would include not only objects, but also the signs that make up verbal and nonverbal language.

- Heroes may be actual or fictional people, who represent models for behaviour.

- Rituals are collective activities, not necessarily useful in a functional way, but important to social cohesion.

- Values are, of course, about moral precepts and beliefs about what is important in life. But they also have an emotional dimension in which the members of the culture have feelings for what is right and proper.

Discourse

Before leaving this discussion of 'what is culture?' we wish to refer again, as elsewhere in the book, to the concept of 'discourse'. Originally, this word referred to a system of language use, and discourse analysis was, and is, the study of how a certain type of language use naturally occurs within a specific group.

Stubbs (1989) provides a useful working definition:

> The term discourse analysis is very ambiguous. I will use it in this book to refer mainly to the linguistic analysis of naturally occurring connected spoken or written discourse. Roughly speaking, it refers to attempts to study the organization of language above the sentence or above the clause, and therefore to study larger linguistic units such as conversational exchanges or written texts. It follows that discourse analysis is also concerned with language in use in social contexts, and in particular with interaction or dialogue between speakers.

Hence we might talk of 'academic discourse' to signal the way that words are chosen and arranged among academics, or 'TV discourse' to signal the way that language is used within television. Remember that the term 'language' may refer to a wide range of codes, including visual forms of communication. The use of language or of codes constructs meanings about various aspects of our world – about how we understand that world.

So, it is easy to see how the link has been made between a 'culture system' and a 'discourse system'. The latter is the distinctive ways in which a particular group uses language and other forms of communication to share their meanings and cultural traditions and values. These meanings are taken for granted as being naturally true. But of course they are not. As mentioned above, **every culture feels that its way of looking at things is the only way**.

Scollon and Scollon (1995) have developed the useful concept of 'interdiscourse communication' to analyse the difficulties that individuals from different cultures or groups meet when they try to share meanings, even when using the same 'language' such as English:

> When as Westerners or Asians we do business together, when as men or women we work together in an office, or when as members of senior or junior generations

we develop a product together we engage in what we call 'interdiscourse communication'. That is to say, the discourse of Westerners or Asians, the discourse of men or women, the corporate discourse or the discourse of our professional organizations enfolds us within an envelope of language which gives us an identity and which makes it easier to communicate with those who are like us. By the same token, however, the discourses of our cultural groups, our corporate cultures, our professional specializations, or our gender and generation groups make it more difficult for us to interpret those who are members of different groups. We call these enveloping discourses 'discourse systems'.

In such cases, it is not just the words that are different, it is the values behind them. There are differences in ways of thinking about how it is proper to treat other people.

4.4 Language and subculture

With reference to previous sections, we are talking here about cultural groupings that might be regarded as intracultural: existing within and alongside a dominant culture. They may be defined by some, including the popular media, in terms of difference from that dominant culture. Their practices and behaviours might be seen to challenge it. They may be represented in a subordinate way, not least if their distinctive behaviours and values appear to challenge that dominant culture. Of course, attributing such a subordinated status is always improper – as in the case of Travellers. Dominant groups seek to support their own status and assert their norms (ideological positions) by diminishing subordinate groups, not least in the ways that they are talked about.

One kind of sociological approach describes at least some subcultural groups in terms of **deviancy** – deviation from norms. Communication about that group – especially the terms of abuse used about members of it – can underline this constructed deviancy: 'lazy students', 'thieving gippos', 'work-shy asylum seekers', and the like. Here, one also sees an interchange between the language used in everyday interactions and the language used in the (right-wing) media. Cultural groups and their status can be fluid – punks of the 1970s are now regarded with affection not outrage, and Johnny Rotten has become a celebrity icon, if not yet a national treasure. Not all subcultures are always regarded as oppositional or subordinate by all members of the dominant culture, least of all those who also identify with subcultures of their own – consider how the Welsh identify with the Scots as sharing a Celtic culture and a history of resistance to the English and to rule from London.

Language defines the diversity of these subcultures, gives them meaning, incorporates and endorses their values. It helps make them distinctive to themselves and to others. It is, of course, true that many aspects of subcultures contribute to this sense of distinctiveness – for example, dress codes (the clothes worn, for example, by Somalians), oral traditions (such as the Northumbrian dialect) and visual communication (for example, British Chinese celebrating their New Year). **Culture is, indeed, a product of communication, and is realized through communication**. The meaning of any cultural group to itself and to other cultures lies in what it says and how it says it.

Subcultures are all around us – gender, regionalism, ethnicity. Just as the notion of a mass audience for the media seems to dissolve the more exactly one tries to define it, so also the notion of a British (or any other) culture tends to dissolve upon close examination. There are many subcultures when one also considers class, occupation, ethnicity, youth, leisure activities and specific groups such as Hell's Angels – so many that it is possible to argue that everyone belongs to a subculture, and the hard thing is to define the core characteristics of a main culture.

Language used by subcultures helps define their sense of identity. Language used *about* them defines how they are understood by the society of which they are a part. This language used by them is often about asserting difference from society at large. Sometimes the intention is even to use conflict, because conflict involving threat from outside causes the group or subculture to focus protectively on its identity, its values and its survival.

In any case, identity can in cultural terms be divided – multicultural – when, for example, one is speaking Punjabi at home and English at work. Subcultures, like identities, are not mutually exclusive. One may be British Asian and male and young and a northerner.

In terms of distinctiveness, the language of youth cultures, for example, may involve using a secondary code that refers to clothing and music through words that are not understood by the culture in general. Youth cultures are also marked by paralinguistic features which in Britain are notable for the adoption of a form of London accent (even by speakers of RP), for slurred delivery with hesitation, for appended phrases such as 'y'know' and 'sort of'.

As mentioned earlier, here identity is mixed up with class and with a notion that borrowing certain restricted code features associates one with working-class values, with something 'genuine'. This has been demonstrated in classic studies of youth cultures (see Hebdige 1979) in which, for example, skinheads adopted shaven heads, industrial boots and forms of work clothing partly as a way of invoking the value of being 'proper working class' – precisely at a time when male manual employment in heavy industry had been collapsing for two decades. These signifers are also about masculinity.

Subculture and values

Language used by and about subcultures also says things, directly or indirectly, about the values they hold and the values that others attach to them. Hippies, Travellers and varieties of drop-out cultures may be seen as counter-cultural, defined by opposition and by what they are not. They oppose dominant middle-class values of acquisitiveness and social achievement, for instance.

Certain speech features may be associated with value positions with reference to other factors such as class. Young Afro-Caribbeans in London have been reusing Creole forms to create a patois which serves the function of both giving them a distinct identity and enhancing their own sense of self-worth and value. And, of course, what they talk about is what they value. It is worth noting that what they are resisting is not only a dominant white culture in a general sense, and what is seen as a threatening police force in particular, but also previous generations of West Indian immigrants, many of whom had sought to shed their patois in order to integrate. There is a whole set of oppositions set up on the issues of age, race, authority, all of which are implicit in language. This is true in terms of language used both by subcultures and about subcultures.

This example relates to interpretations of culture in terms of power. The language of the dominant culture – perhaps typified by the white, middle-class codes used by those who do exercise authority in our society (teachers, the police, politicians) – becomes a mark and symbol of that power, just as using patois, dialect or argot becomes a mark of difference and perhaps resistance. The way that the dominant culture talks becomes naturalised in its dominance. Like being white, it becomes invisible because it is the norm. The values within that talk (and its discourses) become 'normal'.

In this case, the prefix 'sub' becomes associated with subordinate. Others have looked for more neutral terms – Mulvaney refers to Pearson as coining the term 'co-culture' to describe groups that simply exist within a dominant culture (in Jandt 2004). Mulvaney also asserts that: 'differences in world view, language usage and proxemics between the genders are the points of difference which suggest that gender communication is a form of intercultural communication'.

Some may see an identity based only on opposition as being negative in explaining subculture. Rather, one may also look for an active coherence in subcultural groups – for a positive use of communication to celebrate identity – even oppositionally.

> Subcultures aren't just groups of people with common interests that stand in opposition to other groups; they must be doing some kind of cultural work with those interests and that opposition.
>
> (Bell 2001)

Football fans are proud of their clubs and the rituals associated with being a fan. Fandom and subculture spreads into cyberspace. Online game players assume a new identity and use words in new ways, to join in this subcultural group.

To regard women as belonging to a subculture raises some interesting questions about coherence and distinctiveness. Half the human race is not a distinctive group of itself. Yet it is true that many women across many cultures do have the experience of being subordinated, in relation to men and through language use and social practices. Yet again, it is a very different experience to be subordinated as part of a belief system in, say, Ethiopa, to being subordinate in western eyes (but not in one's own convictions) as, say a Muslim woman in Saudi Arabia, or to being subordinated through social commercial practices as a working woman in Britain. A female British Asian may not have issues about being female within her own community, but may have issues that are nothing to do with gender about how she is regarded in the larger community because she speaks Hindi, celebrates Diwali and wears a sari. We will now move on to discuss gendered communication in particular.

KEY QUESTIONS

How far do you think that 'different languages' are used by youth groups to gain a sense of belonging and of being special, and how far are they used to shut others out?

Does it matter that different subcultures have different values regarding subjects such as dating? And how might these be expressed through what is said or not said?

> Is it true that everyone is part of one subculture or another, and therefore there is no coherent main culture in Britain?

4.5 Gendered communication

> ... because gender is a governing ideology within which narratives or scripts are created, gender distinctions occur pervasively in society.
>
> (Crawford 1995)

In the first place it should be said that there are differences in the use of verbal and nonverbal language by men and women. The extent of and nature of such differences is questioned by commentators such as Crawford. She and others, such as Sunderland (2004), also rightly question generalizations about men, women and other gendered groups as being coherent entities. They are too often spoken of as if they are undifferentiated. But, clearly, the term 'women' covers a huge range of difference, based on factors such as age, ethnicity and a variety of cultural histories and experiences. All these factors will affect the way women interact with others. So, for example, one has to be cautious about research evidence suggesting that, along with all women, those in managerial roles show hesitancy in speech patterns because they are women. One might also question whether ideas about assertiveness are entirely valid in the case of this group of women managers.

We need to be careful when making statements about gendered communication. In particular, when considering assertions made out of research one needs to look at the breadth of the sample taken. Even more specifically, one has to question research that relies heavily on sampling of students, simply because these happen to be a segment of the population easily available to researchers. We would also draw attention to the dangers of essentialist arguments, in which it is assumed that there is some kind of core female or male personality. There is no evidence for this, any more than it is evident that we should be talking simply about a choice between masculine and feminine. People are more complicated than that. And we would ask you to look again at the section on identity in Chapter 1. In particular this comments on the dangers of assuming that biological sexuality and the possession of certain kinds of reproductive organs is the same thing (and vice versa) as social gendering – behaving in ways that are described as being male or female.

So, we arguing not for biological determinism but, rather, for social conditioning to explain language acquisition and use.

> Gender differentiation in language, then, arises because . . . language, as a social phenomenon, is closely related to social attitudes. Men and women are socially different in that society lays down different social roles for them and expects different behaviour patterns from them. Language simply reflects this social fact.
>
> (Trudgill 2000)

It remains true that **there is a weight of evidence for differences between men and women in the way that they conduct interactions**. These differences not only identify the gender of the speaker, but they also say things about the nature of the interaction, the nature of the situation, and the way that each of the genders tries to deal with interactions.

The significance of gender differences may also be interpreted according to the values of the interpreter. Borisoff and Merrill (1991) say baldly that 'Numerous studies have established women's superior abilities both as decoders and encoders of verbal messages when compared with men'. Whereas Spender (1980) takes a more implicitly critical stance when she says that 'language has been made by men and used for their own purposes'.

Coates (1991) has surveyed some of this research and focused on what might have been called 'women's style' of presentation through linguistic interactions. She highlights five general linguistic issues:

- Verbosity: there is a widespread belief in our society that women talk (chatter) more than men, yet research findings consistently contradict this.

- Tag questions: such questions, which often end a statement with a tentative question like 'isn't it? . . . or 'OK?' . . . 'agreed?', can seem to be used more by women and imply a less assertive position. However, tag questions are used deliberately to facilitate a conversational interaction.

- Questions generally: research findings so far suggest that women use interrogative forms more than men and that this may reflect women's sense of weakness in interactive situations. However, women exploit questions and tag questions in order to keep conversation going.

- Commands and directives: men tend to use instructions and commands more than women, whose linguistic style is more inclined to be non-hierarchical and more participative.

- Swearing and taboo language: there is little hard evidence on male/female differences in swearing, though the folk-linguistic belief that men swear more than women and use more taboo words is widespread.

One may also distinguish between **language used by women and language used about women**. Both kinds of use identify gender differences and say things about the status of women, the social behaviour of women and the conduct of relationships between the sexes. You should remember that this language also expresses **gender discourses** – ways of thinking about male, female and difference. If this draws attention to speaking and listening, then it also reminds us of the idea of 'mode of address' – a style of communicating that assumes things about the person or audiences addressed, and which tries to put them in a certain kind of relationship with the speaker. If a man talks 'as if a man to a woman' – using certain words and certain inflections – then it is also true that women talk 'as if a woman' to men. In the debates about language, discourse and power it is a kind of reciprocal style of communicating, which expresses how the speaker understands gender and feels about power.

We are, of course, talking generally about western cultures here. But it should also be realized that other cultures may show other kinds of difference in communication, in relation to gender. Some of these differences are extreme. For example, the speech of Carib women or of Siberian women is considerably different to that of the males in many respects. There are plenty of examples of words (like some social practices) being taboo to women in other cultures.

What we would argue about any culture is that the language used is not reflecting realities of gender and socialisation, so much as creating them. If you speak like a woman then that helps construct you as a female. You do not speak in that way simply because you have been born with a certain set of sexual features.

> ... language is not a neutral vehicle in the representation of reality.
>
> (Ehrlich and King in Cameron 1998)

Acquisition of gender definitions

In the first place, if a 'special language' is acquired and used by women in particular, then it must come from somewhere. The same is true of language used about women. Language is pervasive in our lives' experiences. Its influence is there everyday, everywhere: 'gender is constructed in and through every societal space' (Liikkanen in Lull 2001). This language is a substantial part of the acquisition of gender definitions – what it means to be female, how one should regard females. It is Liikkanen again who refers to a degree of gender neutrality in Finnish culture, which is tied in with the language. Finnish has one non-gendered pronoun for 'he'; and 'she'. Nouns do not have a gender, as they do in most European languages. The words 'sex' and 'gender' are not differentiated. Imagine what it would be like if English was like this, and what the consequences would be for how we think about gender.

Forms of address applied to women are particular. The form 'Mrs' is still widely used, and identifies women's marital status, where there is no equivalent for men. It defines the woman in relation to the man. Similarly, descriptors are gender differentiated, not least the application of the term 'girl' to females who are past the age of majority. It is a term that can be seen as belittling women.

Females will learn to use certain kinds of talk and will learn to accept being talked to in certain ways because of their upbringing. We are talking about **socialization**, about address by significant others at home and at school, about peer group talk (not least in the context of games) and about models of talk represented in various media. In the educational context, there is evidence of boys seeking attention at the expense of girls, taking charge of technology, and dominating space/territory:

> ... research at both primary and secondary level indicates that boys (perhaps non-consciously) regard both physical and educational space as primarily for their own use and, by their behaviour as a group, control girls' participation in edu-cational processes and undermine their confidence, especially in 'male' subjects.
>
> (Burr 1998)

One could take the example of female characteristics of hesitancy in speech and deferral to males in conversation (not universal, but frequent). Children will see these communicative behaviours represented in movies and in television drama, and so will tend to internalize and 'naturalize' this behaviour as being acceptable and normal.

Language used about women, even by women themselves, is often demeaning and belittling. More will be said about this in the section below on discourse. But, for example, it is noticeable that diminutive forms of women's names are more common for women than for men and are more commonly used even when they are older. When women are emotionally distressed it is common to hear words such as 'hysterical' or 'emotional' used to comment on this. These words are used to imply that they are 'not coping' or are 'out of control'. Although there is a separate issue of how emotion is expressed differently according to gender, the same kind of behaviour in men is described as being upset or annoyed.

A sense of gender is acquired through the way in which others behave towards the individual. Obviously, other attributes may also be projected onto the individual by these others. A young and conventionally handsome man will be treated differently by others (especially young women) as compared with an aged male.

Equally, there has to be some cultural agreement about how the communication is to be understood. A man can still put down a woman by saying to her, 'You think just like a woman'. But in most situations, the reverse is not true. There would be no irony in saying that a man thinks like a man.

This ties in with the idea that **men are often understood to be the norm in gender terms**, a neutral position – in which it used to be assumed that mankind 'naturally' encompassed women as well. But this norming or neutralizing has never happened for women. Women are very defined by their gender, often in relation to men, and certainly in relation to our cultural histories. It is still women who become wives, who change their names. Men are 'just' men. Epithets addressed to men are still about women. A man may be called 'a big girl's blouse'. A woman is never 'a big boy's shirt'.

Much of one's sense of gender definition is tied in with body image. Obvious displays of sexism and racism take bodily features as the first line of insult and denigration, for example, 'fat slag'. One's body affects how one is treated by others, but also how one sees oneself because ideas about being male or female on the basis of biology are circulating 'out there' anyway.

> . . . being in possession of certain physical features classified as female or male is connected to social, cultural expectations, practices and behaviours.
>
> (Woodward 2002)

Tannen (1996) points out that women are always marked as being female by features such as their clothes (which also relate to body display). As she says, nothing so much applies in reverse to men. Women can adopt male clothes (the power suit) to acquire male status, but men do not borrow women's clothes. They have no need to. They have the ideologically endorsed status.

In general and in linguistic terms we are arguing that two dominant critical views are equally applicable and complementary. One view prioritizes the influence of language and argues that this defines how we think and behave. The other view prioritizes social behaviour and argues that social practices affect how language develops and is used. The latter view is within a sociological perspective described as 'social constructionism'. We would say that these positions are equally arguable, and stand in a dynamic relation to one another.

Interpersonal behaviour, language and gender

> Gender exists not in persons but in transactions.
>
> (Crawford 1995)

When one looks at how women use language there is evidence of differences in nonverbal behaviour. Females touch each other more than men do, they smile more and they use more eye contact. Indeed, such differences are expected of them. For women the communication of gentleness, warmth, tact is seen positively. Women show more listening cues because they do more listening than men. It has also been suggested that listening is seen as a lower-status, passive activity in a male-dominated world. This would tend to reinforce such behaviour. Women do, of course, have the difference of higher voices, but in fact some of the perceived difference is because they use a greater range of pitch than men. Females perceive, respond to and give off cues about feelings more than men. This is the more likely because this behaviour response is socially endorsed as being okay for females. In relation to talk it is more likely that women will use more of these cues because they talk more about feelings than men. Conversely, men have been found to talk about actions, and, of course, their related nonverbal behaviour (NVB) matches this.

This idea of a necessary connection between the two channels of communication fits in with similar points about the connections between role, relationships, perception and communication. In other words, roles create expectations about speech that are gender specific. Equally, it can be said that gender patterns of speech represent gender roles. We make assumptions about how we expect mothers to talk, and how they talk defines them as mothers. Women are often better perceivers than men because they are better listeners: the fact that they use listening cues also elicits the information that helps them perceive others accurately. It is a kind of chicken and egg argument. The same logic applies to the fact that women disclose rather more than men (and disclosure helps improve relationships). Hargie et al. (1994) refer to this as well as to the work of Hill and Stull (1987), which identifies four variables that affect disclosure by gender. These are: situational factors, strength of gender-role identity, gender-role attitudes, cultural gender-role norms. For instance, in western business circles there is a male-oriented view that control of emotion and of disclosure is desirable. Women who want to 'succeed' in business have to modify their usual gender-role behaviour. It has been found that in a number of situations women will adjust their style to obviate any appearance of dominance. At work, women will adopt strategies enabling them to exert authority without being seen as 'bossy'.

Cameron (1998) comments on the difficulties that women experience in a public context, not least in being able to talk about subjects that interest them, or in ways which they prefer. 'In the public domain, and especially the domain of official culture . . . the genres (of language) associated with women have little currency'.

She sums up major debates about gendered use of language in terms of three models:

- deficit – the idea that women are somehow deficient in their use of language, and need to do something about this

- dominance – the idea that use of language is about power, that they are socialised into a position subordinate to men

- difference – the idea that women may be seen as belonging to a subculture or to a different culture, and that there are simply communication problems between the male and female cultures.

We would agree with her position that none of these models is entirely satisfactory.

Nevertheless, what does seem to be unarguable is that women are relatively disempowered in our society, that ideology is a core concept for understanding this, and that language in its widest sense is the essential vehicle for maintaining ideas about disempowerment. We are not convinced by evidence that tends to generalise about men being linguistically incompetent in maintaining relationships or, indeed, women always being competent in this respect. But still it seems that 'women's topics' and women's speech styles are not valued in the public arenas of power – politics, economics and commerce.

It has been found that men and women tend to talk about different topics. They control these topics in different ways. Men talk about work and sports activities. They are competitive. But women talk relatively more often about family and friends and health matters. There is a positive relationship between women's self-esteem and their use of bonding talk. They see this as valuable, and that they are better people for using talk in this way (see Guirdham 1999).

Even where women do talk about 'men's topics', this talk is treated in a gendered manner. Nightingale (in Schirato and Yell 2000) made a study of men and women talking about football, which is summarized as follows:

> . . . not only did women's equal knowledge of and literacy in the game of football (at least as spectators) not count according to the men, but their presence as part of the spoken interaction around football watching was actually ignored, or edited out in the men's report of the interaction. In this case the women's speech, no matter what their contribution, is discounted almost as if they had not spoken.

The way women talk is also different. For example, their speech is usually more fluent and more accurate than that of males. Indeed, they talk in more complex speech structure from an earlier age than do males. However, Sunderland (2004) disputes that there is any innate difference between male and female, and asserts that differences are of performance rather than competence: that if boys perform less well it is because of cultural and environmental factors. Argyle (1992) refers to research that identifies female characteristics such as hesitations, hedges ('sort of'), tags ('didn't I?') and the greater use of 'doubt' words such as 'may' or 'might'. Tannen (1995) reports that women at least appear to apologize and to be self-deprecating. They will use the prefix 'I'm sorry' to sentences. However, this does not necessarily mean that they are apologizing, so much as, for instance, recognizing the other person's feeling of discomfiture. Men tend not to do this.

Crawford (1995) reminds us that any such gendered speech traits may well be a response to social circumstances. We should perhaps be concentrating on context as much as on speech features. She points out that some critiques seem to assume that men's speech traits are the norm ('deficiency' approaches to women's talk). It is not the case that women have a 'problem' with their speech, which should become more like that of men. One might, rather, be saying that there are features of women's talk that are actually more adaptable and flexible than those of men. Women's social awareness may also make them conscious of status and class. This relates to evidence that women more than men tend to adopt prestige dialect and accent.

In mixed-sex conversations men dominate in various ways (loudness and interruption), but also because women are in one sense more socially adroit at maintaining conversations and showing listening cues. They may, in effect, actually encourage men to talk more than they do. They demand less talking time and are prepared to be silent. The related topic of assertiveness is referred to elsewhere, but in terms of gender one can identify the fact that men are more verbally aggressive than women (interruptions again). It has also been found that people are more assertive towards those of the same gender. Other differences are numerous and subtle, and perhaps culturally defined. For example, it is less acceptable for women to use swear words than for men, though things have changed a great deal in the last generation. Women tend to use more words to amplify descriptions of experiences, not least again in respect of feelings they have had.

Of course, if one is arguing for the idea of **gendered performances**, then this is about nonverbal language as much as spoken codes. It is commonplace to refer to gendered signs such as men taking an 'arms spread' position in order to emphasize the masculine breadth of the shoulder area. Similarly, women will commonly make preening gestures such as brushing their hair back (even when it is short!) or fiddling with a necklace, which cause a male conversationalist to lower his gaze from the face to her body area. But such examples are about sexual differences as much as something that is more social and gendered. The 'problem' is that such performance features do happen at the same time as verbally gendered communication.

Equally, there are different uses of NVB which are more about gendered difference. Men will lean into body space or use gesture signs impatiently to show that they wish to 'take the floor'. This, of course, is matched in reverse by women using eye contact and head tilts to show that they are listening, while they wait (perhaps in vain!) for a pause in which they may change their cues and begin to speak.

Tannen (1996) talks about this in relation to women trying to get heard at meetings. Indeed, she refers to various instances of differently gendered styles where, for example, women will make disclaimers ('this may be a silly question but . . .') where men will not. She also gives examples of how men use cues, both verbally and nonverbally, to hold on to conversational control, where women were better at taking turns.

Liikkanen (2001) also sees gendered communication as being about performance when she refers to it as a 'performative role-playing game'. As with many commentators, she talks about the significance of physical and social context. We can relate this back to Tannen's formal meetings. Given the dominating male presence (and history) in many organizations, there will still be a tendency (now diminishing with cultural change) to see the meeting room as a male space. Masculine style will be the norm. All sorts of details can set a gendered tone, from pictures of males on the walls to the gender of the person who pours the tea.

The notion of performance brings us back to that debate between views that, on the one hand, argue that acts of communication are only vehicles for expressing that which is within us (gender difference); and the view that argues that such actions actually construct ideas. Is gender more about performance and appearance, than it is about any essential substance of those taking part? Certainly Crawford (1998) inclines to the view of **social constructionism** in which she refers to language as a set of strategies 'for negotiating the social landscape'.

In this view, there is no reality about gender and difference which exists apart from language. 'The reality constructed through language forms the basis of social organisation' (Crawford 1998).

We can also take account of one of the key ideas from semiotics – that the meanings of signs are not attached to them because of some absolute truth. They are attached to words and to nonverbal cues because we have 'agreed' this should happen. In this case, one is also arguing that certain uses of body language or of words do not have to represent gender and difference: as a culture, we have just come to believe that they do. It is not necessarily manly to use a lot of swear words – we have just come to believe that it is, as much as it is unwomanly to do so. The same is true of ideas about superior and inferior. So if women talk about emotion more than men, and express this more, such expression is only 'better' or 'worse' than men's talk if we agree that it is.

Even where we agree to talk about difference, the reasons for and significance of that difference may still be argued about. For instance, if women do have a different conversational style to men, it may be that is because they have different goals. One observed example is in those masculine conversations that compete for the outcome of proving superior knowledge or status. Women, on the other hand, do not usually talk to compete over how much they know about a subject, so much as to elicit information. Their outcomes are about 'having discovered' rather than 'having told'.

Female gender and discourse

> Through acquisition of language we become human and social beings: the words
> we speak situate us in our gender and our class.
>
> (Kaplan in Cameron 1998)

A discourse can be described as a selective use of language that produces particular meanings about the subject of that discourse. These meanings may usually be described as value judgements about that subject, whether it be children, news or, in this case, women. Discourses are also part of our ideology. They contribute to the total view of the world and of power relationships that are major aspects of ideology. In terms of gender, they incorporate oppositional assumptions about male and female, and so implicitly exclude more complicated notions about gender and sexuality – most obviously that a person may be both masculine and feminine, not either/or. Discourses are expressed through language, and language gives life to the ideas of discourses. As Spender says (1980), 'Language . . . is itself a shaper of ideas'. The notion of language can apply to pictures as much as to words. But given the framework of this book we are concentrating on words about women and the discourse that such words help to create.

Miller and Swift (1979) refer to the naming of women as a way of implicitly demeaning them. That is to say, women are often addressed by their first names, where men are not. Women lose their names (and identity?) when they marry. Many female names are derived from male ones, but rarely has it happened the other way round. Miller and Swift and other writers refer to words that describe the quality of gender and draw attention to the selective nature of these words. They cite a dictionary definition of femininity which includes 'gentleness, affection and domesticity . . . fickleness, superficiality and folly'. You may judge for yourself what such words say to people about the meaning of being female. They often have negative connotations, or suggest some kind of limitation to female ability or potential or character. And so often such words define women in relation to men or as opposed to men. Language assumes that women are 'attractive' – and to men, of course. And the words that are gender specific not only are used rarely about men, they may even be insults when applied to men – males do not like to be called 'pretty'.

Ironically, in the light of what we have already said, part of gendered discourse is words about women that suggest they talk too much. Spender (1980) lists: 'chatter, natter, prattle, nag, bitch, whine . . . gossip'. This language criticizes and denies the value of women talking; it devalues it. Such value-laden meanings of the discourse about femaleness extend into many areas of language use. For example, a woman who is sexually charged and active may well be called a nymphomaniac. The word is not a compliment. There is no such equivalent for men, because it is assumed that it is okay for men to be sexually active.

And then one has to take account of a range of discourses that interlock with one another, and reinforce meanings and their 'natural truth'. For example, there is a discourse of clothing. The great number of terms identifying female clothing has a significance in that it contributes to that part of the gender discourse that says that being female ought to be all about owning clothes, being interested in clothes, wanting to be looked at for the clothes being worn. So it is that female sexuality is firmly linked with ideas about reproduction and motherhood, and, again, with patriarchal notions about marriage. It becomes arguable that we do not rationally construct and control our sense of who we are, so much as become subjected to the histories of our culture, to representations, to discourses.

Nor should it be assumed that the language of such discourses are used only by men. As mentioned earlier, women inhabit the same discourses as men, they perpetuate the language, they operate within the same ideology. Such discourses create ways of women thinking about themselves as much as ways of others thinking about women and femaleness. It is true that women are defined as people-oriented and 'sympathetic'. It does seem that women use conversation and devices of speech towards social and cooperative ends (where men's talk is often about competing and dominating). But this is unhelpful to sexual equality when such qualities and such talk are ultimately not valued through the power structure of our culture.

And all this talk operates within contexts, within social institutions, within the environment that is of our leisure and our labour.

> . . . because using language is a socially situated action, it is clearly embedded in the same sociocultural matrix that supports sexual bias in the work we do, the wages we receive, the expectations that we have of ourselves and of others.
>
> (McConnell-Ginet in Cameron 1998)

We should also be aware that so much of our thinking about gender is tied to a discourse of difference – an assumption that the only way to think about men and women is in terms of how different they are. But, in fact, much research also points to similarities. In saying this we are not trying to contradict a main thrust of this section, which draws attention to gender differences in communication, but we are asking you to be critical, and not think in simplistic terms about language and gender. Consider the complications of language in use, in a wide variety of situations, by a wide variety of people who may happen to be male and female but who are by no means all the same in other respects.

KEY QUESTIONS

What kind of language might parents use to their children that helps establish different gender identities?

In what ways might men communicate with women that reinforces the view that men try to exert power over women, in either social or work situations?

What are the advantages of being female in British culture? Why are these advantages? Has talk got anything to do with such advantages?

4.6 Cross-cultural communication

As mentioned earlier, communication between cultural groups across the world has become relatively common because of processes of globalization. Mexican people go to work in US homes. Polish people come to work in Britain. Malaysian students go to university in Australia. Japanese people take holidays in Europe. British business people go to China. Scientists share projects around the world. Less positively, armies cross cultural boundaries to fight. Refugees join other cultures seeking safety and work. And diplomats cross boundaries to make peace. Given the technologies of transport and electronic communication, there is more intercultural communication now than (probably) at any time in human history. How successful it is, another matter. If one is talking about cross-cultural communication then one is in effect talking about cultural difference – differences not so much of language but of thinking.

Definitions

We have chosen to use the term 'cross-cultural communication' to describe the process of communication from one cultural group to another. It is also important to stress that, in practice, this usually means individuals communicating across cultural differences. This is why we emphasize the importance of interpersonal communication. **Cultures do not talk to each other, individuals do.**

What we said at the beginning of the chapter about defining culture obviously applies here. We also refer again to Scollon and Scollon (1995):

In studies of intercultural communication, our concern is not with high culture, but with anthropological culture. When we use the word 'culture' in its anthropological sense, we mean to say that culture is any of the customs, world view, language, kinship system, social organization and other taken-for-granted day-to-day practices of a people which set that group apart as a distinctive group. By using the anthropological sense of the word 'culture', we mean to consider any aspect of the ideas, communications, or behaviours of a group of people which gives them a distinctive identity and which is used to organise their internal sense of cohesion and membership.

In terms of identifying key factors that appear to define **cultures and their special characteristics**, the work of Hofstede (1981) is often referred to. His four factors are as follows:

- **Power distance** is about the extent of differences of status within a given society or culture, and how far members of that society accept such differences. The USA is very low on this scale – in effect it endorses egalitarianism.

- **Individualism or collectivism** refers to the extent to which a culture values individual achievement and behaviours, perhaps within the framework of the family – or the extent to which collectivist ideals value a much more cohesive approach to social behaviour, in which individualism is disapproved of to a greater or lesser degree. South American countries score highly on collectivism on Hofstede's scale of measurement – but are also high on power distance.

- **Masculinity or femininity** is not so much about gender as such, as it is about the behaviours and values that we associate with gender in the West. So this factor is about, for example, an opposition between societies which value competition and achievement and those which value cooperation and sociability. Cultures which are high in 'masculinity' value material achievement and assign social status to this – for example, the USA.

- **Uncertainty avoidance** is about cultural preferences for or against ambiguity, about a culture's approach to resolving uncertainty. It is about the difference between having strong social conventions and expecting obedience to these – or being more inclined to teamwork, to individualism and to acceptance of outside influences. Countries like Britain and the USA are quite low in accepting uncertainty, whereas Hofstede rated Greece as being very high on this scale.

An alternative but related view of cultural markers is provided by Trompenaars (in Guirdham 1999). He identifies three categories, two of which contain subsidiary points. All of these are about what a culture believes in and how these beliefs are expressed in the way it lives and communicates.

- Relationships with people – including the balance between individualism and collectivism, between valuing emotion or neutrality, between thinking along universal or particular lines.

- Attitudes to time – including the extent to which the culture orientates towards the future or the past.

- Attitudes to the environment.

Problems with communication across cultures

Just as we are most aware of communication when it breaks down, so we are most aware of culture when we experience communication problems. We want to say a little about these problems before looking at the cultural differences that are at the root of the problems. For instance, one kind of problem is that of **discrimination**. This is usually based on simple and visible markers of culture and identity such as gender, age, ethnicity and disability. It is a problem within apparently coherent societies, as well as across evidently different cultures. However, one cannot just say that all discrimination is simply wrong, because this is practised in different ways in different cultures for different reasons. For instance, it may actually be problematic to send a female business executive on a commercial mission to a country where the receiving culture simply does not value women in commercial power-status terms. This is still generally true for Japan. Is it culturally sensitive to recognize this, or is it truly discriminatory not to send the female executive? It is, however, much easier to talk about discrimination and the 'glass ceiling' when one is looking at attitudes towards women in commercial power positions within western societies. In IPC terms we are talking here about perceptual judgements and the attitudes and values that direct attention and inform these judgements.

It is, of course, true to say that the problem of discrimination is tied up with the problem of **stereotyping**, with all the expectations this creates when dealing with others. Stereotyping is itself linked to a problem of assigning people to groups with assumed general characteristics, rather than dealing with them as individuals (even from collectivist cultures) who will display variations from the general norms and behaviours of their culture. In Britain, we would never assume that a Londoner 'stood for' all Britons, so one should not assume that someone from Barcelona is typical of all Spaniards. Because stereotypes refer to a culturally particular set of beliefs, attitudes and values about their subjects, one can see that these beliefs are themselves part of the problem of communication across cultures.

Another problem is the **projection of similarity** onto the person of another culture – this means assuming that they think like you, and that recognizable behaviours mean the same to them as they do to you. Put another way, the problem is to recognize and acknowledge difference, and act on it.

Mulvaney (in Jandt 2004) refers to Laray Brana when identifying six problems for intercultural communication (here glossed by ourselves):

- assumed similarity (for example, of world views or meanings assigned to behaviours)
- language (competence, control and meanings assigned to symbols)
- nonverbal misinterpretations (for example, the 'same' gestures do not mean the same thing)
- preconceptions and stereotypes (see above)
- tendency to evaluate (for example, in terms of assuming other cultures are inferior because they are different)
- high anxiety (which occurs particularly when people feel out of their cultural depth, as when they are travelling/living abroad).

Cultural differences

So, we can see that many of the problems we recognize to do with cross-cultural communication lead us back to cultural differences based on **philosophy and beliefs**.

169

For example, we have already talked about cultures inclining towards an 'individualistic' or a 'collectivist' model. Triandis (1985) notes that people from the latter tend to lay greater emphasis on factors such as age, gender and religion. They look for their own cultural group's norms and authority, and they are concerned with group loyalty and cohesion. People from individualist cultures tend to be less sensitive to the views of others.

Another difference can relate to whether a culture is more scientific/rational in its approach to life; or is more led by religious belief systems. In turn, this could relate to whether people are considered to be fundamentally 'good' or 'bad'. The Judaeo-Christian world view is that 'man' is basically evil and needs to be saved in order to act with love and kindness. The Analects of Confucius, on the other hand, begin with the words: 'Man, by nature, is good; people's inborn natures are similar, but learning makes them different'. Other Chinese precepts may be even more difficult for westerners to take on board: 'The Chinese generally believe that relationships are affected by karma or yinyuan, which is pre-determined by one's previous deeds' (Chuang in Jandt 2004). The Chinese will in fact accept and believe in uncertainty, and do not emphasize with western notions of rationality or linear causality (direct reasons for events and behaviours).

To revisit what was said earlier about difference, refer back to Chapter 1 and our comments on **identity**, and the defining of those who do not belong to our cultural group as 'the other'. Terms of abuse, whether used homophobically within a dominant culture, or used ethnically across national and racial divides, are only one way of constructing what 'the other' means to a given culture, and of prejudicing communication between cultures. They reinforce norms of the cultural group. To call Chinese peoples 'slitty-eyed' is to invoke more than visible difference: it calls up negative emotions and stereotypical assumptions.

Another area of cultural difference is attitudes towards **work and leisure** – which will be different according to cultural views of what these terms mean – as well as attitudes towards ideas about 'acting' and 'living'. Thai culture values reflection and just 'being', whereas US culture is all about getting on with things. In Britain we identify a separation between work and play, but in Latin America this distinction is blurred.

Latin Americans also have their own understanding of **time**. They conceive of it as being about 'now' and being flexible – what others call the '*mañana* syndrome'. By contrast, the industrialized West has turned time into a commodity, into something that is carved up. It has anxieties and urgencies about getting things done. It thinks more about the future. Even in formal situations, in South America, people may be kept waiting for business appointments because of a lack of urgency, because it is normal to do different things 'at the same time', and perhaps because status has to be asserted. This would be unthinkable in Manhattan. In informal situations, a social sense of time is even more tricky. Arrangements to meet simply mean different things to people from different cultures. Cultures that live by the clock will have a sense of time and of social behaviours in which activities are segmented and measured. But elsewhere, without clocks, time is not measured by minutes and seconds: it may be understood more loosely, most obviously measured by the apparent movement of the sun. 'How long' a journey will take becomes somewhat elastic when looked at in culturally relative terms.

The notion of face

Different cultures also have different attitudes towards how direct or explicit one should be in communication. In turn, these beliefs relate to culturally specific ideas about what constitutes politeness. This idea is often constructed through **the notion of 'face'**. Does communication protect the 'face' of the speaker or of the listener? Is it right that it should do this or not? In some cultures it is considered polite and face-saving to conduct business negotiations through a third party, or to convey criticism through someone else. In other cultures this may not be the convention, but one is still supposed to be indirect on voicing criticism – unlike in many European countries! The idea of 'face' is all about the public image of the private self. Everyone wants to be thought well of. But different cultures have different ideas about what is important, about what will cause one to be regarded favourably by others.

Lustig and Koester (2003) describe different kinds of face for the Chinese:

- *lien*, or integrity of moral character
- *mien-tzu*, or prestige acquired through success and social standing.

They point out different behaviours by Japanese and US Americans when they realize they have threatened someone else's 'face'. The Japanese will apologize and will take account of the status of the other. The Americans will take account of the nature of the provocation, and will try to justify what they did or said to cause the threat. They do not apologize. Indeed, the Japanese will readily apologize in public in the case of a trial where it is expected. But the apology is not an admission of guilt, whereas in western cultures it would be seen as exactly that. Apologies in the West, whether from individuals or from organizations, are made reluctantly and usually only after proof of guilt or responsibility.

> Competent face-work, which lessens the potential for specific actions to be regarded as face-threatening, encompasses a wide variety of communication behaviors. These behaviors may include apologies, excessive politeness, the narration of justifications or excuses, displays of deference and submission, the use of intermediaries or other avoidance strategies, claims of common ground or the intention to act cooperatively, or the use of implication or indirect speech. The specific facework strategies a person uses, however, are shaped by his or her culture.
>
> (Lustig and Koester 2003)

Kang (in Jandt 2004) writes about the importance of politeness in Korean culture, which is seen as supporting the 'face' of the other person.

> Korean society consider politeness as one of the most important social virtues . . . they use polite language forms towards older people, frequently tell white lies, and attempt to avoid words which give emotional hurt to others.

Communication behaviours

Let's start with a case situation taken from Scollon and Scollon (1995) which illustrates how different values inform different behaviours, and how those behaviours stand for the values. The problem is that each of the 'players' does not know this. Only when one grows up in the culture does one know the 'rules of the game' and the meanings of the verbal and nonverbal signs. This example may also be tied back to what we have said about discourse systems and the production of meaning.

Two men meet on a plane from Tokyo to Hong Kong. Chu Hon-fai is a Hong Kong exporter who is returning from a business trip to Japan. Andrew Richardson is an American buyer on his first business trip to Hong Kong. It is a convenient meeting for them because Mr Chu's company sells some of the products Mr Richardson has come to Hong Kong to buy. After a bit of conversation they introduce themselves to each other.

Mr Richardson:	By the way, I'm Andrew Richardson. My friends call me Andy. This is my business card.
Mr Chu:	I'm David Chu. Pleased to meet you, Mr Richardson. This is my card.
Mr Richardson:	No, no. Call me Andy. I think we'll be doing a lot of business together.
Mr Chu:	Yes, I hope so.
Mr Richardson:	(reading Mr Chu's card) 'Chu, Hon-fai.' Hon-fai, I'll give you a call tomorrow as soon as I get settled at my hotel.
Mr Chu:	(smiling) Yes I'll expect your call.

When these two men separate, they leave each other with very different impressions of the situation. Mr Richardson is very pleased to have made the acquaintance of Mr Chu and feels they have got off to a very good start. They have established their relationship on a first-name basis and Mr Chu's smile seemed to indicate that he will be friendly and easy to do business with. Mr Richardson is particularly pleased that he had treated Mr Chu with respect for his Chinese background by calling him Hon-fai rather than using the western name, David, which seemed to him an unnecessary imposition of western culture.

In contrast, Mr Chu feels quite uncomfortable with Mr Richardson. He feels it will be difficult to work with him and that Mr Richardson might be rather insensitive to cultural differences. He is particularly bothered that Mr Richardson used his given name, Hon-fai, instead of either David or Mr Chu. It was this embarrassment that caused him to smile.

This short dialogue is, unfortunately, not so unusual in meetings between members of different cultures. There is a tendency in American business circles to prefer close, friendly, egalitarian relationships in business engagements. This system of symmetrical solidarity, which has its source in a western pragmatic view of the function of social interactions, is often expressed in the use of given (or 'first') names in business encounters. Mr Richardson feels most comfortable being called Andy, and he would like to call Mr Chu by his first name. At the same time, he wishes to show consideration of the cultural differences between them by avoiding Mr Chu's western name, David. His solution to this cultural difference is to address Mr Chu by the given name he sees on the business card, Hon-fai.

Mr Chu, on the other hand, prefers an initial business relationship of symmetrical deference. He would feel more comfortable if they called each other Mr Chu and Mr Richardson. Nevertheless, when he was away at school in North America he learned that Americans feel awkward in a stable relationship of symmetrical deference. In other words, he found that they feel uncomfortable calling people Mr for any extended period of time. His solution was to adopt a western name. He chose David in such situations. When Mr Richardson insists on using Mr Chu's Chinese given name, Hon-fai, Mr Chu feels uncomfortable. That name is rarely used by anyone, in fact. What Mr Richardson does not know is that Chinese have a rather complex structure of names which depends upon situations and relationships, which includes school names, intimate and family baby names, and even western names, each of which is used just by the people with whom a person has a certain relationship. Isolating just the given name, Hon-fai, is relatively unusual and to hear himself called this by a stranger makes Mr Chu feel quite uncomfortable. His reaction, which is also culturally conditioned, is to smile.

In this case there are two issues of intercultural communication we want to use to introduce our discussion of intercultural professional communication: one is the basic question of cultural differences, and the second is the problems that arise when people try to deal with cultural differences, but, like Mr Richardson, actually make matters worse in their attempts at cultural sensitivity.

In cross-cultural communication, we need to be aware that **different cultures have different traditions about how the self is presented to others**. People from the USA are, for example, likely to be much more 'personal' in their disclosure and informal in their language use and behaviour than the, traditionally, more reserved British. Differences can also be seen in how much people involve others or remain independent. Within the same culture people can interpret the communication acts of others as being over-friendly or 'distant'.

We will now provide a few more examples of verbal and nonverbal communication that illustrate difference and reinforce the point that **meanings are not universal**. These examples also amplify our points about how language and discourse produce meaning, and about the ways in which different values and ideologies inform the language and behaviour of different cultures. **Interpersonal skills and relationships are culturally determined** and will influence how people build relationships with others.

We should point out here that our particular emphasis here will be on sociolinguistics and language in action. There is, of course, also much that might be said about cultural differences in articulation and in respect of semantics. For example, there are many tonal differences in the utterance of Chinese words – and a change of tone completely changes meaning. Or there are contrasts in vocabulary – cultures that do not have the same range of words for colours that exist in the West. Lustig and Koester refer to the fact that the Tamil language has no word for 'hope'. It is also the case the Polynesians do not have words for 'depression' or 'sadness'.

Verbal communication

Many languages, but not English, have different sets of informal or formal pronouns that signal the closeness of the relationship. For example, in France it would be unusual to address another adult on first meeting as *tu* instead of the more formal *vous*. Similarly, in Spanish there is a pronoun – *usted*, which signals respect when addressed to someone. The cultural difference is not just about knowing the words and using them – it is about understanding the importance of showing respect and acknowledging degrees of social distance in the given culture. This point also ties in with the proposition that there is a relationship between language and thought: indeed, that to use language enhances thinking processes as much as language expresses what has been thought of.

Even within apparently common language groups – and apart from specific variations such as patois or argot (see p. 157) – there may be differences of use and of meaning that can undermine interactions. It confuses US Americans to come across the British usage of the word 'boot' used to identify both an item of footwear and the storage space in the rear of a car.

Language is about syntax as well as vocabulary, and the structure of utterances may also be culturally determined. For instance, as we in Britain we see things, the Japanese organize statements indirectly. They construct observations and ideas around a main point, rather than getting directly to it – the opposite of what we learn to do in Britain or the USA. What we might see as being honest and straightforward, they would see as being rather rude, even aggressive. So even the notion of what one defines as being logical is actually culturally relative. It is also the case that the Japanese prefer brevity in speech, and are content with silences that we in the West might feel are 'awkward'. Lustig and Koester (2003) also draw attention to cultural differences in conversational styles. The British or European Americans would want to 'get to the point', or say what 'they were after'. Not so the Japanese or African Americans, who would approach their needs and intentions behind their conversation in an indirect manner. Lustig and Koester describe the British or European Americans as having an instrumental style in which communication is goal oriented, while the Japanese have a more succinct style that also emphasizes social roles and uses reflective pauses. It is relevant at this point to remark on different nurturing styles across cultures. The Japanese mother does not directly forbid her child to do things – 'don't' is not used. Rather, in an indirect and implicit way, the mother will, for instance, suggest that someone else may be made uncomfortable by what the child is doing (in Tannen 1996).

There are also differences in what a culture expects one should talk about in a given situation. The French expect you not to talk about work if you are having a meal with friends. African cultures expect you to talk extensively about how the family is getting on, when you enter a social interaction.

Cultural rules affect what one says. A typical 'problem' might be what to say if one is pressed to have more to eat, when having a meal in another cultural context. Is it rude to refuse? Is one expected to refuse several times, but then accept? Is the offer not a serious one in that culture, and one is expected to decline politely. And then there are associated behaviours – should one leave some food on the plate or not? should one belch to show satisfaction or not?

Nonverbal communication

Every culture has its own ritual greetings and behaviour patterns for farewells. These can include shaking hands, kissing one or more times on the cheek, bowing, hugging, and so on. Axtell (1991) describes what seem to a person brought up in a non-contact culture as an exotic variety of different greeting rituals, for example:

> Greetings can be downright physical to the point you may want to wear a football helmet and shoulder pads. Eskimos greet each other by banging the other party with a hand either on the head or shoulders. Polynesian men who are strangers welcome each other by embracing and then rubbing each other's back. Among the Matavai, friends who have been parted for some time scratch each other's head and temples with the tip of a shark's tooth often drawing blood.
>
> (Axtell 1991)

One can also refer to the fact that the French have their rules about the number of greetings kisses you may receive or give, once you are known, and according to the degree of friendship or familial closeness. In Mexico the kiss on the cheek is matter of course for relatives. This is not something that is practised as frequently in Britain, though in their lifetimes the authors have seen these conventions shift. The British are much more greetings contactable than they used to be – no doubt because of overseas travel and examples on television.

It is well known that the British are a low-contact culture – use of touch displays – as are the Scandinavians and Japanese. In particular, one will never see British men holding hands, least of all in public. If one did, then there would likely be an assumption that the men were gay. That would not be the case in Greece, where such contact is conventional heterosexual behaviour, just as Muslim males in Jordan might walk arm in arm. On the other hand, there is a Muslim taboo (cultural 'no go' area) regarding males making contact with females (except in private and in a legalized relationship).

The use and meaning of personal space and territory is similarly variable. Generally speaking, those from warmer countries 'need' less space than those from colder areas. What matters of course are the meanings of such uses of space. Someone may be perceived as being 'too pushy' or 'too cold' or 'unfriendly' or 'intrusive', and so on. Cultures use paralinguistic features differently. Latin cultures tend to use a lot of variation in pitch, and their turn-taking cues lead to overlapping speech (what the British might see as interrupting). Asian cultures, on the other hand, tend not to vary pitch so much, sounding relatively monotone to the British. They also leave longer pauses in their turn-taking.

This last point is also one about the use of regulators. Lustig and Koester (2003) refer to research that demonstrates differences in the use of gaze regulators as between European Americans and African Americans. The former gaze at a speaker to show interest and attention, but the latter look away. So European Americans come across as being rather confrontational. They also use a glance and a pause to indicate to the other that it is their turn to speak. Not so the African American, who then ends up talking at the same time as the other person.

Many Asians will laugh and smile when they feel awkward. Western cultures use these signs when they feel pleasure, amusement or want to signal agreement with the other person.

Northern Europeans tend to be restrained in their emotional display: whereas Mediterranean Europeans and Arab cultures will be much more open and active in displays of emotions such as anger or grief, not least in public situations. Ekman (1973) has tried to argue that certain affect displays (of emotion) are universally understood. While it is true that something like anger is pretty universally shown in the same teeth-baring manner, this view is not wholly supported by evidence. And what is more important is *when* such displays are given, for what reason, for how long – if one is to understand what the person is feeling and how strongly.

Enhancing cross-cultural communication

An appreciation of cultural differences can help in effective communication. It is possible to draw inferences and interpret meanings from words and nonverbal behaviour that are quite mistaken if we fail to take into consideration different group behaviours and world views. One should also appreciate that the examples of communication above, the beliefs that inform them, and the social practices that they represent are all features of cultural identity. People from different cultures have different senses of their identity – what it means to be Mexican, what it means to be a man in Iran, what it means to be elderly in China, what it means to be a company executive in Greece.

It may be that in Britain – perhaps because many cities are now so multicultural in their demographics – that there is rather more appreciation of alternative behaviours and their meanings than there was a generation ago. A series of adverts for HSBC bank on British national television advertises it as 'your local world bank'. These adverts illustrate HSBC's expertise, with humorous vignettes of how different cultural behaviours can cause offence to other cultures – for example, the offence given to many eastern cultures by westerners who put their feet up on a table and show the soles of their feet. However, this is not to diminish the very real issues raised by what some would see as a collision of cultures around the world, not least between Muslim and western cultures at the time of writing. One may ask how far does talk between cultures really help understanding? Diplomats are fond of talking about 'dialogue'. But the mere exchange of words is not the same as genuinely taking on different views and making some adjustments to one's own attitudes. Does cross-cultural talk sometimes even become a vehicle for reinforcing dominance – men with women, immigrants with immigration officers, Israelis with Palestinians? Or if talk is informed by empathy can it lead to change?

Babha (in Salamensky 2001) makes an interesting and particular distinction between talk and conversation. He sees the latter as being more social, undirected, sharing, and perhaps interculturally productive – 'conversation depends on a certain kind of culture . . . a perceived notion of community'.

Although many of the examples of difference that we have given above may seem to point to huge difficulties in understanding the communication of other cultures and how they see the world, we want to finish on a positive note. Many people do have a desire to understand others and to get on with them. Globalization is bringing peoples into contact as never before, including even global conflicts. It is therefore in all our interests to recognize difference and to acknowledge the validity of the views of others. Of course, even this view is itself ideological and culturalized – a western assumption that conflicts can and should be resolved. Nonetheless, some essays in the final section of Jandt (2004) describe a range of views and projects relating to inter-cultural understanding. One essay describes the positive effects of multicultural music projects in the Middle East and Bosnia. Another discusses East–West theatre projects in Singapore. There is discussion of the operations of some universities on a global scale. There is evaluation of the effects of new technologies and information exchange. Clearly, cross-cultural communication is happening in a range of spheres and on a scale unimaginable a generation ago.

Even as use of the English language spreads across the planet and raises concerns about other languages and cultural identities, so it mutates into new languages, different patois, new argot. It becomes repossessed by different cultures that have their own world views – witness Indian TV presenters talking half in English, half in Hindi.

By way of contrast, Guirdham (1999) reports a very specific set of measures that describes **areas of competence in cross-cultural communication** (all based on work by G. M. Chen (1988)):

- display of respect
- interaction posture
- orientation to knowledge
- empathy
- relational role behaviour interaction management
- tolerance of ambiguity.

These identify areas in which we can improve communication across cultures:

- through knowledge of the other culture
- through preparation for the interactions
- through management of the interaction.

As elsewhere in this book, we would argue that one can change the way one thinks and adapt the way one behaves in order to get on well with others. We learn communication skills unconsciously through processes of socialization within our own culture. However, it is possible to relearn them and add to them, including to the benefit of our encounters with other cultures.

Lustig and Koester (2003) generate a very similar list – **a behavioural assessment scale for intercultural competence**, based on work by Koester and Olebe (*International Journal of Intercultural Relations in US Organizations*, No. 12 (1988), 233–46).

- 'Display of respect: the ability to show respect and positive regard for another person.
- Orientation to knowledge: the terms people use to explain themselves and the world around them.
- Empathy: the capacity to behave as though you understand the world as others do.
- Interaction management: skill in regulating conversations.

- Task role behaviours: behaviours that involve the initiation of ideas related to group problem-solving activities.

- Relational role behaviour: behaviours associated with interpersonal harmony and mediation.

- Tolerance for ambiguity: the ability to react to new and ambiguous situations with little visible discomfort.

- Interaction posture: the ability to respond to others in descriptive, non-evaluative and non-judgemental ways.'

The ability to acquire and handle these competences effectively does, we suggest, relate to other factors. One needs to:

- recognize the validity of other people's cultural identity

- identify the kinds of problem described above and be prepared to do something about them

- recognize and deal with the kinds of perceptual error that we describe in Chapter 2

- be flexible in one's thinking and one's expectations

- get away from 'cultural centrism', without having to abandon cultural roots, get rid of false assumptions about ideological rectitude – thinking that your view of the world and its values are the only valid views (and especially not saying that other views are simply wrong)

- think diversity, as much as pluralism – 'We are all people, but with diverse ways of thinking and communicating', rather than 'We are different sets of people in different camps'.

Lustig and Koester (2003) talk about:

> individuals who move easily among many cultures. Such people have respect for many varied points of view and are able to understand others and to communicate appropriately and effectively with people from a variety of cultures. Such individuals are able to project a sense of self that transcends any particular cultural group.

We want to end with a note of caution. When dealing with cross-cultural communication it is easy to categorize other people into overgeneralized groupings. Cultural influences are just that; they are not narrow determinants of behaviour or language use. There are considerable variations within any cultural group. It would clearly be nonsense to think that 'all men are task oriented and ignore other people's feelings', in the same way it would be nonsense to say that 'all women are submissive'. Similarly it is not true to say that Japanese people never show emotion, nor that they all display emotions in exactly the same way, to the same degree. The word 'all' is a dangerous word when describing people and cultures.

KEY QUESTIONS

What kinds of differences have you noticed in attitudes and behaviour when you have come across cultures outside Britain – either directly, as when you were on holiday abroad, or indirectly, as when viewing a TV programme?

Looking at the sections above on the concept of 'face', do you think this idea is at all applicable to British culture and the way we communicate in given situations?

In what ways has globalization made cross-cultural communication a key issue for the world today?

4.7 Technology, culture and communication

In this section we want to concentrate on relatively new technologies such as email, mobile phones and uses of the internet. Our interest is in communication between people as enabled and changed by such technologies, which raise new issues around understanding of the Self and identity. The main thrust of our commentary is to draw attention to the significance of how technology has changed our capacity to communicate, especially on a global scale. We do not take a straightforward, technophile position regarding these changes. Rather, we would say that technologies that enable groups such as online communities bring benefits in some ways, but in some respects also diminish our capacity for human communication.

The electronic Self

The following comments should be related back to the section in Chapter 1 on Self and identity. In the first place, technology has in some ways changed the Self that communicates and so has also affected notions of identity. It is obvious, but central to our general line of argument in this section, to point out that **technology intervenes between people**. It may seem to enable communication, but it also transforms it in various ways. And, in particular, the 'social' examples of new technology do not (and cannot) reproduce the conditions of 'real space' interaction. (By this we mean communication that takes place with the participants in the same place at the same time, able to exchange the full range of sensory information.) Technologies change our perceptions of who we are, certainly of who others are – partly because they are actually limiting in communication terms.

However, this is not to take an entirely negative view. Someone may gain a very positive view of themselves precisely because they can use technology to share information on a bulletin board or with a newsgroup. It is just that this a different (technological) context from that of real-life (RL) interaction. At the same time, that person is demonstrating the capacity to present Self (different selves) in a way that would not be possible face to face. So-called **'bloggers'** place personal diaries, with experiences and opinions, on the internet and they will have a certain perception of themselves as they do this. They certainly create perceptions on the part of those others who read the blog! This presentation of Self is little different in principle from those old technologies that people use to write letters or to publish memoirs.

The blogger knows that their reflections will be read by others and that those others do not know or will not meet the blogger.

The difference between the electronic self and the RL self is discussed by Wakeford (in Gauntlett and Horsley 2004) when she refers to research that involved contact with a woman online, which later led to face-to-face contact. Wakeford refers to 'methodological tensions' for the researchers regarding the woman when they met her and she presented in person, as opposed to the woman who presented online. The researchers found that questioning the real person about Web use was affected by their existing perceptions of her online persona. Technology mediates between communicators. It will create different perceptions of the selves involved, and it can be used intentionally to promote a Self that is different from that of the RL self.

There is an interesting question as to how far different kinds of Self are presented, or are, in fact, simply manufactured behind the electronic cover of media that operate dominantly through words on a screen. A number of commentators have been intrigued by the possibilities and actual practices of identity formation on the internet. Sherry Turkle (in Trend 2001) talks of a college junior who played four different characters in three different MUDs (multi-user domains: electronic locations for interaction via text – like chat rooms). She refers to another player whose online self married another projected online character – and some of the players gathered to celebrate this event in real life. On the one hand this may seem like 'only a game', and much like those publicity events manufactured around the weddings of soap stars. Yet in this case one might be concerned about the further comment made by the player when he admitted to an interviewer that he failed to interact successfully in RL. At this point, one might argue that **it is important to make a clear distinction between the Self and identity that exists through RL interactions and that kind of self that is an electronic projection**, lacking the full range of sensory communication.

There is a similar ambivalence about well-documented examples of virtual gender swapping. On the one hand, it can be argued that this is healthy identity exploration within the context of an acknowledged fiction. This is Turkle's argument (in Salamensky 2001) when she talks about 'experiments with identity' and 'a parallel life'. On the other hand, it can also be said that the practice is deceitful, voyeuristic and subversive to the conduct of social relations. It may as well be described as 'identity deception'. It is something that has happened through community sites that are understood by the members to be 'for real', not just on fantasy play sites. One can also argue that, in terms of the development and maintenance of a socially healthy Self, such cyber phenomena as the manufacture of 'heroic' selves or of other gender selves may encourage self-deception.

Jones and Kucker (in Lull 2001) take a neutral view on this: 'online we are not solely or simply expressing cultural identities we maintain offline; we may be expressing ones entirely unfamiliar to us in other realms and repressing others.' This view does, however, assume a certain distinction between online and offline. The problem is that such distinctions are difficult to hold on to if the communicators:

- invest uncritical belief in the authenticity of the online experience, and/or

- simultaneously ignore the lack of RL channels of communication.

One might object here that experience of the online self is similar to that of the telephone, through which we are used to projecting and receiving kinds of identities without the benefit of vision. But there, we would argue, at least there are paralinguistic features available to assess.

Some commentators talk of the benefits to identity of constructing homepages on the Web – a self-exploration process. Cheung (in Gauntlett and Horsley 2004) comments that 'recent research shows that people with uncertain identities have started to use the personal homepage to reflexively explore and reconstruct their identities'. He sees the process as a positive one 'for establishing affirmative identities'. He points out that people may get the benefit of positive feedback. We feel that the validity of this process could only be checked out if it could be found whether those people could carry on successfully both self-presentation and communication in the real world.

Regarding the issue of how one defines the 'real world', there has been critical work that questions the need for this to exist in a material form. Writing by Haraway (2000) and others explores the possibility of leaving behind the body and becoming a valid person in a cyberworld, becoming something new that exists through virtual technology. And Woodward (2002) says: 'One of the claims of visual reality is that it provides the technological possibility of creating identities and forming relationships free from body-based, "real" identities'.

We feel we would have to challenge this view, or at least a claim that such identities are the equivalent of RL experiences. The body may be largely irrelevant to forms of electronic communication; however, these are not the equivalent of RL interactions. They offer a technologically constructed self. **It is precisely the body that provides dimensions of communication, not least those that are affective (to do with emotion), that relate to bonding and intimacy.**

Technology and interpersonal communication

Our reservations concerning the scope and effectiveness of communication via technologies have been made pretty clear. This is not, however, to ignore benefits, conveniences and interesting facets of cultural change. For example, **mobile phones** have expanded the range and frequency of interpersonal contact (although not communication in the full sense). They offer tremendous practical benefits to, for instance, the lone female driver in a broken-down car. There are also strong social reconfigurations, for example, as teenage groups learn to socialize on the back of phone calls. There are kinds of information exchange, for example, for those with phones that have net access. Work patterns have changed, as business and advice is exchanged between people working as they travel on a train. In a general way there has been a collapsing of the distinction between the public and the private, as people conduct intimate conversations while walking through a shopping mall, or can be accessed by anyone (including viral marketers) in any place, so long as the phone is on. The phone communicates through voice, through text and, to some extent, via exchanged still images.

And yet one also needs to qualify these benefits. Contrary to commercial claims, networks are still patchy in their coverage, mainly in rural areas. So one does not have a universal interpersonal tool. Phones are used in selective ways. Young people do a lot of texting because it is cheap, but not as much real-time talking as older people. Picture phones are not being used to exchange images that much – again, because it costs. For some social groups, phones are as much statements about style and fashion as they are a means of communication. Phones are used for functional (and information) exchange, as much as for mediated social interaction. So they have become just one part of our technological repertoire of means of making contact with others, and are certainly not a substitute for face-to-face interactions.

The distinction between making contact, and real-time/real-place communication is an important one. Technophiles can get carried away by the novelty and potential of communication technologies, even to the point of losing sight of the genuine significance of and expansion of our communicative horizons. We have already referred to blogging on the Web. This may have the novelty value of a public confessional, especially when bloggers talk about intimate aspects of their lives. But it also has the real potential to create a more open society and to combat institutional protectionism. Already there are sites on which people talk about the reality of what goes on in working lives, for example within the police forces. And the Baghdad blogger was a useful source of information about what was going on when coalition forces invaded Iraq in 2004. 'Blogs seem part of a new philosophy on the Web . . . the best things are . . . the simple effective phenomena which use the media in a measured, accessible way, and connect people around the world' (Gauntlet and Horsley 2004). Note that this is not an immediate communicative use of technology. It just makes a connection. It is, however, about individual access to media. And it contributes, together with other uses of technologies, to building something called 'global communication' (though one should note that access to this is selective and privileged, in global terms). 'The Net is only one of many ways in which the same people may interact. It is not a separate reality' (Wellman and Gulia, in Wellman 1999).

Email emerged as an accidental application of an early message system named ARPANET, just as texting emerged as an add-on function to the mobile phone. These are examples of how people may drive media development, and to some extent colonize them to carry out communication on their own terms. Email has become well embedded socially as a means of communication between people in the West, though it is by no means universally available or used. Like its 'snailmail' counterpart (that is, the term now used to describe the postal system), it has a wide range of modes and functions. Email:

- enables business communication between individuals, but can also be used by organizations to transmit messages simultaneously to a collection of people

- enables personal contact immediately, between people separated by distance, thus helping to maintain relationships

- can be disposable, or its material can be revisited and reflected upon, on screen or in hard copy.

Bell (2001) says of email, 'its role has been to profoundly restyle communication'. He refers to the personalized style of email wording when he quotes Judith Lee as saying, 'email converts correspondence into virtual conversation'. However, we might suggest that, once again, it is one thing to say that technology has created a supplement to direct interpersonal communication, it is another to suggest that it does the same job. It is revealing that Bell himself admits that all his email is exchanged at the workplace. Even to have a virtual conversation means that one can afford to keep a net connection open pretty much permanently. It is mostly only organizations that can afford unlimited access to broadband, not individuals who want to 'talk to a friend'.

Email is now used instrumentally, on a global scale, to enable organizations to function. It permeates public and private spaces equally. Work-related mail can reach into the home. Advertising mails can also reach into this private space, in the same way that cold calls have become an irritating feature of home phone use (where it was once a much more private technology). Personal email can also get out into the public domain – see the notorious case of the man who posted his girlfriend's intimate musings on to friends and thence into the public domain. This story also reflects on evidence that technology – especially use of the Web – is still about **gendered communication**. Bell (2001) is talking generally about cyber-technologies when he refers to 'the problematic equation of technology with men, the male and the masculine, and the concomitant exclusion of women from what we might call "the circuit of technoculture".' It is Cheung (in Gauntlett and Horsley 2004, p. 63) who refers to a study that demonstrates that in 1999 most homepage authors were men and aged under thirty. He points out that internet access is not only uneven in global terms, but that within this access (according to a Nielsen survey of 2002) female access rates even in the 'developed' West varied between 51.9 per cent in the USA and 38 per cent in Germany. Cameron (1998) comments on women's lack of leisure time and access to net technology. We might add to this an educational context in which young males in schools still grab a larger share of computer time than the girls.

Laura Miller (in Trend 2001) argues that cyberspace is just different, in gender terms, and that one should not try to project real-life values onto it.

'The idea that women merit special protections in an environment as incorporeal as the Net is intimately bound up with the idea that women's minds are weak, fragile, and unsuited to the rough and tumble of public discourse.'

This is all very well, but it is precisely real-life values and behaviours that are projected into cyberspace when women receive sexually suggestive emails and are sometimes 'flamed' by gender abusive comments when participating in community spaces. Miller is right to point out that the notorious example of cyber-rape in the LambdaMOO space (1993) was only a verbally mediated event in a virtual world. Equally, since in our society we regard indecent letters and telephone calls as unlawful, as well as sexist, it is hard to see why new technologies should be regarded as less interpersonal, and their negative gendered use less to be condemned.

Groups and communities on the Web

The construction of online communities through chatrooms, ordinary websites or community spaces is another manifestation of new technologies that put people in touch with one another. Once more, one has to keep a sense of proportion when commenting on the effects of these virtual worlds on people's ability to communicate. They are new, exciting, enabling – but real life they are not. They are just different. They have some advantages, but also some limitations.

Lull (2001) says that 'communications media . . . connect people to each other in ways that overcome the (cultural) barriers imposed by physical distance'; that the internet 'has given tremendous visibility, convenience and power to various cultural and language groups everywhere'. It is true that people can communicate about common leisure, political, religious interests, as well as about broader cultural beliefs and experiences, regardless of where they live. There are many fan sites offering kinds of interaction in cyberspace in relation to specific objects of enthusiasm. Baym (2000) has written persuasively about the emotional rewards that female soap-opera fans gain from sharing their interests and reactions to the narratives. Also, Wendy Harcourt writes about women's groups and internet use (in Gauntlett and Horsley 2004), mentioning, for example, www.womenaction.org. In these cases individuals are mutually supportive, across distances.

And yet it is also true that such **technology underlines separation at the same time as it links people**. This is not the face-to-face interaction of a 'live' group. We are not denigrating the value of such interactions, nor even the sense of belonging that some may achieve. But the debate about what Jones and Kucker call 'socio-emotional information' is a live one (in Lull 2001). Expressing a sense of unity in words on screen is not the same as simply touching someone's arm for real, however much it is acknowledged that people invest themselves and project feelings into cyberspace. It is Jones and Kucker again who admit that 'what goes unsaid by the myriad Internet users, what is not revealed between the lines, is of critical importance, because there is nothing but lines'. We would argue that such absence of information is not the same as pauses and silence in live conversations. Of course, one can make guesses as to why a given user does not write something about themselves or their character on screen. But what we have is a hole in the communication, not a verbal space that has been developed as a signifier over generations.

Howard Rheingold (1993) provides a good example of the enthusiasm and conviction felt by many who share in virtual communities. He refers to gaming communities and to local and global communities, bonded through the net. What is interesting, and perhaps disturbing, is his absorption in what he seems to feel are the realities of the experience. There is an issue around the extent to which such communicative technologies and experiences are an adjunct to real life, or begin to seriously infringe the time given to RL interactions.

Turkle (in Salmensky 2001) gives a positive, but thought-provoking example of an online community when she refers to senior.net, a site that was set up for older people to 'chat'. What she also tells is that her grandmother used to sit in the park, and know that someone would come along and talk to her. On the one hand, it is a positive thing that the elderly should have a safe virtual environment in which to 'meet' others. On the other, it is some reflection on social change if one does not either feel safe sitting in a park, or noone is likely to come along. It is also says something about communication if tapping a keyboard is to be equated with live talk. Turkle also argues for particular benefits of the online experience. One is that virtual communities are formed from people who would not otherwise be able to meet in RL and share knowledge and experience. Another is that online contact often leads to RL contact, even on a global scale. In this case, **technology can be seen as a way of extending human communication, not as providing an alternative to it**: as something that intertwines with everyday life and face-to-face interactions.

Poster (in Trend 2001) sees the internet and its communities as both traditional and new. From one view, much net use is an extension of direct human communication – just like the letter has been a means of addressing people across a distance (but not talking with them). But he also sees something new in features of net communication, such as the ability to reconstruct identity (there are no signs of ethnicity with text in cyberspace) and the access of so many individuals to an electronic form of public space. Furthermore, he claims that 'the age of the public sphere as face-to-face talk is clearly over'. We would dispute this. For a start, there never has been a place where literally all the public could meet at one time. Cyberspace certainly does not offer a new democracy in which all citizens can 'talk' on equal terms – not all have access to it, for a start. In practice, one sees online communities as offering particular benefits for particular people, just as in RL we join certain societies and have certain groups of friends. Nor is there any evidence that groups and interactions in RL have been seriously replaced by the online experience. One might have some concerns about the future of community, but the scanning of any local newspaper will show that groups are alive and well, and that there is a lot of talk going on out there.

In real life, it is hard not to be engaged with people at some level, for some time. Life goes on. Online existence is different. In some spaces one can simply visit as a lurker – the observer at the party. In any case one always has the option of going offline, withdrawing. But you cannot log off life unless you become a recluse or a suicide.

Certainly, new technologies do offer new ways of extending our capacity for communication:

- They can overcome barriers of distance.
- They can help people with common interests to discover one another.
- They can allow people to experiment with their sense of self, even their sexual identity.
- They may allow a building of self-esteem.
- They permit us to play with self-presentation.
- They allow specific social and cultural functions, for example, memorial sites for the grieving.

But they are not the same as real life and face-to-face interaction. They do not permit the range of channels of communication that one enjoys in real life real time and real space (see Fig. 4.2). It is important to distinguish between the pleasures of experimentation with new media – the fun of playing games in cyberspace around the planet – and the actuality of what can be achieved. Chat rooms are places of polemic and deception, as much as offering a frank global exchange of views. Online communities allow a kind of meeting with others – but without material responsibilities. People may be taken out of themselves as they play with a persona in cyberspace, but it is still a real body that sits at the keyboard. Commentators have also been interested in what happens to the body when it is merged with technologies, either in a medical sense or in the use of communication tools. But that body is still a person, and that person is still a communicator. Nor has reality actually caught up with the fiction of writers like William Gibson, so that the brain is 'jacked in' to cyberspace.

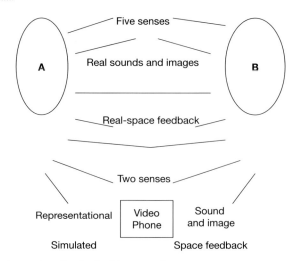

Fig. 4.2 Communication and technological intervention

Critics such as Paul Virilio (1994, 1997) have expressed concern that what we may talk about is itself affected by technology – which, for example, remodels our sense of what war means, and therefore is. But our meaning systems, our discourses about subjects such as war, have always been there, along with languages and codes. Of course, technologies have encouraged the notion of something like 'technowar', in which strategy is mapped on a computer and weapons may be delivered by remote control. Yet war still has its RL dimensions, because it involves people. The USA found, to its cost, that war in Iraq comes down to dead bodies and communication between people about their disappointment and their suffering.

Technologies have become part of all our lives and of our social practices. However, they are not simply life itself. They allow us to conduct interactions in new ways, within limits: they do not replace 'conventional' interactions. They offer some benefits to individuals and to engagement in relationships: they also have disadvantages in respect of limiting the channels available. They help us transcend geographical limitations of space, and yet are limited in the impossibility of their communicators being able to inhabit the same space. They may expand our sense of who we are and where we belong, yet they do not replace our roots in real places with real social histories supported by immediate social networks.

KEY QUESTIONS

In what ways could you argue that technology has improved communication between people?

Has the arrival of new technologies expanded our sense of identity or threatened our sense of self?

In what ways has technology made cross-cultural communication a key issue for the world today?

Review

You should have learnt the following things from this chapter:

4.1 Introduction

- Communication is affected by various cultural features.
- It takes place across cultures and within cultures.
- It involves the dominant culture and subcultural groups.

4.2 Interpersonal communication and questions of culture

- Culture is a total experience, which affects the production of meaning through communication.
- Cultures tend to believe that their values and behaviours are 'naturally' the right ones.

4.3 What is culture?

- Culture is defined by shared values and behaviours, rather than by terms such as nation, race and ethnicity.
- The discourses produced through language in everyday use express the values particular to a given culture.

4.4 Language and subculture

- Language also helps to define the identity of subcultures to themselves and for others.

4.5 Gendered communication

- Gender differences in communication do exist, in terms of verbal and nonverbal behaviour.
- Such differences may have more to do with social conditioning and cultural determination (see 'social constructionism') than with innate biology.
- It can be argued that differences are acquired not given, but are still measured in terms of masculine norms.
- Such differences are recognized in terms of women's ability to notice nonverbal cues, listen attentively, disclose more than men and express emotion.
- Some argue that gender differences have been exaggerated, and are hard to identify in the generality of everyday interactions.
- If language is about difference in performance by gender, as well as

differences in how gender is thought about, then one must also consider the idea of gendered discourse.

4.6 Cross-cultural communication

- Cross-cultural communication assumes a distinctiveness of culture, for example in terms of power distance, individualism or collectivism, gender identity and uncertainty avoidance.
- Problems with communication across cultures include stereotyping, assumption of similar views, different beliefs and different attitudes towards factors such as time and 'face'.
- One can cite many differences in verbal and nonverbal communication that exemplify underlying problems with perception, attitudes and values.
- Cross-cultural communication can be enhanced by a range of strategies ,such as using empathy, being non-judgemental and controlling communication behaviour.
- It is unhelpful and inaccurate to generalize about attitudes and behaviours in another culture.

4.7 Technology, culture and communication

- Technology has changed our sense of self and identity because it affects self-presentation and makes possible new forms of mediated interpersonal communication.
- Technologies of communication remove the element of real-space interaction.
- Technologies have extended communication between people globally and in terms of ease of contact.
- Factors such as gender can still be identified in terms of use and style, in examples of technological communication such as the internet. Technologies such as the Web provide new ways of forming communities, although denying people direct physical contact.

Case situation: The map of love

Read the following short extract from a novel and discuss with others what you think it may say, either positively or negatively, about relationships across cultures.

Isabel . . . throws back the linen sheet and sits up in Layla al-Ghamrawi's big brass four-poster. Through the fine gauze of the mosquito netting she can see, on the wall facing her, the portrait of Sharif Basha al-Baroudi. Now she can make it out only dimly, but she has studied it well. From the heavy gilt frame he looks down at her, the fez set squarely above the high forehead, the eyebrows broad and black, almost meeting above the straight nose. The thick moustache covers the upper lip; the lower lip is firm and wide in a strong, square chin. And all the arrogance of the face is perfectly focused in the eyes: proud, aloof and yet, if you look carefully, sad also. A proud man, in control, holding back. And it is in that face, more than in the face of his father out in the hall, that Isabel sees Omar el-Ghamrawi. Sees him and longs for him. How many times had they met? She goes over them again. The dinner at Deborah's house, the restaurant on Sixth – that was when she had fallen in love: as she watched him cross the room towards her, his hand briefly raised, the smile dawning in his eyes. Then the meeting at college, pausing every three steps to talk to someone just like Amal on the streets of Cairo. It was there, after he had stopped to speak to a bearded young Arab student, that she had asked, 'Are you involved with the fundamentalists?'

'What fundamentalists?' he asked.

'I don't know. Hamas or Hizbollah. Or in Egypt'.

'You should get your fundamentalists sorted – '

'But is it true?'

'Do I look like a fundamentalist? Act like a fundamentalist?'

'No. But that is what they say about you.'

'Not so long ago, Hillary Clinton would have been called a communist for her views on public health.'

'So you're not?'

'My dear child, no. Of course I'm not. Look there's Claudia. What an amazing hat – '

From *The Map of Love*, (Soueif 1999)

Suggested reading

Crawford, M., 1995, *Talking Difference – On Gender And Language*, London: Sage.

Gauntlett, D. and Horsley, R. (eds), 2004, *Web Studies*, 2nd edn, London: Arnold, p. 47.

Guirdham, M., 1999, *Communicating Across Cultures*, Basingstoke: Palgrave.

Lustig, M. W. and Koester, J., 2003, *Intercultural Competence – Interpersonal Communication Across Cultures*, 4th edn, Boston, MA: Allyn & Bacon/Pearson Education Inc.

Schirato, T. and Yell, S., 2000, *Communication and Culture*, London: Sage.

Sunderland, J., 2004, *Gendered Discourses*, Basingstoke: Palgrave Macmillan.

Trend, D. (ed.), 2001, *Reading Digital Culture*, Oxford: Blackwell.

Fig. 5.1 Self-presentation – we put up a mask to front our public performances

Chapter 5

Self-presentation

5.1 Introduction

As we have suggested in Chapter 1 of this book, our notions of **self-image and self-esteem** are crucial to our ability to participate in human communication transactions. Our communication processes – encoding and decoding meanings through shared symbol systems – begin and end in intrapersonal communication.

In this chapter we turn our attention to the public display of Self. In order to do this, we will be relying heavily on the work of the late Erving Goffman, an American social anthropologist and sociologist whose publications reflect his fieldwork in the UK and his USA. His first book, *The Presentation of Self in Everyday Life* (1959) has become a classic, and the metaphor he adopts there of a **'dramaturgical performance'** provides an established terminology for describing the public performances that we play in our daily social interactions. The Reading list at the end of this book provides a note of Goffman's other publications, which reflect his further research into behaviour in public places and enclosed institutions. He was always concerned with observing, describing and analysing the details of how people behave in front of each other and how they treat each other.

Let us begin by noting how Goffman views some of the basic concepts we are exploring in this book and then move on to review some aspects of self-presentation using his terms. These terms include: **persona, performing, staging, teams and roles**.

As you know, Chapter 1 of this book provides a background on how people have come to define the concept of Self. Chapter 6, on transactional analysis, will use a psychological model of the Self and **ego states** as a tool for analysing transactions between people. However, Goffman's view of the self is based on our ability to project a self-image to other people:

When an individual plays a part he implicitly requests his observers to take seriously the impression that is fostered before them. They are asked to believe that the character they see actually possesses the attributes he appears to possess, that the task he performs will have the consequences that are implicitly claimed for it, and that, in general, matters are what they appear to be. In line with this, there is the popular view that the individual offers his performance and puts on his show 'for the benefit of other people'.

(Goffman 1959)

Elsewhere, Goffman has succinctly expressed one of his concerns in the sentence, 'A chief concern is to develop a sociological version of the structure of the self' (Goffman 1961). Later in this chapter we shall review how far each of us is actually a social construction.

In Chapter 3 we explored some aspects of social interaction and social skills. At this point it is worth quoting Goffman's definition of an interaction:

Interaction (that is, face-to-face interaction) may be roughly defined as the reciprocal influence of individuals upon one another's actions when in one another's immediate physical presence. An interaction may be defined as all the interaction which occurs throughout any one occasion when a given set of individuals are in one another's continuous presence; the term 'an encounter' would do as well.

(Goffman 1959)

We are concerned here with public actions – observable behaviour rather than private motives or 'hidden' personalities. The keywords in this chapter are performance and role.

We will now briefly explore some of the concepts that Goffman uses to analyse self-presentation.

5.2 Persona

Essential to the notion of the presentation of self in everyday life is the belief that each of us in our daily life is playing a series of parts. We learn roles for real life as actors learn roles for make-believe. There are, of course, differences between real life and 'the stage'; for example:

- in real life we believe in the part we are playing and create the part for ourselves
- in real life we are performers and audience at the same time, and
- in real life we write our own scripts.

Goffman consciously took some of his terms for discussing the presentation of self from the work of the American sociologist, Robert Ezra Park, and refers to this quotation from one of Park's books:

> It is probably no mere historical accident that the word person, in its first meaning, is a mask. It is rather a recognition of the fact that everyone is always and everywhere, more or less consciously, playing a role . . . It is in these roles that we know each other; it is in these roles that we know ourselves.
>
> In a sense, and in so far as this mask represents the conception we have formed of ourselves – the role we are striving to live up to – this mask is our truer self, the self we would like to be. In the end, our conception of our role becomes second nature and an integral part of our personality. We come into the world as individuals, achieve character, and become persons.
>
> (Park 1950)

We select our behaviours in order to create a desired impression in other people. Hence, we internalize the roles we choose and create a public Self. Goffman believes that, as individuals and as teams, we are seeking in our interactions to 'define the situation' so that others will accept our definition of ourselves, of them and of the situation, and thus we can control other people's responses to us. Other people are led to accept our definition of the 'reality'. For example, in a selling situation the salesperson wants to be able to convince a potential customer of the truth of what the salesperson says; in a teaching situation a teacher wants to be able to convince a student about the validity of his or her arguments.

In order for someone to create the impression they want to, they need to manipulate their conduct, their appearance and the social setting. Other people generally take our behaviour on trust: they infer and attribute to us the qualities that we deliberately give off. **This notion of 'giving off' an impression is essential to understanding self-presentation**. Goffman draws a distinction between the impression that a person 'gives' and the expression that a person 'gives off', as follows:

> The first involves verbal symbols or their substitutes, which he uses admittedly and solely to convey the information that he and the others are known to attach to these symbols. This is communication in the traditional and narrow sense. The second involves a wide range of action that others can treat as symptomatic of the actor, the expectation being that the action was performed for reasons other than the information conveyed in this way.
>
> (Goffman 1959)

It is clear that this idea links closely to that of social skills discussed in Chapter 3. If we are socially skilled, we have learnt to control the apparently coincidental impression that we 'give off' about ourselves. We can, of course, only know people by their behaviour, hence we use the term 'attribution' in describing our perception of others. We have to attribute causes to other people's behaviour. These questions of perception of other people have been discussed in Chapter 2.

Before leaving this section, we wish to note further this idea of the 'mask'. In western cultures, in contrast with some other cultures, we do not wear physical masks except in carnival and masquerade. However, dark glasses – especially mirror glasses – can be used as a depersonalizing mask, and some people have also argued that make-up, hairstyling and dress are also used as forms of mask. We may wish to hide or protect our real selves, or we may wish to create a projected impression of how we want to appear. Fashion magazines provide a regular, rich source of available masks for people to wear in order to face other people.

Smiling has also been described as a mask (Fast 1970). We may keep smiling through the day, but the smile may hide our real feelings of anger, stress or annoyance. We just have a public face we must maintain.

Similarly, we use clothing to mask the body. This masking may cover what we are embarrassed by – both men and women may feel their body shape does not conform to the cultural ideal they would like. Or, masking through dress may be used to make a declaration of group allegiances and professional identity. Such dress could be the graffitied leathers of a biker or the dark suits of bank workers.

This masking may also have a lot to do with cultural values. For example, many women of the Muslim faith (say, Bangladeshi) wear clothes to mask the physical signs of their gender, and to show modesty and restraint. The priests of many cultures, including British Christians, wear robes and regalia that both emphasize their distinctive role and mask the ordinary human being within.

Also, some professions mask the individual person to create an impersonal social role. In the case of surgeons and their teams, the physical mask is used for hygienic reasons, but it also has the effect of hiding the person and helping their professional performance. A surgeon performs operations on other people that are so disturbing to contemplate that the ritual of hospitals serves more than just medical purposes. The whole paraphernalia of the place licenses behaviour that would be intolerable anywhere else.

Controlling our performance, both verbally and nonverbally, and hence defining the situation and leading the audience to adopt our view of the situation is what we now want to explore.

KEY QUESTIONS

Describe what are, in your opinion, four key characteristics of the persona of a schoolteacher. Compare your answers with those of other people.

How does the concept of persona relate to ideas about self?

5.3 Performance

This term, taken from drama, implies some notion of deceit – that is, seeking to appear to be something that we are not. However, this is not the sense in which we wish to use the word here. **We can present a performance that we believe is true and sincere and which we**

want observers to believe. Goffman rather unnervingly writes that 'one finds that the performer can be fully taken in by his own act; he can be sincerely convinced that the impression of reality he stages is the real reality'. Surely this is true for most of us for most of the time. We believe that we are presenting ourselves, our attitudes, ideas and actions. We are playing an unconscious role; we believe we are being ourselves. We believe in the impression that is being fostered by our own performance.

Certainly at the other end of the spectrum it is possible to conceive of a 'cynical' performance, in which an individual has no belief in his/her own act and no concern with the beliefs of the audience. He or she is merely and deliberately putting on a performance to deceive – things are not what they seem. An example of this is, of course, the 'confidence man' who sets out to deceive in order to rob his victim. Another example, of a 'con' that is played because the audience demands its, would be the doctor who prescribes a placebo because the patient insists on some treatment.

A moral dimension does, of course, come into this. We can expect that things are as they appear to be. Or, as Goffman puts it, 'society is organized on the principle that any individual who possesses certain social characteristics has a moral right to expect that others will value and treat him in an appropriate way'. In any particular performance, of course, we do not reveal ourselves completely and may, indeed, deliberately not disclose certain parts of ourselves. This issue of managing our self-presentation and our perception of identity is fully described in Goffman's book *Stigma: Notes on the Management of Spoiled Identity* (1963). People who are stigmatized or labelled in some way as 'abnormal' will manage information about themselves and not disclose information about themselves to some observers.

Goffman's contention is that without being dishonest or insincere, we do put on a performance to create a desired impression whenever we are in the presence of others. His observations of these performances were largely carried out in work situations, total institutions (mental hospitals, prisons or the armed forces), or in domestic situations where groups or individuals were consciously seeking to create an impression on other people. If we want to succeed in creating this impression, we need to perform not only verbally, but more especially nonverbally where our 'real' feelings may leak. As we have noted in Chapter 3, people tend to rely more on nonverbal messages about other people than on the more consciously controlled verbal messages.

It is perhaps useful to think in terms of *degrees* of performance. You might like to reflect on your own communicative behaviour: are there moments when you feel you are not engaged in any sort of performance and can you define degrees through which your performance becomes more consciously played as the audience and social situations change? There are structured situations as in an interview, a first date or a formal occasion, when your performance to create the desired impression is at its most staged. The idea of presenting performance suggests that an audience is needed: do you think we also perform for ourselves? Or when alone (or with a very intimate partner) do we drop the performing mask? Perhaps our giveaway is when we are conscious of being 'on stage' and then retreat 'back stage' where we can relax. We look next at this idea of staging.

KEY QUESTIONS

Performance

Describe two contrasting performances displayed by an individual in two different situations (for example, when receiving a ticket for a parking fine or when making complaints about the lateness of a train).

How does the concept of performance relate to ideas about attribution and the use of strategies?

5.4 Staging

As we manipulate our conduct and our appearance, and our verbal and nonverbal communication channels for a personal performance, **we also manipulate our physical contact to create the appropriate setting**. On a theatrical stage we have make-believe performers playing roles in front of a real audience. In real life the situation is rather different because participants are both performers and audience at the same time. This can lead to difficulties and Goffman spends a good deal of time discussing the **front stage** and **back stage** performances. The front stage is the public performance area where a careful manner and appearance are maintained. This front will provide the appropriate setting (of furniture, décor, physical layout and other items) for the desired performance. We can observe such staged fronts most deliberately created in, for example, shops, office reception areas, living rooms or on ceremonial occasions. For example, devout Jewish families mark their Sabbath with a formal laying out of the table, including relevant symbolic 'props'. There is a breaking of bread and other ritual behaviours.

Key notes for front stage performances are politeness and decorum. The notion of front presupposes an area back stage where different norms of behaviour and decorum operate. This is the area where performers can drop their public mask, where different language norms can be used. Here the stage props are kept. A particularly clear example of this front/back can be found in restaurants, where the stage door from private kitchen to public restaurant can mark a rapid change of décor, atmosphere, language and behaviour. One well-expressed example of this Goffman used was taken from George Orwell's *Down and Out in Paris and London* (1951):

> It is an instructive sight to see a waiter going into a hotel dining room. As he passes the door a sudden change comes over him. The set of his shoulders alters; all the dirt and worry and irritation have dropped off in an instant. He glides over the carpet, with a solemn priestlike air. I remember our assistant *maître d'hôtel*, a fiery Italian, pausing at the dining room door to address his apprentice, who had broken a bottle of wine. Shaking his fist above his head he yelled (luckily the door was more or less sound proof) '*Tu me fais* – do you call yourself a waiter, you young bastard? You a waiter! You are not fit to scrub the floor in the brothel your mother came from. Maquereau!'

Words failing him, he turned to the door; and as he opened it he delivered a final insult in the same manner of Squire Western in Tom Jones.

Then he entered the dining room and sailed across it dish in hand, graceful as a swan. Ten seconds later he was bowing reverently to a customer. And you could not help thinking, as you saw him bow and smile, with that benign smile of the trained waiter, that the customer was put to shame by having such an aristocrat to serve him.

It is comparatively easy to accept the idea of staging a performance in a public place such as a shop or a restaurant. We can also accept that in private workplaces people are on stage; for example:

- A supervisor is likely to dress differently, have a separate space and use 'props' such as worksheets, instruction manuals, pens, measuring rules, desks, and so on, depending on the nature of the work.

- An executive is likely to have a personal stage area with props such as desk, special chairs for him or herself and visitors, tables, cabinets, personal computers, executive toys, pictures on the wall, plants, bookcase, magazines, and so on, as well as a secretary/PA to create a team performance.

These examples are all, of course, semi-public. Do we also use our home as a stage? We would argue that we do. Certainly, homes have areas of front and back stage and some audiences are admitted to different stage areas. We wear different costumes in the bedroom, bathroom, kitchen, and we have carefully chosen the props in each room according to our own tastes, self-image and financial state. In the presence of guests and visitors, the members of the household may be expected to act as a united 'cast', which creates problems sometimes for young children who do not maintain the role. They may fail to understand why a meal is being eaten in a different room on different plates with different cutlery and with different norms of behaviour than an everyday meal: 'Use your napkin, dear' – 'I don't usually have one'; 'Wait until everyone is finished before you get up, dear' – 'I've finished eating, why can't I get up?'

Staging by one or more performers for an audience (who, in turn, are performers) is, of course, all calculated as a means of **'impression management'**. Many of the examples cited by Goffman are from shops where the salespeople are at pains to create a particular impression for their customers. A long-running comedy series on British television, *Are You Being Served?* depended for a good deal of its humour on the subcultures of front and back stage in a department store. The communication behaviour in front of customers was rather different from that when the performers were alone. These performers acted as a team when on stage. We will now go on to look at this idea of teams.

KEY QUESTIONS

Staging

Describe ways in which a living room or a receptionist's office can be set up as a 'stage' for a 'performance'.

Explain how the staging of a performance might affect the outcome of an interaction.

5.5 Teams

Teams are concerned not only with the presentation of self, but also with a united presentation of a social establishment. In order for a social establishment – whether a family, a school, a hospital, a shop, a church or a business – to manage the impression it gives off, it must create teams that can perform together. This team has the task of coordinating their individual activities to maintain a given projected definition of the situation. When an outsider enters the establishment, the team wants its definition of this situation and the interactive relationship to be the controlling one, the one accepted as real. For example, in a school the teachers and the head are expected to present a front to angry parents who may wish to complain. A member of the team will not criticize another colleague in front of the parents, but may do so later back stage. For a team to maintain a staged performance they need to maintain loyalty as team members; discipline to cope with any faux pas that may occur and to keep up the public performance; and circumspection to plan ahead and to maintain the audience's perceptions in line with the desired impressions. Embarrassment may occur if the team is caught in some sort of false presentation, in the same way that an individual may feel embarrassed if he or she is caught out in performance. The team will, of course, share secrets not divulged to non-team members and may develop its own secret codes. One nice example given by Goffman, which refers to a store, is as follows:

> Now that the customer is in the store suppose she can't be sold? The price is too high; she must consult her husband; she is only shopping. To let her walk (i.e. escape without buying) is treason in a Borax shop. So an SOS is sent out by the salesman through one of the numerous footpushes in the store. In a flash the 'manager' is on the scene, preoccupied with a suite and wholly oblivious of the Aladdin who sent for him.
>
> 'Pardon me, Mr Dixon,' says the salesman, simulating reluctance in disturbing such a busy personage. 'I wonder if you could do something for my customer. She thinks the price of this suite is too high. Madam, this is our Manager, Mr Dixon.'
> Mr Dixon clears his throat impressively. His is all of six feet, has iron grey hair and wears a Masonic pin on the lapel of his coat. Nobody would suspect from his appearance that he is only a special salesman to whom difficult customers are turned over.

'Yes,' says Mr Dixon, stroking his well-shaven chin, 'I see. You go on, Bennett, I'll take care of Madam myself. I'm not so busy at the moment anyhow.'
The salesman slips away, valet-like, though he will give Dixon hell if he muffs the sale.

For a full account of teamwork in presenting a social establishment, we suggest you read the appropriate sections of Goffman's *The Presentation of Self in Everyday Life* (1959) or *Asylums* (1976). The latter book, dealing with total institutions, shows how staff and inmates both develop sophisticated team performances. Particular examples of impression management by mental-hospital staff are staff/patient parties, theatrical performances, institutional displays or open days.

We suggest that you observe team performance in action when you are next in shops, restaurants and other social establishments. It may also be possible to observe interesting cultural nuances – for example, the busy working café at lunchtime contrasted with a more upmarket restaurant in the evening, or an Italian-run pizzeria contrasted with an English-run pub. Try to identify front and back stage areas, how the staging of the physical context has been managed, and how the performers treat their audiences.

5.6 Roles

Earlier in this chapter we drew attention to the notions of persona, mask, role, character and person. We present ourselves, our personalities, through performing roles in the presence of others. So far we have reviewed the idea of performing individually and in teams and the idea of staging. Now we wish to look at the concept of roles, which Goffman defines as follows:

> Defining social role as the enactment of rights and duties attached to a given status, we can say that a social role will involve one or more parts and that each of these different parts may be presented by the performer on a series of occasions for the same kinds of audience or to an audience of the same persons.

The way we play a role via our parts suggests some consistency based on the personality and self-image of the person. We engage in roles that are patterns of behaviour considered appropriate for a specific audience and a specific social context. For a general discussion of role-playing you could refer to *More Than Words* (Dimbleby and Burton 1992). In this section we will concentrate on the nature of roles played in team performances for managing an impression.

There are three crucial roles in maintaining a team performance:

- those who perform
- those who are performed to
- outsiders who neither perform in the show nor observe it.

Those who perform know the impression that is to be fostered, possess the secret information of the establishment and have access to front and back regions.

In addition to these three prime roles in a performance, Goffman (1959) also notes what he calls **discrepant roles**, which bring a person into a social establishment in a false guise. These include:

- The role of informer who gains access to back stage and secret information, then openly or secretly shows it to the audience.

- The role of 'shill'* who acts as though he or she were a member of the audience but is in fact with the performers. He/she normally presents a model for the type of audience response that the performers want. Such shills may be a part of an occasion, such as a sale to provoke customer interest or response.

- The role of inspector who pretends to be a member of the audience but is in fact checking on the performers. Would a writer of a restaurant report reveal his or her identity to the waiter before eating the meal?

- The role of agent from another team spying on the performance.

- The role of go-between who learns the secrets of two teams on different sides. For example, a factory supervisor may have to play as part of the management team and also as part of the workers' team.

- The role of service specialist who specializes in the construction, repair and maintenance of the show that their clients maintain before other people. These include architects and interior decorators, hairdressers and others who deal with personal front, and others – such as economists, accountants, lawyers, who provide factual information for the display.

These descriptions suggest almost conspiratorial games being played. More will be said about another view of 'games people play' in the next chapter.

The final comment in this section about roles and games concerns the audience. Often the audience for a performance will have access to a back stage area or access to some information that the performing team do not want to share with the audience, but will tactfully not acknowledge or exploit this in order to maintain the performance and the definition of the situation that has been projected by the performers. Perhaps this is most obvious in a performance for children, where adults in the audience know the 'secrets' of the staging but do not spoil the performance by sharing their knowledge – the pretence of the performance is maintained.

5.7 Personal style

In our discussion of self-presentation so far it is possible to lose sight of the Self in our concentration on performance, staging and teams. However, **within these public behaviour patterns there is a consistency of personal style and identity**. We play a role in our own personal way, revealing our own attitudes, experiences and responses to the situation. We draw our own conclusions about how we can individually create the impression we desire.

---

* Shill is an American word that means 'a person who poses as a customer in order to decoy others into participating, as at a gambling house, auction, confidence game, etc.

Goffman concludes his study of the presentation of self in everyday life with the following significant comments:

> In this report, the individual was divided by implication into two basic parts: he was viewed as a 'performer', a harried fabrication of impressions involved in the all too human task of staging a performance; he was viewed as a 'character', a figure, typically a fine one, whose spirit, strength and other sterling qualities the performance was designed to evoke.
>
> (Goffman 1959)

This 'character' is equated with the concept of Self and, in turn, the Self is a product of performances and other people's reactions to them. It results from one's social interactions. For further details about this you should refer back to Chapter 1.

Similarly, we create an identity of the Self from a life history that is a single continuous record of social and biographical facts. A chilling sequence in Goffman's book *Asylums* concerns the stripping of personal identity that happens to someone taken into a total institution, whether a prison, a religious institution, mental hospital or the armed forces. The term that Goffman uses to label this process is **'self-mortification'**. By this term he means the way in which personal possessions, clothes and the freedom of action that we take for granted as autonomous adults are taken from the individual. However, the individual may be a willing participator in this in order to redefine their self-identity in line with what they want or feel they need, or in line with what their close associates feel they need. In the context of a mental hospital this effect is summarized as follows:

> I am suggesting that the nature of the patient's nature is redefined so that, in effect if not by intention, the patient becomes the kind of object upon which a psychiatric service can be performed. To be made a patient is to be remade into a serviceable object . . .
>
> (Goffman 1976)

Time spent in a total institution is a disruption of a life career by which self-identity is shaped. Each of us can review our life career and draw conclusions from it that confirm or deny our self-image.

The Self is a private matter only known, and not fully, by oneself through intrapersonal communication. But it is also a public construct, a result of public performances and interactions with others. We all seek to present ourselves by creating a specific desired impression and by defining the social situation. Questions of controlling people and situations are fundamental to the notion of communication. In the next chapter we will look at another perspective on the controlling games people play, but before we close this chapter, we want to create a checklist of skills arising from the ideas outlined here.

5.8 Presentation skills

So far we have been describing, analysing and giving examples of how individually and in teams we present ourselves and create a 'public performance' in social interactions. In terms of effective communication it is possible to identify a number of presentation skills that we use in our social performances.

- Reflect on the other person's view of you, on the persona that you wish them to perceive. It might even be possible for you to find out something about the other person or other people involved. Think how they may respond to you.

- Reflect on what you would like the outcome of the interaction to be (apart from the matter of your image). Consider what you can do to achieve that outcome.

- Reflect on the social situation involved, think about what would be appropriate for you to do and say in order to be seen in a positive light. This idea may include factors like the roles of others, or the role that others might assume you to take on.

- Reflect on yourself, on your strengths and weaknesses. Determine to build on your strengths and to overcome your weaknesses.

- Consider the stage where you will present yourself, and think about how you can use it to help put across what you want. This might even include organizing the props on that stage.

- Consider what verbal and nonverbal behaviours you can use to represent your desired persona – and then, of course, use them.

- Perhaps try practising your performance in some private back stage area.

Again, you may think that this kind of reflection, decision making and deliberate action seems rather calculating. Remember what we have said about the fact that all humans do carry on this kind of organized behaviour in many ways and at many times – for example, when trying to form intimate relationships, when trying to carry out their jobs successfully. If your motives and the preferred outcome of the interaction are positive, then there should be no moral problem.

In order to contextualize this list of skills it is worth considering a number of situations in which we wish to present ourselves.

- An obvious one is an interview, where, clearly, we want to be seen in a positive light. Many people prepare what they will say at interviews in terms of facts. But it is also relevant to consider how you wish to be perceived, and therefore how you should behave to achieve this image in the eyes of the interviewer.

- There are also relevant work situations for many people who have to deal with the public or with clients. Again, the skill of self-presentation largely depends on control of communicative behaviour, to control the impression that is formed by the other person.

- A more intimate situation is one where one wishes to present positively to someone with whom you want to form a good social relationship. The same principles of personal management skills apply and people are subconsciously aware of this when they spend time choosing what to wear and even rehearse what they might say.

- Presentation might also include more formal performances in education or in work when talking to a small group of people. Although there are particular needs here to prepare the content and structure of what one is going to say, presentation skills still apply.

If you are in a college or school situation then you might benefit from having a group brainstorming session on what you all think are the qualities and abilities that make a person an effective communicator and presenter. When people do this exercise, in addition to suggesting language skills, nonverbal and social skills, they often mention a phrase such as 'personal confidence'. Perhaps the three main sources of confidence (a belief that you can succeed in interactions with other people) are these:

- a positive self-image
- a knowledge of communication processes
- being prepared and rehearsed for performing and presenting yourself to others, especially in front of a group.

Review

You should have learnt the following things from this chapter:

5.1 Introduction

- The importance of self-concept in communication and ways in which we seek to present ourselves in everyday life.
- The terminology used by Goffman, based on a dramaturgical metaphor, including performance, staging and roles.

5.2 Persona

- Persona suggests the idea of mask, of a way of performing roles – which, in turn, leads to a notion of self-identity – a consistency of role performance.

5.3 Performance

- We can perform sincerely or cynically.
- We can regulate our verbal and nonverbal behaviour, our conduct, appearance and objects around us to create the impression of ourselves that we believe to be true.
- We inevitably perform and display public behaviour patterns when in the presence of others.

5.4 Staging

- We manipulate physical context to create a suitable stage for our performances.
- We perform differently in front stage and back stage regions. The back stage is kept secret from the audience and from other teams.

5.5 Teams

- In social establishments we perform in teams, which develop patterns of behaviour and secret languages to maintain a team presentation so as to manage the impression that the audience receives. Examples can be seen in any social organization, from family to factory, from hospital to restaurant.

5.6 Roles

- Teams presuppose performers, observers and outsiders who neither perform nor observe.
- Additionally, there are specialist or discrepant roles to aid the team or a rival team or the audience.

5.7 Personal style

- Within this notion of performance lies a concept of self-identity that is a social product of other people's reactions to our role-playing performances.
- Each of us has created an identity based on a life history or career that is both private and public.
- Total institutions disrupt the individual's social public identity kit in a mortification of the Self.

5.8 Presentation skills

- These skills include:

  - defining desired outcomes
  - awareness of self and of context
  - control of communicative behaviour to present a desired persona.

Case situation: Privacy

Read the case situation below and try answering the following questions:

- What kind of things do you think that Collins would say to his patient that would be consistent with his self-presentation?
- How does the extract illustrate the ideas of back stage and front stage?
- In what ways does the extract show connections between the ideas of role and performance?

Mrs Purvis's mouth was an inhuman orifice, packed out with cotton wodges focused on the damaged tooth. The gum tissue had a distinctive tinge where the anaesthetic had turned it into unfeeling flesh. She shifted uneasily in the chair as he started to drill once more in order to finish undercutting the section he was working on.

Peter Collins smiled reassuringly and muttered something soothing as he started on the now nearly finished cavity. His patient rolled her eyes. His hands smelled of pale disinfectant and were perfectly clean. She tried to ignore the gurgling instrument in her mouth and gazed at the crocodile on the poster on the ceiling, with its disconcerting smile and clean, clean teeth.

Peter finished his work as briskly as ever, though it was the end of his working day. He sneaked a look at the clock and hoped that his stomach wouldn't betray his humanity as he leaned over the patient to finish the shaping of the filling with deft, quick scrapes. His legs were beginning to ache, but only he knew that. His white medical coat encased him protectively. His assistant had dark rings under her eyes. But she also maintained a firm pleasant manner. She admired him, his coolness in the face of daily dental crises, his certain manner as he asked her for things, his patience in dealing with the laboratories and the suppliers.

Mrs Purvis left at last, with a lopsided smile. He was pleased. He knew that he had done a good job. Her gratitude was appreciated. He complimented his assistant on her share of their good day's work, and they cleared up the instruments and the debris. Finally, she, too, left and he was able to shut up the rooms at the front of the house and to retire upstairs to his sitting room and the tree-clad view over the little park where he had once played with his children.

His children were now grown up, he was divorced and he lived on his own. It was a kind of pleasure to let his body slump into an armchair. He enjoyed the lonely privacy of his room where he was not on view, where no one expected anything of him. Which is why he was not pleased when a minute later the telephone rang.

It was a colleague, who should have known better than to ring him at this time. But still, the call was only a matter of enthusiasm. She had been to a conference on conservation techniques, and soon Peter found himself out of his chair and pacing up and down, asking her questions. A curious observer from the park might have seen this tall, rather stooping figure crossing and recrossing the window frame, shaping the air with his hands.

Suggested reading

The following books by Erving Goffman provide a number of perspectives on how we present ourselves and interact with others in a variety of contexts. In several of these books he deals with the 'problems' of self-presentation and interaction in total institutions, in public places and for people who feel in some way stigmatized:

The Presentation of Self in Everyday Life, 1959, Harmondsworth: Penguin.
Encounters: Two Studies in the Sociology of Interaction, 1961, Indianapolis: Bobbs Merrill.
Behaviour in Public Places: Notes on the Social Organization of Gatherings, 1963, New York: Free Press.
Stigma: Notes on the Management of Spoiled Identity, 1963, Harmondsworth: Penguin.
Interaction Ritual: Essays on Face-to-face Behaviour, 1968, 1967, Harmondsworth: Penguin/ New York: Anchor Press.
Asylums, 1976, Harmondsworth: Penguin.
Gender Advertisements, 1979, London: Macmillan.

Fig. 6.1 Transactional analysis – the parental ego state may operate outside the role of parent

Chapter 6

Transactional analysis

By far the greater part of all social intercourse is in the form of play.

(Berne 1961)

6.1 Introduction

Why examine TA?

In the first place, the simple answer to this question is because we believe it works! We have been looking at various approaches to interpersonal communication in this book: at ways of explaining why we communicate in the way we do, how we carry on that communication, what conditions it, what regulates it. Transactional analysis (TA) offers another approach that provides some very plausible answers to these questions of 'Why?', 'How?' and 'What?' They may not be the only answers, nor is it the only approach. But it is useful in that it makes sense, and in that its ideas can be put into practice. **Understanding of TA can enhance one's own communication skills, and can also be used to understand the communicative behaviour of others**.

Transaction and communication

The starting point for TA is 'the transaction'. Eric Berne, the psychologist who created transactional analysis, identified a basic fact of interaction that can be recognized and then built upon. We might say that, in effect, he identified building blocks of communication. In his widely known work *Games People Play* (1964), Berne described these as follows:

> The unit of social intercourse is called a transaction. If two or more people encounter each other . . . sooner or later one of them will speak, or give some other indication of acknowledging the presence of the others. This is called the transactional stimulus. Another person will then say or do something which is in some way related to the stimulus, and that is called the transactional response.

The present and the past

In this section, and in some later remarks, we have drawn on and adapted from Stewart 2000. Transactional analysis assumes that present communication behaviour is a response to events and experiences in the past. In terms of making an analysis it is assumed that there are four modes that one may recognize and analyse (see Berne 1961):

- behavioural – which is about the behaviours within a given ego state (see below) for a particular person

- social – which is about noticing ego states of the responses which a given person gets from others

- historical – which is about how a given person may talk about the past, about those around them and about childhood in particular

- phenomenological – which is about a mode of communication in which the person is not merely remembering, but 'talking' as if that past is really present.

6.2 Ego states – Parent, Adult, Child

Fundamental to TA are the **three 'ego states', 'Parent', 'Adult' and 'Child'**, which are used as a description of personality. Encoding and decoding of communication starts and finishes with these three ego states. Everyone has something of Parent, Adult and Child in them. **The presence of these ego states affects communication** in a given situation, depending on which state or combination of states predominates at that time. Particular verbal phrases and nonverbal behaviours are associated with given ego states. Someone who bangs the table and says 'I won't' could be said to be **Child-like**, *though not childish*. Berne makes an important distinction here when refusing use of the colloquial term 'childish' and so trying to avoid the value judgements associated with it. It is important to bear in mind throughout that these behaviours (and forms of language) are unconsciously adopted by people, often as a result of earlier experiences in life.

So, it is important to understand that **adults can be Child-like, and children can be Adult-like**. Certainly it is true that the Child ego state (with its associated behaviours) is the one that is first laid down in early years, and that the Adult comes later. But it is also true that people of young years are perfectly capable of behaving Adult- or Parent-like. Indeed, Harris (1970) argues that the child learns both Child and Parent from the moment of birth, and has learnt most of the associated attitudes and behaviours by the age of five. He suggests that **learning of the Adult starts only a little later, at the age of ten months**.

A possible misuse of TA theory (and in assessing people generally) is to assume that Child, Parent and Adult are necessarily associated with certain ages or roles. You need to bear this in mind because too often our communication is founded on assumptions about others, based on careless readings of their communicative behaviour (see also Perception). There is also the matter of the self-fulfilling prophecy being involved here – that people who are treated Parent-like may respond by being Child-like, but that young people who are treated Adult-like may indeed respond by being Adult-like themselves, even at the age of, say, seven years.

We will now summarise each of these ego states.

The Child

The Child is impulsive, instinctive, emotional and full of feelings. The Child may have negative manifestations such as temper and sulking, but it will also have positive aspects such as love and fun and curiosity.

The Child-state is one in which emotions and reactions are on the surface. In effect, we re-live the young person (Child) that we once were, when the Child takes over. Not surprisingly, this state tends to take over at times of high emotion or stress. People also flip into the Child-state and its patterns of communication because in their experience it has proved to get them what they want. Grown people lose their temper in arguments, sometimes because (perhaps subconsciously sometimes) they know that uninhibited rage is so disturbing to the other person that they will give in to them.

When describing these ego states in a book, of necessity we state them in sequence on the page. But it is important to realize that, as with the communication process in general, these three ego states do not necessarily happen separately or in sequence. All of us have all three ego states within us. All of these may manifest themselves during the course of one conversation. It is not the case that one exchange has to happen in one ego state. So, if one considers the example of an argument again, during this someone might switch from Child rage (shouting) to Parental admonition (perhaps using the threatening finger), and then to Adult reason (saying, 'Yes, but let's look at the facts').

Variations on the child

TA theory also recognizes that ego states can have their own variations. In the case of the Child, one can recognize at least three common variations, described as the Natural Child, the Adapted Child and the Little Professor.

- In the first case of the **Natural Child** our original description above still largely applies. This child is uninhibited in its behaviour: it is both fearful and curious, affectionate and aggressive, sensuous and self-indulgent, enjoys games but is also self-centred.

- But **the Adapted Child** has been trained through contact with grown-ups. It has learnt strategies for coping with grown-ups around it that are still within the realm of Child, and that reflect its view of itself and its self-esteem (of which more later). The Adapted Child may be described as compliant (it gets by through obeying grown-ups passively without question); withdrawn (it avoids others or perhaps 'dreams' its way through life and its problems); or procrastinating (it defers decisions and actions). If you think that you know grown-up people like this then you are probably right! People learn behaviours young. People in various kinds of work may behave like this because they are reacting to their boss from this Adapted Child-state. They learned to cope with adults with status in these ways at a young age, and they keep on doing this with comparable adults when they are older.

- **The Little Professor** is, on the other hard, most likely to be recognized at a young age. This version of the Child ego state is one in which the Adult is emerging. To an extent, it comes out of the curious and self-centred aspects of the Natural Child. In this case, one recognizes creative qualities, use of intuition as the rational mind develops, and attempts at manipulation ('I promise to be good for a week if you let me have . . .').

Child behaviour

So the characteristics of these three versions of Child can be said to construct personality: the Self from which communication comes and which adjusts to communication received. But then these characteristics are themselves inferred from communicative behaviour. So what are these behaviours? To make a brief selection (which you may be able to add to through observation), there are the following typical uses of speech. (Remember when reading these that different kinds of Child utterance do not have to come from children):

- The Natural Child might say things like: 'Wow!', 'Great!' and other exclamations, or 'Hey, come on, let's have some fun'.
- The Adapted Child might come out with: 'Okay, if that'll make you happy'; 'It wasn't me'; 'I wouldn't have said anything like that'; 'I didn't mean to upset you'.
- The Little Professor might come out with: 'You'll be sorry you did that'; 'I'm going to have to tell X about you'; 'I'd be glad to run that errand for you, but I need a lift to the shops later'; 'That's a mean thing to say'; 'It's not fair to expect me to be like her'.

Nonverbal behaviours might be those such as paralanguage in which the speaker is whining about injustice, complaining about someone else, trying to aggravate, wheedling their way into someone's favour, or exclaiming loudly as they excuse some mistake. The ingratiating tone of someone asking permission for action is probably the sign of an Adapted Child. Raw laughter and fast talk is the enthusiasm of the Natural Child. These behaviours may be matched and reinforced by kinds of body language. When found out in an error, people sometimes throw a temper tantrum as a kind of defence. When things go wrong they may slump in despair and look tearful. Adult women have been known to try and get their own way by fluttering their eyelashes and putting on a naive, wide-eyed expression. Insulting gestures and faces are also part of this Child-state. Putting up a hand at a meeting for attention is a reversion to a Child-state gesture. Pouting and nail biting are nonverbal signs of the negative aspects of this state, whereas jumping around and looking animated is a sign of the positively excited and enthusiastic child.

You should, by now, have grasped the point that a lot of these Child behaviours are to be seen in adults. To behave like a Child is not necessarily a bad thing. Indeed, many would argue that it is healthy to express the Child within us if this means giving space to our curiosity, and expression to our positive emotions towards others.

The Parent

The Parent ego state is one in which we behave like a parent, a figure with status who directs the life of another (originally the young child), and who establishes standard and

values. The beliefs and consequent behaviour patterns that we inherit at an early age are accepted uncritically (it is in an adult function to criticize). To this extent, while TA firmly believes in the capacity for growth and change, it also recognizes the heavy influence of the parent. Parental ego state, attitudes and behaviours are learnt from our parents. We absorb them and reuse them, often unconsciously, usually uncritically. The epitome of this state is to be seen in utterances such as, 'It was good enough for my father so it's good enough for you.' This is, of course, no logical basis for any belief or a justification for any behaviour! Still one may even observe children repeating parental utterances as part of their play, and hence their process of socialization. Many a hapless doll has been admonished to sit still and behave or it won't get any sweets. That same person, older in years, will practise the same threats in the same ego state on real children in order to obtain compliance. Parents may threaten to withdraw favours or reward in order to get their children to do what they want. Grown people may use the same device in order to influence the behaviour of others around them. In each case it is the Parent speaking, using the arguments and attitudes that were laid down in childhood.

Variations on the Parent

In fact the Parent is not always directive or even punitive. **Two types of Parent may be recognized: the Nurturing Parent and the Controlling Parent**.

* The Nurturing Parent can, broadly, be seen in a positive light. This Parent is caring, offers rewards, and protects the child. The behaviour of this Parent is sympathetic and comforting. These characteristics are important when read in conjunction with the later section that explains feelings of 'being OK' or 'not OK'. A Nurturing Parent can help the child to feel OK about itself and its relationships. Obviously, an overprotective parent can smother a child and can inhibit the growth of the Self. A child who is smothered cannot achieve autonomy. Misplaced protection and reward may be seen in parents who, for example, overfeed their children. In effect, they may try to feed away anxiety and distress, and, of course, merely create another set of problems. But if qualities of true care are present then this kind of distorted Nurturing Parent should not emerge. A truly Nurturing Parent does not give a child everything that it wants when it wants it.

* The characteristics of the Controlling Parent are less attractive. There will be firm and immediate opinions about the child's behaviour and motivation. This Parent will be proscriptive, and will make quick judgements about the child. This Parent is authoritarian and punitive, moralizes and makes heavy demands of the child. Such a Parent ego state will pre-judge a child's behaviour, shaping a sense of guilt as much as of conscience. This kind of Parent is the one who generates things like the work ethic, and worst of all, makes the child feel guilty about failing even when it has done its best. This is the Parent who drives the child to succeed on the parent's terms. This is the parent who is prone to say 'It serves you right', or 'I told you so' when perhaps the child needs comfort rather than admonition.

Parent behaviour

Once more, we can read the ego state through the communication: the Controlling Parent will have a stock of 'do and don't' phrases. They will tend to use imperative utterances such as 'You must eat up your greens', 'You really shouldn't do that', 'For goodness sake, be good when your aunt comes', 'You ought to do your homework now', and so on. Or 'Come on, try harder now, don't be such a coward', 'You really are a bad girl', 'You stupid boy!', 'That's very naughty', and 'How could a child of mine grow up to be such a little wretch!' Perhaps the most identifiable phrase, which all parents will have delivered, at some time or another at least, in exasperation to the question 'Why?' from their child, is the infamous '. . . because I said so!'

On the other hand, the Nurturing Parent will also have typical utterances: 'Don't be afraid, it will be all right', 'Here, this will make it better', 'Don't worry. I'll talk to your teacher'. Or again, 'Why don't you let me help you do that?' and 'If I were you I would try the blue crayon'. They will also use terms of endearment in address such as 'Darling' or 'Honey', and give compliments such as 'That's a really good idea', 'You really are an angel', or 'What a good boy/girl', 'That's pretty smart', and so on.

These verbal utterances are, of course, paralleled by nonverbal behaviours. The Controlling Parent has a repertoire of expressions of disapproval that could be described as frowning, hostile, disdainful and the like, with all the specific associated uses of lowered brows and fixed gaze. The Nurturing Parent will look happy, admiring, encouraging and use a lot of smiling.

Other body signs might be characterized in terms of lack of contact and of 'locking off' in the case of the Controlling Parent, but in terms of open gestures and touching in the case of the Nurturing Parent. The latter 'gives strokes', and so teaches the child to do likewise. ('Giving strokes' refers to any sign of approval or reward that has a positive effect on the child.') The Controlling Parent points the finger, uses height, looks down the nose or shakes the head. The Nurturing Parent will give the pat of approval or the hug of comfort. Similarly, one can compare paralanguage, where the Controlling Parent offers the gentle tones of sympathy or the bright tones of encouragement.

From what we have said about social skills, it will be very clear that TA is to be associated with these – or lack of them. The Parent ego state is very much alive in the grown-up:

- People try to win arguments or intimidate others by employing Parent communication behaviour.

- People comfort others in distress by replaying their memories of Nurturing Parents and what they did for them.

- As we point out elsewhere in this chapter, it is not uncommon for communication problems to be explicable in terms of people communicating Parent-like when the other person does not want to play along with this. Wives do not take kindly to husbands trying to be the Controlling Parent when trying to argue them out of the proposed purchase of a new car. And even the Nurturing Parent can irritate if it is a colleague at work saying 'Let me help you', when the other person wants some straight adult discussion of a problem.

Again, the value of this approach to interpersonal communication is that you can observe it at work for yourself. You can look for the utterances, and can consider whether or not barriers to communication are set up through inappropriate utterances out of an inappropriate ego state (see also 'crossed transactions' later on).

The Adult

The Adult ego state is one that is characterized by detachment and logic. It is, one might say, most obviously represented through the character of Mr Spock in the TV series *Star Trek*, whose dominant characteristic is that of being logical. The Adult is a calculator, a reasoning person, one who is not swayed by emotion. In one sense, the Adult ego state is attractive because it is about truth and objectivity, and because it is a state of self that most obviously signifies sense and maturity. But it is worth remembering that the whole person has something of all three ego states in them and available to them. The Child, with its feelings and curiosity, is important as a foil to the moral arbitrator of the Parent and the impersonal reasoning of the Adult.

In the Adult-state there is no room for assumptions or dreams. The Adult is an information handler and decision maker. The Adult part of us gives and takes in information relevant to the interaction or situation being experienced at a given time. It listens actively as part of that information gathering. It correlates information and evaluates it. It calculates possibilities and probabilities. It thinks about cause and effect. It constructs models of physical and social reality from data. It weighs up new information against previous data and previous models. The Adult-state comes into play when we are problem solving, which happens most obviously when we are at work. But the Adult can be there at any time or place – and probably should be there at times when it tends to slip away from us, such as when we are making our minds up about buying some expensive item of clothing that attracts us, and in situations when logic as well as emotional response should come into play.

Adult behaviour

In terms of characteristic verbal utterances, the Adult asks questions, explores and analyses. The Adult is likely to ask, 'How did it happen?', 'Where is your evidence?', 'Why did you do that?' or 'Who says that is so?' The Adult will deal with problems by saying, 'Let's look at the facts first', rather than, for example, making a Child utterance such as 'I'm fed up with this thing always going wrong'. The Adult will recognize false argument and say something like, 'Fair enough, you're expressing an opinion, but that doesn't make it a fact,' or 'Okay, that's decided then. We'll meet on Thursday at 10.30.'

The nonverbal communication of the Adult is restrained and neutral. It may underscore some point of logic, but will not attempt emotional inflection. In terms of paralanguage, it uses a level tone, using emphasis for meaning, to underline questions or to signal a change of point in an argument.

The body language used in this ego state is also marked by an absence of features, as much as by active distinguishing signs. Posture is alert and responsive, matched by even eye contact, which obeys social conventions already referred to (e.g. turn-taking). Gestures are used to describe, say, physical characteristics. Gaze provides feedback and acknowledgement of the other person. One would expect to note reflective listening techniques. This state is one in which the person is attentive, clearly thinking about what the other person is saying, and shows confidence in their own abilities and their own worth.

KEY QUESTIONS

Describe the behaviour of a grown person who is acting like an Adapted Child.

In what ways could a Controlling Parent or a Nurturing Parent have a negative effect on another person?

6.3 Scripts

Definitions

'Scripts' are an example of long-term structuring of time. A script is described by Berne as a 'life plan'. Like other TA elements, these are developed in one's formative years and thereafter shape all our actions and interactions. It is important to emphasize that scripts are not pre-ordained, though they are very explicable if one looks at the individual's experiences when growing up. They can be changed or modified. Again, it is the case that recognizing one's life script is halfway to changing it. The script does, of course, affect our communication style, how we use communication and how we interpret communication offered by others. People's feelings about themselves and about others will be written into their scripts. These attitudes are also formed through early experiences.

A script, in a general sense, comprises a view of the Self, a view of others and a view of the world, implicit in the plan of action that it represents. It also follows that such views and such a plan will affect attitude and the individual's overall communications style. **Scripts could be described as model stories that the person carries in the head and that will influence every interaction.** So a script shapes the way in which communication is used, as well as the purposes for which it is used.

For example, disappointed parents may be 'telling' their boy child too often that he has 'failed' because he didn't make a home run or should have done better at school assignments. It is not hard to see that the boy is likely to write himself an 'I'm useless' script – and then to fail because he expects to fail. Similarly, if a girl child is always being 'told' that she is good looking and she will have no trouble finding a good guy when she grows up, then her script is likely to incorporate ideas such as 'Beauty is everything'. She is likely to grow up thinking that how she looks is more important than how she is, and to be disappointed when she finds that all the guys she attracts are not 'good'. Scripts are formed in two periods:

- In early childhood, experiences and unconscious decisions form the **'script proper'**. This is when the child is operating in a very emotional way, pre-speech, responding to nonverbal cues. This script is irrational, and forms out of the survival drive or hunger, and things like fear, loss and death. It might be, for instance, that experiences of parents withdrawing their love (which they probably experienced from their own parents) lead the child to internalize the idea that 'I can't trust that person', and so to grow up not trusting others because they fear rejection.

- The **'counter-script'** comes later in childhood, responding to parental performance, to parental demands, to hearing views about subjects such as race. This script counters or modifies the script proper. It is developed largely in response to the verbal injunctions and prohibitions of the parents and tends to embed the views and prejudices of the parents in the child.

Both kinds of script are inside us, and may need to be confronted if they are having a negative effect on our lives. We may repeatedly play out the same storyline, making the same kind of mess of relationships over and over, or seeing ourselves getting nowhere in our careers, feeling frustrated, feeling that something is wrong.

A script will distort one's perception of oneself and others, so that these then match the script beliefs. The script will influence one's view of reality, so that certain aspects of reality – things that are observable to others – are simply discounted in order to strengthen the script. So scripts will incorporate these 'script beliefs', which may need to be challenged. This distortion of reality and of perception may be seen in the performance of redefining transactions (see p. 222).

Payoffs

Scripts, like games, may have payoffs for their uses. And like games, Berne has some alluringly colloquial titles for scripts which, he says, are rather like slogans printed on the script-owner's T-shirt. For example, one such slogan is 'You Can't Trust Anybody'. The contention is that people who live by this script actually seek situations where this thesis will be proved. Then comes their payoff because they can turn round and say, 'I told you so'. (This person is also saying, in effect – looking to the next section – 'I'm OK but they are not OK.'

Script types: winners and losers

In general terms, one could say that **scripts fall into paired categories**. One pair is about optimism and pessimism, in which people write themselves positive or negative views of themselves and of the likely outcomes of any action they may take. Another pair would be described in terms of fatalism and determinism, where the person would script themselves as being either more, or less, in control of their lives and actions. Again, this will have a lot to do with communication style, and with the inflections of paralanguage and body language in particular. Berne refers, here, to **winners and losers**. It is likely that those who see themselves as winners from an early age will have qualities of confidence and drive in their social interaction. These qualities, being about attitude and emotion, are most powerfully expressed through nonverbal behaviours. In other words, we are back to the situation where it can be argued that TA principles and terminology only become real, can only be tested, through observing and interpreting communicative behaviour.

Berne argues that we decide whether we will be winners or losers at a very early age, because of some particular formative experience of success or failure, or perhaps because of what parents say about success or failure. For example, parents might repeatedly use a phrase such as 'Do you want to grow up like your brother?' to a young boy. The older brother is on the streets and in trouble with the police. The parents see this as an awful warning. But for the kid brother the answer to the question might be 'Yes!' because he sees the brother as having a good time and always having money in his pocket. Such is the material from which scripts are constructed. But, we should emphasize, there is much of this kind of material, there are many scripts and they can be reformed during the various phases of maturing for the individual. What we are trying to explain is the nature of the script and its origins. For proper detail you should refer back to Berne's work.

Scripts are limiting

Berne sees scripts and games as not only being predictive but also as being limiting. Even winner scripts are not a good thing because, for example, they may push the **script-driven person** to try to win at all costs, even at the cost of their relationships or of their own lives.

An example of a loser's script is one in which a woman sees herself as a born victim, but one who must keep on suffering to prove that she is a victim. She is the one who marries the violent or abusive male because she can then play games such as 'Kick me' – which is, in Berne's terms, the slogan on the back of her sweatshirt. Of course, on the front she wears a brave face. The script line for the front is about being tough and about being able to keep going for the sake of the marriage. Somewhere in the past she became imbued with parental views about the importance of never giving up at any price. This was a Controlling Parent who allowed no space for autonomy, decision making and simply learning when to give up on a bad deal. She gets what she 'wants' – plenty of kicking to confirm her script and her dominant game plan. But she doesn't deserve this. She needs to be allowed to break free. She needs to feel OK about giving up on the man. A psychotherapist working from a TA perspective would try to get her to recognize this, and to free herself of that script. Of course, to do this the psychotherapist would have to decode her communication and to communicate effectively with her.

Stewart (2000), refers to Goulding and Goulding (1979), who identify twleve common examples of script prohibition that can dominate people's lives.

- I mustn't exist.
- I mustn't be me.
- I mustn't be a child.
- I mustn't grow up.
- I mustn't make it.

- I mustn't do anything.
- I mustn't be important.
- I mustn't belong.
- I mustn't be close.
- I mustn't be well (I mustn't be sane).
- I mustn't think.
- I mustn't feel.

He elaborates on these. For example, 'I mustn't grow up' is explained in terms of parents who do not want to let go because their own Child wants to hold on to a child to play with. Sometimes people with these scripts end up being carers for aged parents. They may be seen to avoid responsibilities, to respond to stress with emotional displays, to want someone else to take charge in their relationships, and even to display child-like communication behaviours and utterances.

Tragic outcomes from scripts

The worst effects of scripts are those that involve things like self-harm. These three worst-case scenarios are summarized as being about 'killing , harming or going crazy'. Counsellors and therapists talk about regaining control and heading off these outcomes by a process of 'closing the hatches', in which the person has to genuinely deny such kinds of script lines, from an Adult position. For tragic outcomes especially, and for other kinds of prohibition and negative behaviour, the idea is to stop the person from storing up bad feelings and, in effect, beating their head against the proverbial brick wall. To recognize the script line can start a process through which it is deleted. Just as communication has helped construct the script in childhood, so more communication can rewrite the script. Bad scripts are not inevitable or perpetual.

KEY QUESTIONS

Describe, as honestly as you can, the main features of your own life script.

Explain how a life script might impede the personal growth of an individual, or might have a negative effect on their relationships.

6.4 Transactions

We have already described the transaction as a basic unit of social interaction in which some verbal or nonverbal signal is offered, recognized and responded to between people in different or similar ego states. Transactions can be as brief and ephemeral as that nod of recognition that British people offer one another as they pass each other in their place of work for the nth time. Or one may have an elaborate series of transactions through an animated conversation, with switches of ego states and their associated types of utterance. The point of looking at transactions in communication terms is that they are the act of communication itself. Description of transactions also leads one to an understanding of why conversations can have positive or negative outcomes:

- There are two dominant types of transaction recognized in TA theory, the 'complementary' and the 'crossed' transaction. Berne describes these as working on one level.

- But he also recognizes those transactions that involve a sense of irony, innuendo and phatic communication (see Glossary). He identifies these as working on two levels and calls them 'angular' or 'duplex' transactions.

We go on to give a brief explanation of these transactions below, each illustrated by a figure. You will also find written examples in the first two Case situations at the end of this chapter.

You need to bear in mind that each person in an interaction has the three ego states present, each with the potential to influence the style of communication that is used. The key question is, will the styles adopted match one another or not? Will they continue to match through the interaction?

Complementary transactions

A complementary transaction is one in which the styles match because the ego states are complementary (see Fig. 6.2). The ego states balance one another out. Someone opens a conversation out of a particular ego state; the other person recognizes this and feeds back communication that complements that first utterance. And so it goes on for as long as the participants choose. They have adjusted to one another. This is not to make any judgement

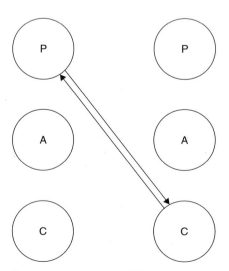

Fig. 6.2 A model for a complementary transaction (after Berne 1972)

on what they say or how well they express themselves. Nor is it even to approve how they choose to match one another. So, for example, one might have complementary Adult-to-Adult talk between two engineers discussing the cause of a pipeline failure. Or one might have a Parent–Child transaction in which a supervisor speaks as Controlling Parent and a clerk responds as Adapted Child:

Supervisor: You ought to pull yourself together. You can't go on coming in late.
Clerk: I'm sorry, you're right. I promise it won't happen again.

You might feel that the clerk should not have responded in this way, but the fact is that the response matched and the communication continued smoothly. With reference to the model we have a transaction in which the lines remain parallel. You might consider what other kinds of complementary transaction there could be and work out appropriate communication behaviours. For example, two people swapping zany jokes might be thought to be operating as Child to Child. Two people exchanging instant (but unsupported) opinions about the moral decline of the young could be Parent to Parent.

Crossed transactions

A crossed transaction is one in which our model's lines cross and the ego states are not complementary (see Fig. 6.3). Because it can illustrate and explain breakdowns in communication, this transaction is one of the most useful pieces of TA theory. In this transaction the response to an utterance – whether at the beginning of or partway through an exchange – does not match the style and ego state of that utterance. This would be the case where the young person does not respond as expected to some parental injunction, such as 'Don't fiddle with that toy or you'll break it!' A reply such as 'I'm trying to find out why the motor isn't working' is perfectly reasonable and Adult. Sadly, it is quite likely to invoke a

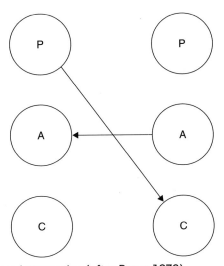

Fig. 6.3 A model for a crossed transaction (after Berne 1972)

hardening of the parental approach: 'Don't argue with me! Put it down when you're told to.' Such are the opening gambits of family rows. Looking back to the supervisor and the clerk, you decide here what is the nature of the cross if the clerk says, 'I am together. But I've had some problems to deal with.'

Would it still be a crossed transaction if the clerk were to say, 'Get off my back. Anyway, you're no angel about timekeeping yourself. So don't preach to me.' Is there also a switch of ego states here?

Angular transactions

An angular transaction is one in which on one level the speaker talks as if to one ego state, but covertly is addressing another ego state (see Fig. 6.4). People who try to wind up others are practised in this kind of double dealing. On the face of it, a statement such as 'Charlie was having a good time at last night's party' may sound innocuous. But if the speaker is talking to Charlie's girlfriend who thought he was at home, then they may not get an Adult response, such as 'Oh, I wonder why he didn't tell me that he was going'. We leave you to imagine what the more likely reply would be, and what ego state it comes out of!

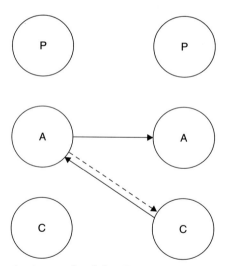

Fig. 6.4 A model for an angular transaction (after Berne 1972)

Duplex transactions

The duplex transaction is one in which the exchange takes place in parallel on two levels (see Fig. 6.5). These may be described as the **overt social level** and the **covert psychological level**. In this case two people may appear to talk to one another as Adult to Adult, but in fact there is another level of meaning and exchange in operation. For example, consider a group of people who are trying to help one of their members install an alarm system in his or her

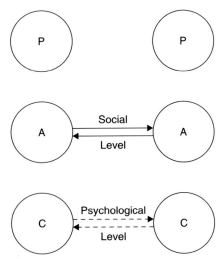

Fig. 6.5 A model for duplex transaction (after Berne 1972)

home. Two of the group may be coming up with all kinds of adult utterances: 'Why don't we try wiring the sensors round this way?' or 'I heard it was best to put the pressure pads under a window.' Now, this kind of talk exchanged between the two seems unexceptional. But if it happens at a considerable rate, and if the other group members know that the two concerned both pride themselves on their practical knowledge, then they may perceive that unspoken psychological level of transaction, which is basically about competition. They are talking Adult, but on a Child level are really saying, 'I'm smarter than you are!'

The most common example of a duplex transaction is the 'girl meets boy, and they are attracted to each other' situation. In this case the conversation may be on an apparently Adult social level: 'What did you think of that TV show about the couple who adopted a child?', and so on. But the two people concerned may be very well aware that underneath the reasoned talk they are also operating an emotional transaction.

In fact, this is where an all-embracing communication approach is helpful, because we would say that for this covert transaction to take place there must still be some communicative signs that make up this transaction, and which one could identify. In other words, it is not just a matter of vague intuition that the couple are communicating emotionally, Child to Child, saying, 'I like you and would like to know you better'. The covert level would be nonverbal. The couple would be talking through two channels and in two ego states at once. The reasoned verbal level is what apparently justifies the contact. But the important messages, so far as they are concerned, are being fed back and forth through body language. In effect, it is like carrying on two conversations at once. There are two sets of transaction, or two levels and means of communication. In this way, one can see a demonstration of the fact that principles of transactional analysis and of communication are complementary, and inform one another.

Redefining transactions

A development in TA following Berne's original ideas looks at how transactions may start in one mode and then shift. The following exchanges are characterized by ways in which the speaker, in Child-state, shifts ground to avoid a response to questions or a topic that they find threatening.

Tangential transactions

In this case the person goes off at a tangent, shifting the issue from where the exchange started.

Person A: Do you think we should be spending more time together?
Person B: I don't know how I'm going to cope with all the pressure at work.

(B's response is not wholly irrelevant, but it is a Child, shifting to talk about its concerns, and not addressing the issue raised by A.)

Blocking transactions

In this case, the issue is avoided by starting an argument about it, usually by quibbling about definitions.

Person A: Do you think we should be spending more time together?
Person B: How much time do you want? I mean, there's time and time, isn't there?

KEY QUESTIONS

Write a conversation that illustrates a crossed transaction.

Explain how an understanding of transactions would be useful for a trainee teacher.

6.5 Hungers

Just as Berne's notion of a transaction bears close analogy with a single act of communication, so also his idea of **hungers** looks very much like the notion of communication needs. In both cases the essential idea is that any act of communication, including those that may be defined as social, must be motivated by something. There must be an impulse, a drive to initiate that communication or transaction.

We will summarize analogies between TA and communication study at the end of this chapter. For the moment it is enough to say that the three hungers that Berne argues drive all transactions and can be easily compared with types of communication need.

- **Sensation hunger assumes a need in all humans for stimulus.** Social interaction provides such a stimulus and satisfies the hunger.

- **Recognition hunger is described as a need for sensations provided by another human being**. It is perhaps rather more personal than the general sensation hunger. It is about personal recognition from an individual.

- **Structure hunger** is about a need to create order and be a part of social structures – hence the drive for humans to form groups.

One could say, by way of summary, that these three points may explain why people have an inbuilt need to talk to one another, why they want to form special relationships with one other person and why they want to be part of groups. In other words, this is an explanation of why communication takes place.

6.6 Time-structuring

Another premise of TA is that social interaction is organized by people over periods of time in various ways. These ways of organization have at least two general characteristics:

- one is the time period of the interaction: long- or short-term
- the other is the degree of habit or predictability involved in the interaction.

Transactions occur within these various types of time-structured activity. You will need to read the books by Berne that we have already referred to if you are interested in going into this in detail. However, we intend looking at one kind of short-term and one kind of long-term activity in the next sections. It is worth grasping the point of time-structures here because, once more, we can see useful analogies with mainstream communication theory.

How time-structures relate to communication

An example of how time-structures relate to communication is that the principle of time-structures suggests that communication is organized within units of activity. These units are more or less predictable in their content, in the nature of interaction, in the use of communication. For instance, Berne describes **rituals** as a short-term activity, and there is no doubt that these are characterized by extremely repetitive patterns and uses of communication. (**Work** is described as another short-term activity, but this is less predictable in communication terms.)

In one sense TA theory and communication theory reinforce one another's ideas. In another sense they throw different kinds of light on basic processes of social interaction that concern both approaches. Berne sees rituals as being 'highly stylized exchanges': entirely bound, one might say, by conventions. Berne argues that they are a safe form of interaction, which may have the merit of giving strokes as part of the behaviour, but which are also limiting. In Communication terms we would be interested first in the fact that Berne effectively confirms the proposition that much communication is learnt (nurture not nature!). We would also be interested in the content and treatment of relevant exchanges:

'Morning, Mrs Brown. How are you this morning?'
'Oh, I'm fine. Terrible weather again isn't it?'
'Yes, really dreadful. Thanks.

There are covert messages beneath these habitual exchanges. There is information about relationship, understandings, social bonding – whether one calls these exchanges transactions or communication. Communication theorists may be more interested in the production, process and effect of such exchanges, while Berne is more interested in the psychology behind them, and in the implications for those involved. But, in the end, the one approach informs the other.

To take one last example, Berne refers to **pastimes** as the kind of social action typified by people's fairly predictable exchanges when meeting each other at social events, for example:

'Hello, my name's Michael. I'm a client of Peter Mountford. Do you know him?'
'Oh, hello, yes, I know Peter. Do you know his brother, John?'

Berne is interested in the way that we organize such interactions, in the extent to which we may put ourselves in a kind of straitjacket by repeating some formula of conversation. This is very useful because it deals with the significance of certain kinds of use of communication. Again, we might also see this as a way of recognizing **conventions** in practice, or of exploring **covert messages**.

So now let's move on to look in more detail at two particular kinds of time-structuring described by Berne, both of which can tell us quite a lot about how and why we use communication. These are 'Games' and 'Racketeering'.

6.7 Games

There is really no substitute for reading Berne's deservedly popular book *Games People Play* (1964). This offers many examples of different types of games, and says a lot about human interaction and motivation. It talks about ways in which we try to manipulate each other, or try to achieve some sort of psychological victory or satisfaction – what we mentioned earlier as (in Berne's terms) the payoff. But the main characteristics of games can be explained fairly easily, and these enable one to appreciate how they are superb examples of communication in action. An examination of games tells us a great deal about how and why we use verbal and nonverbal language.

Games are an example of short-term structuring of time. They are a form of social interaction. Berne describes games as 'sets of ulterior transactions, repetitive in nature, with a well-defined psychological payoff'. He says that 'all games involve a con' because the players, or the initiating player, are pretending to say and mean one thing, when in fact they are really manipulating the interaction and the other person towards some kind of conclusion which pleases them. **Usually a game does involve one person trying to 'put something across' another person**. Berne has actually created a whole vocabulary to describe game elements.

Game terminology

The victim in a game is called the **mark**. A weakness in the mark that is used to **hook** the mark is called the **gimmick (G)**. This gimmick may be something like ill temper or fear of conflict, which the manipulator arouses and uses in order to 'put one across' the mark. The **switch (S)** describes the point in the interaction when the manipulator uses some phrase that changes the direction of the conversation so that the mark is caught out and feels that he or she has been made to feel stupid or inferior in some respect. It is also at this point that the **crossup (X)** occurs. This describes the confusion that the mark feels at having been caught and may also be represented by confusion and breakdown in the conversation itself. The end of it all is the **payoff (P)** when the manipulator has scored a point (their payoff) and the mark collects a feeling of inferiority (their payoff).

The two important communication elements are first the **Con (C)**, which is what the first player says to the other one when trying to hook them. Then there is the **response (R)** that the second player makes if hooked.

So, picking up on our key letters above, one can actually express a game in terms of a formula that summarizes how one game element leads to another. That is:

$$C + G = R \rightarrow S \rightarrow X \rightarrow P$$

Examples of games

Berne gives his games colloquial titles that summarize their dominant characteristic, and which employ some key phrase from the game – perhaps the switch line. The archetypal game is called 'Why don't you – Yes but.'

In this simple game the manipulator uses an excuse or raises an objection to every suggestion the victim makes, so that eventually the victim is blocked into silence and is made to feel powerless or useless. He may also feel angry at having been drawn into what in the end seems to be a pointless conversation. If he expresses that anger then the manipulator has gained a double payoff by making the victim lose his temper as well. What the manipulator does not want, of course, is for the victim to say something like, 'I don't think you seriously want help'. In this case the game would be blown, and, to an extent, the victim would have turned the tables on the manipulator. To be able to do this we need to able to recognize when others are playing games with us.

The conversation for this game might run something like the following:

'I'm feeling really depressed. I owe three assignments and I just can't seem to get down to any of them.'
'Why don't you take a break and go out for a good time? It could make you feel better.'
'Yes, but I'm so broke I really can't afford to go out this week.'
'Well, why don't you go and see the teachers and ask for a postponement?'
'Yes, but I did that before. I can't ask them again.'

'So why don't you ask Jane for some help? I know that she's up to date with her work.'

'Yes, but she's got problems of her own. She just split up with her boyfriend.'

. . . and so on, until the conversation dies with the victim feeling a failure and the manipulator feeling smug and vindicated in the excuses for not attempting the assignments.

Berne groups games in various categories, such as **life games**. In all groups one can see certain archetypal forms of game giving rise to versions special to that group. One archetypal game is called 'Now I've got you, you son of a bitch', in which the manipulator 'catches out' the victim in some way, almost always as a result of a situation that has been deliberately engineered in which the victim is led to the edge of an elephant pit.

One variation that Berne describes is a **marital game** called 'Frigid woman'. This one is an interesting example because it certainly doesn't have to depend on a conversation, though talk is likely to enter into it. Explaining this in narrative form (because it can be dominantly about nonverbal communication), the sequence look something like this.

> The wife makes it clear that sexual relations are out of bounds and repugnant to her. The husband accepts this situation. The husband is the **mark**. The wife then proceeds to use her **gimmick** to hook the husband. She offers nonverbal signs of sexual availability, but nothing too overt. These signs, which are often ambiguous in meaning, such as bath towel that may or may not intentionally have been allowed to slip, increase in frequency and effect. Finally, the husband decides that an offer has been made and proceeds to take it up. At this point the wife **pulls the switch**. It may even be the first time that a verbal transaction takes place. She asks him what he thinks he is doing, or something like this. The payoff for him is that he is left looking stupid, is guilty of breaking the 'rules' of their relationship, and may even feel guilty about his sexual drives. The wife's payoff is that she has 'caught him out' and got a moral buzz from doing this. The point of the payoff is emphasized if he starts protesting.
>
> (Berne 1964)

One interesting aspect of the switch is that it puts the victim in what has been called elsewhere a 'double bind'. The victim is damned if he does and damned if he doesn't. If the husband persists in his advances after the switch, he may not be playing the game as perceived by the wife, but he is still likely to feel guilty, and his behaviour can be used by her against him, perhaps in some later argument. Equally, he cannot win by saying nothing or even by apologizing. It is too late. Even trying to expose the game by discussing her behaviour and their relationship is likely to lead to a destructive argument if she persists in her moral position.

Game roles

We have been using words like 'victim' to describe the behaviour of people in games. In fact, it is proposed that **there are three main roles one can see in games and, indeed, in scripts**.

- There are **persecutors**, who are usually the initiators and manipulators in a game, who try to make someone else suffer.

- There are **victims**, who may be the victim of a manipulator, but who may also try to manipulate others by claiming victimization when this is not actually true.

- There are **rescuers**, who can be helpful people, but who again may actually manipulate others by trying to make them grateful and dependent by doing things that are not wanted or asked for.

In fact, manipulative game roles can always be described as **illegitimate roles**. But there are also **legitimate roles** and role behaviour in life where the role player is not getting some kind of secret 'kick' and payoff from the transaction. People really are victims if they are denied promotion at work because of their gender. Counsellers can be seen as legitimate rescuers if they are helping other people to sort out their lives. And, although it seems a strange way of putting it, people who have a socially endorsed position that demands that they control the behaviour of others are actually acting legitimately. For example, a judge, a teacher or a parent may be seen as persecutor, but it is accepted that it is okay for them to behave this way as part of 'agreed' socialization.

Games and relationships

Games are negative and are destructive to relationships. The game initiator usually does not feel OK about themselves (see below) and is trying to create a relationship that helps them take out anger on others. This helps them feel better by making others feel worse – and this then reinforces their negative feelings about themselves because these are what they want to wallow in.

Games are about dominance and submission in relationships. They may be about the struggle to achieve this on the part of one person or another. They may also be about attempts to reinforce an existing situation. Those who use an illness or a disability in order to get a payoff from others are enacting the illegitimate role of victim. They are exploiting their condition. When it is an ageing parent who is the person that is ill it can be hard for their carers to acknowledge that they are the victim of a game. But still this may be the case.

It is also hard for people to admit that relationships based on habitual games are also flawed. It is very easy for others especially to say something like, 'Oh, they're always like that. He doesn't mean to hurt her. They always kiss and make up after it is over.' But this does not alter the fact that games are being played. It also suggests that the people involved are locked into bad scripts, as discussed earlier.

KEY QUESTIONS

Write the dialogue for a game that you have had first-hand experience of (perhaps a variation on one that you have read about!). Try using the formula given in this book.

Why do people play games, and why shouldn't they?

Racketeering

This is the second kind of time-structuring. Again, it is manipulative and something like games, but without the switch. In this case people are said to have 'racket feelings' which they want to be 'stroked' by others (see English 1976). So they are manipulative towards others, usually out of a Child-state. Getting the strokes is the payoff. One may link this with the kind of person who is a victim seeking out a rescuer. One may link it with games such as 'Poor me', where the game player is out for sympathy – for having their Child-state and (for instance) some sense of 'being hard done by' stroked and so reinforced.

Racket feelings are often learned in childhood. Racket feelings are not genuine feelings but displaced feelings, substituting for what are called 'authentic feelings'. Authentic feelings are about emotions such as fear, sadness and happiness. A racket feeling might be expressed as, for example, anger towards a parent who, the person has convinced themself, has in some way let them down in childhood – perhaps by walking away from a failing marriage. The anger conceals an authentic feeling of great sadness for something that has been lost. These substitute emotions are used to manipulate others, to get a response. One has to distinguish quite finely between the two sorts of feeling. For example, sadness because you are grieving for a loss is an authentic feeling. But 'putting on a sad face' to get attention is not authentic.

These emotional performances are also called 'rackety displays'. The display may be detected in more than observable communication. It may be seen in how people talk about their internal states. This may link for instance with ideas about hypochondria – people who talk a great deal about how 'bad' they are feeling, may in effect be looking for attention from the Parent. In extreme cases, actually being ill is also okay because at least it still gets attention – any attention is better than none. Rackety displays are repetitive patterns of script behaviour.

Another form of display is described as 'fantasizing' best- and worst-case scenarios. People may have permanent fantasies (as opposed to passing wishes) about their ideal male or female partner. These show a disconnection from reality and from the Adult-state. This is tied up with their script and script beliefs. For example, a female in a given relationship may project a fantasy about the reliable, resourceful male onto her partner. Her life script describes her as being in a relationship with a competent male. In fact, the male may be quite incompetent at holding down jobs or at managing practical tasks.

However the rackety display is put across, if it gets the response the person wants, then it reinforces the internal beliefs and ensures that more displays will happen.

6.8 I'm OK – You're OK

The phrase 'I'm OK – you're OK' is one of what TA describes as **'life positions'**. There are four of these positions (see Fig. 6.6), as follows:

1. I'm not OK – you're OK

2. I'm not OK – you're not OK

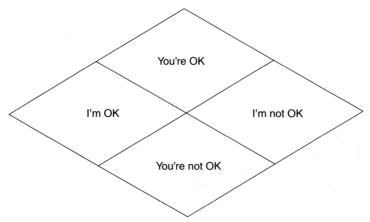

Fig. 6.6 The OK diamond – four states of being

3. I'm OK – you're not OK

4. I'm OK – you're OK

It should be said at the outset that, like scripts, positions are laid down in childhood but they are not set in concrete. It is possible to change your position and your script.

> Our childhood position was arrived at pre-verbally and was based on feelings about how life seemed to us then. The I'm OK – You're OK position is based less on feelings than on conscious thought, faith and the wager of action. It is a decision to reject our childhood assumption and to assert that we are no longer helpless, dependent children.
>
> (Harris and Harris 1995)

'I'm OK – you're OK' is a good position to be in. It means that one feels good about oneself and about the other person. **The significance of being OK or Not OK is that it shapes and predicts a person's approach to interaction – and so, of course, to the communication that is the essence of that interaction.**

We first need to acknowledge the fact that feelings are real for the person who experiences them. Whatever their source, however strange they may seem to others, they are there. Harris and Harris propose that, in fact, every human starts off feeling Not OK because of the birth trauma, and that the destructive nature of games can be traced back to this life position and a desire to work it out. It is also asserted that we do have complete memories of childhood, even if we do not recall them consciously. Harris and Harris (1995) say that however 'good' the parent, the child will have negative feelings because there are bound to be some prohibitions in the course of growing up, never mind episodes when the parent becomes stressed or angry. The baby human wants to get the OK person (parent) to be good to them because the baby feels Not OK. Looked at from one point of view, it becomes another way of explaining how communication starts. If the baby is going to get the grown-up to do something they have to get this across. And if they are going to know what the grown-up feels then they have to recognize and decode communication.

Positions and scripts

Furthermore, Harris and Harris say that position 1 of the first year of life is then either confirmed in years 2 and 3, or the child shifts to position 2 (I'm not OK – you're not OK) or position 3 (I'm OK – you're not OK). But **to reach position 4 (I'm OK – you're OK) there has to be some conscious decision, and not everyone makes this shift**. In other words, many people go through life feeling that either they and/or others are Not OK. This rather gloomy state of affairs does, of course, affect attitudes, relationships and the communication that is part of these. Such life positions are fundamental to the kind of script that a person writes for herself or himself. One half of the equation writes a script, the other half a **counter-script**. This would mean that for position 1 a person might write a script in which they punished themselves for feeling Not OK. Or it might mean that they write a counter-script in which they try to emulate (and win the approval of) the OK person. They are always trying to win the approval of some grown-up, who in later life might be the girlfriend or the boss.

This desire for approval has everything to do with parents. So often the person whom we are really trying to please is the remembered parent inside ourselves. They have inspired the Parent-state that we have internalized and the parent is seen as being OK by the child. It may well be that as grown-ups we have to use the Adult inside ourselves to revisit memories of our parents and to deal with that inner Parent-state. We might have to recognize that our parents were not, in fact, OK all the time.

For a start, they can send us mixed messages, not least if they themselves are actually in conflict – as opposed to having different positions on some issues in life. If the child has conflicting parents then he or she is in a no-win situation because whatever they do they cannot please both parents. And then there are the 'Don't' messages that we have referred to above. Some of these messages are about the material world – 'Don't play with matches'. But over-protective parents can induce a state of mind in the child where he or she ends up never doing anything remotely risky or exciting. And it is the psychological, inferred 'Don't' messages that are the most insidious: 'Don't be child-like, ever' (because big boys don't cry, because mummy needs a grown-up little helper now daddy isn't well, and so on).

Shifting positions – consequences

One important reason for shifting position might be to do with whether or not the child receives 'strokes' from the parent. This idea of offering rewards and approval to others has elsewhere been described as a social skill. Put colloquially, being pleasant to other people improves their feelings for you, your feelings for yourself and the quality of communication between you. Nowhere is this more true than in childhood. There is overwhelming clinical evidence that love and affection are far more important to the development of children than are physical comforts (within reason, of course). Jules Henry, in his book *Culture Against Man* (1973), has described movingly and tragically how well cared-for middle-class children nevertheless were disturbed and withdrawn for lack of physical and verbal affection.

It is, in fact, important both to receive strokes and to learn how to give them. The most important strokes are those that we receive in childhood, from parents. But as adults we also need others in order to receive this kind of recognition. In some respects one might say that we form relationships to receive strokes on a reliable basis from someone else. Such strokes may come in the form of verbal praise, or through small gestures such as being touched approvingly.

Not to receive strokes as a child is damaging and can generate negative scripts. Harris and Harris describe 'unhappy achievers', who have had strokes held back in various ways. One example is the perfectionist parent who is never satisfied with their child's achievements. Their communication is always about, 'Well, why didn't you come first, come top, get one hundred per cent'. For these parents, you could always do better, good is never excellent enough. And if this verbal behaviour is reinforced by the withheld smile, the withheld hug, then the child is likely to turn into a driven and troubled adult.

A child who does not receive messages about being OK and being loved, mainly in terms of body contact, may decide to change its life position. It may shift to position 2 (I'm not OK – you're not OK). In this case a possible life script could involve self-destructive and disturbed behaviours, the sort which will cause the child to end up in institutions because this individual feels bad about everyone, including him or herself. Their particular time-structuring is an extreme one identified as **'withdrawal'**. In effect, this person's communication may break down or become incoherent. This person cannot make meanings effectively because social interaction is too painful to bear.

This area of TA, therefore, helps explain why communications do not take place or why some people seem unable to interact according to the social conventions learnt and used by most of us. Examples of this are protective strategies used by people in response to that inner voice of the parent who has used the same strategies to deal with perceived threats. Such strategies are withdrawal, intellectualization, intimidation and ritual behaviours. For instance, people who use intellectualization may well fear feelings so they rationalize about situations or about something another person said, so that they do not really have to deal with that person's fears, or even their expressions of love. An example of a ritual (repetitive behaviour pattern) might be when a person suddenly discovers the need to go to the toilet or make a cup of tea whenever their partner or child starts to open up emotionally loaded topics (for example, talk about sex).

Similar conditions of upbringing may cause a shift to position 3 (I'm OK – you're not OK). The child may not just lack stroking, it may have been positively brutalized. There is no doubt that for such a child, others are Not OK. It has decided that others are to blame for its situation, but it also decides that it is not to blame. The Adult in the developing mind reasons this out. So this child writes scripts in which this can also lead to destructive behaviours. At the least it predicates a tendency to paranoia. It may also lead to criminal and violent behaviours, easily justified when one believes that others are wrong anyway. Someone in this position could become very successful in material terms. Their feeling about being OK in themselves would lead to very positive communication traits, where they might talk with confidence and assurance. Their attitude that others are not OK might lead them to be pretty ruthless in business deals, for example, so bringing material success and further confirming a view of themselves as being OK. There might well be arrogance in their communication style. This kind of person might behave 'correctly' but would not give strokes to others.

It is a TA precept that, even with the possibility of achieving position 4 through self-knowledge, still one must remember that the other positions are around. In particular the 'I'm not OK' attitude is always there as an early experience. It can be dealt with, but cannot be simply wiped off a slate. Put rather simply, it means that if one listens to the way that people talk, even some perfectly pleasant people, one might recognize anyone dropping into one of the two positions in which they are Not OK.

Harris and Harris refer to Schiff (1975) when they emphasize the importance of positive messages, of 'dos' as much as 'don'ts'. These are very important when coming from parents. Three key messages are:

1. You can solve problems.

2. You can think.

3. You can do things.

These are all about autonomy and bringing out the Adult in the young person.

Dealing with it

Harris and Harris also suggest other ways of dealing with, for instance, the unhelpful parent within us. One of their 'parent stoppers' is to 'break the body set'. In this case they are suggesting that the tensions and anxieties created by a controlling parent within us are expressed through nonverbal behaviours – clenched jaw muscles. If we are self-aware enough to identify such signs of tension, then we can consciously control them – relaxation. And then (as principles of NLP would agree) changing our outer behaviour affects our inner state.

They also talk about ways in which people handle confusion – what we might also call stress. In this case they describe four unhelpful things that people often do, which we now explain (with adaptations):

- they withdraw from the situation (do not deal with it)

- they postpone action (put off dealing with it)

- they speed up everything (doing a lot in order to suppress it)

- they become passive (let the situation roll over them).

Helpful ways of dealing with confusion are (among others):

- think – respond rationally through the Adult, do not let the emotional Child take over

- ask for clarification – get the other person to talk and explain, rather than just going into anger or panic mode

- write – put on paper the things that are causing confusion and anxiety: sometimes these turn out not to be what originally got you going, and solutions seem clearer when it is all laid out in writing.

6.9 TA and interpersonal communication

To recognize positions such as feeling Not OK in action is to understand why a person talks the way they do, because one is able to infer something about their self-image and self-esteem. In such cases recognition of nonverbal behaviour is crucial – the signs of emotion and feelings. Here, the idea of semiotics and transactions come together. The sign carries a (unspecified) meaning. A transaction is an exchange of signs. The semiotician and the analyst are both concerned to identify signs and to find ways of ascribing meaning (because of what other signs suggest, for example). The semiotician talks about connotations, or 'real and hidden meanings'. This is what the TA analyst is after, too.

To recognize such positions in oneself is to achieve some self-knowledge and potential for change. There is an intimate relationship between the Self and acts of communication, between inward and outward aspects of a person. TA may conceptualize the Self in terms of ego states, where social psychology and communication studies talk about personality, but the principle of identifying some kind of self-construct remains the same. Similarly, when Berne talks about 'hungers', others may talk about needs. But once more, there is a common principle – to recognize driving forces within. Change in either the inner or outer aspects of a person means a change in the other. If one is looking for change, in a sense it does not matter which of the two one changes first. Control of social interaction means control of communication. It is perfectly possible to learn at least some uses or patterns of communication that represent social skills. But the content is bound up with the form. So it would be our contention that in learning what to say – for example, in order to gain others' approval or to express approval towards them – one cannot help but learn the values and beliefs that motivate that communication. Put another way, we are saying that there is a limit to people's ability to say something without meaning it and without being caught out. All forms of words are used for the first time at some point. With practice their meaning becomes really felt.

Scripts are about who we are and how we behave, and so is the study of interpersonal communication. In that scripts include ideas about feeling OK or Not OK, we would argue that one can also make a comparison with ideas about self-esteem. To feel OK is clearly to rate oneself positively. One might also draw an analogy with what we have already said about positive or negative self-image.

And, finally, we would argue that TA games are pretty much like communication strategies in action. They are manipulative and try to achieve what one could describe as negative outcomes to the interaction.

In all the above ways, TA gives us another angle on social interaction. It provides valuable insights and helps reinforce ideas such as those about the connection between social performance and inner states of being.

6.10 TA skills

TA skills are based on essential perceptual skills – recognizing what is going on with another person and recognizing our own behaviour. One then has to do something about what has been perceived. We would also advise our readers to be cautious and humble in making judgements and in taking action. It is possible to obtain specific training in TA skills and this takes time and care. So, in what follows we are trying only to describe a few skills and to suggest basic actions that may improve your dealings with others:

- Try to tune yourself to **be aware of the more obvious verbal and nonverbal utterances of others that signify one ego state or another**. Look out for the most obvious cues, such as the parental 'ought' and 'must' or child-like shouting or arm waving.

- Stay tuned to your own utterances and try to control both your NVB and what you say, so that you **represent the ego state you want**. For example, if you think it is important to be Adult then stick to the relevant nonverbal control and reasoned statements that you think are right, and do not respond to someone else's Child by being child-like yourself.

- Having become aware of the ego state of another, **try to make an immediate decision about how you want to sound in response**. If someone else is giving off Parent signs, you do not have to respond as a Child or compete in trying to out-Parent them.

- Think about how others have been dealing with you and you with them – everyone does! But in particular, **think if you have been playing games**. If you have, consider why, and whether you might not get on better if you were more straightforward in what you say. If you **think that certain other people tend to play games with you**, perhaps to make you feel bad if you do not do what they want, then try to sort out what it is in you that lets you become victim, and what sort of things they say to put you in a double bind. Ideally, one notices a game as someone is playing it on you, but you have to become quite skilled to actually pick this up as it is happening.

- When you have sorted the hook and the mark, then decide what you are going to do about it. **The skill is to break up someone's game without causing a row**, if you can avoid it. With hardened game players this may be unavoidable, though all you have to say is something like, 'I can see you are trying to get me to do X and I'm not prepared to go along with it.' But you may also recognize that friends are playing games because they want to make themselves feel OK by making you feel Not OK. Because they are friends, you might want to use some basic assertiveness skills, for example, 'I don't want to do X, but why don't we do Y tomorrow?'

- Finally, we think it is worth trying to **practise the skill of analysing your own life script**, which may include your own games. Nobody really wants to be the victim of a bad script. You need to recognize habitual ways in which you deal with situations and with others, to recognize how you feel about your life and about the future. For example, do you put things off a lot? Do you tend to assume that you cannot cope with situations? Do you assume that things will go wrong, and avoid actions because of this? Then it may be that you have cast yourself in the general life role of victim. It may be that you often act out of the Adapted Child ego state.

- Then you can decide whether or not you want to practise further skills in changing and controlling how you deal with others and deal with situations. You can try consciously to do things differently. You can tell yourself that you will not make excuses, you will say 'yes' sometimes and not 'no' every time and you will politely refuse to do things that you do not really want to do.

The situations in which these TA skills may apply are, of course, as various as the wide number of encounters that we have in everyday life. However, it may be useful to recognize a few typical situations. For example:

- Encounters in education, at any level, throw up the Parent–Child transaction. The problem is that this is often not appropriate, especially at higher levels, where the encouragement of intellectual skills means precisely that one would expect Adult encounters.

- In friendship groups it is not uncommon to find people who play games, in order to achieve and maintain power and status in the group. In the workplace, people's life scripts may emerge as they talk about their jobs and their aspirations, and as the patterns of the ways in which they deal with situations and people at work emerge over months and years.

You may find it useful to look for examples of TA in action, out of these situations. Also with people you know and trust, you could discuss TA concepts and the related communication behaviour of others and of yourself. The acquisition of knowledge and understanding is one kind of skill. The use of these, their application, is another kind of skill.

Review

You should have learnt the following things from this chapter:

6.1 Introduction

- Why it is useful to study TA as a student of communication?

6.2 Ego states – Parent, Adult, Child

- These are Parent, Adult, Child, with different variations on Child and Parent.
- They are characterized by certain uses of verbal and nonverbal communication.
- These are one way of describing the personality, which is likely to influence all communication.

6.3 Scripts

- A script is a life plan formed in childhood and carried into adult life.
- Scripts, like games, have payoffs for the user – which explains why they are used.

- Scripts are generally optimistic or pessimistic, are about winners or losers.
- Games are chosen to fit scripts and to confirm their plan.
- Scripts influence the communication style adopted by the individual.
- Scripts limit the autonomy of the individual and are best revealed and exorcized.
- Scripts can be revealed by analysing the communication (transactions) of the people concerned.
- Scripts are laid down early in life (when they are known as the 'script proper'), and then modified in later childhood (the 'counter-script').
- Scripts may involve prohibitions against 'what we must not do'.
- Scripts often come out of needing to seek the approval of our parents.

6.4 Transactions

- There are four types of transaction: complementary, crossed, angular, duplex.
- They involve an exchange between various combinations of the ego states in any interaction between people.
- Crossed transactions offer an excellent explanation of the causes of breakdown in communication between people.
- Angular and duplex transactions help explain how we may communicate on two levels at once, and offer both covert and overt messages.
- Tangential and blocking transactions are used by speakers in a Child ego state in order to redefine a transaction to their own convenience.

6.5 Hungers

- There are three of these, described as sensation, recognition and structure hungers.
- These hungers underlie all transactions and even the development of ego states in the child.
- Hungers are the equivalent of needs in communication studies.

6.6 Time-structuring

- Social interaction – and, by implication, communication – is organized in long and short blocks of time.
- Short blocks are described as rituals, games or work, among other things.
- Long blocks are scripted.
- Such structuring reinforces communication ideas, such as that of the convention.

6.7 Games

- Games are short blocks of interaction in which one person tries to manipulate the other and gain some psychological advantage.
- Games are designed to make the victim of the interaction feel stupid, inadequate and frustrated, but to make the manipulator feel good.
- Games describe communication used in conflict and, when analysed, may reveal the sources of the conflict.
- Games may be referred to aspects of communication theory, such as covert messages, or the issues of when communication is intentional or not.
- Racketeering (or rackety displays) is about emotional manipulation of others, communicating out of a Child ego state in order to get strokes.

6.8 I'm OK – you're OK

This describes an ideal life position for every person, which can only be achieved through coming to terms with the Not OK position which every child is thought to adopt.

There are three other positions:
- I'm not OK – you're OK
- I'm not OK – you're not OK
- I'm OK – you're not OK.
- Receiving strokes is important if the child is to feel OK about others.
- These positions shift as the individual matures.
- Some positions cause the individual to become disturbed or criminal.
- These positions create scripts and counter-scripts.
- All these life positions are to be recognized through the communication behaviour of the individuals concerned.
- In that they are fundamentally about self-esteem, so these life positions are bound to affect the uses of communication by that individual.

6.9 TA and interpersonal communication

There are a number of comparisons to be made between the terminologies of TA and communication studies. Examples of overlap are:

- signs and transactions
- needs and hungers
- the Self and ego states

- self-esteem and scripts
- strategies and games.

6.10 TA skills

These skills include:

- recognizing ego states in Self and in others
- controlling responses
- refusing to play games
- recognizing life scripts.

Case situation 1: A complementary transaction

Look back at the model for a complementary transaction. Then see if you can answer the following questions about the story below.

What ego states are displayed by the characters involved? How are these displayed?

Write a passage showing that age has nothing to do with the expression of ego states.

Mrs Martin plucked at her cheek anxiously and reviewed her kitchen with some apprehension, having just got home from work. She liked things to be in their place and they were not. She was a neat person, in profile and in dress, who characteristically pulled her skirt or her dress into line every twenty minutes. They had to know their place. Now she badgered some breadcrumbs from the breadboard and seized a teacup from the draining board in order to give it a proper wash behind the ears. The freshly baked cake that she had spotted when she came in was an interloper that she did not know how to deal with.

'Hello, dear.' Her mother came into the kitchen. 'You're home nice and early. I've only just had a cup of tea, but I can soon make another one.' 'Hello.' And a kiss to anoint the forehead from a dutiful daughter. 'It's all right. Don't fuss. I can put the kettle on myself.'

'Whatever you say, dear.' Her mother seated herself placidly.

Mrs Martin placed the kettle precisely between the teapot and the coffee grinder. 'Mother, there was no need for you to make that cake. But thank you, of course.' Ellie Williams studied her hands. 'I thought Danny might like it. I'm sorry if you'd rather I hadn't. He always says how much he likes my cakes.'

Mrs Martin folded her arms as she looked down at her seated parent. 'Now don't misunderstand me, mother. I'm very grateful for what you do. But you shouldn't try to do too much. You ought to get your afternoon rest.'

Her mother smiled placatingly. 'Oh, but I have had it. I feel fine. I just thought it would save you trouble. I know how hard you and David work.' Mrs Martin patted her mother on the back encouragingly. 'I appreciate that. Now why don't you'd go and rest on the lounger. I'll bring you your tea in a minute.'

Case situation 2: A crossed transaction

Look again at the model for a crossed transaction. Then see if you can answer the following questions about the dialogue below.

Which phrases show which different ego states?

At what point does the lecturer switch ego states, and which ego state does the lecturer switch to?

Try rewriting the end of the dialogue to show a positive outcome to the interaction.

Lecturer: Morning, Lesley. I'm glad you've come. I've wanted you to tell me why you're so far behind with your assignments.

Student: Er – yes, I'm sorry about that. I was going to come and see you.

Lecturer: Well, about time. You must get a grip on yourself. We can't have you wasting your time, can we?

Student: It depends on what you mean by wasting time. I calculate that I have spent 37 hours reading and making notes for your last two assignments. And according to my record book those are the only two I owe you. Is that right?

Lecturer: Er – I think so . . . but that's not the point. You ought to be able to keep up with the assignments if you're going to make it through the course.

Student: I see. Have you any reason to think that I won't make it?

Lecturer: Lesley, if I were you I would concentrate more on actually getting things done.

Student: I don't think that's quite fair. By all means let's look at the situation. I'd like to have some suggestions about how I should rearrange my schedule, bearing in mind that I am covering three other subjects as well.

Lecturer: Look – don't get smart with me, young lady! I get pretty fed up with you people coming to my office and moaning about how much you have to do. I should show you my workload sometime – and no one cares about that. My advice to you is to get on with it, or you'll be sorry.

Case situation 3: Games – If you really loved me (a variation on 'Corner')

Read the dialogue that follows, showing a game. See if you can decode the game through answering the following questions:

Who is initiating the game?

What is the gimmick involved?

Where does the switch take place?

Can you tell anything about the scripts or life positions of the people involved?

This dialogue is between a young couple who have been going out together for some time. The man has just come round to see the girl at her apartment. Helen lets Nick into her apartment in the early evening. He is in a cheerful mood and is carrying his sports bag. They make conversation and eat a light meal that she has prepared.

Nick: That was great. Thanks. Don't forget that I'm doing the same for you tomorrow night.

Helen: Nick! As if I would. But don't expect me before 7.30. I said that I would call in to see Mum and Dad on the way home.

Nick: No problem. My masterpiece won't be ready until 8.30. But don't worry, I'll soften you up with wine as soon as you get there.

Helen: Now, not too much of that, or I won't be able to drive back.

Nick: I'll work on that as well.

Helen: I bet you will . . . So, how did the game go?

Nick: Terrific – didn't I say? It was pretty close actually. But so what – it means we're through to the next round. So Friday is our next big day, if Terry has recovered.

Helen: Oh, Nick I was hoping we could catch that new movie on Friday.

Now, gentle reader, at this point we have to reveal that Helen 'knew' very well that the next round of the local tennis tournament was to take place on Friday. But, truth to tell, she was feeling just a little bit jealous that her husband-to-be was off on his own playing tennis. Helen preferred togetherness, and felt that a tennis racket should not come between the two of them. Nick is now on the horns of a dilemma.

Nick: Helen, I'd have loved to see the movie. But it was always on the cards that we'd be playing on Friday. How about Saturday?

Helen: Nick, you know I promised Mum and Dad that I'd take them to see Uncle Bill. It's pretty difficult for them to get out since Dad had his stroke.

Nick: I know that. I guess I had forgotten about Saturday. But the movie is on next week, too. And I can't just walk out on Terry and the tournament.

Helen: Hey, what about me! What about our relationship? Damn it, Nick – if you really cared . . .

Suggested reading

Berne, E., 1964, *Games People Play*, Harmondsworth: Penguin.

Berne, E., 1972, *What Do You Say After You've Said Hello?*, London: Corgi.

Harris, A. and Harris, T., 1995, *Staying OK*, London: Arrow Books.

Harris, T., 1970, *I'm OK, You're OK*, London: Pan.

Fig. 7.1 Group interaction – at any age

Chapter 7

Communication in groups

Groups and meetings at work certainly can be wasteful of time and effort, frustrating and accomplish little . . .

Groups are absolutely essential to modern work and without them any enterprise is likely to flounder . . . .

(Reid and Hammersley 2000)

7.1 Introduction

What is a group?

Like most words in daily use, the term 'group' has a wide range of meanings according to the context in which it is used. In general, it refers to **a collection of people who interact in some way and share some common goals or interests**. Hence it can refer to a small group of, say, two to twenty people in face-to-face contact (which will be the focus of this chapter), but it can also refer to very large groups of people that might include thousands or millions – for example, any particular profession or employment category with shared values and interests (such as teachers or civil servants or students or hairdressers) might be described as a group. Each of these terms will conjure up a set of pictures in your mind that would probably differ depending on whether you are inside or outside that group. We categorize – and, indeed, stereotype – people according to their group memberships. Some of these groups may be accidental (e.g. age, gender); others may be achieved through our own efforts (e.g. social clubs, work organizations).

Kelvin (1969) sums up these different definitions of the term group as follows:

> From a psychological standpoint it is probably sufficient to distinguish between only two kinds of basic groups: there are the face-to-face groups to which the individual belongs in a strictly physical sense, and there are the stereotype reference groups to which he 'belongs', in the sense that he identifies himself with the norms and values of the stereotype. The common element in both cases is expectation. In essence a group consists of people, who know, or believe they know, what to expect from one another.

We can refine this notion of a group being defined by **mutual expectations** if we identify more precisely some of these expectations. In describing how groups communicate, we usually think in terms of:

- **role differentiation** (different ways in which the members behave and ascribe status to each other)
- **patterns of leadership**, a **set of norms** and **rules of membership**.

In seeking to analyse how groups communicate there are three aspects that we need to concentrate on:

- How group members communicate and interact with each other: these are usually known as **group processes**.
- How groups are formed in order to achieve certain tasks or goals: this is usually known as a **task performance**.
- How groups are structured in various ways, which means that individuals occupy roles, have status and power and conform to a certain extent to **group norms**.

Group tasks and group processes

We shall concentrate on two broad fundamental aspects of groups in this chapter:

- the tasks of groups
- the processes of groups.

The tasks of groups

This includes the goals, purposes and problem-solving aspects of groups. We choose to belong to groups or to form groups in order to achieve stated goals for ourselves and for the group. In addition to the overtly stated aims there may also be 'a **hidden agenda**' for group activities. Under this heading we include what we have previously referred to as the '**content of the interaction**': what the communication and group processes are about.

Processes of groups

This includes the nature of the interactions between group members and the relationships that develop. It is the social dimension of groups that leads to group cohesion, interdependence and issues of role relationships and leadership. Often, in group communication a good deal of energy is spent simply on the 'group dynamics' in order to develop and maintain a set of individuals as one cohesive group.

But before we look at these, it is useful to remind ourselves why people join groups. Adrian Furnham (2002), in his comprehensive text, *The Psychology of Behaviour at Work: The Individual in the Organization*, lists five important reasons why people join and work and socialize in groups:

- Security: Groups provide safety in numbers, protection against a common enemy.

- Mutual benefits (goal achievement): By joining together, group members can work to ensure attainment of shared goals and benefits.

- Need to be social: Groups satisfy the basic need to be with others, to be stimulated by human companionship.

- Self-esteem: Membership in certain groups provides people with opportunities to feel good about their accomplishments and to identify with others from the same group.

- Mutual self-interest: By banding together people can share their mutual interests, such as hobbies.

Your groups

What groups do you belong to? You may like to pause and create a list of your group memberships. As we have suggested, some may seem to be accidental (e.g. family, age, gender, social class). Others may be more consciously sought (because they fulfil your perceived needs). Others may have been urged upon you (e.g. a committee, working party, task group) because a larger organization or a larger group of people wanted to achieve a particular purpose and mobilized a small group to work towards it.

So, we choose some groups and have others assigned to us by birth. We also usually belong to a number of groups at the same time. Some communication behaviour carries from one group to another; other behaviours change because of notions of appropriateness. For example, someone might retain a cheerful, jokey persona from school peer group to Baptist youth group, but would change when it came to the chapel service. This change of communication style does, of course, change the dynamics of the group: roughly, who talks to who, in what way, how and why. You will also be able to see that these dynamics vary from the fairly unstructured patterns of chat at school, to the (probably) more organized activities of the youth group, to the very structured and ritualized patterns of communication and interaction in the religious service.

The groups we belong to and how we behave within them also relate to matters of culture or subculture. A youth group in any city will behave generally much like any other: they will want to meet somewhere, to talk about the same things. But then particular kinds of group behaviour will depend on the exact subculture they choose to belong to.

The conventions of behaviour within a given subculture shape the communication of the groups belonging to that culture. Social conventions often relate to factors such as age and gender. If you are female, white and British you will have a relatively free involvement in youth group activities. It is accepted that you can interact with males in such groups. But if you are an Asian female then this is frequently not the case. Or again, if you are African-Caribbean in background then you may well feel that your ethnicity affects how you behave within various groups.

Such cultural differences make the study of communication very interesting and help us understand all the better how concepts such as role or convention really do have meaning in our lives.

In the rest of this chapter we will look at a number of key concepts for groups, as well as some of the issues that they raise.

7.2 Goals

We often join and form groups because we believe that 'two (or more) heads are better than one' or because 'many hands make light work'. These clichés sum up the common view that an effective group can:

- call upon increased thought power

- get greater access to information and ideas

- distribute responsibility to accomplish aims, and

- have a more coherent and committed approach to fulfilling any task.

This idea is succinctly stated by Judy Gahagan (1975): 'a group of people is considerably more than the sum of its parts'.

The explicit tasks of a small group might include:

- Research and fact finding: for example, a research group might be asked to investigate the causes of an accident.

- The pooling of ideas and information: for example, an environmental pressure group might wish to collate information on a particular ecological area.

- Recommending a particular course of action: for example, a working party might be set up to suggest ways of improving productivity in a workplace.

In addition to overtly stated aims of a group, there may also be 'a **hidden agenda**' of other unstated aims. In the setting up of a task group to investigate productivity, an unstated aim may also be to create a reason for workers from different parts and levels of an organization to meet together simply to engender better relationships and mutual trust. Explicitly or implicitly, groups always have those two dimensions of task:

- the content of their work together, and

- relationship, the social processes of their interactions.

We form and join groups to accomplish tasks that could not be accomplished by individuals alone, and also to foster social relationships and a sense of belonging. We also create our social identity through group memberships: a theme that was explored in earlier chapters of this book.

The psychological term that is used to describe the way in which individuals can achieve more by working with others is '**social facilitation**'.

Research has shown that individuals achieve more and perform better when other people are present to observe them, and also that individuals working as a group are more effective in performing a task than an individual working alone. There has been a good deal of social psychological research into this since the 1920s, which is well summarized by Donald Pennington (1986) in his book *Essential Social Psychology*. The research suggests that groups can solve problems faster than individuals. However, in terms of person-hours this may not be more economic, and in **'brainstorming'** to generate novel ideas, four separate individuals will generate a greater number and more original ideas, than four people working together.

In recent years there has been a great deal of concentration on groups working as teams to achieve set or agreed goals (see below the section on Teams). Many books, training manuals and organizations have explored how people working in teams can help or hinder the achievement of goals or effective decision-making processes.

There are some clear advantages in taking decisions in a group rather than as an individual, for example:

- a broader range of expertise and skills
- the ability to generate more ideas in a brainstorming session
- the ability to generate more information
- the ability to share workload
- the ability to see other people's mistakes
- a wider ability to evaluate possible decisions, and
- increased commitment and motivation because of group loyalty.

However, the process may be a lot slower and tensions within a group can lead to a failure to take responsibility and lead to risky decisions.

7.3 Cohesion

One of the assumptions behind the idea of group working is that a group of separate individuals can harness their separate talents and unite them to achieve more than they could achieve separately. This is self-evident in that to achieve many large-scale work tasks we have to organize people into working teams with divisions of responsibility and labour. However, the notion of group cohesion goes further than merely identifying a team of performers such as was described in Chapter 5.

Davis (1969) identified **'group behaviour'** as a function of three classes of variables:

- person variables, such as abilities, personality traits or motives
- environmental variables that reflect the effects of the immediate location and larger organization, community or social context in which group action takes place, and
- variables associated with the immediate task or goal that the group is pursuing.

Individual group members may have joined the group because they share a mutual interest in achieving a specific task. They may be prepared to adapt their individual ambitions in order to gain the benefit of group effort. Alternatively, an individual may have joined a particular group simply because he wishes to be with other members of that group, that is, for purely social reasons. These three variables clearly interact and influence the development and effective working of individuals within a group.

Work groups or leisure groups offer both specific activities and social reward – a sense of belonging and of friendship. People stay in jobs they do not particularly like sometimes because they value greatly the social dimensions of their work group. Someone might join a drama group because they believe they would value the social exchange and sense of togetherness as much as making a play.

Stages of group formation

Groups consist of interacting individuals. These interactions become part of the social experience of the group and it is usual to describe stages through which a group becomes more cohesive and the individuals accept a way of working together. Tuckman (1965) suggested that there are four developmental stages that a new group will go through:

- **Forming** – anxiety, dependence on a leader, members find out about the task, the rules and nature of the situation.

- **Storming** – conflict between individuals and subgroups, rebellion against the leader, resistance to rules and demands of the task.

- **Norming** – development of stable group structure, with social norms, conflicts resolved, cohesiveness developing.

- **Performing** – interpersonal problems are solved, the group turns to constructive solution of problems, energy is directed to the task, some degree of cohesiveness is achieved.

In 1977, Tuckman added a fifth stage that many groups also go through:

- **Adjourning** – the time when the group disbands and says farewell because its task is completed. Of course, not all groups disband, and some carry on even though they may have reached the appropriate time to adjourn.

Not all groups will necessarily go through these five identifiable stages, but the issues mentioned here will usually be part of the experience of a group as it develops into a cohesive group of individuals.

For example, it is now common for a collection of individuals to join together to form a **pressure group**. At the start the founder members need to define their purposes and their strategies, and to designate specific roles such as chairperson, secretary, public relations person, and so on, according to the task. However, when the group is formed, it is likely that some people may believe that the group is not putting the right stress on certain issues or not using the most appropriate tactics – indeed, not achieving what they joined to achieve. At that point some members may opt out, but those left will probably have developed a greater trust and commitment. The views of the group will be confirmed and the social interactions will be more group-oriented. They will work with greater confidence and cooperate to achieve the, now agreed, aims of the pressure group. You may like to think of groups you know or belong to. Have they gone through some or all of these stages?

Any group of people is necessarily in a dynamic situation, that is, the relationships and the processes of the group can never be static. Hence, the notion of group cohesiveness is not something that can be seen as the ultimate aim of a group. A group may seem to be working in a cohesive way, but then tensions can arise that may damage that group identity. **Cohesiveness is generally regarded as characteristic of the group in which the forces acting on the members to remain in the group are greater than the total forces acting on them to leave it**. A cohesive group reflects a high level of interpersonal attraction and a desire for mutual association. The shared experience of the group and the familiarity with each other can lead to effective working relationships and pleasurable personal experiences.

Kell and Corts (1980) used the metaphor 'immature–mature' to describe the life and growth of a group. They characterize a mature group as having the following qualities:

- 'There is a growth, rather than a loss, of selfhood in the group – which can lead to a high sense of self-concept and competence for all group members.

- The mature group exists in an atmosphere of trust and friendship.

- The mature group shows a uniform concern, a positive regard for the least, the loudest and the best of its members. Ideas and other contributions are weighed according to their value and not according to who expressed them.

- The mature group uses positive nonverbal communication to help each member to participate and to struggle with issues, personalities and with themselves. A system of mutual support develops and is demonstrated by the ease of nonverbal communication between the group members.

- The mature group strains; it adapts to points of disagreement. Groups can cope with disagreement, crisis and conflict.

- The mature group is marked by members who are ready and willing to relinquish any position in the group for the general benefit of the group.

- Finally, the mature group has a good time. Membership of a group can lead people to actually love the experience of being with group members.'

Group think

Any group that exhibits these characteristics of a mature group can surely be said to be a cohesive group. Such cohesiveness seems to be a desirable aim for any group to pursue. If the individual can find fulfilment in the group task then the group could be expected to work effectively. However, we need to be aware that such cohesiveness can lead group members to be totally concerned for maintaining the relationships of the group and, in so doing, downgrade or neglect the tasks for which the group came together. This notion has been characterized as **'group think'**. Janis (1972) has made a study of this phenomenon, which can occur in a highly cohesive group that is striving for unanimity of opinion rather than a realistic appraisal of the situation they are in. Group think has been defined as 'a deterioration of mental efficiency, reality testing and moral judgement that results from in-group pressures' (Janis 1972).

Janis argues that a group can become so cohesive that it develops symptoms of group think, which he lists as:

- illusion of invulnerability
- collective rationalization
- belief in inherent morality of the group
- stereotypes of out-groups
- direct pressure on dissenters
- self-censorship
- illusion of unanimity
- self-appointed mind guard.

He and others refer to several significant political movements of decision making, such as Pearl Harbor, the escalation of the war in Vietnam and the Watergate affair, as evidence of group think operating among a close circle of politicians and their advisers. The effect of this group think was a kind of smugness, even stupidity, in which the presidential team ignored uncomfortable information in its discussions and made bad decisions. Pearl Harbor 'couldn't happen', Vietnam could be conquered, no one would find out about Watergate – or so they brought themselves to believe.

For a group member, group think means that he or she loses the ability to think independently or to criticize other members of the group or what the group is proposing. Certain religious sects actually encourage group think in order to subdue possible criticism and to reinforce the validity and very existence of the group. This phenomenon also ties in with ideologies. Those who adhere to a particular ideological value system may also want to believe that such values are inherently right and all others are wrong. Religious and political groups have lapsed into this position throughout history, from Calvinists who believed that only their followers could go to heaven, to versions of Communism with an equally bigoted view of their own rightness. In a personal sense it is, of course, comforting to the Self to believe that one belongs to the only 'right' ideological position. It makes the person feel OK, and may be used to justify all kinds of behaviour towards others.

KEY QUESTIONS

Describe the main features that give identity to a group of football fans and to a group of soldiers.

What in your opinion gives cohesion to a family?

7.4 Roles

We have used this term in several different sections of this book. The word is used with different emphases in different contexts, which often reflects whether it is a label being used from a sociological or a psychological perspective. In this book we are trying to use the insights from both sociological and psychological studies to analyse communication processes. **Fundamentally, role refers to a notion of public behaviour (rules, norms, expectations) that the person believes is appropriate for the situation and his or her position in it**.

In any group context, it is inevitable that individuals adopt roles vis-à-vis the other people present. In Goffman's terms, we 'perform' to manage the impressions other people receive from us and to define the situation as we see it. People are assigned **status** in any particular group according to the role they play. For example, in family groups we tend to have very clear role designations as daughter, son, mother, father. These roles are certainly being redefined nowadays and changed in specific family contexts and in broader social contexts, but nevertheless the labels do suggest notions of relationships and status. In work groups, once again, we can see clearly assigned roles and relationships that they reflect.

Shaw (1981) suggested there are three different aspects to this overall concept of role playing in groups: the **expected role**, the **perceived role** and the **enacted role**:

- the perceived role is the behaviour that the person believes he or she should enact
- the enacted role is the actual behaviour that the person engages in
- the expected role is the behaviours thought appropriate by others in the group.

If these three are in harmony there will be little, if any, conflict between the role player and other members of the group. However, if there is any difference between any two or all three it often results in group conflict. If perceived and/or enacted roles differ greatly from member expectations, the person occupying the role may:

- be put under pressure to conform
- be asked to vacate the position, or
- unusually, attempt to change the expectations of other members of the group.

We adopt roles as a normal part of our public behaviour. The social or group expectation of a particular role will be interpreted by the individual, according to his or her self-concept and his or her reading of the social situation and the expectations of others. Hence, each individual performs a role in accordance with his or her personal attitudes, values, beliefs, perceptions and experience (see Fig. 7.2).

KEY QUESTIONS

Describe the various roles taken on by members of your family in different aspects of their lives.

How does a sense of role affect the way that people communicate?

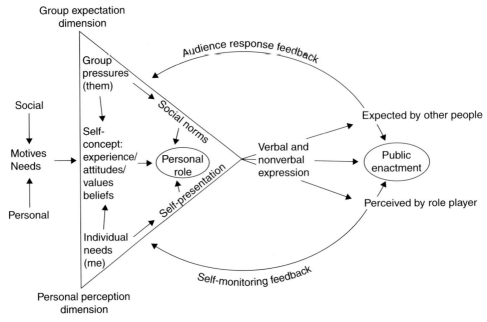

Fig. 7.2 A model for role playing – the interface of me and them

7.5 Teams and team working

Traditionally the word 'team' referred to a team of animals pulling something. Later it was used to describe a sports team; now teams have become the essential building blocks of every organization. People are expected to work as part of permanent and short-lived project teams. Being 'a team player' is one of the qualities that many companies seek in their employees.

The theory of teams, based on some of the benefits of working in groups outlined above, implies that teams can provide all sorts of benefits. These are often listed as:

- increasing productivity
- improving communication
- doing work that ordinary groups cannot do
- making better use of resources
- being more creative and efficient in problem solving
- enabling better quality services and improved processes.

Effective teams can achieve all of these. But not all teams work effectively, for many different reasons. These may include:

- members having their own agendas
- confused objectives
- unresolved roles among members

- conflicts between members

- poor leadership

- lack of team trust, and

- lack of appropriate expertise and resources.

To tackle some of these issues, many researchers have sought to analyse team working and team roles. One of the most often cited writers on team working is Meredith Belbin (1993), who has developed a widely used framework for describing nine complementary roles for effective teams.

The nine team roles as described by Belbin (1993) are as follows:

- '**Plant**: creative, imaginative, unorthodox. Solves difficult problems. But also ignores details. Too preoccupied to communicate effectively.

- **Resource investigator**: extrovert, enthusiastic, communicative. Explores opportunities. Develops contacts. But also over-optimistic. Loses interest once initial enthusiasm has passed.

- **Co-ordinator**: mature, confident, a good chairperson. Clarifies goals, promotes decision making, delegates well. But also can be seen as manipulative. Delegates personal work.

- **Shaper**: challenging, dynamic, thrives on pressure. Has the drive to overcome obstacles. But also can provoke others. Hurts people's feelings.

- **Monitor evaluator**: sober, strategic and discerning. Sees all options. Judges accurately. But also lacks drive, and ability to inspire others. Overly critical.

- **Teamworker**: co-operative, mild, perceptive and diplomatic. Listens, builds, averts friction, calms the waters. But also indecisive in crunch situations. Can be easily influenced.

- **Implementer**: disciplined, reliable, conservative and efficient. Turns ideas into practical actions, but also somewhat inflexible. Slow to respond to new possibilities.

- **Completer**: painstaking, conscientious, anxious. Searches out errors and omissions. Delivers on time. But also inclined to worry unduly. Reluctant to delegate. Can be a nit-picker.

- **Specialist**: single-minded, self starting, dedicated. Provides knowledge and skill in rare supply. But also contributes only on a narrow front. Dwells on technicalities. Overlooks the big picture.'

These roles were described after Belbin and his colleagues observed several hundred teams engaged in management games and exercises. Their observation scheme was based on Bales' interactive process analysis (see below). A questionnaire was devised to enable people to identify which roles they might most easily assume. It can be used as a tool to design a 'perfect team' or to analyse why a team is not working effectively – for example, if all members have the same strengths and weaknesses.

Peter Hartley (1997) comments that perhaps the most fundamental implication of this approach is that all roles are valuable, unlike approaches that suggest that some roles are destructive and negative. While we might debate the various roles as described above, they do provide a useful way of appreciating that an effective team does need a balance of different strengths among its members.

There is also a recognition that teams do not simply form and perform without some care being taken of the needs of individual members and of maintaining the team as a team. At the heart of a successful team is open and effective communication processes, where individuals are assertive but not aggressive and take note of the needs of other members and of the team as whole.

Michael West, in his practical guide *The Secrets of Successful Team Management* (2004), sets out the basis for effective team building. He suggests the team needs to take time out from their regular work to focus on task performance. His list of topics for discussion highlights the requirements necessary for a team to continue working effectively as a coherent group:

- recent team successes and difficulties
- team objectives and their appropriateness
- the roles of team members
- quality of team communication
- team meetings (frequency, content and value)
- team decision making
- organizational support for innovation
- conflict resolution in the team
- organizational support for skill development.

It is clear from the interest in teams in all sorts of organizations that team members who have knowledge and skill in interpersonal communication are more likely to be effective team members and leaders.

Within organizations, people now also develop 'virtual teams' where the members may never meet face to face, but work as teams from remote locations. Using email and intranet or the internet, people can keep in contact in real time. However, it is difficult to develop a true team coherence remotely (see Chapter 4 for more discussion on aspects of communication and technology).

KEY QUESTIONS

Sir Ranulph Fiennes, the explorer and extreme sports enthusiast, has said: 'Whenever feasible, pick your team on character, not skill. You can teach skills, you can't teach character.'

Do you agree with this view?

List some of the skills that Fiennes might want in his team, particularly interpersonal communication skills.

List qualities that Fiennes may be thinking of by using the word 'character'.

7.6 Analysis of group dynamics

A number of ways have been developed to analyse the contributions to group dynamics and the roles that people play in regard to the task of the group and the social processes of the group. These methods can, for example, deal with the amount of communication that is going on in a group, with the qualities of that communication, with its frequency and with the directions in which communication seems to travel between group members. There are three principal ways of recording these analyses, as described below.

Participation in a group

You can record levels of participation by drawing a circle to represent each member of the group and placing a mark in the circle for each time the person speaks (see Fig. 7.3). For example, in a group of five people labelled A to E, we could record the participation of each person. This sort of analysis can indicate who is speaking most in the group. However, this is obviously an unsophisticated recording device, since there is no way of recording people's listening involvement or people's nonverbal interactions with other group members.

Interaction in a group

To record the interaction between people in a group we can use the same circles as in Fig. 7.3, but indicate the particular verbal contributions between specific people and to the group in general. This sort of diagram is often called a 'sociogram'. Figure 7.4 is an example of how a record of a group meeting might appear. From this we can see that, for example:

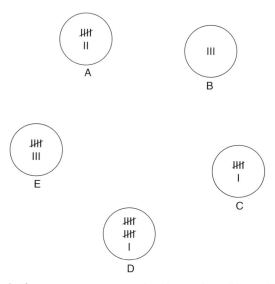

Fig. 7.3 Participation in the group process – scoring the number of times that each group member speaks

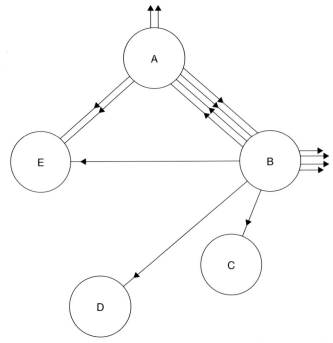

Fig. 7.4 Participation in the group process – representing lines of communication as group members interact

- person A spoke generally to the group twice, spoke to person B twice and spoke to person E twice;
- person B, on the other hand, spoke generally to the group four times, spoke twice to person A, once to person C, once to person D and once to person E.

The patterns of speaking and interaction between each of the people can thus be recorded.

If one wished to use such a record to indicate group communications, it would be useful to have each group member describe their own experiences of the group interactions as part of the debriefing since, once again, this sort of recording offers no information about people's nonverbal communication or their listening, or their intrapersonal thoughts concerning themselves and the group. This can only be revealed as far as people are able and willing to discuss their own perceptions.

Interaction process analysis (IPA)

Bales (1950) developed a coding system for analysing group processes, which he called interaction process analysis or IPA. This is based on the assumption that all behaviours, both verbal and nonverbal, occurring in small groups can be described within four main headings: positive and negative socio-emotional behaviour and information giving and information seeking concerned with the task of the group. Once again, we can see that the dimensions of the task and content of the group (as opposed to the social relationship dimensions of the group) are fundamental to this analysis.

Figure 7.5 reproduces Bale's interaction process analysis chart, which can be adapted as a grid for recording group communication processes – as shown in Table 7.1 (analysis sheet for observing communication). If you are planning to use a grid such as this (and you can, of course, draw up your own particular headings), you need to brief the observers carefully so that they are as consistent as possible in recording both verbal and nonverbal communication from each of the group members.

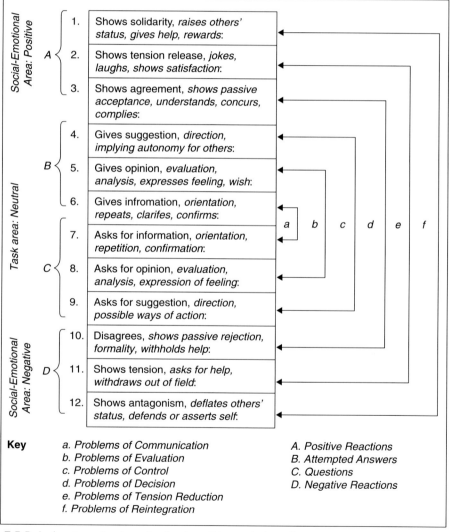

Fig. 7.5 Bales' system of categories for describing and observing group processes and communication (Bales 1950)

Types of Group Communication		People				
		A	B	C	D	E
	Tasks					
1	Giving information					
2	Questioning/seeking information					
3	Organizing ideas					
4	Clarifying ideas					
5	Summarizing					
6	Evaluating					
7	Deciding					
	Relationships					
8	Encouraging					
9	Harmonizing					
10	Sharing/gatekeeping					
11	Listening					
12	Relieving tension/compromising					
	Individual needs					
13	Blocking					
14	Seeking attention					
15	Dominating					
16	Not involving					

Table 7.1 A score sheet for recording the types of and quality of contributions in group interaction

In our experience of using these sorts of interaction analysis grids, we find that it is very important in the debriefing period to have each member of the group compare their own perceptions of their performance and other people's performances with that of the outside observers.

We suggest you might like to use this recording technique for a small group, either in your college or school class, or among a group of friends. You can set up a simple decision-making task for this purpose. An example might be to have each member of the group choose a well-known person from history and then for the group to decide which of those people chosen has made the greatest contribution to human happiness.

A number of books on communication processes indicate various other networks of communication among groups of five people. If you want to follow this up you can find these networks in, for example, James Davis's *Group Performance* (1969) or Dimbleby and Burton's *More Than Words* (1998). Networks of controlling communication in groups usually lead to certain members of the group gaining positions of dominance. Dominance, of course, may not be the same as group leadership, to which we will now turn.

7.7 Leadership

Issues of leadership, and particularly what makes an effective leader, have long been the concern of social psychologists and other students of human behaviour. **In previous generations the favourite theory was that leadership was a function of personality**. However, most students of leadership would now see this as an extremely limited view.

A more modern view of leadership sees it as a function of several variables. These do include the leader's personality and behaviour, but also cover:

- the composition and function of the group
- the social context
- the structure of the group
- the nature of the task, and
- whether the leader can be described as effective or ineffective in mobilizing the group and completing the initial objectives.

Peter Hartley (1997) describes the 'problem' of leadership. He goes on to say that despite the enormous literature on the topic of leadership, both from practitioners and social scientists, we still do not have a definitive account of what it means to be an effective leader across a wide range of situations. Many universities have established centres for leadership, and one of these in the United Kingdom, Leadership Southwest at the University of Exeter, has felt it necessary to publish a research report entitled 'What Is Leadership?' (Bolden 2004).

In this report Richard Bolden states that despite the recognition of the importance of leadership, there remains a certain mystery as to what leadership actually is or how to define it. Among many views, there are those who view leadership as the consequence of a set of traits or characteristics possessed by 'leaders', with others seeing leadership as a social process that emerges from group relationships. Whatever view we may favour from our own experiences, it is generally agreed that leadership involves the art of communicating with other people to persuade them to follow the leader's vision and objectives.

Northouse (2004), in his *Leadership: Theory and Practice*, identifies four common themes in the way leadership now tends to be conceived:

- leadership is a process
- leadership involves influence
- leadership occurs in a group context
- leadership involves goal attainment.

He then defines leadership as a 'process whereby an individual influences a group of individuals to achieve a common goal'. The mystery lies in just how that process works – which has led to many hypotheses and theories to seek to explain it.

Tedeschi and Lindskold (1976) suggest that three components of leadership can be identified as the most significant:

- '**Social influence**: This refers to how far a person can direct and control other people's behaviour, attitudes and opinions and persuade group members to conform to assigned roles and group norms. This notion stresses that an effective leader must be able to conform to assigned roles and group norms. This notion stresses that an effective leader must be able to form satisfactory relationships with group members and influence the social, group dynamics.

- **Behaviour**: This refers to the leader's ability to clarify group objectives, make decisions and suggest ways of achieving objectives. This suggests that an effective leader must have an informed understanding of the tasks that the group is seeking to complete. The leader must be seen to be able to match those tasks in his or her own behaviour.

- **Authority**: This can be a result of the leader being assigned a role of authority, for example by being nominated or elected, or it can reflect other people's perceptions of his or her authority in being able to achieve the group's goals and manage the situation.'

Hence, rather than stressing the individual personality, modern views of leadership stress the ability of a person to perceive the task that is set and to handle personal and social relationships.

Adrian Furnham (2002) classifies the major leadership theories into three groups.

- Leadership *trait* theory assumes there are distinctive physical and psychological characteristics that explain leadership effectiveness.

- *Behavioural* leadership theory assumes that there are distinctive styles that effective leaders continually use: these may be variously classified (i.e autocratic, democratic, laissez-faire – see below) or based on models that specify dimensions such as task or person orientated (see Fig. 7.6 on page 268).

- Situational leadership (or contingency leadership) theories assume that leadership style and effectiveness vary from situation to situation.

The **trait approach** is often described as the 'great person approach', with the view that leaders are born rather than made. These traits may include personality characteristics, intellectual and emotional abilities, interpersonal styles and general ability factors. According to this view, leaders lead by force of personality rather than a range of learned methods and skills. Such traits as vigour, persistence, originality, self-confidence, stress tolerance, ability to influence others, capacity to structure tasks and willingness to take responsibility for the consequences of your actions all seem to be examples of what a leader requires.

The **behaviour approach** stresses that it is what leaders actually do rather than their personal qualities that unlocks the mystery of leadership. Behaviour was analysed, for example, in terms of how far leaders showed consideration for others and built relationships with those they led; or alternatively how far they concentrated on structuring the tasks that were involved. Of course, both areas of activity are necessary. But some leaders may tend to be directive in their dealing with people, some may seek to coach people to do their tasks, some support their people and some delegate more to other people. A leader's behaviour can be categorized on a spectrum from 'commanding/directing' at one end, through 'consulting/persuading', to 'delegating/empowering' at the other. Each of these approaches can be effective according to the situation. However, generally it is expected that most leaders seek to persuade and take people with them rather than simply direct.

The **situation approach** is based on the premise that abilities, qualities and skills of a leader are to a large extent determined by the demands of the situation. The situation can be described in terms of:

- the relationship between leaders and followers, and
- in terms of tasks to be accomplished.

The behaviours of a leader lead to a range of leadership styles that the leader can deploy according to her/his interpretation of what is needed. A situational leader also recognizes that leadership does not rest with a single person, but is deployed by people who are able and willing ('empowered') to lead others throughout the group or organization.

Leadership styles

Research has also been carried out on leadership styles. These are usually classified under three headings: **authoritarian, democratic or laissez-faire**. These styles were used in a class experiment by Lewin et al. (1939) to demonstrate how leadership style affects group performance. Ten- and eleven-year-old boys working in groups where they had to carve models from bars of soap were exposed to these three leadership styles:

- Authoritarian leaders made all the decisions for the group, did not participate in group activities, assigned boys to tasks without saying why and made changes without consultation.
- Democratic leaders made decisions only after consultation with the group, were friendly to group members, participated in group activities, gave reasons for praise and criticism and offered help when required.
- Laissez-faire leaders played a passive role, did not attempt to direct or coordinate the group and made neither positive nor negative evaluations of the group.

The democratic style of leadership was found to produce highest morale in the group and the greatest friendliness and cooperation; however, groups with this style of leadership produced fewer soap models than those under authoritarian leadership, though the models were of higher quality. The boys also kept working in the absence of the leader. The authoritarian style resulted in more models being made, but misbehaviour occurred when the leader was absent. Poorest performance was under the laissez-faire style of leadership. Here fewest models were produced and misbehaviour occurred all the time. However, the boys were friendly towards the leader. After the boys had experienced each type of leadership style they were found to prefer the democratic approach most. In summary, group performance in terms of quality of models made and group cohesiveness was highest with the democratic style of leadership.

A further style of leadership could be described as 'collective' style. In this case no one person would be designated as the leader of the group and each member of the group would be assigned equal status and power, and actions and decisions would be a matter of consensus within the group. In practice, within such a group different leaders might well emerge according to different tasks and situations.

All of these styles are described in terms of the relationships between leaders and followers. Goleman, Boyatzis and McKee (2002) set out a view of leadership that is built on emotion:

> Great leadership works through the emotions. No matter what leaders set out to do – whether it's creating strategy or mobilizing teams to action – their success depends on how they do it. Even if they get everything else right, if leaders fail in this primal task of driving emotions in the right direction, nothing they do will work as well as it should or could.

They argue that effective leaders need to develop emotional resonance with those they seek to lead, rather than dissonance, which comes from negative emotions. Their concept of 'the new leaders' comes from recent thinking about emotional intelligence and multiple intelligences (see page 23).

They suggest that there are six leadership styles and that the most effective leaders can switch between styles according to the situation. Each style is described in terms of how it builds resonance, its impact on the emotional climate of the organization and when it is most appropriate to use. The six styles they describe are:

'Visionary:

- Resonance – moves people towards shared dreams
- Climate – most strongly positive
- Appropriate – when changes require a new vision, or when a clear direction is needed

Coaching:

- Resonance – connects what a person wants with the organization's goals
- Climate – highly positive
- Appropriate – to help someone improve performance by building long-term capabilities

Affiliative:

- Resonance – creates harmony by connecting people to each other
- Climate – positive
- Appropriate – to heal rifts in a team, motivate during stressful times, or strengthen connections

Democratic:

- Resonance – values people's input and gets commitment through participation
- Climate – positive
- Appropriate – to build buy-in or consensus

Pacesetting:

- Resonance – meets challenging and exciting goals
- Climate – because too frequently poorly executed, often highly negative
- Appropriate – to get high-quality results from a competent and motivated team

Commanding:

- Resonance – soothes fears by giving clear direction in an emergency
- Climate – because so often misused, often highly negative
- Appropriate – in a crisis, to kick start a turn around, or with problem people.'
  (Goleman, Boyatzis and McKee 2002)

At the root of all of these styles is the knowledge that leaders only achieve results through communicating with, and emotionally engaging with, the people they are seeking to lead.

There are no conclusive answers to these issues of leadership. Perhaps some sort of conclusion might be drawn in stressing that all groups have both the task dimension and the social dimension. An effective leader within a group will be able both to contribute towards the completion of the task and maintain the social relationships of the group. To do this a leader requires considerable communication skills in order to manage other people and to achieve group goals. Theoretically, a person who has effective communication and social skills – an ability to express and to read verbal and nonverbal messages, to perceive other people's needs and to maintain open social relationships – is likely to be an effective leader. He or she will be able to persuade other people and gain other people's trust and loyalty.

In this discussion of leadership, inconclusive though it is, it is possible to say that an effective leader of a group is not the person who dominates and imposes his or her will on the group but is rather a facilitator for the group task and is sensitive to the social dynamics of the group.

One also needs to recognize that notions of leadership have a cultural dimension. Subcultural groups such as Hell's Angels have a positive attitude towards an authoritarian style that is more extreme than that of the main culture within which they exist. Equally, cultures other than those of the western nations also have differing views about leadership.

These issues of leading and managing small and large groups and teams of people will continue to be debated and observed. The last words in this section are intended to provoke further debate about all of this:

> If the 1980s were the *me* decade and the 1990s the *we* decade, how is this reflected in management training? Nearly everyone works in groups, and business success is, we are told, dependent not on individuals but on teams. It really is true

that the chain is only as strong as its weakest link. Heterogeneous teams do best: those with overall ability but whose members each had different skills, preferences and approaches that complemented each other. Just as people may have to be trained to become leaders, they may also have to be trained to be followers. Training programmes now focus on how to build, sustain and manage a team; how to assess your favourite and most comfortable role when operating a team; how to select individuals with a team in mind and how to be a better team member.

(Furnham 2002)

KEY QUESTIONS

Describe the leadership qualities that you admire in other people.

Explain why different kinds of leadership may be appropriate in different situations.

7.8 Norms

The concept of 'norm' is often used both in describing people's behaviour in small groups and in large-scale sociocultural groups. In its widest sense a norm can be said to be **a standard against which the appropriateness of behaviour is to be judged**. Within a group there may be overtly stated rules and expectations for behaviour, but unwritten standards will also develop.

Davis (1969) suggests that norms vary in a number of respects:

- Some norms (perhaps most) apply to overt behaviour, while others seem to guide subjective states when the individual is faced with uncertainty.

- Some norms are formal, in that they are written or otherwise conspicuously and intentionally adopted by a group (rules or operating procedures).

- On the other hand, many norms are informal in their origin; they arise from the interaction of the group members over time. Working norms emerging in this way may even occasionally be in conflict with the formal group norms that ostensibly govern behaviour in some particular case. Formal norms are not necessarily equally evident to all group members; but in most small groups that have existed for a time, there is little likelihood that norm violations occur frequently without the awareness of most of the members.

With regard to what we described earlier as reference groups, norms can be quite clearly observed. For example, a particular profession may have clearly stated codes of conduct for its members. A particular group may signal its adoption of norms through clearly visible clothes or other symbols. These could range from turbans for the Sikh male, to a wrist band for a charity group supporter, to uniform for a member of the police force. A pressure group might consist of members who display quite different behavioural norms, but whose views on a particular issue are following a set pattern. For example, members of an organization like Greenpeace may adopt very different norms in their general social behaviour, but will share the same opinions about treatment of endangered species and the need for conservation in general.

The concept of norm presupposes that some individuals will deviate from the norms of the group to which they belong. Obviously, each of us is a member of a number of groups and these may have different norms. At some time in our lives these may lead to conflicts which we shall have to resolve. If we feel particularly attracted to one group to which we belong then we are likely to be prepared to conform to the norms of that group. If we want to be identified as clearly part of a particular reference group then, again, we are prepared to conform to the norms of that group. Our self-esteem may be closely tied to the social identity that comes from particular group memberships. Someone who wants to be identified with a local group of heavy-metal fans will adapt their appearance and behaviour (including communication) in order to be accepted by that group.

It is one of the assumptions of this book that individual processes of perception and experience are dynamic, and that group processes are also dynamic. Hence, we would not expect that an individual member of a group or the group itself can remain in a static norm state. It may be that a member of a group is content to follow the norms of that group for a certain period, but then something might occur in his or her life that could lead to a desire for deviation from this norm. As we said in an earlier section, excessive conformity to group norms can lead to a sterile state of group think.

In concluding our remarks on norms, we wish to stress that they are not imposed on groups from the outside. They develop as a result of the interactions between the individual members of the group and, hence, themselves change and develop with the group. Research has shown that if there is one deviating person in a group then he or she may be isolated and excluded; however, if two people deviate in a small group then they may well be able to move the whole group across to their new norm.

KEY QUESTIONS

Describe what you believe are the norms of an ethnic group and a youth group that you know about.

Explain how being in a group can change the norms of behaviour (and values) shown by someone as compared with their behaviour as an individual.

7.9 Conflict

In the past few sections we have been discussing groups as if they take on a life of their own through cohesiveness and norms of behaviour and belief. It is impossible to conceive, however, of an active group of individuals maintaining a position of 100 per cent cohesiveness and conformity for a long period. Inevitably there are going to be challenges to the norms of the group and conflicts between individuals. **These conflicts may arise from several sources**. One of these may be simply the personal differences in needs and aims of the members of the group. These personal needs may well change over a period of time. Another source of conflict may be as a result of the roles that people are playing. A role that is expected within one group may conflict with a role that the same person is expected to play in another group. Such role conflict may reach the point where the person has to change his or her role position.

Obviously an individual is playing a range of roles in his or her life – indeed, in any one day. As the context and group expectations change, so the role player's behaviour will change, but, of course, he or she remains the same person. If one is taken over completely in a role without maintaining some personal consistency, then other people become anxious about 'who the real person is' or about honesty and reliability. We interpret roles according to our own beliefs as well as other people's expectations (see Fig. 7.2, above).

Playing different roles can create personal tensions and conflicts – for example, if at work you are expected to play a subordinate role but at home you need to play a leading role, then the latter may become excessively dominating to compensate for frustrations at work. Or, if you are 'the boss' at work you may want to play the boss at home when you are expected to be part of an egalitarian family group. You may be able to think of other 'role conflicts' that can arise from shifts in context and expectations.

Within groups, people are assigned different status levels. Once again these will change over time and the process of change may be a cause of conflict.

Managing conflict

In order to maintain the group, individuals often avoid conflict situations. Many social psychologists and practical communicators writing about conflict suggest that conflict should not be ignored but should be faced and resolved. Blake et al. (1964) suggest that **we can manage conflicts in three ways**:

- **Avoidance**: We often avoid conflict or potential conflict in the hope that if we ignore it then it will go away. Sometimes we seek simply to smooth over problems and do not face up to the sources of the difficulty. In such cases the conflict will often reappear in some other form and is not likely simply to disappear just because we wish it would.

- **Defusion**: This strategy is used when a person involved in a conflict decides to hold off until tempers have cooled. Alternatively, we might seek agreement on minor points and avoid the bigger problem that lies beneath them. Sometimes these defusion strategies can work; sometimes they are only a form of avoidance.

- **Confrontation**: In confronting a problem we can seek one of three outcomes. First, we can reach a win–lose situation. This may come about because 'the boss' imposes his or her ruling on a situation. Often this sort of problem is resolved by one side dictating the terms and the other side inevitably losing. Another strategy is the lose–lose strategy. In this case people involved in conflict may simply decide that neither of them will have their way and hence the conflict will end. Sometimes both people can decide to have part of what they want and give part of what they want. This may be a sort of compromise. However, a compromise can also be more positively sought and lead to the third strategy, which is a win–win strategy. This is generally described as the most desirable way of confronting a conflict. In this view people treat conflict as an issue to be solved, not a fight to be won and take the view that nobody has to lose completely. Time is spent defining the specified and unspecified sources of the conflict and working at alternative solutions that will satisfy both parties. It was suggested that this could be a form of compromise. However, this suggests that both parties do, in fact, lose in finding a solution. The more positive view of the win–win strategy is to see a new solution being developed by the parties to the conflict that actually leads to a new consensus, which resolves the problem. Neither party wins or loses, but each contributes to the resolution of the conflict.

In the group context, the main source of conflict is behaviour that is individually oriented as opposed to behaviour that takes note of the needs of other group members and of the tasks and social processes of the group. Earlier in this chapter we have stressed the task and group relationship dimensions of groups, illustrated in Figure 7. 5 (Bale's interaction process analysis) and Table 7.1 (analysis sheet for observing communication). These group dynamics can be developed by a mutual acceptance of group norms and differentiated roles, and by a desire to put group cohesiveness before separate individuals' needs.

However, in a group of people there are inevitably overt and covert tensions between the demands of the task, the group's maintenance needs and the individual's needs and motives. It is possible to summarize these tensions and the conflicts that have been explored in this chapter, as shown in Figure 7.6 – task, group and individual demands.

Nolan (1987c) stresses that for effective group meetings it is not possible to have one person (even if he or she has the status of leader) who manipulates the rest of the people. Such manipulation is likely to lead to overt or covert conflict. Nolan expresses this idea forcibly:

> even if one party should 'win', the loser will not take it lying down: he or she will fight back, subvert, refuse to co-operate or undermine in one way or another. The win–lose contest becomes lose–lose as the loser sets up a return match on his or her own ground which that person is sure to win. If we are to have successful meetings, we must get away from the idea that 'meetings are manipulation'.

7.10 Problem solving

It will be no surprise to those of you who have read this far in this chapter to be told that problems that arise in a group may need to be solved in either the task dimension or the social dimension. In the previous section on conflict, we primarily looked at conflicts in the social dimension. In this section we concentrate more on problems and their resolution in the task dimension. **It is useful to draw a distinction between open problems, which require a creative imaginative approach, and closed problems, which require a more analytical and factually based approach.** In broad terms, a group is probably more able to deal with open problems, since it can call on the imaginative resources of a large number of

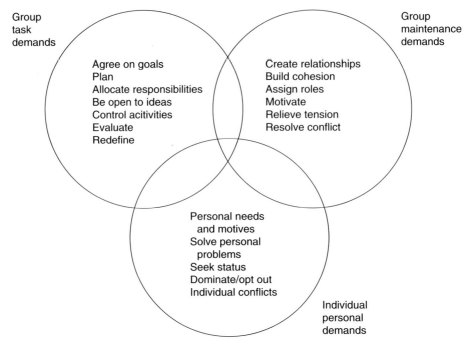

Fig. 7.6 A chart to describe task, group and individual demands

people, than it is to deal with closed problems. However, having said that, a group of people who have specialist knowledge can be very helpful in providing information to resolve a closed problem. In this case, however, it is likely that ultimately one person is going to have to take the decision about which particular solution they want to follow.

Whatever the problems are, for a group to be effective in tackling the problem there needs to be an openness to ideas and a willingness to listen to all the members of the group. If the group is restricted by notions of specified roles for group members, clearly designated status for group members, or constricting norms of what is suitable behaviour and thinking processes, then it is not going to be an effective vehicle for problem solving. Once again, we think here of the idea of group think, in which a group of people can be confined within their own universe and unable to step outside their thinking and feeling processes to see that they are deluding themselves and are remote from the real world outside the group. Perhaps the conclusion to be drawn here is that a closed group with an unchanging membership is likely to become somewhat sterile in its thinking processes.

7.11 Communication in groups: some concluding remarks

Individuals

It is a truism to say that a group consists of two or more individuals. However, it is important to remember this because each member of the group has his or her own needs and motivations. Their relationships and performances in front of other people will be influenced by their self-concept and their attitudes, values, beliefs and past experiences. They will have developed their own communication styles, which will include particular verbal and nonverbal strategies for expressing themselves and for interpreting other people's communication. Each member will inevitably be performing in front of other people: each person is seeking to manage the impression they give off and to define the situation. The personalities and characters of each individual will need to adjust to those of other members of the group if the group is to work as a group.

Interpersonal factors

For a group to come into effective existence, there needs to be a sharing by each member of the group. This sharing will depend on the perceptions that each person has of every other person in the group. It will also reflect the expectations they have of each other and of the group as an entity. Each person will be adopting certain roles vis-à-vis the other persons in the group. Notions of appropriate behaviour and mutually accepted performances are important. In order for a group to become a mature group, degrees of trust and familiarity need to be developed between the individual members on a one-to-one, interpersonal basis.

The quality of verbal and nonverbal interactions will determine the strength of the group. In general, we are taught to think of communicating with each other as speaking to each other. However, in a group, each member is going to spend more time listening to other people than speaking. Being sensitive to other people's feelings and emotions, most of which will be conveyed nonverbally, is a crucial element in group communication. This nonverbal interaction will be largely responsible for creating the climate of the group, which determines how open and supportive it is. The development of this climate will be one of the determinants of the group norms. These are developed from within the group and are likely to reflect the needs of the individuals within that group.

Differences between interpersonal and group communication

Finally, in this chapter, we want to stress that there is a basic difference between individual and group communication. In a one-to-one situation we are presenting our Self according to our self-concept and our perception of the other person(s) and the social context. When we are part of a group, however, the dynamics of the group, its tasks and social relationships mean that we are more conscious of playing a role and of being concerned with the group. The group, when it is working cohesively, develops a life of its own, of which the individual members are merely a part – we subordinate our individual needs and motives for the sake of the group.

The focus of this chapter has been on small groups, but at the start of the chapter we also referred to membership of large-reference stereotype groups that influence our self-perceptions and behaviour. As a teacher, for example, one is constrained by notions of professional responsibility and conduct that might include a tendency to take control in a situation, to care for pupils and to speak and behave in a way that provides a socially acceptable model of behaviour.

Another dimension of group behaviour to note is 'crowd behaviour'. If an individual feels totally submerged in a group so that the usual personal responsibilities, norms and inhibitions of behaviour disappear then some individuals feel free to behave in ways that are out of character. The power that comes from group membership enables people to achieve more than they could alone; but group membership can also be used as a mask to cover individual responsibility and to give licence to perform what individually would be unthinkable. Such group-dominated behaviour is at its most extreme in what Goffman (1976) called 'total institutions', such as the army or a religious order, where a person is denuded of individuality. This notion is described as **deindividuation** and is used to explain why people in crowds will commit acts of violence and not feel individually responsible for what has been done.

Eiser (1986) reports the work of Reicher (1984), which suggests that people shift their attitudes when in a group because there is a shift in their social identity. Their sense of who they are and what they should or should not do becomes bound up with the group. In 'normal' life our group memberships influence our self-concept, our roles and our personal attitudes, but they do not rob us of our individuality. The strength of a group grows out of the strength of the individuals in it and their social interactions.

7.12 Group skills

Once again, we would say that there are two broad areas of skill in group participation:

- one set is to do with recognizing what is going on;
- the other is doing something about what we have recognized.

Clearly, the kind of group that we are involved with influences what we might mean by being skilled. If one is with a group of friends then it is not appropriate to exercise leadership skills in the same way that one might at work. If one is in the middle of a team game it is not appropriate to stop and evaluate the worth of the captain's request for you to take some particular action now! On the other hand, it is surprising how many skills are broadly appropriate across a range of groups. It is as important to contribute to harmony and cohesion in a family group as it is in a peer group.

Group skills ride on the back of other interpersonal skills, not least of which is being able to listen properly and constructively to others. These skills are distinctive in that one is talking about behaviour (verbal and nonverbal) that contributes positively to the well-being and the working of the group as a whole. Group skills also overlap with what one can recognize as skills in problem solving or decision making. Items 1 to 9 of the Bales categories (Fig. 7.5) offer one kind of summary of skilled behaviour. The following list is a variant on this and includes an indication of communicative behaviours.

1. To offer information and ideas
   'How would it be if we did X?'

2. To develop ideas and information (recognize worth of other's ideas)
   'That's good. And we could do X' (*leaning forward into group*).

3. To evaluate ideas and information
   'So how would that work in practice? What would happen if . . .?'

4. To ask for others' contributions or evaluation
   'So what do you think about X?' (*direct gaze held on respondent*).

5. To summarize ideas and opinions
   'So what we seem to be saying is X. Is that right?'

6. To suggest courses of action
   'Then why don't we do X?' (*looking round the group*).

7. To praise and recognize others' contributions
   'That's a really good idea!' (*smile and direct gaze*).

8. To offer supportive action
   'All right – well, I'll put the leaflets through the door.'

9. To offer humour
   (*making a joke about a problem, using laughter*).

In terms of leading or managing groups in a formal sense it is usual to require adaptability and a wide range of skills in leaders. However, effective leaders of small groups are not usually so much directive in their communication as good at bringing things together and at moving things on, so skills 5 and 6 are particularly ones to be valued in a group leader.

Teams are a particular type of group, which have clear aims and assigned roles for its members. Meredith Belbin (1993) has analysed team working processes and describes nine different types of roles that he believes individuals may adopt in teams:

- Plant, who solves difficult problems but also ignores details
- Resource investigator, who explores opportunities but is also over optimistic
- Co-ordinator who clarifies goals and promotes decision making but also can be seen as manipulative
- Shaper, who has the drive to overcome obstacles but also can provoke others
- Monitor/evaluator, who sees all options but also lacks drive
- Teamworker, who listens, builds, averts friction but also may be indecisive in crunch situations
- Implementer, who turns ideas into practical actions but also may be somewhat inflexible
- Completer, who is conscientious and delivers on time but also can be a nit picker
- Specialist who provides knowledge and skill but also dwells on technicalities.

A team may not have all of these roles, but they indicate the sorts of complementary activities and behaviours that help to create an effective team of people.

Positive, constructive communication in groups can be seen in a wide range of situations. To be skilled as a group member one simply has to think about what one is saying and how one is saying it. Ask yourself, 'Am I saying something that will help the group?', '. . . that will please other people?', '. . . that will help sort something out?' These skills could cover working with others at some task in a job, or organizing a birthday treat for a member of your family without them knowing about it, or just talking with friends at a party. Look back at what this chapter tells you about negative or self-oriented behaviour to see how this underlines the existence of skills. We feel better for working positively with others: we often benefit in practical as well as in emotional ways.

Review

You should have learnt the following things from this chapter:

7.1 Introduction

- A group is a collection of people who interact in some way and share some common goals or interests.
- We belong to small groups (2–20 people) and to large (possible millions of people) reference stereotype groups.
- We belong to groups through accident (e.g. gender, age) or through achievement (e.g. committee or employment).
- We can analyse processes of groups in terms of tasks – overt and covert goals of the group – and in terms of maintenance of relationships.
- In groups we find mutual expectations, role differentiation, patterns of leadership, sets of norms, rules of membership.

7.2 Goals

- We belong to a variety of groups with a variety of aims.
- The concept of 'social facilitation' suggests that individuals achieve more and perform better when other people are present to observe them.

7.3 Cohesion

- Cohesive group behaviour is a function of three variables:

    - personal abilities, characteristics and motives
    - environmental factors of the context of the group
    - task to be achieved.

- **Stages of group formation**: To achieve group cohesion the following stages are often necessary:

    - forming the group identity
    - rebelling within the group
    - developing norms of group behaviour
    - cooperating to solve the problems and to fulfil the agreed goals.

- **Group think:** A small group can become so cohesive that it becomes separate from the outside world and confined within its own limits of thoughts and behaviour.

7.4 Roles

- Roles refer to a notion of public behaviour (rules, norms, expectations) that the person believes is appropriate for the situation and his or her position in it.
- People achieve status through the roles they play.
- It is useful to divide 'role' into three aspects: the perceived role of the individual; the expected role as perceived and expressed by the group; and the enacted role, which is the actual behaviour displayed by the individual.

7.5 Teams and team working

- Teams are a particular type of group, with clear aims and assigned roles for its members.
- Meredith Belbin has analysed team-working processes and describes nine different types of roles that he believes individuals may adopt in teams:

  - Plant, who solves difficult problems, but ignores details.
  - Resource investigator, who explores opportunities, but is overoptimistic.
  - Coordinator, who clarifies goals and promotes decision making, but can be seen as manipulative.
  - Shaper, who has the drive to overcome obstacles, but can provoke others.
  - Monitor/evaluator, who sees all options, but lacks drive.
  - Team worker, who listens, builds, averts friction, but may be indecisive in crunch situations.
  - Implementer, who turns ideas into practical actions, but may be somewhat inflexible.
  - Completer, who is conscientious and delivers on time, but can be a nit-picker.
  - Specialist, who provides knowledge and skill, but dwells on technicalities.

  A team may not have all these roles, but they indicate the sorts of complementary activities and behaviours that help to create an effective team of people.

7.6 Analysis of group dynamics

- We can observe and describe group communication processes through:

    - participation of group members
    - interaction of group members
    - interaction process analysis:
    - positive (group-oriented) social emotional contributions
    - negative (self-oriented) social emotional contributions
    - task contributions.

7.7 Leadership

- Leadership is now perceived as a function of several variables:

    - personality and behaviour
    - composition and function of the group
    - social context
    - structure of the group
    - nature of the task
    - whether the leader can be described as effective or ineffective in mobilizing the group
    - completing the initial objectives.

- **Leadership styles**: It is possible to see four major styles of leadership: authoritarian, democratic, laissez-faire, collective.
- **Leadership skills** can be summarized as:

    - Openness – ability to receive and respond to group members' ideas
    - Information – apparent knowledge base for group problem solving.
    - Persuasion – ability to influence others.

7.8 Norms

- A norm is a standard against which the appropriateness of behaviour is to be judged.
- A group develops its own norms of thought and behaviour, but these are not static – they develop as the group develops.

7.9 Conflict

- Conflicts arise from the personal differences of individuals and from different role expectations. They also arise from demands of the task, the group maintenance and the personal needs of members.
- Managing conflict. We can manage conflict in three ways: avoidance, defusion or confrontation.

7.10 Problem solving

- Problems exist in both the task dimension and the social relationship dimension of groups.
- Groups are effective in solving problems where they are open to ideas and willing to harness the contribution of all members.

7.11 Communication in groups, some concluding remarks

- A group develops as a result of the interaction between individuals and their own needs and motives and the desire to form a group.
- For a group to function effectively its members need to agree on mutual roles and norms of behaviour.
- Each member of the group needs to contribute verbally and nonverbally to develop a mutually supportive climate.
- In group communication, individual members subordinate their own needs to those of the group, but to submerge individual needs totally to those of the group can lead to extreme results.

7.12 Group skills

- These skills include:

  - giving and evaluating information within the group
  - giving and evaluating ideas
  - suggesting actions
  - recognizing the worth of others and of their contributions.

Case situation: Who runs this project?

Read the extract below, about group behaviour in a meeting, and try to answer the following questions:

What is revealed about conflict in groups?

What is revealed about leadership?

If you were talking to this group of people about their behaviour, what advice would you give them to improve their cooperation and communication?

The last time they had a meeting Joe had noticed that Pauline appeared to be totally bored for most of the time. She spoke only twice, mostly just shuffled her papers, avoided eye contact and drew elaborate doodles around her agenda. Every letter on the left-hand margin became an illuminated manuscript.

He hoped that today she would get involved. Competition for contracts was tough. So the project needed her. Anyway, Joe knew that she had a lot to contribute because he had watched her really pull things together on the Waterstones' project. She had transformed the graphic design of the leaflets. He glanced around the table as people shuffled their papers, waiting for something to happen.

Maybe she was disappointed because, again, it was Jane who was asked to be project leader. Everyone knew that Pauline had more experience and artistic flair than Jane. But then Pauline was a bit arrogant, she didn't really listen to other people. She seemed to even despise her colleagues, though he didn't care. But he could see why Calvin wouldn't have her as leader. People needed encouragement. There was Bob who was desperately trying to get a job out of London and who seemed really to have lost interest. Lindsey had only just joined the company and seemed too worried about not making a mistake, though she had good experience. There was Marc who was new and very green, but promising. Joe himself was very comfortable with his own niche.

Jane looked round the group trying to attract attention. 'Okay, let's start,' she said. 'Last time we agreed on broad approaches to this promotion. The exhibition is the centrepiece for creating a positive image. Considering our client's interests we're going for an ecology theme. So – Bob, you were going to come back today with ideas about how we can develop the theme, bearing in mind we have a month to deliver. What have you got?' She focused on him directly.

Bob looked at the ceiling and twiddled his pencil. 'Yeah – well, I haven't actually got much on paper yet . . .' 'Typical!' muttered Pauline, looking down, but knowing they could all hear . . . Bob glared at her. 'But I have given it some thought and I reckon we could go on the back of the Greenpeace logo, so long as we don't make it too obvious. You know, endangered species and all that. We're already into a safe image in the brochure mockup: Pollution free. In fact, we could borrow some material and blow it up for the exhibition. Lindsey has taken some photos and tried composites to show how everything blends in with the surroundings.' He turned to Lindsey with a flick of an eyebrow. She nodded.

'Yeah, well I did take some. But they were really for the brochure and the display ads. I'm not really sure how they would look blown up.'

'Is anyone round this table sure about anything!' Pauline's Yorkshire accent fell with a bang into the discussion. 'I don't feel we have a proper coordination policy here. Nobody has made clear what the budget is. So we don't know how far we can go with colour. We haven't discussed video. Can we get video? Do you actually know the real budget, Jane? Or are you in the dark as well? Video would make all the difference, and we still have time to put it together. Let's get on with it.'

'Wait a minute!' Jane pushed herself forward and looked round at the rest of the group, but avoiding Pauline. 'Let's hold back a minute. We haven't decided that at all.' She glared at Pauline. 'We're not ready.'

'And never will be at this rate,' snapped Pauline, leaning across Joe and looking daggers. 'We've actually met twice now and got nowhere. Completely wasted our time.' She was largely right, thought Joe. 'If Bob couldn't bring in something more than a vague idea then he should have said so. I suppose he will expect Lindsey to rescue him again.' The room snapped with atmosphere, everyone was wide awake and sitting up.

'Now wait a minute, Pauline. We're not going to get anywhere if we just attack one another . . .'.

Suggested reading

Adair, J., 1986, *Effective Teambuilding*, London: Pan.

Belbin, M., 1993, *Team Roles at Work*, Oxford: Butterworth-Heinemann.

Furnham, A., 2002, *The Psychology of Behaviour at Work: The Individual in the Organization*, Hove: Psychology Press. (See Chapters 10, 11, 12.)

Goleman, D., Boyatzis, R. and McKee, A., 2002, *The New Leaders: Transforming the Art of Leadership into the Science of Results*, London: Time Warner.

Gudykunst, W. B. (ed.), 1986, *Intergroup Communication*, London: Edward Arnold.

Hartley, P., 1997, *Group Communication*, London: Routledge.

Kell, C. L. and Corts, P. R., 1980, *Fundamentals of Effective Group Communication*, New York: Macmillan.

Reid, M. and Hammersley, R., 2000, *Communicating Successfully in Groups*, London: Routledge.

Shaw, M., 1981, *Group Dynamics*, 3rd edn, New York: McGraw-Hill.

West, M., 2004, *The Secrets of Successful Team Management: How to Lead a Team to Innovation and Success*, London: Duncan Baird.

Fig. 8.1 Communication, culture, process and signification

Chapter 8

Critical perspectives

Critical theories . . . are aimed at producing enlightenment in the agents who hold them
(Geuss 1981)

8.1 Introduction

In this final chapter we want to set out some critical perspectives that provide different angles
on what is important in communication and how it can be understood. We will link these
sets of ideas back to the preceding text, not least because we have, for example, already said
quite a lot about communication and culture. Although this book is dominantly about
human communication, it exists in a relationship with the more all-embracing area of
communication studies – which, in turn, links and overlaps with academic disciplines such as
media studies, sociology, psychology and cultural studies. A critical perspective is in itself just
one way of making sense of that which it criticizes. Critical perspectives comprise ideas about
how the object of study may be analysed and understood, and may well generate their own
terminology.

To give you some examples of what we mean:

- In terms of media one might be looking at how media technologies have extended the
  capacity for interpersonal communication, or at ways in which mode of address in media
  performances connects with communication performance in real life.

- In terms of psychology we would refer you back to ideas about intrapersonal processes as
  they affect behaviour.

- In terms of sociology one could be making connections through examination of group
  behaviours and social interactions.

- In terms of cultural studies we could be talking about the cultural context that affects
  communication behaviour.

So, in part we are referring to issues generated by these critical positions – some of which
issues have already been referred to. But the chapter will also open up new ideas about critical
perspectives and their related issues, so that you have a better understanding of how
interpersonal communication fits in with a bigger picture.

Because of the links back that we are making – and because we are already providing a summary account of critical perspectives – we do not give a further summary in the form of a review section at the end of this final chapter.

8.2 Communication as a process

The **process approach sees communication as being active** (something that is about 'doing'). It is **dynamic** – an activity that is ongoing and always subject to change. It is **irreversible** – what is communicated cannot be taken away, but only added to the sum of our knowledge and experience. It is **continuous** – that is to say we will always communicate something when in the presence of others (for example, even if we are silent), and we will even carry on communicating when we are alone (because we are always taking in and dealing with outside experience of some kind).

As a process, any communication activity must relate in some way to all the previous experience of the communicators, and to the entire culture that surrounds them. So it is also about **history** and about **context**.

We have already said that the process of communication between people is one that starts and ends with the Self. We regard what is happening within us (see the psychology of communication) as being all of a piece with our communication behaviour outside the Self, outside what goes on in our heads. NLP (see Chapter 3) supports this view in the way that it demonstrates that external behaviour can affect internal constructs as much as Self drives behaviours. This dynamic and symmetrical view within the process approach is also exemplified by ideas about **encoding and decoding**. We have to 'put together meaningfully' that stream of symbols that we call speech given to others, as much as we have to make sense of them when their speech is received.

And this draws attention to the fact that the process approach also sees communication as the continual construction and making sense of meanings. To be alive is to communicate. To communicate is to be in a state of continual interaction with our world. The most significant part of that interaction is our dealings with other people.

Communication is, indeed, active. It is about our behaviours, which influence the behaviour of others and which produce changes, just as others influence us.

Because of our different needs, we are continuously trying to present our Selves in different ways to different people in different situations. We are continuously adapting our thinking and our behaviour. Part of that adaptation is in response to others. The roles we adopt shift according to how we feel inside, how we want to be seen, how we are being treated by others, what we feel is appropriate, what outcomes we want for the interaction.

The way in which we present ourselves to others, and negotiate interactions, can be understood through the concept of **'mode of address'**. Originally, the term comes from the work of the linguist Roman Jakobsen. Jakobsen's model of an exchange between people brought out the importance of context and of the style of speech used. He distinguished between the addresser (the one who talks to) and the addressee (the one who is talked at):

- He saw the language used by the addressor as being about an emotive quality – the person who addresses looks to produce an effect on the person being talked to.

- For the addressee, however, he saw the language functions as being conative – that is to say, the listener is trying to make sense of what the speaker has to say (the connotations or meanings of their utterance).

Jakobsen (1990) analysed and described what he saw as structures in common uses of speech. He used and developed Saussure's work, and helped give rise to the birth of **structuralism** in the 1960s, and to the work of Roland Barthes in particular (about which we talk more below).

Ideas about mode of address have been developed by various critics. The concept draws attention to, for example, the relationship with the receiver that the use and style of speech is intended to set up. It is about notions of what is appropriate to a given situation or context. It has been extended into understanding media talk – especially how audiences are addressed by, for instance, radio or television. The idea is further extended to include features of a programme (such as titles music), which also contribute to the relationship set up with the viewer or listener. Of course, in the case of the media, this relationship raises particular issues about the exertion of media power over the audience, or about the promotion of ideological positions. The reason for setting up a pretend relationship between, for example, a DJ and the audience, is both mediated by technology and ultimately motivated by commercial interests. Day-to-day and face-to-face communication between people is, in general, a social affair, motivated by a variety of social and personal needs.

KEY QUESTIONS

What questions and problems are raised when technologies such as the mobile phone intervene in the communication process?

Can one accept that communication is entirely a result of socialization?

What capacity do we have to monitor something like communication with others, when it appears to be so 'natural'? And do we then have the capacity to change the way we behave?

8.3 Semiotics and communication as text

This approach is much concerned with the signs that we use in communicating and with the meanings generated by these signs. It is also concerned with structures and patterns in communication and within interaction. Semiotics, which has its roots in language study, offers terms through which to identify specific parts of communication in any form, and through which to explain ways in which meaning is constructed. It is tied in with the critical movement known as 'structuralism', which, at its most basic, can be understood as proposing that there are organizing principles or structures behind all forms of communication.

One of the better-known concepts that came out of this critical approach was that of 'binary oppositions' – the principle of opposites shaping the way that we think about the world: the opposition between words about male and female gender, for example.

Structuralism has its roots in linguistics, and the work of critics such as Jakobsen (see above) and Ferdinand de Saussure. Saussure also created what we now call 'semiotics', when, for instance, he conceived of language as a sign system. Among many ideas, he realized that signs only have meaning in respect of their difference from other signs; and that the meaning of any sign is not naturally tied to the sign itself.

Semiotics is concerned with how we internalize the production of meaning from external signs recognized in communication activity. Words and nonverbal signs have to be decoded internally. The process of decoding becomes the production of meaning. In general, meanings may be seen as being about our understanding of the world. Such understandings will, in turn, affect how individuals encode languages and their meanings.

Semiotics proposes that sign symbols are organized within what are called **paradigms** – one example of such a 'set of signs' would be the alphabet. We must have knowledge of these structures within us before we can decode any form of communication.

Further kinds of categorization or structure would be what semiotics calls 'codes' and 'syntagms':

- A **code is a coordinated sets of signs**, perhaps working at a **primary level** (the English language), or perhaps at **secondary level** (the 'codes' used in television news).

- **Syntagms are structures within codes** – such as a sentence, which is an organized set of word signs.

The idea of structure and organization also implies that there are rules that govern the pattern of the structure. These rules are called **'conventions'**. They help make sense of signs by organizing them into a pattern. Through these patterns meanings emerge. For example, a photograph is merely a collection of colours of more or less intensity unless we 'know' what the parts of the picture signify, unless we can 'see' how the parts relate to one another to make a whole. The signs, the structures, their meanings, are all learnt. Once learnt, they can be used. For instance:

- we learn the 'rule' that a large object (which also has to be recognized!) that obscures a smaller object in a photograph is 'in front' of it

- we learn to see a two-dimensional image as a three-dimensional representation.

So these signs, structures and their meanings exist within ourselves, and are recognized and understood through intrapersonal communication. It is important to remember that meanings are actually created within our minds and are not the same thing as the signs themselves – whether these signs are words or gestures or pictures. It is a central precept of semiotics that the meanings of a sign are arbitrary.

We can say that perception of others is about recognizing the signs of communication for what they are, and then making sense of them.

Once we have identified as words the sounds that someone makes, or the hand movements that they make as gestures, then we may attempt to attach meanings to these. We do not, of course, decode every single sign individually and laboriously when looking for meaning. Rather, we look at collections of signs, at a complete statement, at a set of body movements, and then make sense of the signs collectively, using the categories and rules that we have learnt.

Signs may signify many different things. In isolation they are relatively ambiguous. When we read the word sign 'bow', we do not know whether it is an action or an object unless it is placed within the linguistic context of a whole sentence or paragraph. If the sign is also a **signifier** in semiotic terms, then what it may mean is described as the **signifieds**. So perception is also about making choices of possible signifieds in order to decide on what the actual meaning is in a particular case. **Signification** is the process of making meanings.

Semiology is interested in social interpretations. So a sentence that runs, 'Bow to your superior knowledge' might be analysed by a semiologist in terms of the symbolic significance of 'bowing down'. But a communication student might analyse the phrase in linguistics terms and as a statement within an ongoing exchange.

It is also useful to be aware that semiotics recognizes different qualities of sign used in codes (communication). Fiske (1990) refers to Pierce when explaining that signs can be described as symbols or indices or icons:

- **Icons** are signs that refer directly to what they stand for – picture images, for instance.

- An **index** is a sign that just refers to something else indirectly – the smell of coffee drifting down a street refers to the fact that there is coffee somewhere.

- And **symbols** are signs that refer to something quite arbitrarily – like words as signs within writing.

In critical terms, semiotic analysis of what it called **'the text'** merges its interests with those of the later movements of cultural studies and postmodernism. A picture might be analysed as a text, as much as a novel. So, in terms of interpersonal communication, we could argue that a chunk of talk can be analysed as much as something more obviously coherent textually – like a letter to a friend.

Communication and social interaction can be viewed as an exchange of signs between people. If all communication is made up from signs, then we can only exchange information, ideas and meanings through signs. We are joined through signs. All relationships are conducted in terms of symbols. We can never deal in the original experience, the actual idea, but only in the signs that stand in place of the experience or the idea. To this extent it is a second-hand world that we live in.

The various forms of communication that we deal in can be described as codes (see above) – that is to say, English language or computer users' language are examples of primary and secondary codes, respectively. Visual forms such as the language of photographs or the language of comics are also codes.

Social interaction can be seen as being structured in terms of codes and of the segments of these labelled syntagms in the language of semiotics. More importantly, interaction is bound by conventions. These rules operate on a primary level, where for instance the rules of grammar help make sense of verbal signs. But there are also conventions binding secondary codes, and the use of communication in, for example, various social situations. If we agree that we would use a certain kind of language in, say, a religious ceremony, then we are saying that we would select certain signs appropriate to this occasion. We would expect by convention to use these. We would understand their meaning through conventions.

Many of the semiotic terms above owe their development to the work of Roland Barthes. In terms of meaning, he introduced two important terms – **denotation and connotation**. These distinguish between two levels of meaning in a text.

• Denotation is about what is immediately referred to in the real world.

• Connotation is about deeper meanings that are referred to – 'ideas about' what is denoted.

The terms are frequently used to explain the difference between something like a painting of a horse (the object denoted) and ideas about 'horse-ness' (the connotations). But there is no reason why one cannot see the same process working in the spoken and written word.

Barthes also introduced the idea of **mythologies**, when exploring meanings in texts, using semiotics as an analytic method. In our view, his mythologies are closely tied in with ideology. Myths are things we want to believe in, for example, masculinity as being about independence and physical prowess and nation as being about patriotism and common beliefs. Barthes demonstrated that texts (in the widest sense of the word) are full of mythologies about what we think is true and valid, but that this 'truth' does not necessarily stand up to analysis. There is not much difference in effect between myths and ideological positions. Motherhood is a mythology much invoked in our everyday talk as well as in media texts. By this we mean that ideas about it are invoked. For example, one of those ideas is that all women naturally want to become mothers. This simply is not true. We are not saying that many women do not or should not want to become mothers. But we would ask where this mythology comes from, who benefits from it – whether at least some women become mothers because of the influence of mythologies rather than because they decided this was a need coming from within themselves and their relationships.

Symbolic interactionism

This phrase refers back to the work of Mead (1934), in particular, and is of interest to communication students because of its emphasis on interaction between people. As an explanatory approach to interactions between the Self and others, it emphasizes the distinctiveness of human exchanges in using and recognizing symbols. This is about the importance of spoken language and nonverbal signs. It draws attention to the way in which we are able to reflect on our own actions – and, indeed, to think about who we are and how we wish to express ourselves. It also remarks on how we can try to think ourselves into the position of the other person who is trying to communicate with us.

Critics such as Blumer (1969) developed interactionism into ideas about how we create the very notion of society through interacting with others – communication makes things real. Society cannot exist apart from the interactions that make it happen.

Goffman (see Chapter 5) developed interactionist ideas into the area of face-to-face interaction. He was interested in the ways in which we construct ideas about our Self to others and to ourselves through presentation of Self. We are different selves in different social situations.

Issues and questions raised

If the link between a sign and its meaning is arbitrary, can this explain all failures of communication?

How far are the 'structures' suggested by semiotics innate or learned, and what are the implications of this?

Is reality just another meaning produced through communication?

8.4 Communication within a Marxist perspective

Marxist views of communication and culture have been developed and modified over many decades. As an analysis of economics, politics and society, they have tended to be more relevant to macro views – large and general views of what is going on and how. To this extent, and in respect of communication studies, they are more applicable to the media than to understanding human communication and face-to-face interaction. However, we would argue that there is some connection, not least in relation to, for example:

- the behaviour of groups of people as media audiences, or
- in relation to the connections between social communicative behaviour and models of the same thing as represented in the media.

Given the widespread assumptions about media influence, it is a pity that more research has not been done into modelling of interpersonal behaviours on the basis of media representations.

If we summarize a Marxist perspective on media communication, then we see that, for instance, this view of the media – audience relationship – is dominated by an assumption that the media do things to people. The media are part of capitalism and its interests, and inevitably promote views of the social élite – the ruling class – and promote the dominant ideology, which serves to maintain the power of this élite. Capitalist ideology believes in the production and consumption of goods. Critics like Adorno and Horkheimer, writing over half a century ago, saw the then developing mass media as, rather, 'mass culture'. They talked about the **culture industries**, trying to emphasize how in their view the 'quality' of what they thought of as culture was being turned into nothing but big business, producing goods not art.

Media programmes or magazines are examples of such goods. Goods may also be called 'commodities'. Belief in 'materialism' (the importance of commodities) then affects the way that we value everything else in our lives. Even our social relationships could be valued in terms of these commodities. The process of defining social values and relationships in this way is called **'commodification'**. The energy that is behind capitalist media industries comes from the force of economic determinism, that is, the behaviour of media institutions is determined by economic factors. The economic base of society is founded on the labour of workers. The media are run in the interests of the wealthy and of wealth creation, which remains the privilege of the few. The media may be seen as part of the **superstructure** of society in a Marxist model, where ideology is at work. This ideology affects workers (the economic base of the model) and their understanding of the exchange value of their labour and of the goods that they produce.

Marxist ideas relate to the argument that control over the means of production and distribution of goods leads to control over the ideas that are (in the case of media) within those goods. It seems reasonable to argue that such control represents some sort of power and influence. In particular, **Marxist criticism produces variations on the idea of 'false consciousness', in which social institutions generate false ideas about social relations**. They produce ideas – through representations, for instance – about status, power, class, which are made to seem true and valid when they are not. An unequal society is made to seem falsely and yet naturally acceptable.

The manufacture of this false consciousness is part of the invisible exercise of power – or **hegemony**. It springs from a **dominant ideology** – a particular and prevailing view of the world, of how it should be, of its values, of power relations. It maintains and conceals that ideology. Ideology is about a system of beliefs that benefit those who have social, economic and political power, but that work against the interests of those who do not have such power. For example, there is a prevailing belief that everyone has the capacity to work, that they should work, that work is good. This belief drives government efforts to question the situations of the disabled on incapacity benefits or single mothers on social benefits. It makes it hard for some employees to have their stress-related illness and nervous breakdown recognized as valid or even true. It may invoke a related belief that somehow the retired and low-income earners are less worthy citizens than those in full employment. It certainly invokes beliefs that Travellers or those who choose a dropout lifestyle are somehow deviant and 'odd'. And we would say that these ideological beliefs (or 'positions') must be contained within forms of communication. It is the use of words such as 'work-shy' or 'shirkers' by ordinary people, as well as by certain politicians, that gives life to beliefs and keeps ideology in circulation.

Antonio Gramsci made a significant contribution to the development of Marxist ideas in conceiving of the exercise of State power on society as having two forms:

- The one he described as coercion – the use of institutions such as the army or the police.

- The other is that of consent – the use of institutions such as the media or education.

We would point out that both media and education are 'ideas industries' that produce meanings about our world, but are also very much about communication. This is not to say that the teacher or the news announcer is a conscious mouthpiece of government. But it is the case that behind the teacher is a curriculum prescribed by the State, and behind the announcer is State regulation of a kind (e.g. OfCom) as well as an editorial system dominated by the discourse of consensus (as opposed to disagreement, opposition and change). But again, our point is not so much to get into a debate about media influence, as to point out that if there is some 'pressure for consent', then it is partly exerted through human communication. This may be an electronic representation through the TV screen, or face-to-face in a learning situation. In either case it is about speech and body language, and related notions in this book.

It also follows from the above that **hegemony is there in our everyday lives because ideology is also ever present in our thoughts**. One would have to accept that our perceptions of others, as well as our perception of media material, are filtered through some naturalized view of how the world is and should be. The beliefs and values that are part of the Self (and its schemata) must also, in the Marxist model, include views about social difference, views about which social groups are seen as having power (industrialists?), and about which are not (the disabled?). If you believe in the existence of class and the notion that it is a kind of social difference based on wealth and privilege, then Marxism may interpret that belief for you. We are talking about a view of the world that is received from without, but constructed and endorsed from within ourselves. We are talking about the effects of communication from various socializing sources, and about intrapersonal processes.

A relationship between Marxism, media and human communication can be seen in some of the ideas of Raymond Williams. In *The Long Revolution* (1965) he links the media and objects of mass production, as being part of a cultural revolution. He proposes the interchangeability of the terms 'culture' and 'society'. For him, **meanings about a culture are expressed in forms and acts of communication** (often social, but not exclusively so). He talks about what he calls 'structures of feeling', with reference to the idea that culture is something lived out in everyday life. He talks about recognizing the importance of people's response to the media, as much as seeing media as 'imposing' on us.

And it is true that talk about the media – about what is going on in soap operas, for example – is very much part of everyday conversation. But even this kind of 'casual chat' may still be ideological. Someone could make a comment about 'that daft cow getting what she deserved'. The comment is not referring to real people in a real world. But it is about the attitudes of a real person who does inhabit a real world, which happens also to include TV programmes. The comment is sexist and ideological in that the term of the abuse and the assumptions about what people 'deserve' come from a certain view of the world, stand for a particular set of beliefs.

If hegemony works to maintain one set of views, one set of values, even as other views may contest these – then it works as much through social interaction as through interactions with the media. The masculinity of car racing is constructed both through its media representations (the dominance of male drivers and commentators, and so on) and through the assumptions behind day-to-day conversations. On the other hand, hegemony may also be understood to be about a struggle between views trying to achieve dominance. In some examples one can see this happening 'live' – as with the political and social debates about the merits of passing laws to forbid 'smacking' children.

Marxist ideas can also help explain the nature of social interactions through comments on capitalism and commodification. Parents who offer cash to children for household labours are endorsing a capitalist model. If these parents said, 'It's Saturday morning, let's all spend an hour cleaning the house', this would be a more socialist and collectivist position. Equally, parents who 'bribe' the children to achieve good exam results are applying materialist incentives, are commodifying the process of study and its recognition.
The certificate comes to be worth cash as much as self-esteem. Parents who give their children cash 'to go to the shops and buy something' because they (the parents) are 'busy', are turning time into money (and perhaps giving their money rather than their time to their children).

Issues and questions raised

If ideology is invisible and pervasive within our communication, then how far can we really 'stand outside' it? Is something called 'objectivity' really possible?

What is the difference between the power of words used in everyday interactions and the power of words used within the media?

In terms of hegemony, what different views of the environment can you see struggling for dominance in public debates?

8.5 Communication and the study of culture

Culturalist approaches to communication are wide-ranging and have been the substance of an entire chapter (4) in this book. Even sections that follow in this chapter – postmodernism and feminism – could be subsumed under this heading. Cultural studies are interested in history, geography, urban spaces, the context in which things happen. They borrow from anthropology – for example, ethnographic approaches to audience studies in which media researchers have gone into the homes of people to hear them talking about media as they watch and listen to it.

Cultural studies may in part be about the Arts – what tends to be called still 'high culture'. But, in practice, it has been very much about **popular culture** – about what people do in shopping malls, or what they do with products like personal music players, or how they think about animals from their experiences of visiting zoos.

Culture is an all-embracing term, and in a sense the rise of an academic discipline called cultural studies has been a reaction against other subjects that have perhaps attempted to put ideas and topics into boxes. For instance, we could argue that **there is not much difference between culture and communication because culture is lived through communication**.

Cultural approaches are interested in groups, identity and difference, as we have already explained. Your sense of who you are, where you belong, who you belong with, is, we would say, only made real through communication – your dress codes, how you talk, details of your nonverbal behaviour. So everything that we have said about the Self, about self-presentation, about group behaviour, is about culture as well as about the conduct of interpersonal communication.

We are very happy with the idea of overlaps between what are called academic disciplines and between critical approaches to understanding any object of study – whether it is a conversation, a magazine or a cathedral.

As communication theorists we are interested in understanding how conversations produce meanings, and might use semiotic analysis to help us. Cultural analysis can also be wide-ranging in the tools of analysis and explanation that it uses. A culturalist interested in, for example, a cathedral would want to see what meanings this produces and how. This person might use semiotics as part of analysis and explanation. They might use the idea of the cathedral as a text (taking a term that has its origins in linguistics and literary studies and applying it to any object or experience which may be analysed). They would explore symbolism, the history of the cathedral and, most importantly, how it is used and understood by those who enter it – visitors as much as worshippers. Popular culture has itself been studied by people who might describe themselves variously as Marxists, structuralists, postmodernists and feminists.

Paul Du Gay (1997) and others have pinned cultural analysis to a relationship between five concepts, which we now explain in basic terms, and with reference to this book's emphasis on communication.

- **Representation** is about how we construct or represent ideas about the world – we can do that through talk or through the media.

- **Identity** is about our sense of who we are, where and how we 'belong' – we work this through from what we are told by others, from using our perceptual processes, from 'making it real' in the way that we talk and behave towards others.

- **Production** is about the production of meanings, the production of goods that have meanings – so while for the culturalist this includes such things a designer clothes, for us it also includes the 'production of' conversations, chants at football matches, group behaviours.

- **Consumption** is about using what is produced – for the culturalist it would be about what we do with the clothes or the movie we watch ('do with' in terms of understanding). You will see here that cultural studies has an affinity with media studies. It is easy to understand production and consumption in terms of media material. In terms of this book, the best analogy is with the idea of decoding – the consumption of talk comes to be about how we make sense of it and what we do with what we have heard. This could, for example, include talk on the telephone or talk from the radio. Talk also becomes associated with ideas of consumption and commodity when it is part of social behaviours that include other commodities – going to the movies, going shopping.

- **Regulation** is about ways in which institutions (mainly those of government) may control or limit what is produced and how, and what is consumed and how. Again, this is most easily understood in terms of the media. Thankfully, we do not live in an Orwellian state where there are attempts to control your conversations and interactions with others. And yet, it is possible to think of examples of regulation in face-to-face communication. In fact, we referred earlier in the book to 'regulators' – signs that help control conversation and turn-taking. But in a more social sense you might consider, for example, the regulation of talk in learning situations – those where the student is supposed to do the listening, or the silence of examination halls. We are not saying that such regulation is without sense or represents some abuse of power. But it exists. As do examples of the regulation of mediated speech – you are not free to say what you like about anyone or any subject over the radio (or in public for that matter). Incitement to religious hatred has now been made against the law.

With reference to groups, Parekh (in Du Gay 1997) provides an interesting set of **definitions of culture for a recognized cultural group**:

1. A body of beliefs through which the group members understand themselves and the world, and assign meanings to their social relations and behaviours.

2. Values and norms of behaviour which regulate social relations, inform ideas of 'goodness', and are behind key life events such as birth, marriage and death.

3. Rituals and expressive arts which communicate collective emotions, experiences and self-understanding.

4. Conceptions of a distinctive history and of difference from other groups.

5. Cultivation of a common social character (including elements such as motivation and temperament).

You should be able to see how we have touched on many of these ideas in this book, including what we have said about self-concept, about identity and about social interaction. (For more on ideas about media and culture, see also Burton 1999.)

The culturalist would also be interested in subcultures, how they display their identities, what holds them together, what use they make of cultural artefacts. Again, we would wish to emphasize here the overlap between so-called discrete disciplines, although the sociologist would be more interested in how the subculture relates to other groups and to society as a whole. But, whatever discipline the critic is coming from, they could all be interested in issues of empowerment and disempowerment for that subculture. All of them might find the concept of ideology to be relevant.

In communication terms, signs of regional identity might be mainly analysed in terms of dialect and accent. But a cultural analysis might range wider in explaining that identity with relation to history, place (geography), leisure patterns, and so on.

Cultural analysis also recognizes wide and diffuse bonds that link people together, even globally. There is here, again, an overlap with communication in the use of different language. For example, though its use is diminishing, Yiddish is still spoken, written and understood by communities in the USA, in Israel, in Eastern Europe. But Jewishness is also (apart from the obvious fact of religion) about a sense of the Jewish past, about a certain kind of humour, about a sense of belonging. Culturalists use the word **'diaspora'** to describe this feeling, this kind of identification. There has been analysis of those aspects of history, place, common experience, myths and rituals, which it is suggested, create a black diaspora ranging from West Africa to the USA – obviously linked to a background of slavery and slave trading. We would also argue for the importance of communication within this concept of diaspora, both as an expression of identity and as linking separated communities. A literal and contemporary example of this linking is in the website for Tamil communities, which makes a global connection, back to the original cultures in southern India and Sri Lanka.

Here, we also see a link between ideas about communication and those about **globalization**. This term is often associated with the global spread of western economic power, with media imperialism, with international commerce, with the rise of information technology and use of the internet. In fact, globalization is much more complicated than that. For a start, it is not true that it is all about the dominance of the West. There are many influences flowing around the planet, not least in terms of music and popular culture. Economically the world may be dominated by the USA, but it certainly is not the only global influence. Eastern countries are very important in this respect. In terms of its being about the flow of goods and ideas, globalization is not that new – these 'flows' have been going on for centuries. Western sciences and mathematics are very much built on the influence of Arabic cultures, going back several hundred years.

In terms of globalization being about more frequent contact between cultures, based on things like the technologies of travel and the culture of tourism, we have already commented on this earlier when looking at cross-cultural communication (page 167). Globalization has led to the spread of the English language as a medium in activities as diverse as aircraft control, diplomacy and commerce. But it is not the most widely spoken language on a global scale. And cultural contacts draw attention to the central importance of what meanings are produced and understood, and how and when communication takes place. (For more on globalization see Burton 2005.)

In that communication is one kind of cultural activity, ideas about self-presentation link with a culturalist perspective. However, while a communication analysis would link with psychological perspectives on, for instance, what that presentation might be saying about emotional state, a cultural analysis might be more interested in the more culturally specific signs of the performance – for example, how 'Chavs' dress, linked to how they fit into popular culture in Britain in the twenty-first century.

KEY QUESTIONS

How do social groups use both talk and display signs to represent ideas about themselves to the rest of society?

In what ways might culture constrain what we say, and how?

How far is communication on a global scale affecting people's sense of their identity, or even leading to something described as 'global culture'?

8.6 Communication and postmodernism

As a critical 'movement' **postmodernism is closely linked with the rise of cultural studies**. It is a set of ideas, rather than a discipline as such. But whichever keyword one starts from, both tend to lead to study of the text, and to the relationship of the audience with the text. In this tendency to particularity, postmodernist approaches can be seen as being at the other end of a spectrum from process approaches, which want to take into account everything that has bearing on the object of study, which may be a newspaper or a conversation. In the 1980s, reception studies exemplified this shift, in that they preferred to look at specific audiences reacting to specific texts in specific situations – and avoid seeing audiences as large groups, especially as groups that behaved coherently. Analysis influenced by postmodernity would ignore the place of the institution and the overview – on the assumption that making sense of this larger and complicated view just is not possible.

For postmodernists the text is sufficient unto itself. The **postmodern text** is one that is full of ironies and intertextuality; it is understood by reference to other texts; it is about form as much as content; it is driven by style as much as any well-shaped narrative; and it is not interested in big moral conclusions. Stuff happens.

Some have tried to argue that postmodernism is only valid in terms of criticism within the arts — reactions against modernism in painting or architecture. Others disagree, and have argued that in many spheres it is a way of thinking that reacts against ideas about unity and overall explanation for how things are, and accepts kinds of chaos and fragmentation. It might be saying, 'Don't look for the meaning of life, just look for what gives your life meaning for the time being'. Human communication is both informed by the arrival of such ideas, and its language is the means of expressing such ideas.

Whether **postmodern perspectives** are applied to sociological analysis, media analysis or communication, they **generally react against the idea that there can be certainties and structures**. They oppose the efforts of Marxist analysis to construct a 'big picture' of what is going on in society (including media). They discount attempts to construct meaningful theories about the power relations between large social institutions. The argument is that this cannot be done – there are too many complicating factors to be able to construct a meaningful overview. All one can do is to examine the particular.

However, we as authors do not agree with this and would argue that it is just as important to try to propose models of what is happening on a grand scale as it is to make detailed analysis of particular subjects. In communication terms, this means that it is, for example, as important to establish some overall principles for stages of group bonding as it is to analyse the behaviours of specific groups in specific circumstances. Of course, there is the problem of cultural relativism – the meaning and use of communication behaviours is relative to the culture that uses them. But we would point out that, at the same time, cultures do not exist exclusively. All cultures communicate about family, and have various groups that bond through communication. All cultures have rituals to do with birth and death. All cultures have notions of joy and sorrow, even if they express these in different ways, for different reasons, at different times. Postmodernism argues, on the other hand, that there are no absolute truths, there are no certainties about how society operates, there are no universal ideals to which we can all aspire.

Postmodernism and cultural studies come together in a celebration of popular culture – again, as some kind of reaction against earlier twentieth-century views that culture means 'high culture', the material of high Art. A postmodern analysis of culture, including media, would point to the way in which 'image' has become everything in our society. One becomes a celebrity because of appearing on the celebrity medium of television, not because one has done anything that is worthy of being celebrated on some scale of achievement. **In the postmodern society we are all for consumption**, for being what we wear, not what we are. In this society **the distinction between social reality and media reality is blurred**. Indeed, some postmodern critics argue that there is no difference. What we read and watch becomes as true as what we live directly, because both are about lived experience.

It was these kinds of point that Oliver Stone was trying to make in his film *Natural Born Killers* (although many critics failed to see past the violence in it). In a world of consumption for its own sake, of celebrity-dom, of 'style is everything', of 'reality is everywhere', the protagonists in the film embarked on a killing spree – living out comic-book fantasies, abandoning long-term morality for short-term fame.

All this relates to the study of human communication in a variety of ways. It has a bearing on the formation of Self and of identity, on the way in which one conceives of one's relationships with others. A postmodern view would see individuals as using communication to present a Self that is about style and performance, about public appearance, about the smart one-liner, rather than about a larger structure of relationships informed by a general set of beliefs. By this argument, what has been called the cynicism and selfishness of some social behaviours is linked to a weakening of social structures (the family, the school, the community) and expressed through ways in which people talk about themselves and their attitudes towards others. We are not saying that we entirely agree with this view. But it is at least arguable that an analysis of communication behaviours can be linked with, for example, a postmodern view that there is no perfect society to which we can aspire. Postmodern uncertainties simultaneously are expressed by, and lead to, communication that avoids the maintenance of relationships. If people do not believe in the importance of working on relationships, then they will not talk in ways that do that work: if you do not talk to each other in constructive ways then you are also implying that you do not care, that you have a certain view of the world.

We are also in sympathy with **the postmodern emphasis on close analysis** – many examples in this book have been about the significance of details of verbal and nonverbal signing. Similarly, we would agree that kinds of context are very important to the production of meaning, and to understanding what meanings may be intended in a given situation.

Postmodernism has been associated with 'discourse analysis' – previously referred to on page 154. An influential example of this has been seen in the writing of Michel Foucault. He has, for instance, proposed that the way that madness has been talked about, written about and photographed tells us a lot about what it means, at a given time. Communication about madness reveals how we think about madness. Its meaning is constructed by this communication (words or images) and this meaning is changeable. He examined texts in which the discourses of female gender and madness come together to construct the nineteenth-century myth of female hysteria. Again, we would agree that forms of communication are used to *construct* the truth, as much as to express anything that can be demonstrated to be already 'out there'.

Issues and questions raised

In what ways can we see changes in habits of eating and taking meals (e.g. the TV dinner) as changing how communication is carried on within the family?

Is communication becoming less formal than it was (e.g. in respect of letter styles or of how we address people in everyday life)?

How could discourse affect the way that a child develops?

8.7 Communication and feminist analysis

We have, again, already alluded to this critical perspective throughout the sections on language and gender. In general, feminism is concerned with (mis)representations of female genderness, with the construction of textual meaning, with women as audiences for texts, with the nature of social relations. It has also been much concerned with the exercise of power, in social and political terms. It sees women as being subordinated to men in western culture.

In many ways feminism is about using existing critical tools such as semiotic analysis or discourse analysis, but mainly in the cause of **understanding how gender comes to be given meaning**. There is interest in the connections between representations and gender difference as it is lived in our society.

There are different feminist approaches allied to different critical traditions, as described below:

- **Marxist feminism** would see gender inequality as a further evidence of ideology in action, of the oppression by the powerful of the powerless via unjust social and economic structures – in much the same way that Marx conceived of class oppression.

- **Psychoanalytical feminism** critiques texts through, for example, Freudian or Lacanian readings. In the first case, comment might be made about patriarchal dominance or about fear of female sexuality on the part of males – many Hollywood action films can be read in this way. In the second case, comment might be made about 'the mirror self', about women seeing themselves in media images as being looked at by men. This continues to perpetuate the subordination of women in society.

- **Radical feminism** would see this subordination in terms of sexual oppression and the manipulation of women's sexuality.

As Gunter (1995) puts it, with reference to gender representations in the media:

> For feminist media theorists, the media are seen as principal instruments in conveying stereotypical, patriarchal and hegemonic values about women and femininity. The mass media are instruments of (male-dominated) social control.

Feminism would also relate media representations to social practices, arguing that social structures, behaviours and attitudes still support the idea of patriarchy. In terms of social practice, for example, it is acknowledged that in many industries there is still a 'glass ceiling' that makes it difficult for women to obtain senior management positions. Sometimes it may be that attitudes are revealed through ways in which women are talked about, or even talked to, within an organization. Sometimes what is not said is more important than what is said. Sometimes appointment processes may put weight on masculinized behaviours, approaches to decision making and uses of communication. And in any event – as with ethnic issues – the statistics reveal that there is a problem of unequal achievement.

Feminist critical perspectives and terms interact with those of cultural studies. For example, feminist analysis might work through ideas about identity and difference. It would explore questions about what it is to be female. There are those who strongly question the approach that talks about female as being 'different' to male, not least because that makes male-ness a kind of benchmark for female-ness. They would also question the use of the concept of binary oppositions as being equally unhelpful – female as the opposite of male. We have already pointed out that some critics argue that the way words are used in life situations suggests that there is not much difference, if any, between male talk and female talk.

Feminism also has to take on issues and representations that do not simply pivot on gender. It is clear that how women are represented, how they think about themselves, is complicated by other issues such as religion and race. One is never simply female. This recognition of complexity in making a feminist critique is sometimes referred to as **'Third Wave Feminism'**, which accepts that identity may have dimensions beyond that of being female. This reminds us of the idea of multiple identities. It also draws attention to the fact that for women in some parts of the world issues of injustice for them may be more to do with race (and how both men and women are treated) than mainly to do with their gender.

But in all respects feminist critiques do place weight on how women are shown and talked about. They comment on ways in which women are empowered or disempowered.

KEY QUESTIONS

Do you agree that females are disempowered by the ways that they are talked about in our society?

What do you think are the main differences in the ways that men and women see themselves? What part does communication play in this?

How could questions of culture affect the issues that matter to women in contemporary society?

8.8 Conclusion

So, in this chapter, we have looked at a number of major critical perspectives and their key terms, we have explained them, and we have tried to relate them to communication in general and to interpersonal and group communication in particular. We have pointed out where these perspectives overlap or borrow from one another. Having done this, our central arguments would be:

- that these perspectives rely on the human capacity for communication
- that they throw light on what it means to communicate
- that direct communication between people is central to our social structures and our social relationships
- that everything we call culture is both manifested and valued through this communication
- that communication is about the production of meanings

- that our well-being as individuals, as couples, as group members, depends on how we understand and deploy our ability to communicate with one another.

Suggested reading

Burton, G., 2005, *Media and Society, Critical Perspectives*, Maidenhead: Open University Press.

Fiske, J., 1990, *Introduction to Communication Studies*, 2nd edn, London: Routledge.

Glossary of communication terms

This list provides a brief definition of the meaning and use of some important terms in communication studies. We also suggest that you consult the index of this book for terms defined in the text. Finally, for further information on terms you will find the following works useful:

- Harre, R. and Lamb, R. (eds), 1986, *The Dictionary of Personality and Social Psychology*, Oxford: Blackwell.
- O'Sullivan, T., Hartley, J., Saunders, D., Montgomery, M. and Fiske, J., 1994, *Key Concepts in Communication and Cultural Studies*, 2nd edn, London: Methuen.
- Watson, J. and Hill, A., 1994, *A Dictionary of Communication and Media Studies*, 3rd edn, London: Edward Arnold.

Attitude: in terms of interpersonal communication, this refers to our mental orientation towards another person. Basically, attitude is measured in terms of the degrees of hostility or friendliness that we feel towards that other person. Attitudes are founded on beliefs that we hold as a result of previous experience.

Attribution: refers to the mental process through which we assign characteristics to another person. These characteristics may also be called their 'attributes'. These will include aspects of personality, emotion, and attitude. Attribution theory attempts to explain how we carry on this mental process. (See also *perception* and *judgement* in the main text.)

Beliefs: are convictions that we hold, mainly to do with social reality and social relationships. They are concepts that contribute to the Self, and which act as reference points when perceiving other people and when carrying on social interaction. Beliefs define how we think things are and how we think they should be.

Code (Encode and Decode): refers to a system of signs bound by cultural conventions. There are many types of communication code – for example, verbal, nonverbal and graphic – through which we generate and share meanings. **Encode** refers to our putting information into signs for other people. **Decode** refers to our interpreting signs from other people.

Cognition: is the mental process through which we recognize external stimuli (signs) and then assign them to categories to try to make sense of them. The term refers to both the ways in which we take in information and the ways that we organize that information in our minds.

Cognitive dissonance: describes anxiety that arises from a sense of inconsistency between one belief that we hold and another, between what we believe and what we think we should believe. It may also arise as a result of our doing something that we then realize is inconsistent with our beliefs. An advertiser may arouse a sense of this dissonance when they suggest that a caring parent will use their product. If one of the audience does not use this product then they may feel that they are not caring – hence the anxiety.

Commodification: refers to the economic effects of capitalism and marketing, through which social relations and cultural artefacts are turned into commodities, or goods. For a simple example, think of the ways in which romance and love are sold for Valentine's Day. Then consider how this affects interpersonal relations.

Communication: means many things to many people. Essentially, it is about the creation and exchange of meanings through signs. Communication between people is a process in which the signs of verbal and nonverbal language are used in an attempt to make known that which otherwise only exists in the minds of the communicators. What is made known may be many things – experiences, ideas, feelings. How well these things are made known depends on the signs selected for use, how well they are used, and how far the communicators share agreement about what the signs mean anyway. There are many other ideas about what defines communication, including those that propose communication must be intentional. Distinction has been made between process, semiotic and cultural approaches to studying and defining communication. This book has proposed that such distinctions are largely unnecessary.

Competence: refers to the psychological and the behavioural abilities that enable one to fulfil certain functions. (*Performance* is the actual goal-directed behaviour resulting from this competence.) **Communicative competence** refers to our ability to use appropriate means of verbal and nonverbal communication (as well as communication technology) to achieve goals through interaction with others. **Social competence** refers to our ability to use social skills to manage social interaction through appropriate verbal and nonverbal behaviour. **Linguistic competence** refers to our ability to use written and spoken language in an appropriate range of registers to express ourselves and to share meanings with other people. **Emotional competence** is a learned capability based on emotional intelligence (see below) that results in effective interpersonal performance at work and in personal and social life.

Context: describes the physical, social and cultural environment in which communication takes place and draws attention to the effects of such environmental factors on the way that communication is carried on. For example, we relate differently to people depending on whether we are communicating in what we consider to be a public or a private place.

Conventions: are a system of culture-based rules and practices defining how signs are used within codes, and how behaviour takes place within social interactions.

Cultural studies: is the study of cultural behaviours, the interaction of cultures, and the meanings produced by specific cultures. It focuses on the relationship between the ideas that inform a culture and the practices through which these ideas are revealed. Cultural studies often concerns itself with the characteristics of subcultures and with the relationship of these to the main culture. To this extent it is also concerned with cultural or social divisions and with the ways that these are both represented and naturalized.

Culture: a comprehensive term embracing all those factors which make the lifestyle and beliefs of a given group distinctive – for instance, in terms of social behaviours, religious practices, shared history, creative productions. We have argued that culture is made real through communication. Refer back to Chapter 4.

Deindividuation: refers to the lessening of social, moral and societal constraints upon individual behaviour; and to a belief that one may cease to be responsible for one's own behaviour, and can allow group identity and norms to take over this responsibility.

Diaspora: describes the sense of shared cultural identity that is important to groups that may be scattered geographically, such as Jewish peoples.

Difference: a critical term that draws attention both to what members of a given group may have in common and to what they feel is identified as being different about them – usually expressed through the attitudes of a dominant culture towards a subculture.

Discourse: is a term used in linguistics to refer to verbal utterances and texts that are longer than a sentence. The term is also used elsewhere by extension to identify other longer types of discourse – e.g. 'television discourse' could mean the characteristic modes of verbal and visual representations in broadcast television. In terms of cultural studies, 'discourse' refers to the use of language (in its broadest sense) to construct representations and particular ways of understanding these (e.g. the selective use of words or pictures about people of Arab origin which demonizes them). **Discourse analysis** looks at the production and structures of discourses. Such an analysis would investigate the structure of paragraphs and texts, as in a monologue or in an interaction between two or more people. It seeks to explain how one utterance follows in a rational, rule-governed way to create a meaningful sequence and structure to communication. A cultural version of discourse analysis would examine communication to see what was selective and constructed about it, which represented the subject in a particular way (e.g. a film which showed Arab people as terrorists or untrustworthy, as opposed to showing Caucasian people as being good and law-abiding.

Ego state: is one of the three primary states identified in transactional analysis theory. The three primary states are those of Adult, Parent and Child. Ego state describes a particular kind of Self that will affect attitudes towards another person, as well having its own characteristic communication behaviour.

Emotional intelligence: is the ability to be aware of our own and other people's emotions and to be able to use this awareness to build effective and fulfilling relationships. This concept developed from ideas about multiple intelligences (see below). One of the intelligences described is **interpersonal intelligence**, which is the ability to understand other people – what motivates them, how they work, and how to work cooperatively with them. Another type of intelligence is **intrapersonal**, which is the ability to form an accurate, truthful model of oneself and to be able to use that model to operate effectively in life. Emotional intelligence has five domains: knowing one's emotions, managing emotions, motivating oneself, recognizing emotions in others and handling relationships.

Empathy: is being able imaginatively to enter into another person's feelings and experiences, without filtering these through one's own beliefs, values and experiences. When we empathize we imagine why it would make sense to behave as another person is behaving.

Feminism: a critical approach to texts and communication that is interested in how women are constructed as a gender. Such an approach often looks at discourses and representations, explaining how women are disempowered within patriarchal societies. The use of speech is central to how women see themselves and are seen, in terms of social relations.

Games: is another concept attached to transactional analysis. Games are recognizable episodes of social interaction in which one person will attempt to gain psychological advantage over another.

Giving strokes: See Strokes, below.

Globalization: describes a process in which economic and political institutions now increasingly operate on a global scale. This process is intertwined with developments in technology that support global communications in order to enable these operations, but which also develop interactions between peoples (for example, through tourism).

Group: a collection of people who interact in some way and who share common goals or interests. These can be **small groups** (people who interact face to face), **reference groups** (stereotypes with which individuals identify or are identified) and **statistical groups** (defined as simply having one or more characteristics in common). A **virtual group** refers to a collection of people who do not meet face to face but who communicate via electronic means, such as emails or the World Wide Web.

Halo effect: is that 'perceptual barrier' results from allowing one feature of another person to dominate our attention, with the effect of excluding or diminishing the importance of other features.

Hegemony: a term that describes ways in which one set of beliefs (often the dominant ideology) works via social, economic and political institutions to promote that set of beliefs as being naturally true.

Icon: in semiotic terms an icon is a sign that looks like the thing it is meant to stand for. Pictures of people are iconic: names of people are not.

Identity: that sense of Self which has cultural dimensions – a sense of belonging to a certain place and group with a certain history and certain ways of behaving. Identity is manifested through the use of communication. See also Difference, above.

Ideology: is another term about which whole books have been written. Fundamentally, it stands for that coherent set of values and beliefs that is dominant in a culture and which is particularly held by those social groups who have power. To this extent an ideology is often seen to be repressive of alternative views of society. It must be represented through communication, and is usually there by implication. Ideology is also necessarily concerned with social and power relationships and with the means through which these are made apparent.

Idiolect: is a personal repertoire and capacity for language use (e.g. vocabulary, syntactic structures, register, accent) resulting from our own knowledge and experience.

Index: an index is a sign that refers indirectly to the thing it stands for. If we hear a knock on our door, this 'indexical' sign refers indirectly to the presence of someone outside the door.

Interaction: is the exchange and negotiation of meaning between two or more participants located within given social contexts. It may consist of behavioural events that occur merely because people happen to be in the presence of others, or it may be more focused through mutual engagement of the people concerned. See also Transaction, below.

Interpersonal communication: is any form of communication (both verbal and nonverbal) between two or more people face to face.

Language: refers to the whole body of words (vocabulary) and ways of combining them (grammar) that are used by a nation, people or race.

Leadership: refers to the ability a person has to persuade, or to require, other people to follow him or her and to fulfil his or her aims. Leadership implies the ability to challenge the status quo, to communicate a new vision, direction and strategy and to motivate and inspire others.

Leakage: refers to the notion that nonverbal behaviour or unconscious physiological feedback may contradict our more consciously controlled verbal communication and give away how we really feel. In practice, it is not possible to separate verbal and nonverbal channels since they interact in our self-presentation, intentionally or unintentionally.

Marxism: a critical approach to economic and social relations that emphasises the unequal disposition of power in society. Since the original writings of Karl Marx, his ideas have been much modified, to explain, for example, how ideology works to privilege those who operate dominant institutions such as the media. This inequality permeates even the talk of everyday communication. See also Hegemony, above.

Meaning: what is signified by the messages conveyed through the signs that we give off and that we perceive. We assign meanings to all human behaviours through agreed cultural conventions.

Mode of address: a term that originally referred to examination of speech styles, but which now refers more widely to ways in which any communicator 'talks' in a certain way to set up a relationship with the addressee.

Modernism: In terms of art, modernism is a term used to describe works in which the emphasis is on structures and patterns, perhaps at the expense of naturalistic representation. Picasso and cubism is one expression of modernism, just as art deco or the work of Van de Rohe is another example within design and architecture.

Multiple intelligences: is a concept developed by Howard Gardner, based on a theory that human capacity should be seen as being more than just intellectual competence (IQ). He has suggested that we can identify several types of problem-solving intelligence which reflect a person's interests and talents, including linguistic, musical, logical-mathematical, spatial, bodily-kinaesthetic, intra- and interpersonal, and naturalist.

Myths/Mythologies: tie in with the work of Roland Barthes and the concept of **connotations**. Texts contain meanings that are ideological, and, at the same time, mythical beliefs about everything – from what it takes to be a 'real man' to the possibility of 'getting back to nature'.

Neurolinguistic programming (NLP): describes the notion that each person has internalized a particular pattern of language use and physiological/neurological behaviours, according to a personal programming of perceptions, experiences, knowledge and imaginings.

Nonverbal behaviour: People cannot not behave in the presence of others. The effect is that we are giving off messages through means other than speech all the time. These messages may be intentionally encoded and represented, in which case one can talk of **nonverbal communication**. But they may be unintentionally given off, though still decoded by other people. In this case one is dealing with nonverbal behaviour.

Paradigm: is a set of items (very possibly signs) that clearly belong to one category. The alphabet is a paradigm of letters from which words are constructed. Similarly, nonverbal signs form a coherent category and are a paradigm. When the signs operate together according to **conventions** or rules, then one has a **code**. Paradigms can be culture specific – that is to say, only that culture recognizes that a particular set of items 'goes together'. Often paradigms coexist. A pack of playing cards includes the paradigms of cards, of number, of suits, of kings and queens.

Paralanguage: the term used to describe the ways in which words are spoken, including features such as volume, pace, intensity, stress, pitch, tone, emphasis, quality of voice, articulation, accent and other sound factors that are often interpreted in terms of certain emotions ('She/he sounds sad/happy/stressed', etc.). Like other forms of communication behaviour, we can consciously seek to control our paralanguage, for example, to sound confident and relaxed in an interview.

Perception: is that part of the interpersonal process of communication through which we make judgements on another person in terms of their attributes. In respect of interpersonal communication, it includes both sensory recognition of verbal and nonverbal behaviours, and also interpretation of these.

Perceptual set: is much the same as a **schema**: that is, a related set of notions or of information held in the memory, which form a category of ideas or of experience.

Performance: refers to the idea that each of us performs in various roles when presenting ourselves to others and when interacting with others. See also **Competence**, above.

Personality: a set of traits that it is believed are characteristic of the individual, and which describe their distinctive qualities. There are alternative views of personality as being relatively fixed, with a core, or as being mobile, changing its characteristics according to need and situation.

Phatic communication: is communication that often serves to confirm social relationships. It is often represented through small, nonverbal signs of recognition and of bonding between people and within groups.

Postmodernism: the term describes a reaction against modernism, and its beliefs in the importance of structure and patterns, as well as against the idea that one can construct grand models to explain things like communication. Postmodernism tends to celebrate style above content, the use of irony and referentiality, in respect of all forms of communication. It permeates all disciplines. It is associated with reception studies and the study of popular culture – with specific critical projects as much as with grand designs.

Prejudice: is about prejudgements. People who have pre-formed attitudes and values that they immediately call up when perceiving the behaviour of another person can be said to be prejudiced. It is often supposed that these predispositions are negative. But this need not be the case. One may be prejudiced for as much as against.

Presentation: See Self-presentation, below.

Racketeering: a term from transactional analysis that identifies those kinds of **Game** in which the players seek to manipulate the victim into giving **strokes**. See Strokes, below.

Redundancy: is about the degree of predictability in a message that aids accurate decoding and that may strengthen social relationships. So, what is redundant are those elements of encoding that are not strictly essential to conveying meaning, but which seek to reinforce the message or foster a relationship that will help with the sharing of meaning.

Register: is that stylistic variation of language use that may change according to situation and context. It also includes choice of vocabulary, use of syntax and paralinguistic features.

Ritual: refers to repetitive and highly convention-bound behaviours that have become a matter of habit. Our communication behaviours are full of rituals in certain situations. Meetings of Freemasons or of Girl Guides include ritual communication, especially at the end of the meeting. But even informal social interaction may become ritualized – for example, what members of the family say and do at breakfast time.

Role: is a socially defined pattern of behaviour that reflects specific expectations, conventions and norms. It will inform the regulation of interaction and of relationships. It includes a notion of public behaviour that the communicator believes is appropriate to the situation and to his or her position within this.

Role conflict: is experienced by people who feel that the behaviour patterns of a role that they are expected to play conflict with the patterns of either a role which they would prefer to play or with the patterns of a role that seems just as appropriate.

Saliency: refers to the relative dominance or importance of, for example, certain features of another person's behaviour as this is perceived. Certain behaviour may have saliency because it fits in with expectations or because it fits in with some previous experience of the perceiver in which such behaviour was important.

Schemata: are ways of organizing our knowledge and experience, including the categorizing and grouping of items of information. We call on these schemata to check new information and to make evaluations of people. See also **Perceptual set**, above.

Self-concept/Self-image: is defined as an internalized view that we have of ourselves. One important element of this **self-esteem**. The Self also includes the ideas of the Self as seen by others, the ideal Self and the Self as we believe we are seen.

Self-disclosure: refers to a revealing of Self to others. Self-disclosure involves getting to know oneself more honestly and includes the idea of building relationships with others (because disclosure also means offering trust to another person by telling them something about oneself).

Self-esteem: is about how we rate ourselves. We have degrees of self-esteem, rating ourselves more or less positively. We may rate ourselves in terms of elements such as social attractiveness or skills.

Self-presentation: is public behaviour that we use for various reasons: to present ourselves to other people in order to match an ideal self-image, to enact what is perceived to be an appropriate role, to influence others' view of us, to define the situation in our own terms or to influence the progress of the interaction – or any combination of these.

Semiotics: refers to the study of signs, of sign systems and of their meanings.

Sign (Signification): a sign is a sign because we agree that it is. Any small piece of behaviour – whether it be a sound that we call a word or a movement that we call a gesture – only becomes a sign because we have learned through a socializing process that it is, in fact, meaningful. The particular meaning, or **signification**, of a sign is also socially agreed. Learning to talk is the same as learning to recognize one code of signs, to acquire the agreed meanings of those sound signs. Signs have no meanings in themselves.

Social cognition: is that process through which a person acquires, assimilates and organizes knowledge of events and of social reality. Through this process we come to 'know' the world and to use this knowledge to interpret our perceptions.

Social constructionism: describes a view of communication behaviour (and with relation to social psychology) that notions such as reality are constructed and are part of social processes – that these notions do not exist as absolute truths outside such processes.

Social facilitation: refers to the idea that individuals can achieve more by working with, or in the presence of, other people than they can on their own.

Socialization: describes those processes by which a person becomes a participating member of society, through learning how to live (and interact successfully) in that society. The term includes the idea of assimilation of sociocultural values, attitudes, conventions and norms of behaviour. It is not necessarily a passive personal process, but can include negotiation and rejection of a socially constructed consensus.

Social reality: is constructed in the mind. Communication helps us to share the social reality that we have constructed in our heads, and to agree on what this includes. This reality includes beliefs about our roles, our relationships and the structure of society, as well as the values that underpin all these things. This reality is for us as individuals the truth of what society is like, what rules it lives by, what it believes in.

Social skills: are sets of goal-directed, interrelated social communication behaviours that can be learned and which are in the control of the individual. These skills include the ability to control and monitor the information that we give off to others, and to interpret information that others give off to us through verbal and nonverbal behaviours.

Spiritual intelligence: is not one of the currently accepted list of multiple intelligences (see above), but it has been suggested that it should be seen as a separate competence. It can be defined as the intelligence with which we address and solve the problems of meaning and value: the intelligence with which we can place our activities and lives in a wider, richer, meaning-giving context.

Stereotype: is a generalized and simplified social classification of individuals or groups that represents incomplete assumptions and judgements about these people. Such categories are often seen in a negative light, as being fixed, prejudiced and closed to modification through future knowledge and experience.

Strategy: is coordinated, communicative behaviour designed to achieve specific purposes and goals in social interaction.

Strokes: in terms of social interaction and social skills, one is said to be 'giving strokes' when one gives some signal of reward and recognition to another person. Praising someone in verbal terms, together with a friendly glance and a pat on the back would be a commonplace example of giving strokes.

Structuralism: describes a critical approach that emerged in the 1960s and that argued that forms of communication (texts) can be described in terms of structures or patterns. These structures also help make and exchange meanings. Structuralism can be associated with

semiotics (an ordered approach to the production of signs and their meanings); to modernism (see Postmodernism, above); and developments in a range of disciplines, such as linguistics and media (narrative analysis).

Symbol: a sign that bears no literal relationship to what it refers to. It stands for something else because there is a social agreement that it should do so (see also Icon, Index, above). The word 'giraffe' is symbolic. It does not literally represent a giraffe in any way. But a picture of a giraffe would be iconic because it does literally represent the animal.

Symbolic interaction: refers to the fact that interaction between people takes place through symbols. Also, the communication behaviours involved may be culturally symbolic. If a male opens a door for a female and says, 'After you', that person is, first, using word symbols to control behaviour and, second, symbolizing a culturally determined view of the relationship between men and women. Here, we are back to the nature of communication itself. This interaction through symbols is a way of negotiating meanings between people.

Syntagm: is a combination of signs from within a paradigm that, through the operation of conventions has come to have meaning as a unit. A sentence is composed of letter and word signs and can be seen to be a unit on its own. It obeys the rules (conventions) of syntax and grammar. The meanings of syntagms are understood only through their relationship to one another. In a piece of writing the meaning of one sentence can only be fully understood by looking at another sentence.

Team: refers to a group of three or more people who work interdependently, combining different skills and operating in different roles to achieve a set of mutually agreed goals.

Text: a term that now describes any example of a piece of communication, from a photograph to a speech.

Transaction: in terms of transactional analysis, this is the smallest unit of interaction that can be identified as taking place between two people. So a glance given and received could be considered to be a transaction. In more general terms, a transaction can be defined as interaction where two or more people mutually and simultaneously take one another into account. In the transaction these people will work out their role relationships and conduct their interaction by a set of rules. Such interaction is focused and goal directed.

Reading list

The following is a selection of books and other references that we have used in the preparation of this book.

There are also, of course, a number of websites that have relevant and often up-to-date information about interpersonal communication. We have decided not to make a list of such sites we have used: many are limited and partial in their information, for example, often advertising books or courses. We suggest you use keywords to make your own web searches.

Abercrombie, D., 1968, 'Paralanguage', in *British Journal of Disorders of Communication*, No. 3, 55–99.

Adair, J., 1986, *Effective Teambuilding*, London: Pan.

Aitchison, J., 1976, *The Articulate Manual: An Introduction to Psycholinguistics*, London: Hutchinson.

Altmann, I., 1972, *The Reciprocity of Interpersonal Exchange*, 80th Meeting of the American Psychological Association.

Anderson, S. and Williams, D., 1985, 'Cognitive/affective reactions in the improvement of self esteem', in *Journal of Personality and Social Psychology*, No. 48, 1086–97.

d'Ardenne, P. and Mahtani, A., 1992, *Transcultural Counselling in Action*, London: Sage.

Argyle, M., 1973, *Social Encounters*, Harmondsworth: Pelican.

Argyle, M., 1973, *Social Interaction*, London: Tavistock.

Argyle, M., 1988, *Bodily Communication*, 2nd edn, London: Methuen.

Argyle, M., 1992, *The Psychology of Everyday Life*, London: Routledge.

Argyle, M., 1994, 1983, 1967 *The Psychology of Interpersonal Communication*, 5th edn, Harmondsworth: Penguin.

Argyle, M. and Dean, J., 1965, 'Eye Contact, Distance and Affiliation', in *Sociometry*, No. 28, 289–304.

Argyle, M. and Henderson, M., 1985, *The Anatomy of Relationships and The Rules and Skills Needed to Manage Them Successfully*, Harmondsworth: Pelican.

Argyle, M. and Trower, P., 1979, *Person to Person*, London: Harper & Row.

Arnold, M., 1932, *Culture and Anarchy*, Cambridge: Cambridge University Press.

Asch, S., 1946, 'Forming impressions of personality', in *Journal of Abnormal and Social Psychology*, No. 41, 258–90.

Atkinson, J. M., 1984, *Our Masters' Voices: The Language and Body Language of Politics*, London: Methuen.

Atkinson, J. M. and Heritage, J., 1987, *Structures of Social Action: Studies in Conversation Analysis*, Cambridge: Cambridge University Press.

Atkinson, M., 2004, *Lend Me Your Ears: All You Need to Know About Making Speeches and Presentations*, London: Random House.

Axtell, R., 1991, *Gestures: The Do's and Taboos of Body Language Around The World*, New York: John Wiley.

Babha, H., 'Just Talking' (with Sander Gilman), in Salamensky, 2001 (see below).

Bales, R. E., 1950, *Interaction Process Analysis*, Cambridge, MA: Addison-Wesley.

Bandler, R. and Grinder, J., 1979, *Frogs into Princes: Neurolinguistic Programming*, Moab, UT: Real People Press.

Bannister, D. and Agnew, J., 1977, 'The child's construing of self', in Landield, A. (ed.), *Nebraska Symposium on Motivation, 1976*, Lincoln: University of Nebraska Press.

Barker, L., 1984, *Communication*, New Jersey: Prentice-Hall.

Barthes, R., 1973, *Mythologies* (trans. A. Lavers), London: Granada.

Baxter, L. A., 1986, 'Gender differences in the heterosexual relationship rules embedded in break-up accounts', in *Journal of Social and Personal Relationships*, No. 3, 289–306.

Baym, N., 2000, *Tune in, Log On – Soaps, Fandom, and Online Community*, Thousand Oaks, CA: Sage.

Beattie, G., 1983, *Talk: An Analysis of Speech and Non-Verbal Communication in Conversation*, Milton Keynes: Open University Press.

Beattie, G., 2003, *Visible Thought: The New Psychology of Body Language*, London: Routledge.

Beck, A., Bennett, P. and Wall, P., 2004, *Communication Studies: The Essential Reader*, London: Routledge.

Belbin, R. M., 1993, *Team Roles at Work*, Oxford: Butterworth-Heinemann.

Bell, D. F., 2001, *An Introduction to Cybercultures*, London: Routledge.

Berger, C., 1974, *The Acquaintance Process Revisited*. Paper for the International Communication Association, referred to in Patton and Griffin, 1981 (see below).

Bern, D., 1967, 'Self perception', in *Psychological Review*, No. 74, 183–200.

Berne, E., 1961, *Transactional Analysis in Psychotherapy*, London: Souvenir Press/New York: Grove Press.

Berne, E., 1964, *Games People Play*, Harmondsworth: Penguin.

Berne, E., 1969, *Layman's Guide to Psychiatry and Psychoanalysis*, London: Souvenir Press.

Berne, E., 1972, *What Do You Say After You've Said Hello?*, London: Corgi.

Berry, R., 2000, *Freud: A Beginner's Guide*, London: Hodder and Stoughton.

Berry, R., 2000, *Jung: A Beginner's Guide*, London: Hodder and Stoughton.

Birdwhistell, R. L., 1968, 'Kinesics', in *International Encyclopedia of Social Sciences*, No. 8, 381–399.

Blake, S. M., Moulton, J. and Shepard, A., 1964, *Managing Intergroup Conflict in Industry*, Houston: Gulf.

Blumer, H., 1969, *Symbolic Interactionism: Perspective and Method*, Englewood Cliffs, NJ: Prentice-Hall.

Bolden, R., 2004, *What is Leadership?*, Exeter University: Leadership South West.

Bolton, R., 1986, *People Skills – How to Assert Yourself, Listen to Others, and Resolve Conflicts*, Sydney: Prentice-Hall.

Borisoff, D. and Merrill, L., 1991, *Listening in Everyday Life*, Maryland: University of America Press.

Brigham, J. C., 1971, 'Ethnic stereotypes', in *Psychological Bulletin*, No. 26, 15–38.

Burr, V., 1998, *Gender and Social Psychology*, London: Routledge.

Burton, G., 1999, *Media and Popular Culture*, London: Hodder & Stoughton.

Burton, G., 2005, *Media and Society, Critical Perspectives*, Maidenhead: Open University Press.

Butler-Bowden, T., 2003, *50 Self-help Classics*, London: Nicholas Brealey.

Butterworth, C. and MacDonald, M., 1985, *Teaching Social Education and Communication*, London: Hutchinson.

Cameron, D. (ed.), 1998, *The Feminist Critique of Language*, London: Routledge.

Carnegie, D., 1938, *How to Win Friends and Influence People*, Tadworth: World's Work.

Carrol, J. and Payne, J. (eds), 1976, *Cognitive and Social Behaviour*, New Jersey: Erlbaum.

Chuang, R., 'An examination of Taoist and Buddhist perspectives on interpersonal conflicts, emotions and adversities', in Jandt, 2004 (see below).

Chen, G. M., 1988, 'Relationships of dimensions of intercultural communicative competence.' Paper presented at the 79th meeting of the Eastern Communication Association, Baltimore, MD (see ERIC document reproduction service, no. ED297381).

Civil, J., 2003, *Assertiveness: Your Personal Trainer*, London: Spiro Press.

Clifford, E. and Clifford, M., 1967, 'Self concepts before and after survival training', in *British Journal of Clinical Psychology*, No. 6, 241–8.

Coates, J., 1991, *Women, Men and Language: A Sociolinguistic Account of Sex Differences in Language*, London: Longman.

Cooley, C., 1902, *Human Nature and Social Order*, New York: Charles Scribner & Sons.

Coopersmith, S., 1967, *The Antecedents of Self-esteem*, Los Angeles: Freeman & Co.

Corner, J. and Hawthorn, J., 1990, *Communication Studies: An Introductory Reader*, 2nd edn, London: Edward Arnold.

Crawford, M., 1995, *Talking Difference – On Gender and Language*, London: Sage.

Davis, J. H., 1969, *Group Performance*, Reading, MA: Addison-Wesley.

Deaux, K. and Wrightsman, L. S., 1984, *Social Psychology in the Eighties*, London: Brooks/Cole.

Derlega, V. and Berg, J. (eds), 1987, *Self-Disclosure: Theory, Research and Therapy*, New York: Plenum Press.

Dickson, A., 1988, *A Woman in Your Own Right – Assertiveness and You*, London: Quartet.

Dimbleby, R. and Burton, G., 1998, *More Than Words: An Introduction to Communication Studies*, 3rd edn, London: Routledge.

Duck, S., 1993, *Relating to Others*, Oxford: Oxford University Press.

Duck, S., 1994, *Dynamics of Relationships*, London: Sage.

Duck, S. 1986, *Human Relationships: An Introduction to Social Psychology*, London: Sage.

Duck, S. and Perlman, D., (eds), 1985, *Understanding Personal Relationships: An Interdisciplinary Approach*, London: Sage.

Du Gay, P. (ed.), 1997, *The Production of Culture/Cultures of Production*, London: Sage/Milton Keynes: Open University Press.

Duncan, S., 1972, 'Some signals and rules for taking speaking turns in conversation', in *Journal of Personality and Social Psychology*, No. 23, 283–92.

Dwyer, D., 2000, *Interpersonal Relationships*, London: Routledge.

Eiser, J. R., 1986, *Social Psychology*, Cambridge: Cambridge University Press.

Ekman, F., 'Cross-Cultural Studies of Facial Expressions', in Ekman, P. (ed.), 1973, *Darwin and Facial Expressions*, New York: Academic Press.

Ekman, P., 1982, *Emotion in the Human Face*, Cambridge: Cambridge University Press.

Ekman, P., 2004, 2003, *Emotions Revealed: Understanding Faces and Feelings*, London: Weidenfeld & Nicolson.

Ekman, P. and Davidson, R. (eds), 1994, *The Nature of Emotions: Fundamental Questions*, New York: Oxford University Press.

Ellis, A. and Beattie, G., 1986, *The Psychology of Language and Communication*, London: Weidenfeld & Nicolson.

English, F., 1976, 'Racketeering', in *Transactional Analysis Journal*, Vol. 6, No. 1, 78–81.

Erikson, E., 1972, *Childhood and Society*, Harmondsworth: Pelican.

Erlich, S. and King, R., 'Gender-based language reform and the social construction of meaning', in Cameron, D. (ed.), 1998 (see above).

Fast, J., 1970, *Body Language*, London: Pan.

Festinger, L., 1954, 'A theory of social comparison processes', in *Human Relations*, No. 7, 117–40.

Festinger, L., 1957, *A Theory of Cognitive Dissonance*, Evanston, IL: Row, Peterson.

Fiedler, E., 1973, 'The trouble with leadership training', in *Psychology Today*, February 1973, 23–9.

Fiske, J., 1990, *Introduction to Communication Studies*, 2nd edn, London: Routledge.

Furnham, A., 2002, *The Psychology of Behaviour at Work: The Individual in the Organization*, Hove: Psychology Press.

Gahagan, J., 1975, *Interpersonal and Group Behaviour*, London: Methuen.

Gahagan, J., 1984, *Social Interaction and Its Management*, London: Methuen.

Gardner, H., 1993, *Frames of Mind: The Theory of Multiple Intelligences*, 2nd edn, London: Fontana.

Gardner, H., 1999, *Intelligence Reframed: Multiple Intelligences for the 21ˢᵗ Century*, New York: Basic Books.

Gauntlett, D., 2002, *Media, Gender and Identity: An Introduction*, London: Routledge.

Gauntlett, D. and Horsley, R. (eds), 2004, *Web Studies*, 2nd edn, London, Arnold, p. 47.

Gergen, K. and Gergen, M., 1986, *Social Psychology*, New York: Springer Verlag.

Geuss, R., 1981, *The Idea of a Critical Theory: Habermas and the Frankfurt School*, Cambridge: Cambridge University Press.

Glass, L., 1992, *He Says, She Says – Closing the Communication Gap between the Sexes*, London: Piatkus.

Goffman, E., 1959, *The Presentation of Self in Everyday Life*, Harmondsworth: Penguin.

Goffman, E., 1961, *Encounters: Two Studies in the Sociology of Interaction*, Indianapolis: Bobbs Merrill.

Goffman, E., 1963, *Behaviour in Public Places: Notes on the Social Organisation of Gatherings*, New York: Free Press.

Goffman, E., 1963, *Stigma: Notes on the Management of Spoiled Identity*, Harmondsworth: Penguin.

Goffman, E., 1968, 1967, *Interaction Ritual: Essays on Face-to-face Behaviour*, Harmondsworth: Penguin/New York: Anchor Press.

Goffman, E., 1971, *Relations in Public: Microstudies of the Public Order*, Harmondsworth: Allen Lane.

Goffman, E., 1976, *Asylums*, Harmondsworth: Penguin.

Goffman, E., 1979, *Gender Advertisements*, London: Macmillan.

Goffman, E., 1981, *Forms of Talk*, London: Macmillan.

Goleman, D., 1996, 1995, *Emotional Intelligence: Why It Can Matter More Than IQ*, London: Bloomsbury.

Goleman, D., 1998, *Working with Emotional Intelligence*, London: Bloomsbury.

Goleman, D., Boyatzis, R. and McKee, A., 2002, *The New Leaders: Transforming the Art of Leadership into the Science of Results*, London: Time Warner.

Gonzalez, J., 'Cultural fronts: Towards a dialogical understanding of contemporary cultures', in Lull (ed.), 2001 (see below).

Goulding, M. and Goulding, R., 1979, *Changing Lives Through Redecision Therapy*, New York: Brunner/Mazel.

Gray, J., 1992, *Men Are from Mars, Women Are from Venus*, London: Thorsons.

Gross, R. D., 1992, *Psychology: The Science of Mind and Behaviour*, London: Hodder & Stoughton.

Gudykunst, W. B. (ed.), 1986, *Intergroup Communication*, London: Edward Arnold.

Guirdham, M., 1999, *Communicating Across Cultures*, Basingstoke: Palgrave.

Gunter, B., 1995, *The Representation of Women on Television*, London: John Libbey.

Hall, E. T., 1969, *The Hidden Dimension*, New York: Anchor Books.

Hall, E. T., 1973, *The Silent Language*, New York: Anchor Books.

Hamilton, D., 'Cognitive biases in the perception of social groups', in Carrol and Payne (eds), 1976 (see above).

Haraway, D., 'A Manifesto for Cyborgs', in Kirkup, G., Janes, L., Hovenden, F. and Woodward, K. (eds.), 2000, *The Gendered Cyborg*, London: Routledge.

Hargie, O. (ed.), 1986, *A Handbook of Communication Skills*, Beckenham: Croom Helm.

Hargie, O. and Dickson, D., 2004, *Skilled Interpersonal Communication*, London: Routledge.

Hargie, O., Saunders, C. and Dickson, D., 1994, *Social Skills in Interpersonal Communication*, London: Routledge.

Hargie, O. (ed.), 2003, 1986, *The Handbook of Communication Skills*, 2nd edn, London: Routledge.

Harre, R. and Lamb, R. (eds), 1986, *The Dictionary of Personality and Social Psychology*, Oxford: Blackwell.

Harris, T., 1970, *I'm OK, You're OK*, London: Pan.

Harris, A. and Harris, T., *Staying OK*, London: Arrow Books.

Hartley, P., 1997, *Group Communication*, London: Routledge.

Hartley, P., 1999, 1993, *Interpersonal Communication*, 2nd edn, London: Routledge.

Harvey, C., Banks, W. C. and Zimbardo, P. G., 1973, 'Interpersonal dynamics in a simulated prison,' in *International Journal of Criminology and Penology*, No. 1, 69–79.

Hastie, R. (ed.), 1980, *Social Perception*, Hillsdale, NJ: Erlbaum.

Hayes, J., 2002, *Interpersonal Skills at Work*, London: Routledge.

Hayes, N., 1984, *A First Course in Psychology*, Walton-on-Thames: Nelson and Sons.

Hayes, N. and Orrell, S., 1993, *Psychology: An Introduction*, 2nd edn, Harlow: Longman.

Hebdige, D., 1979, *Subculture – The Meaning of Style*, London: Routledge.

Heider, E., 1958, *The Psychology of Interpersonal Relations*, New York: Wiley.

Hewson, J. and Turner, C., 1992, *Transactional Analysis in Management*, Blagdon: The Staff College.

Hickson, M. L. III and Stacks, D. W., 1993, *NVC: Nonverbal communication – Studies and Applications*, Oxford: Brown & Benchmark.

Hill, C. and Stull, D. E., 'Gender and self-disclosure: Strategies for exploring the issues', in Derlega and Berg (eds), 1987 (see above).

Hodges, B., 1974, 'The effects of volume on relative weighting in impression formation', in *Journal of Personality and Social Psychology*, No. 30, 278–381.

Hodgkinson, L., 1987, *Smile Therapy: How Smiling and Laughter can Change your Life*, London: Optima.

Hofstede, G., 1981, *Cultures and Organisations – Software of the Mind*, London: HarperCollins.

Honey, P., 1988, *Face to Face*, London: Gower.

Howitt, D., Billig, M., Cramer, D. et al., 1989, *Social Psychology*, Oxford: Oxford University Press.

Jakobsen, R., 1990, *On Language*, Cambridge, MA: Harvard University Press.

Jandt, F. (ed.), 2004, *Intercultural Communication: A Global Reader*, London: Sage.

Janis, I. L., 1972, *Victims of Groupthink*, 2nd edn, Boston, MA: Houghton-Mifflin.

Jenks, C., 1993, *Culture*, London: Routledge.

Jones, S. and Kucker, S., 'Computers, the Internet and Virtual Culture', in Lull (ed.), 2001 (see below).

Jung, C. G., 1957, *The Undiscovered Self*, London: Routledge.

Kang, K. H., 'Koreans' politeness strategies', in Jandt (ed.), 2004 (see above).

Kaplan, C., 'Language and gender', in Cameron (ed.), 1998 (see above).

Kell, C. L. and Corts, P. R., 1980, *Fundamentals of Effective Group Communication*, New York: Macmillan.

Kelley, H., 1967, 'Attribution Theory in Social Psychology', in *Nebraska Symposium on Motivation*, No. 15, 192–238.

Kelley, H., 1969, 'Attribution Theory in social psychology', in Levine, D. (ed.), *Attribution Theory in Social Psychology*, Lincoln: University of Nebraska Press.

Kelley, H., 1971, 'Attribution: Perceiving the causes of behaviour', in Jones, E. et al. (eds), *Attribution*, New Jersey: General Learning Press.

Kelvin, P., 1969, *The Bases of Social Behaviour*, London: Holt, Rinehart & Winston.

Knight, S., 2002, *NLP at Work*, 2nd edn, London: Nicholas Brealey.

Langer, E. and Dweck, C., 1973, *Personal Politics: The Psychology of Making It*, New Jersey: Prentice-Hall.

Layder, D., 2004, *Social and Personal Identity*, London: Sage.

Lewin, K., Lippett, R. and White, P. K., 1939, 'Patterns of aggressive behaviour', in *Journal of Social Psychology*, No. 10, 27–99.

Liikkanen, M., 'The question of cultural gender', in Lull (ed.), 2001 (see below).

Livingstone, S., 1987, *Accounting for Relationships: Explanation, Representation and Knowledge*, London: Methuen.

Luft, J., 1969, *Of Human Interaction*, Palo Alto, CA: National Press Books.

Lull, J. (ed.), 2001, *Culture in the Communication Age*, London: Routledge.

Lustig, M. W. and Koester, J., 2003, *Intercultural Competence – Interpersonal Communication across Cultures*, 4th edn, Boston, MA: Allyn & Bacon/Pearson Education Inc.

March, J. and Simon, H., 1958, *Organisations*, New York: John Wiley.

Markham, U., 1993, *How to Deal with Difficult People*, London: Thorsons.

Markus, H., 1977, 'Self schemata and processing information about the self', in *Journal of Personality and Social Psychology*, No. 35, 63–78.

Marsh, P. (ed.), 1988, *Eye to Eye: How People Interact*, London: Sidgwick & Jackson.

Maslow, A., 1984, *Motivation and Personality*, New York: Harper & Row.

McArthur, L., 1972, 'The how and what of why: causal attributions', in *Journal of Personality and Social Psychology*, No. 22, 171–93.

McConnell-Ginet, S., 'The sexual reproduction of meaning', in Cameron (ed.), 1998 (see above).

McGuire, W. and Padawer-Singer, A., 1976, 'Trait salience in the spontaneous self concept', in *Journal of Personality and Social Psychology*, No. 33, 743–54.

McGuire, W., McGuire, C., Child, P. and Fujioka, T., 1978, 'Salience of ethnicity in the spontaneous self concept', in *Journal of Personality and Social Psychology*, No. 36, 511–20.

Mead, G. H., 1934, *Mind, Self and Society*, Chicago: University of Chicago Press.

Mehrabian, A., 1971, *Silent Messages*, New York: Wadsworth.

Miller, C. and Swift, K., 1979, *Words and Women*, Harmondsworth: Penguin.

Montgomery, M., 1986, *An Introduction to Language and Society*, London: Methuen.

Morgan, J. and Welton, P., 1986, *See What I Mean*, London: Edward Arnold.

Morris, D., 1977, *Manwatching: A Field Guide to Human Behaviour*, St Albans: Triad Panther.

Mulvaney, B. M., 'Gender differences in communication, an intercultural experience', in Jandt (ed.), 2004 (see above).

Myers, G. and Myers, M., 1992, *The Dynamics of Human Communication*, 6th edn, New York: McGraw-Hill.

Nierenberg, G. L. and Calero, H. H., 1973, *How to Read a Person like a Book*, London: Heinrich Hanau.

Nisbett, R. and Ross, L., 1980, *Human Interference: Strategies and Shortcomings*, Englewood Cliffs, NJ: Prentice-Hall.

Nolan, V., 1987a, *Communication*, London: Sphere.

Nolan, V., 1987b, *Problem Solving*, London: Sphere.

Nolan, V., 1987c, *Teamwork*, London: Sphere.

Noller, R., 1980, 'Gaze in married couples', *Journal of Nonverbal Behaviour*, No. 5, 115–29.

Northouse, P. G., 2004, *Leadership: Theory and Practice*, 3rd edn, London: Sage.

O'Connor, J. and Seymour, J., 1990, *Introducing Neurolinguistic Programming*, London: Aquarian.

O'Connor, J. and Seymour, J., 1994, *Training with NLP: Skills for Managers, Trainers and Communicators*, London: Thorsons.

O'Sullivan, T., Hartley, J., Saunders, D., Montgomery, M. and Fiske, J., 1994, *Key Concepts in Communication and Cultural Studies*, 2nd edn, London: Routledge.

Park, R. E., 1950, *Race and Culture*, Glencoe, IL: The Free Press.

Patton, R. and Griffin, K., 1981, *Interpersonal Communication in Action*, New York: Harper & Row.

Pease, A., 1992, *Body Language*, Sheldon Press.

Pease, A. with Garner, A., 1989, *Talk Language: How to Use Conversation for Profit and Pleasure*, London: Simon & Schuster.

Pederson, P. (ed.), 1985, *Handbook of Cross-cultural Counselling and Therapy*, Westport, CT: Greenwood Press.

Pennington, D., 1986, *Essential Social Psychology*, London: Edward Arnold.

Pennington, D., Gillen, K. and Hill, P., 1999, *Social Psychology*, London: Arnold.

Persaud, R., 2001, *Staying Sane: How to Make Your Mind Work for You*, 2nd edn, London: Bantam Press.

Persaud, R., 2005, *The Motivated Mind: How To Get What You Want From Life*, London: Bantam Press.

Price, S., 1996, *Communication Studies*, Harlow: Longman.

Prior, R. and O'Connor, J., 2000, *NLP and Relationships*, London: HarperCollins.

Radley, A. R., 1974, 'The effect of role enactment on construct alternatives', in *British Journal of Medical Psychology*.

Reicher, S. D., 1984, 'The St Paul's riot', in *European Journal of Social Psychology*, No. 14, 1–21.

Reid, M. and Hammersley, R., 2000, *Communicating Successfully in Groups*, London: Routledge.

Rheingold, H., 1993, *The Virtual Community: Homesteading on the Electronic Frontier*, New York: Harper.

Rogers, C. R., 1990, *On Becoming a Person: A Therapist's View of Psychotherapy*, London: Constable.

Rosenberg, M., 1965, *Society and the Adolescent Self-image*, Princeton: Princeton University Press.

Rosenberg, R. and Jones, S., 1972, 'A method for representing and investigating an implicit theory of personality', in *Journal of Personality and Social Psychology*, No. 20, 372–86.

Ross, L., Berkowitz, L. (ed.), 'The intuitive psychologist and his shortcomings: distortions in the attribution process', in 1977, *Advances in Experimental Psychology*, vol. 10, New York: Academic Press.

Salamensky, S. I. (ed.), 2001, *Talk, Talk, Talk – The Cultural Life Of Everyday Conversation*, London: Routledge.

Saussure, F., de, 1983, 1916, *A Course in General Linguistics*, London: Duckworth.

Schachter, S., 1964, 'The interaction of cognitive and physiological determinants of emotional state', in Berkowitz, L. (ed.), *Advances in Experimental Social Psychology*, New York: Academic Press.

Schiff, J., 1975, *A Cathexis Reader*, New York: Harper & Row.

Schirato, T. and Yell, S., 2000, *Communication and Culture*, London: Sage.

Schultz, R., 1976, 'The effects of control and predictability on the psychological well-being of the institutionalised aged', in *Journal of Personality and Social Psychology*, No. 33, 563–73.

Schultz, W., 1958, *Firo: A Three Dimensional Theory of Interpersonal Behaviour*, New York: Holt, Rinehart & Winston.

Schultz, W., 1966, *The Interpersonal Underworld*, Palo Alto, CA: Science and Behaviour Books.

Schwartz, J. and Schaver, P., 1984, *A Prototype Approach to Emotional Structure*. A paper given at the American Psychological Association Convention, referred to in Gergen and Gergen, 1986 (see above).

Scollon, R. and Scollon, S. W., 1995, *Intercultural Communication: A Discourse Approach*, Oxford: Blackwell.

Sentis, K. and Markus, L., 1979, *Self Schemas and Recognition Memory*, Unpublished paper, referred to in Gergen and Gergen, 1986 (see above).

Shaw, M., 1981, *Group Dynamics*, 3rd edn, New York: McGraw-Hill.

Shilling, C., 'The body and difference', in Woodward (ed.), 1997 (see below).

Shotter, J., 1984, *Social Accountability and Self-hood*, Oxford: Blackwell.

Soueif, A., 1999, *The Map of Love*, London: Bloomsbury.

Spender, D., 1980, *Man-made language*, London: Routledge & Kegan Paul.

Stein, S. and Book, H., 2001, *The EQ Edge: Emotional Intelligence and Your Success*, London: Kogan Page.

Stewart, I., 2000, *Transactional Analysis Counselling in Action*, London: Sage.

Stubbs, M., 1989, *Discourse Analysis: The Sociolinguistic Analysis of Natural Language*, Oxford: Blackwell.

Sunderland, J., 2004, *Gendered Discourses*, Basingstoke: Palgrave Macmillan.

Tajfel, H., 1969, 'Cognitive aspects of prejudice', in *Journal of Social Issues*, No. 25, 79–97.

Tajfel, H. (ed.), 1978, *Differentiation between Social Groups: Studies in the Social Psychology of Intergroup Relations*, London: Academic Press.

Tajfel, H. and Fraser, C. (eds), 1986, *Introducing Social Psychology*, Harmondsworth: Pelican.

Tannen, D., 1991, *You Just Don't Understand: Women and Men in Conversation*, London: Virago.

Tannen, D., 1992, *That's Not What I Meant: How Conversational Style Makes or Breaks Your Relations with Others*, London: Virago.

Tannen, D., 1996, 1995, *Talking from 9 to 5*, London: Virago.

Tedeschi, J. T. and Lindskold, S., 1976, *Social Psychology: Interdependence, Interaction and Influence*, New York: J. Wiley.

The Mindgym: Wake Your Mind Up, 2005, London: Time Warner.

Theobald, T. and Cooper, C., 2004, *Shut up and Listen: The Truth About How to Communicate at Work*, London: Kogan Page.

Ting-Toomey, S., 1991, *Cross-cultural Interpersonal Communication*, London: Sage.

Trend, D. (ed.), 2001, *Reading Digital Culture*, Oxford: Blackwell.

Triandis, H., 'Some major dimensions of cultural variation in client populations', in Pederson (ed.), 1985 (see above).

Trudgill, P., 1983, *Sociolinguistics*, Harmondsworth: Penguin.

Trudgill, P., 2000, *Sociolinguistics, An Introduction to Language and Society*, 4th edn, London: Penguin.

Tuckman, B. W., 1965, 'Developmental sequence in small groups', in *Psychological Bulletin*, no. 63, 384–99.

Turk, C., 1985, *Effective Speaking: Communicating in Speech*, London: Spon.

Turner, J. C., 'Social comparison, similarity and ingroup favouritism', in Tajfel (ed.), 1978 (see above).

Videbeck, R., 'Selfconception and the reactions of others', in Argyle (ed.), 1973 (see above).

Virilio, P., 1994, *The Vision Machine*, London: BFI.

Virilio, P., 1997, *Open Sky*, London: Verso.

Watson, J. and Hill, A., 1994, A *Dictionary of Communication and Media Studies*, 3rd edn, London: Edward Arnold.

Weiner, B., 1985, 'Spontaneous casual thinking', in *Psychological Bulletin*, no. 97, 74–84.

Wellman, B. and Gulia, M., 'Netsurfers don't ride alone', in Wellman, B. (ed.), 1999, *Networkers in the Global Village*, Boulder, CO: Westview Press.

West, M., 2004, *The Secrets of Successful Team Management: How to Lead a Team to Innovation and Success*, London: Duncan Baird.

Wheen, F., 2004, *How Mumbo-Jumbo Conquered the World*, London: Harper Perennial.

Wilkinson, J. and Canter, S., 1982, *Social Skills Training Manual*, London: Wiley.

Williams, R., 1965, *The Long Revolution*, Harmondsworth: Penguin.

Williams, R., 1983, *Culture and Society*, Columbia: Columbia University Press.

Woods, C., 2003, *Everything You Need to Know at Work: A Complete Manual of Workplace Skills*, London: Pearson.

Woodward, K. (ed.), 1997, *Identity and Difference*, London/Milton Keynes: Sage/Open University.

Woodward, K., 2002, *Understanding Identity*, London: Arnold.

Wyer, R. and Srull, S., 'The processing of social stimulus information', in Hastie (ed.) 1980 (see above).

Zohar, D. and Marshall, I., 2000, *SQ – Spiritual Intelligence: The Ultimate Intelligence*, London: Bloomsbury.

Index